To Luigi
IANNUNZIO

Enjoy — DR Smith

Beaches of Belmont

& Other Short Stories

by **D.R.** *Smith*

To my new friends

"...every smile dear, and every life precious;
we're all in it together"

D.R. Smith

Beaches of Belmont
& Other Short Stories

ISBN: 978-0-615-22026-0

Published by Andover Training Stables & Associates
Printed in the United States of America
by Signature Book Printing, Gaithersburg, MD

Acknowledgements & Credits

To Catherine Zajac, Chicago IL: a special thanks of gratitude to a valued friend to whom I'm indebted for her trust, generosity, and unwavering belief in this book; making it all possible.

Erik S. Snyder, Murfreesboro, TN: a dear friend whose generous technical support has been most appreciated

Photo Credits
(following portfolios can be found at "morguefile.com")

Dawn Turner, Bisbee, AZ: *The Magic of Moses, Poet's Pantry*
Darren Hester, Macon, GA: *Hogs 'N Hens*
Sanjay Pindiyath, Hong Kong: *Play On, Maestro*
George Imrie, Scotland: *Jesters on flap*
JP McMann, Ontario: *Author's Forum*
Kevin Connors, Amsterdam, NL: *A Worst Way Wee*
Ray Forester, U.S.: *A Kiss from Alex*
Simon Chapman, England: *The Idiot*
Lisa, Edinburgh, Scotland: *The Price of Loyalty*
Clara Natoli, Rome, Italy: *Hardly Heathens, Rhubarb Wine, The New Yorkshire Times, The Whispering Stone, Freckled Face of Fear, Twelve Labors of Hercules*

Andrea Cassetta, Sarasota, FL: *Path of Evil*
Joel Guerin, Lexington, KY: photo, *54 Excuses*
Feebleminds-gif.com, United Kingdom; *True Name*

Personal Dedication

 Every now and then, chance events and people come together that ultimately have a significant impact on one's life… two such people having inspired this effort, and it is to them I dedicate this book.

Vincent Zecca, a WWII B-29 belly gunner became a most revered friend; one of the finest human beings I had ever known… He was a gentleman of the highest order, and I was grateful for the time spent sharing ideas and experiences that inspired *Beaches of Belmont*; and in whose honor, the main character bears his name.

Vince passed away only a week after the first draft was rushed to his hospital bedside. I'll never know if he had the chance to read it, but in spirit, I'd like to believe he had, and that I've done justice in honoring my dear friend, and his legacy.

The second person of whom I'm immensely proud is my soul mate, Deborah, whose undaunted support, encouragement, and especially her patience… having given up countless hours of personal time normally enjoyed together in order to foment the production of this effort. I couldn't ask for a more genuine, loving fan.

Aside from Vince and Deborah, I have also been blessed to have known other such special people. You *know* who you are, and it is to you as well, that I wish to express my sincere gratitude for your enthusiasm, and above all, your friendship.

D.R. Smith

The Itinerary

Beaches of Belmont

& Other Short Stories

Beaches of Belmont
by D.R.Smith

Burma Road

Spring, 1944— and the world was mired in war. April showers seemed endless in North Carolina. It was near midnight, yet the woods still dripped from a day-long drizzle. Our fatigues were wet, and boots caked with sand as Tony and I snaked our way through Burma Road; code name for our secret shortcut across a wooded area linking Fort Baxter to an all-girl campus on the edge of town.

"*Damn* you, Vince. Careful with them branches, for crissake." Tony cursed in as loud a whisper as he dared. MPs could be *anywhere* on base, and sound carried in those woods.

"Sorry," I lied, knowing we had to be quiet, but I couldn't resist letting a spry branch slap his face with cold rainwater.

We thought MPs might be looking only for us; it never dawning on us spies and sabotage were real concerns. Recruits were shipping in and out of Fort Baxter like changing factory shifts. Technically, we *were* AWOL, though we didn't see the harm risking a fortnight in the stockade for a few stolen hours smooching with good-looking college gals.

"Quick! Cut the light." Tony pulled at my shoulder, pressing a finger to his lips. MPs were approaching, patrolling the perimeter. We squatted motionless behind low pines until they passed. Once clear, we dashed across the open lane giggling like a pair of juveniles, each clutching a bottle of Old Crow.

We made it to the barracks without being seen and crept inside, careful not to wake anyone. Most were sleeping soundly, exhausted from a day's hard training. Tony placed his whiskey at the threshold of our platoon leader's door, a spot from which it always disappeared by first light. I put mine in my foot locker for sharing with the squad later in the week. I gingerly slipped into my bunk bemoaning 05:00 reveille knowing I'd be dragging by about mid day. *But oh what a night*, I sighed, and smiled myself to sleep.

For weeks, the Army had been trying to turn a bunch of us undisciplined boys into men. The physical strain was one thing, but from mid January, everyone was pensive tracking the news of brutal fighting at Anzio and Monte Cassino. Papers said Hitler's Luftwaffe had been severely depleted, paving the way for Allied bombing raids over Germany and pounding his armies along the Atlantic Wall.

We sensed Uncle Sam was about to hand us tickets to front-row seats *somewhere* in Europe's theater of operations. No one knew exactly when or where, but latrine chatter laid short odds that the long-anticipated invasion of Nazi-occupied Europe was near.

Antonio Mosconi and I were as concerned as anyone, though we seldom took anything seriously. We met making rail connections at Grand Central in New York, and have been inseparable since. We were both streetwise, big-city tenement Turks; pretend-to-be outfit toughs from poor Italian neighborhoods. I was from Boston, and Tony was born in the Bronx, but grew up in Newark: "where men are men, and sheep are noivus," he always blustered.

We fathomed ourselves a couple of bulletproof privates enlisting only a few years after high school. During opening weeks of training, a few guys called us the Mutt and Jeff misfits. We'd laugh it off, but in some respects, I suppose we did fit the mold of Bud Fisher's popular comic strip.

Tony was about four inches taller, and slender at just over six feet. He was one of those enviously handsome types; girls finding him irresistible, swooning and carrying on like he was a Hollywood heartthrob. His perfect olive complexion, quick-witted inner-city suave, and a warm, disarming smile drove local southern belles nuts. I ran with him if for no other reason than to be guaranteed a shot at castoffs.

I was the *Mutt*— "a Sicilian mutt," guys joked. Short, no neck, and barrel-chested; built like a hairy tombstone that sprouted limbs. Though I had thick forearms and biceps the size of most guys' thighs, I was deceptively quick, like a seasoned welterweight.

My buddies called me Vince or Zeck, short for my last name of Zecca. Either was far better than *Plug*, a hated moniker I inherited from street bookies milling around the Italian Social Club a half block from my home. At times, they'd book action on local High School football, and the Malden Gazette once wrote the flattering line: "Zecca singlehandedly shut down Medford's running game, plugging every gap in Malden's line."

'Plug' may have seemed apropos to those goombahs, but what they didn't know was, aside from looking like one of their bouncers, I played a mean trumpet that would give Harry James an orgasm. My music helped getting girls to hang around, too. During dance breaks, they'd flirt and carry on with the band as though we were real celebrities. Sometimes I'd have them clambering to kiss me after I boasted my lips were so sensitive, I could pick the morning dew off a rose petal.

* * *

Thank God the day stayed on the cooler side following the prior day's rain, although temperatures had risen high enough for me to be drenched in sweat.

We hiked fifteen miles before noon, with bayonet practice and hand-to-hand combat scheduled for later in the day. Plans were to simulate battlefield conditions with an overnight bivouac and a return trek at first light. For me, the worst part about bivouacs was spending miserable nights in sleeping bags on the cold, hard ground, or *worse* as happened to a few guys— waking up with a big snake coiled against your body for warmth. I *hate* snakes. Had I woke with one wrapped around my neck, t'hell with reveille; the bugler would be blowing taps for the outfit's first heart attack casualty.

I was worn out and my feet were killing me. The Army expects dropouts and provided trucks to haul their wimpy asses back in line, but I refused to break formation. Pabst and panties can be damned, for this was the moment I regretted midnight antics the most— *but only for a little while;* my grin returned.

Frazer kicked at the soles of my boots. "You two Guinea fowl flew the coop again last night, didn't ya?" I didn't bother looking up from beneath my helmet; only smiled with my head resting against my field pack. "I swear; you two heathens would chase a skirt into hell. But you watch. One of these days, they're gonna pull a surprise bed check and you'll be spending your nights in irons."

I ignored him, confident we had the routine figured out to avoid such possibilities. Frazer meant well; a terrific guy, always looking out for us 'heathens'.

Howie, or "Rubber Legs" was renowned for his dancing skills, but we also called him "Father Frazer"; not because we felt anyone over twenty-three should be called *Pop*, but he was an agnostic Jew prone to anoint us with priestly blessings.

Nearby, I heard a familiar brand of Hooterville hee-haws. Aside from Tony, Rufus "Woofie" Mullins was one of the first guys I befriended upon entering the service. Rufus was a huge, yet kindly yokel from the hills of Eastern Kentucky. At 6'-6", his massive frame bulged with hardened muscles developed from endless hours shifting tons of quarry stone. He was a hulking ox— *only not as smart as one.*

Tony may be the pretty one in the outfit, but I was the more observant. Fate showed her mystic face in Virginia; making the giant bumpkin our ally when our paths crossed as scores of recruits gathered for changing trains to North Carolina. I spotted a shifty loudmouth I'd seen before during physicals. He was from New Bedford, a predominantly Portuguese fishing port south of Boston. He and a shill were operating a three-card-Monte scam; cheating the big lummox out of his money. I intended to expose the fraud, and let

Tony in on my plan. Tony moved off to one side to watch my back as I pushed my way into the game.

"Hey scum, remember me?" The bum pretended not to know me. "So you're swindling guys around here now, huh? Well this dude's off limits; comprende, *Jose?* He's one of *my* buddies, chump." Guys backed away sensing certain trouble when I ordered the thief to give back the money.

"Oh, yeah? Well your friend's a dim-witted loser, fatso. So why don't you shut your fat guinea face and get lost?" he snarled, reaching for Rufus' money.

Tony impressed me, and several others looking on. Newark street life must have taught him how to use a switchblade. Before I could act, he snapped a shiv at the dude's hands quicker than my eye could follow, pinning several bills to the ground.

Rufus struck like a viper. His massive hand swallowed the sleazy bum's face and slammed his head to the ground. The shill sprung to his feet and swung at me, but my quickness and strength surprised him. In one motion, I parried the punch with my forearm, snatched his collar, and held him at arms' length. He tried breaking my grip, but my tightly coiled fist held firm under his chin, locking his jaw in position. I cocked the other fist, and was about to hammer him into next week when the simpering bastard grimaced and begged me not to hit him, insisting we keep the money. I let him go for fear I'd break his jaw anyway, but sent him sprawling on his belly, out of the way.

Tony leaned over to retrieve his blade, and in doing so, he whispered something in the bum's ear. I coaxed Rufus into letting the dude go before blood spurted from his eyeballs. Rufus obeyed but never shifted his glare while gathering his money.

Rufus thanked us and introduced himself as we walked away. He kept calling me his guardian angel, grateful for having saved him from being duped of 'Momma's saved-up goin' away money.' Once by ourselves, I asked Tony what he said to the two-bit con artist.

"Oh, nuttin' special," Tony winked. "I told him youz was Pappy's favorite nephew, and if he so much as *spits* to get even, one phone call and his ol' man will be woikin' a new job as crab bait by da end o' da week." I understood Tony to mean Carmen Pappalardo, a notorious gangster frequently in the headlines in New England.

"You told him *what*? The only Pappy I know is in Lil' Abner— like Woof Woof here." I flubbed Rufus' name, but he didn't seem to object, and so it stuck. We enjoyed a knee-slapper. Woofie hooted the loudest though he hadn't a clue who we were talking about.

"Oh yeah," Tony interjected, looking up at the big Kentuckian. "Uh— Woofie is it? Just one more thing; don't youz *evah* call Vince your guardian angel again. *Evah*."

Woofie sensed seriousness in Tony's quiet, yet stern voice and nodded obedience.

"Y'see, it's like this my friend. I'm a superstitious kind o' guy, and *angels* can only come from dead people, understand? Well he ain't dead, and I ain't dead. And we ain't gonna *get* dead, either— cuz I'm also a very *lucky* guy, and since I don't intend to get whacked in this here war, that means Zeck can't be nobody's angel. Cuz where he goes, I goes too. Capisce?"

Woofie's face morphed from exuberance to looking as if he broke his Momma's heart.

"Tell youz what; you can look at Zeck as like your protector— someone you can trust and respect. Ah, kinda like a boss as some like to say in my neck of da 'hood."

"Gee, I'm sorry, er— boss. I didn't mean nothin' bad on ya. I was only tryin' to say thanks." Woofie looked back at Tony. "I— I don't want him to be no dead people— and from now on, where yoots two goes, I goes too." Woofie beamed, spoofing Tony's strong accent.

"What are youz, some kind o' smartass?" Tony grinned. "Yeah, yeah; f'get about it. You're in like Flynn, big guy. Hey, Vince; how you like them apples, huh? It looks like y'gonna be da boss o' this outfit, ya big slug."

All in it Together

New recruits came from all points of the compass and ranged in type from skilled collegians to barely literate; from rugged plow-boys to timid Mama's boys. About the only thing in common, most grew up feeling the belt-tightening of the depression.

Aside from the dramatic response to Pearl Harbor, many of us answered the call to arms believing the Army was our only chance at becoming more than the kids we really were. Despite the risks, the Army satisfied a means to learn skills, improve prospects for the future, seek adventure, and travel to places we had only dreamed of; something the depression never allowed.

Recruits were stripped of individualism and melded into a common personality that functioned and depended on one another with the beat of a collective heart. Group camaraderie boosted confidence and helped instill a strong sense of unit identity that kept morale high.

Everyone pitched in, each helping the other cope with the mental and physical demands of training, homesickness, or for many; their first attempts at mastering simple domestics like making bunks, pressing clothes, and sewing uniforms.

Guys quickly sorted themselves out, mixing and matching into closer friendships while learning to live with the personal quirks of others. Every outfit had its pain-in-the-ass jerk, but I got lucky with my twelve-man squad.

We were part of 3rd Platoon, B Company. Led by a terrific First Lieutenant C.B. Estes, we worked together and got along swell. Whether intra-squad or Battalion strength, units became fused with a strong sense of pride, rivalries sprouting like forest mushrooms. Aside from field maneuvers and team sports like soccer or softball, boxing exhibitions were a common basis for lofty prestige, especially among Company Commanders.

Each platoon was assigned to one floor of a two-story barracks, and during opening weeks, a fateful blend of swing and sass not only tightened the knots of our closely-knit unit, but also unveiled surprising talents that won favor with high-ranking Company brass.

Our platoon was constantly squabbling with the one above us. Though we never violated a minute past lights out, we were fed up with their obscenities, threats, and gripes about our taste in music, or accusing us of being too noisy at night.

"Ah, go blow it out yer barracks bags," we'd yell back. "Swing is king!"

A hayseed with a thick southern accent hollered: "come now, my brothers. Y'all need to cut with the cussin' and carryin' on, and settle things like it says in the Bible's 1:Samuel."

We figured some wannabe preacher dude thought he could mediate an amiable turn-of-the-cheek, but soon learned the rascal had another part of the Good Book in mind.

Upstairs had a 6'-3" *Goliath* named Shiloh Bragg, a bully who hated Yankees, Jews, Blacks, Micks, Wops, or just about *anybody* that didn't chew tobacco or worship Johnny Reb's Bars and Stars.

He was always crowing of being named after the Civil War battle in which his great-grandfather was a General opposite Grant's Union forces. He may have been taller than most in his outfit, but in our eyes, he was an ignorant barroom brawler of medium build who pranced around his barracks boasting how he used to beat up local pig farmers in some backwater village in southern Alabama.

"Y'all got five days to pick somebody and square off against Shiloh in the gym's ring. Three rounds, six o'clock Friday. Four cases of beer to the winner unless y'all are a bunch of low-down Yankee chicken-shits and wanna call it quits right now."

Benny yelled back. "Are you cotton pickers sure you wanna buy us beer, *and* listen to swing all night, too? We got a former golden glove boy in the outfit, ya know." The crafty Benny just tossed the baited hook back upstairs, and this time, *they* bit.

"Bring 'im on, you Jewop pilgrim. We heard about your pal. Golden gloves or not, he's a has-been that ain't even close to being a heavyweight."

Benjamin Shapiro was a quiet, yet street-savvy ghetto Jew from Rahway, New Jersey. Soon after arriving at Fort Baxter, he became best friends with Frankie D'Simone, a tough ex-reform school kid who grew up in nearby south Newark; "where *both* sides of the tracks were wrong," they'd joke.

During early phases of orientation and training, platoons were only vaguely familiar with one another. Benny didn't lie, but merely said we *had* an experienced fighter in the outfit, *not* that we intended to send D'Simone into the ring. Word had it Frankie was damned good with his dukes, and despite his lesser height and weight, he felt confident he could easily handle Bragg, but we had other plans.

For psychological effect, we sent the pint-sized Willis McKenzie upstairs to negotiate terms. *Little Mac* was in my squad, though the entire platoon adopted the feisty imp as its *Scottish* leprechaun.

Willis was a good looking, sandy-haired rascal with a playful wit and natural, permanent grin. The oldest of eight from a small cattle farm in northern Indiana, he was the size of a jockey who barely made Army weight minimums. What he lacked in stature, pound for pound, he more than made up for in heart. Given his size, he was at first shy, but always game for action; winning rapport with everyone in the outfit. Mac returned ten minutes later with both thumbs in the air.

"I told those yahoos to put up or shut up, and bumped 'em to six cases of beer and two bottles of whiskey. No draw, no rematch, no cancel; either win or forfeit. Both units to have the booze in Estes' room by tomorrow or the fight's off." Satisfied, all eyes fell upon our *David*.

"Ha," Woofie smirked. "I seen that Shiloh fella from across the ball field— shovin' on little guys and struttin' around barkin' bullshit like he was a General hisself. Shoot, he ain't nuthin' but a blowhard. Built up a little muscle tossin' hay bales around maybe, but got legs like broom sticks. I don't know nuthin' about boxin', but I'll be an egg-suckin' coonhound if I cain't whup that pig-slopper one handed."

Benny raised his hands to quell scattered laughter. "Don't worry about the knowhow, Woofie. We don't make it public knowledge, fellas, but trust me, Frankie ain't no slob; he's the real deal." Shapiro patted Frankie's shoulder. "He'll show ya the ropes, right Frankie?"

"Yeah, sure. We're all in it together, ain't we?"

Frankie smiled, and huddled us closer in laying out his plans. "Let's all meet in the barracks tomorrow afternoon. No gym work yet, Woof. First, I'm gonna teach you a little one-two technique— *then* we go to the gym and show you off. With what I got in mind, that pig turd will tuck his tail up his ass and the beer will be ours *before* the weekend. Where's our little Irish leprechaun hiding?"

"Over here, Frankie; and I'm Scottish, you Guido twit." Mac grinned, poking his head around Tony's shoulder.

"Ha, ha. Whatever you say, squirt; same soup, different veggie. Now listen. That Shiloh character loves to pick on little guys, right? So day after tomorrow, you get him riled up so he'll follow you to the gym at around five. I'll do the rest."

"You got it, Frankie."

The next day, every squad was eager to pitch in however they could. Two guys collected for the booze and picked up our ante from the PX. Someone else had a friend in motor pool, and for a carton of Camels guys chipped in, he got his buddy to torch a pair of heavy trailer hitch-pins to fit Woofie's hands.

I enjoyed working with Frankie, and got to know him better watching him coaching Woofie. I liked his style; he had that laid back class and quiet self-confidence I admired in people. Between Frankie's boxing savvy and my linebacker talents, we spent the afternoon teaching Woofie how to time his weight and balance for maximum power at impact. Frankie brought some of his gear to Baxter, and using a padded target mitt, showed Woofie how to line up the arm bones with the wrist and knuckles for making ram-rod hits.

"He's not as quick as I'd like to see," Frankie said, "but he's still a decent athlete with *incredible* power seldom seen in any fighter. In fact, Woofie's downright scary; *exactly* what we want, Vince. This is gonna be fun."

Frankie was a superb coach; precise, methodical, and patient with his giant student. His demonstrations of speed and combos that hit like steam pistons left no doubt he had seen the ring before.

The next day, half the platoon hovered over Frankie's shoulder, gloating over the promise of beer as they watched him tape Woofie's hands around the steel hitch-pins. Hoots and whistles applauded the final touch as Frankie stretched a pair of striking mitts over Woofie's massive fists.

"Christ almighty!" Mac grimaced. "Look at the *size* of this guy— and those *clubs*. I know Bragg's a half-wit goon, but you ain't gonna let Woofie hit the bastard with those pins in his fists, are ya? He'll *kill* the guy, Frankie. We don't need beer that bad."

"Relax, Mac. There ain't gonna be a fight— leastwise, *not* with Woofie if Bragg insists on doin' battle. I've seen bullshit guys like this before. You watch; he'll vanish like a popcorn fart when he gets a peek at King Kong about to stave in his ribcage. Just do as I say; go upstairs and distract those bums while we hustle Woofie off to the gym. Give us time to set up and then make sure you get them down there in about an hour."

We threw an overcoat over Woofie's shoulders just as Lt. Estes approached. "Ten-hut!"

"As you were. You boys got a dice game goin' on, or what?"

"No, sir," we parted, making room.

"What's this I hear about a boxing match? Lt. Berriman just sent a few of his boys down and filled my room with beer and whiskey."

We explained how the situation started, and how we intended to end it. Estes smirked.

"Thought so. I bet Berriman a bottle of Old Crow myself." Lt. Estes eyed Woofie top to bottom, stopping at Woofie's fists beneath his overcoat. "So, those whiny brats think their tough guy is up against D'Simone, huh? Humph, either way, I'd *still* bet, but you boys had better tell 'em to bring a priest if they go through with it." Estes chuckled and went back to his room as a group of us encircled Woofie and herded him off to the gym.

Little Mac followed within a half hour, wearing a sleeveless tee-shirt, shorts, and D'Simone's sixteen-ounce sparring gloves over his hands. We laughed at the comedic sight; the oversized gloves looked big enough for Mac to hide under.

"What the hell are you doin' with those? You look ridiculous."

"Maybe so, but you said to get the son-of-bitches down here, Frankie. So I hung these around my neck, went upstairs and told 'em I was on my way here to help the champ get the kinks out. But first, I begged them to let me off my whiskey bet. Then I told 'em not to show up cuz the champ was rusty, and didn't want anyone to see him practice. They told me to eat shit, and my bet still stands. Give 'em a few minutes, Frankie; *they'll* be here," Mac grinned.

D'Simone started Woofie running in place until breaking a good sweat before moving him to the gym's heavy bag. Frankie then asked him for a series of quick-paced, yet *easy* combos. Though only half force, the tight leather mitts reinforced with hidden steel pins amplified the impact of each thunderous wallop. A few curious GIs gathered around and watched in awe as the giant newcomer drilled the heavy bag.

"Mac's right. Here they come now," Benny said, who had been keeping an eye on the door.

Frankie asked Woofie to turn up the steam to his pile drivers. My head throbbed as I and another heavyset Corporal did our best to shoulder the bag, trying to keep it steady and from tearing loose the turnbuckles holding it to the rigging.

Frankie acted like he didn't see them and let a few more bone-crushing, jaw-breaking blows resonate before he thankfully put a halt to the violent pounding.

"What are you lowlifes doing here?" Frankie challenged. "You stooping to spying now?"

Shiloh and about a dozen of his mates sauntered up to us, their eyes fixed on Woofie's bulky physique; his sweaty biceps looked like mini V-8s behind a pair of battering rams.

"Who's that guy? I thought I was fightin' you; the golden gloves boy," Shiloh said, looking down at Frankie.

"You thought wrong. You boneheads said to *pick* somebody and to bring him on. So we did. We only *said* we had a fighter in the group— and fair warning, Bragg, we do. Only I'm his trainer, not that he really needs it since his last big fight," Frankie lied.

Mac needled Shiloh. "Cheer up Bragg. Since you love Jesus so much, you'll get to meet him come Friday. And since you and me still have our whiskey bet, I'll be sure 'n put it back on your grave— *after* I pass it through me kidneys first."

"That wasn't me spoutin' off, you dim-witted runt. It was that idiot preacher's kid, Simpson. He's the one with the big mouth."

"Oh? Not from where I'm standing."

"Shut your twisted face, you cocky little snot-rag. Why I otta shove that scotch up your scrawny Yankee butt and smack you good 'n silly." He raised a hand to cuff Mac.

Woofie knocked me and Frankie aside and got in Shiloh's face. "Touch one hair on his head, and you'd better send one of yer shit-eatin' pals to fetch a medic, cuz I'm fixin' to pound yer guts up 'n out yer eyeballs." Both platoons knew Woofie meant every word.

Shiloh's face went white. He stood looking *up* at a gorilla who outweighed him by at least eighty pounds; a gorilla whose wicked hammer-blows were still fresh in Bragg's mind. Frankie gently nudged Woofie aside.

"You'll only kill him, Woofie, and he knows it. I can see it in his eyes. Besides, he's bare knuckled— like me. How 'bout it Shiloh? You said you expected me; the *smaller* guy. Why wait 'til Friday? Let's get this over with now. It's about time you found out what it's like to fight a pro instead of some yahoo from that swamp you call home. Yeah, you heard it right, Bragg— a *pro*. I'll hit you forty times and open your face up for crow meat before you know where the first one came from. So whad'ya say, bigmouth— care to take your best shot?"

Tension hung thick, primed to explode into a platoon brawl as we edged closer, each of us eying one of Shiloh's buddies we'd likely drop first. Little Mac eased the standoff when he wedged between Frankie and Shiloh, bouncing on his toes, aping the famed profile of *The Boston Strongboy*, John L. Sullivan.

"And while Frankie's beatin' your brains out up there, I'll be down here doing a little speed bag number on your balls." Mac rolled the big gloves at Shiloh's crotch causing him to flinch and step back in natural reaction.

I burst into laughter, and soon, both groups were laughing at the skinny little nutcase dancing around looking like a stick figure shadow boxing.

Shiloh found his tongue and sneered at his backers. "This is all a set up. Why should I be the one to chance a beatin' for the likes of you bums over booze? It looks like y'all out some beer, fellas, cuz the fight's off. And if any you guys don't like it, tough shit. Mama didn't raise no fool, and anyone who says I'm yellah had better say it out of reach, or wish they hadda."

Shiloh glanced at Woofie, but gave the *pro* a more thoughtful, final measure; his eyes reading D'Simone's intense warning for the last time before bloodshed. Shiloh bulled past his silent backers and stormed from the gym, slamming the door in the face of his stunned cronies on the way out.

Mac laughed. "'*Chance* a beating,' the dumb bastard said? How about a sure thing? And talk about chances, what chance do you fellas reckon I'll have of collecting my scotch?"

"Pretty good I'd say if ya tell 'im Woofie *loves* the stuff," Tony quipped.

While giving Shiloh and friends time to disappear, we watched Woofie have his fun beating the life out of a nerveless heavy bag. GIs ended workouts and circled around, many cringing at each ferocious boomer. Ironically, it was the fearless little leprechaun who provided the uproarious finale after he goaded Frankie into putting on an amazing show rattling the gym's speed bag.

Still wearing the heavy sparring gloves, Mac wanted a go, but his poor timing repeatedly failed to keep the bag in motion. Frustrated, he let loose a final haymaker that nearly missed. The glancing blow carried his momentum forward just as the bag's sharp rebound hit him square in the face. The unexpected sting snapped his head back in reaction.

"Umph," Mac hammed it up, staggered, and fell flat on his back. Frankie counted him out, and held the bag up in triumph.

"Ladies and gentlemen," Frankie bellowed. "At one minute, thirty-eight seconds of the first round, Speedo Baggi defeats Rocky Macarooni by a knockout, and is *still*, the undisputed, *Leather*-weight Champion of the World."

The gym resounded with hoots and whistles, but erupted into guffaws when Benny, mocking deep-throated formation commands, began barking orders. Eight guys in on the impromptu skit scurried into a two-man column a few inches apart, standing at attention like pall bearers. Four of us then hoisted a *lifeless* Mac and laid him prone atop their shoulders, crossing his arms over his chest.

"Le-ft; le-ft; le-ft, raht, le-ft," Benny marked cadence; the eight stepping in place until the rest of us fell in behind as honor guard. "For-ward, harch!"

Suppressing snickers, every soldier in the gym came to attention and held military salute. Another GI caught up in the tomfoolery triggered the ringside bell at solemn intervals until our column left the gym. Woofie, the odd man out, brought up the rear, his overcoat flowing like a Napoleonic cloak as our procession marched out the gym and back to the barracks for collecting our spoils.

We waited until Friday's raucous sing-along before parsing out the beer. Minutes before honoring 22:00 lights out, we serenaded the muted mutts upstairs with a *slightly* revised chorus of "Good Night Ladies". It sparked a bit of sore-loser retaliation with their version of bunkhouse blues that brought about an end to the bickering.

At 02:00, they picked up heavy foot lockers and dropped them in unison about every fifteen minutes. After the third tumultuous jolt, more than half our platoon was up and ready to teach them a new lights-out lullaby. But our platoon leader beat us to the punch.

Lt. Estes bounded the stairs and had a private chat with his apathetic counterpart. We learned that *nobody* messes with Lt. C.B. Estes when his collar is stiff. He assured Lt. Berriman, and *both* platoons, that we'd all be singing soprano if we hosted any more jam sessions or insisted on furthering the pissing match. From then on, both units were kept too pooped with daily field training and endless miles or marching for anything more than meals or sleeping. A week after the feuding ended, Major Baldwin paid Lt. Estes a surprise visit after evening chow.

"Ten-hut!"

"At ease, gentlemen." Major Baldwin and Lt. Estes came to my section of the barracks and stopped at Woofie, who was leaning against his bunk.

"So you're the big guy I've been hearing about, eh? Rufus James Mullins," Major Baldwin said, glancing in his file folder. "Lot of stories floating around about you, Mullins— like you killed two guys in the ring awhile back. But I don't see anything in here about it. So what's the scoop?"

Woofie smirked. "Shoot, sir. I ain't never been in no dang ring, and I ain't never kilt nuthin' I ain't et, before. But prob'ly woulda come close if that Bragg fella had swatted Mac like he was gonna. That's prob'ly what you heard, sir; bunch o' henhouse jaw-jackin'."

"I see. So you're saying it's all hyped-up gossip? You didn't falsify papers to get into the Army, did you? Because if you did, that would be a serious offense, Mullins."

"No, sir. I wouldn't do nuthin' like that. All I did was beat up on that danged old bag and make a lotta noise like I was told. Tell him like it was, boss." Woofie nervously glanced at me.

"There's no need, Mullins; I believe you. It does explain a few things, but the truth is, I came over here hoping to find me a good heavyweight after hearing how King Kong shook the dust from the rafters. Given your size, maybe I could still use you; *despite* what it says in here about your limited—"

"Excuse me, sir." I interrupted. "I'm Private Zecca, Woofie's—ah, I mean Private Mullins' best friend, sir. Rufus has confided in me about his personal life, and please, no disrespect intended, but maybe some things should best be left confidential, don't you think so—sir?"

"Hmm." The Major's eyes narrowed on me. "Your name again, soldier?"

"Private Vincent Zecca, sir. If he gives me permission, perhaps I can shed some light on what happened in the gym, and likely a lot more about certain things in your file, but in private, sir."

"Is that so, Mullins? You can't speak for yourself?"

"Um, no sir. I mean yes, sir," Woofie stammered. "I mean he's the boss, sir. There ain't nuthin' he don't know about me, but I cain't talk as good as him."

I saw the confusion and sensitive fear welling in Woofie's eyes as Major Baldwin paused and scanned another page.

"I see," Baldwin nodded, closing his folder. "You got chutzpah, Zecca, and I like that in a soldier. Perhaps my excitement of finding a big heavyweight muddled my thinking. Very well then, Zecca, Estes' office."

I spent a half hour with Major Baldwin, a first rate and savvy officer I found to be sensible and easy to talk to. He followed me out and shook Woofie's hand.

"Zecca's filled in many blanks, Mullins. He said he's proud of you and respects your efforts. Keep up the good work, soldier, and stick with it. So, which of you are D'Simone and Shapiro?"

"Over here, sir." Frankie shot me a quizzical look from the other side of the room as he and Shapiro came forward.

"Zecca said if I was looking for a fighter, that you'd be my boy. He seems quite impressed with you, D'Simone; thinks you really know your stuff. Says you won a golden gloves championship once. Is that so?"

"Zecca's not correct, sir."

My heart nearly stopped. Aside from handling Woofie's secret, I buoyed the Major's hopes of landing a top boxing prospect, and *still* kept them together. *Hell of time to make a liar out of me, D'Simone.*

Frankie grinned. "Actually, it was eleven, sir: two Inter-City, a Metro, and eight City, State, or Mid-Atlantic Regional titles between New York and New Jersey."

"Jesus— are you a prize fighter?"

"Technically, not yet, sir. Those were amateur championships; *big* ones, but still open amateur. I was just about to turn pro when duty called."

"Hell of a string, D'Simone. What's your overall record like?"

"I won forty-seven bouts, thirty-eight by knockout with only one loss; and *that* was to Ray Robinson for the Inter-City Golden Gloves Championship in 1940."

"*The* Ray Robinson— like in *Sugar* Ray?"

"Yes, sir. I was only eighteen, yet still floored him in the second round, but they gave him the split decision."

"Sounds like you've been up against the big boys, D'Simone."

"Well, he was my toughest bout, sir; lightning fast." Frankie slightly flushed.

"I know who and what he is, D'Simone. Ring Magazine named him *Fighter of the Year* two years ago. And I also know that Zale's in the Navy, and about Graziano's big problem with the Army last year. It's not my first day in Dodge, son."

"Sorry, sir; didn't know." Frankie's blush reddened. "Then you may have seen pieces in local rags about a newcomer from Jersey— called 'the Iceman'? If so, that would be me, sir."

"D'Simone, D'Simone," the major reflected, trying to link the name to an article he remembered seeing— "yeah, the one the papers said was turning pro: 'who hits so hard, he'll lay 'em out for the morgue. Sure, the *Iceman*; the one they say could be the next Jake LaMotta. That's you?"

"That be me, but my country came first, sir. The pros can wait. I'm only twenty-two, so we'll see where it goes from here."

Hearing that, I kept thinking how close Bragg had come; a twitch, a feint, a single wrong word, and he'd have been hamburger.

Baldwin stroked his chin, eyeing Frankie top to bottom. "How much you weigh, son?"

"Hundred-sixty-five, but I can make middleweight in a couple days if that's your question."

"I see, and uh, Zecca also said you and Shapiro were a team. How's that?"

Frankie seized the cue. "In or out of the Army, sir, Shapiro's my trainer and corner man. I've never had better and *won't* fight without him. We're always together, sir; like a good mortar team— he loads, I explode."

"Ha, ha; a guy with wit, *and* grit. Well, I suppose it does make sense. Zecca did say you were a straight shooter; all biz. Okay, done."

Frankie could have asked for a blue-eyed babe and a staff car and got them, I mused. The Major glanced at the rest of us standing around.

"I'd love to have a good middleweight, and given your big-league stats, I'd say you could end up top banana in the entire Army; maybe whip a few smartasses in upper weight brackets as well. I'd be happy as a clam at high tide if you'd consider joining my roster, soldier. You'd have everything you needed, and every opportunity to shine. I take damned good care of fighters who make me happy, if you get my drift. I know you're probably settled in here, D'Simone, but what do you say? Think you'd be interested in new quarters?"

"Yes, sir. I do like my outfit, but if I'd still be with Company B and my buddies are close by, I don't see why not. Shapiro too?"

"Wouldn't want it any other way. If he's that good a trainer, maybe he can help develop a few of my other prospects. How about it, Shapiro, you up for the task?"

"Depends on what clay I have to work with, sir. But if you give me the authority I need to keep them focused, then I promise I'll do my best to turn them into masterpieces of violence."

"Ha, ha; *masterpieces* of violence. You have great attitude, boys. Looks like my trip over here is turning out to be better than I thought." Major Baldwin looked at Lt. Estes. "We have a few items to chat about, C.B. You in a trading mood?"

"My pleasure, Major. I know you like bourbon, and as luck has it, Lt. Berriman sent me a fresh supply last week. And ah, Mosconi!"

"Yes, sir."

"If memory serves me right, the Major enjoys a good cigar with his whiskey now and then. Any chance you'd be willing to sell me a couple of your Cubans?"

"No, sir! They're not for sale, but on the house for you, sir."

"Is that so? Well, much obliged then, Mosconi. What'd I tell ya, Moe? Do I have me a good group here, or what?"

"The best, Estes. The best; let's chat."

Lt. Estes winked at me as he guided Major Baldwin to his office. While they sipped through horse trading, the guys pounced on me eager to know what I said to Baldwin. I told them the Major agreed with me; that Woofie could knock over a half-track, but unless his opponent was chained in place, Woofie was *not* his man.

"And that's where you came in, Frankie. I told Baldwin after watching you work with Woofie, I knew you were no novice in the ring. I figured you were good, but have to admit, you floored me when I learned you're world class. As for you two as a team, I told the Major he couldn't find a more effective pair. Baldwin said he trusted my judgment, and it felt good hearing that from top brass. So do us proud, paisan."

"Count on it, Vince. I got a good taste of joint-life doing a stint in juvie when I was twelve. I've kept my nose clean ever since, and don't intend to ever look back. Thanks for the vote of confidence. You're my kind of garlic-snapper, paisan. We'll stay in touch."

"I figured as much. You'll be missed, but it's for the best. From what Baldwin was saying, it sounds like you guys are in for some nice perks, too. So what the hell, run with it and leave the ground-pounding to us."

"Vince is right, *Iceman*," Tony added. "Grab the brass ring while ya can. We'll take care o' them Nazi's. You just give the Stars and Stripes plenty to write about, capisce?"

Shapiro shook my hand. "Thanks for keeping me and Frankie together, Vince. That was class."

"Hey, glad to help," I said, brushing it off. "Baldwin agreed the change in venue meant Frankie could train, and keep his skills sharp under your guidance instead of some bent-nose leech in Jersey City."

JJ interrupted. "Enough about those two palookas, whadja say about Woofie? What's he hidin'; are we losin' him, too?" Jim Aaron Yarnes, Jr., or "JJ", was the squad's stone-in-its-shoe, a nitwit from West Virginia coal country, though I suppose he was not a total reject, but more of a naive nuisance who meant well and tried hard most of the time.

"You really wanna know what I said— in *private*, moron? Okay; Woofie didn't kill *two* guys; it was *eight*— and *all* of 'em just for nosing into his personal business. Can you imagine if word got out we had a maniac in the outfit who snaps like a summer twig when somebody annoys him? Why, you might even be the next poor slob to trip his trigger, JJ. Y'never know.

Woofie tapped him on the shoulder. "Hey, junior. What was it you was wantin' t'know about me?"

"Nuthin', Woof." JJ blushed. "I gotcha's. Don't mind me. I'm a moron like the boss said. Sorry, won't happen again."

"Five minutes, lights out, you twittering pack o' schoolgirls!" C.B. yelled. "Anyone not in their bunk when I drop the switch gets next latrine duty!" The chatter stopped and we scattered, sounding more like an attic full of mice when the lights *go on*.

A couple days later, we gave D'Simone and Shapiro a quiet sendoff pending transfers to cushy *clerical* posts at Baldwin's HQ. We split a case of beer and polished off the last of Mac's scotch, sent courtesy of the *honorable* ones upstairs who refused to be tainted by Bragg's welshing on his bet with Mac.

More changes soon affected the outfit. Wholesale shifting of troops was common during this phase of training. Platoons were adjusting; balancing talents into more effective combat units. GIs were discovering aptitudes and honing skills for manning specialized duties needed anywhere from Army Air Corps crews to zither players. If one could do it, the Army had a need for it.

On the flip side, Lt. Estes finagled a shrewd trade from Baldwin. We struck pay-dirt with the arrival of Corporal Chase Fairchild; our new squad leader.

An inch taller and slightly heavier build than Tony, Chase was a class act; respected by GIs and officers from several platoons within B Company. He was the eldest son of a prominent horse breeder from Kentucky's bluegrass, who, contrary to his parents' firm stance, enlisted while a junior at Princeton.

"I *had* to serve; before the war ended, Zeck. It's my duty. I'm not a spoiled blueblood or afraid of combat— *despite* what callous slobs may think. I even fudged a little about my education levels so I'd be treated like any other regular guy. But oh boy, did I ever catch it from the folks," he chuckled. "They pitched a *fearsome* fit, but understood my views and came around in the end. I gave them my word I'd finish my degree, as well as get my Masters as soon as I returned to civilian life."

Though he exemplified wealth and polished upbringing, Chase was as fun-loving and unpretentious as anyone in the outfit. He also happened to be blessed with a divine tenor's voice equal to the finest of virtuosos; the *perfect* topping for our musically-flavored group.

Advanced training wore on at about the same pace as Shiloh wore out platoon pals. Shiloh grew increasingly sullen; finally boiling over when he set upon on a 5'-8" whipping boy from another platoon.

The 'no good Yankee Mick' was a draftee out of a Chicago street gang; an Irish tough with an excessive mean streak. While on maneuvers, push came to shove, and without warning the punk planted a heavy boot into Shiloh's groin. Though a cheap shot, the spat should have been over, but the alley rat kept kicking a downed and beaten Bragg who suffered a badly smashed nose and two cracked ribs.

Despite Shiloh's reputation, he was still part of 2nd platoon. In his defense, four mates pounced upon his attacker and delivered punishing field justice of their own. Soon after, the Army sent the draftee to the stockade, and discharge papers to Shiloh on account of his undesirable conduct and inability to adapt as fit for soldiering, similar to dozens of others culled from the Army.

I was never a fan of Bragg's by any stretch, but in some ways, I felt sorry for the miserable lout; thinking he arrived at Baxter with more baggage than socks and underwear.

Clinging to their fading Civil War heritage, I suspect his family filled his head with a litany of Deep South tutelage, nurturing a false sense of confidence that made him a bully. In their eyes, he was next in line to change the world at war; the heir-apparent to preserve the family's legacy, his portrait hanging alongside Grand Pappy Bragg. But it was not to be.

Within weeks, he trudged home disgraced, an official reject, a blight on the family tree. *A pity, Bragg; by picking on all the little guys, you became one.*

Fort Hamilton

Advanced training whizzed by quicker than Chinatown cabbies. Drill instructors pushed us hard as we scrambled over, under, and through obstacle courses; marching our asses off lugging full field packs and rifles for miles with our heads baking inside steel helmets under a blazing sun. Several passed out, but the toll would have been worse had it been the height of summer.

The frequency of bivouacs increased as did everything else we had to do; and to do them all *quick*. Digging fox holes, going through mess, or no matter what the task; the '*do it quick, quick, quick*' drove me nuts.

We learned about the tools of military mayhem by caring for and firing 30 caliber M1s, Browning automatic rifles, light and heavy machine guns, mortars, bazookas, grenades, high explosives, mines, and artillery. They made us crawl under barbed wire and into slimy drainage ditches as live machine gun fire zipped overhead. If not schlepping it, we were listening to it at lectures and films covering topics from hygiene to camouflage and chemical warfare.

The day finally came when we got orders to ship out; *our* turn to prove our battle braggadocio as the latest band of Yankee Doodle Dandy's anxious to punish the Axis Powers. We were leaving behind memories, pleasant or otherwise, with newly arriving recruits likely viewing our departure with envy.

Guys handled orders in different ways. Some itched to see combat, others wrestled with mild anxiety to outright fear of having to first navigate U-boat infested waters, let alone of squaring off against a determined enemy in a *real* war.

We'd even heard of draftees who either ate, or did *something* to themselves to avoid going, but there were plenty of replacements for the bastards. As for the Mutt and Jeff misfits, we remained our usual don't-give-a-rat's-ass selves— ready for whatever the Army threw at us. Perhaps it was our way of repressing worries that we'd ever taste home-cooked lasagna again. For now, the Army threw us weekend passes, and we planned to use them carousing with a collection of female fans in town.

Weeks ago, we found a cheap hotel and for seventy-five cents each, we split a room with two double beds for saying goodbye to a few special coeds; not so much with words, but with long embraces. Tony was getting impatient and poked his head into the showers.

"Snap it up, Zeck. Leave some hot water for the kitchen, for crissake. We're gonna be late."

"Hold ya hoss's, handsome. I'm doin' a Maytag mash."

A few guys paid to have their clothes cleaned, but Tony and I figured on saving the fare for more important things like booze and broads. Laundry to us meant heaping our clothes in a pile, soaping the body and the duds, and then stomping hell out of them while showering. I suppose I had been taking more time than normal, lingering under the hot spray while sifting through a medley of thoughts. Perhaps the reality of leaving the relative comfort of Fort Baxter was sinking in.

Officers stressed the need to keep our mouths shut; not to write home that we were leaving, let alone in what strength, type, and timing of transports were involved. We weren't told our final destination; only officers were privy to such veiled plans. But wherever it was, it would likely be a POE, or Port of Embarkation. Like it or not, our stay in North Carolina was over.

We spent our last days cleaning barracks and packing. Baxter's warehouses were stacked to the rafters with foot lockers and barrack bags stuffed with what meager possessions we had. Two hours before departure, the camp was abuzz with activity. Columns of trucks hauled battalions and equipment to loading platforms; everyone in a festive mood, yet no one seemed to be talking.

Normal chatter converted to song as squads improvised musicals as they worked. There were songs for hefting equipment, songs for loading trucks, and even a song for boarding the troop train led by Chase, our platoon's operatic maestro. Civilians often stopped to listen, many joining in the chorus much to our delight.

Once aboard, we were read a long list of do's and don'ts— like don't leave the train and talk to civilians at station stops along the way. Late in the afternoon, the trained pulled away from the loading depot. The trip was painfully slow, averaging fifteen miles-per-hour over illogical routes to avoid possible saboteurs. After passing bridges with sentries posted, we realized security was not taken lightly. Although we didn't know where we'd end up, town signs along the way told us we were heading in a northerly route.

Coaches were built at the turn of the century; the original wooden interiors were dirty and stained from old soot and years of use. The narrow bench seats were hard as hell with matted horsehair for padding, covered by well-worn leather.

We spent a terrible night tossing and turning. No one got much sleep as guys were angled every which way, constantly shifting position trying to get comfy. The following day we rolled into a large switching yard, stopping on a siding somewhere in D.C. as we could see the Capitol and the Washington Monument off in the distance. C.B. Estes passed word of a layover pending linkup with an inbound train due in about three hours.

A day prior to leaving Baxter, Major Baldwin shuffled several officers; promoting Lt. Estes to Captain and new CO; Chase bumped to sergeant, though still our squad leader. Given the tiresome, dust-plagued trip, Estes bent the rules and allowed platoons a chance to stretch their legs, but warned us to keep our mouths shut, stay close to the rail yards, and avoid civilians.

Tony and I were grateful for the breather and wasted little time wandering, hoping to find relief for parched throats. We ambled upon a place called the Whistle Stop; a small, yellow brick tap-and-grill on the edge of a spur catering to rail workers. Judging from its decorum and filled with rail workers ending shifts, we saw no harm in going in. A yard this massive must see military trains every day.

Everywhere I'd been, I was amazed at how supportive civilians truly were of the war effort, or expressed sincere regard for troop welfare. Whistle Stop patrons were no different.

Nick, the burly but jovial bartender, charged us only half price for drinks. His generosity stretched what was left of our month-end finances, but we still tapped out after sampling shots from one end of the back-bar to the other. Tony emptied his pockets.

"Get a load o' this shit, Zeck. It's pathetic. All I got left 'til payday is a whoppin' seventy-three cents."

"Don't feel bad, Rockefeller. You're richer than me." I dropped two dimes and a quarter beside it. "Look at that— two buck privates and not two bucks between us."

We laughed and resumed milking our last affordable shots as we spotted Frazer coming in behind two privates we didn't recognize.

"Frazer! Over here," Tony called, flagging him toward the bar.

"Hiya, fellas. Figured you two alkie-hounds would sniff a trail to the nearest gin mill. Shots, too, I see."

"Yassah, Father Frazer." Tony waved his hand along a row of bottles. "We started at that end and now we're up to there." Tony pointed to a scotch.

Frazer grinned at Tony's slight slurring. "Keep on mixing shots like that, and the train won't need a *woo-w-o-o-o* of its own."

"Yeah, maybe so, but how's about I buy youz a drink so youz can hoot-a-choo-choo with us?"

"Okay, don't mind if I do. And may God bless you my son for the kindness." Frazer ordered an untried brandy.

"Make it three— no, four. Get yourself one, too Nick," Tony ordered. Nick poured and stood by waiting to be paid.

"Well, don't just stand there looking like a cross-eyed putz; pay the man. You said you were buying."

"Um, I think I'm gonna stand here and look like a cross-eyed putz. How you like them apples?"

Frazer matched Tony's lopsided grin. "Come on, Tony, the guy's waitin'. Ante up."

"Um, I'd love to, Dad, but you'll have to loan your bastard son an advance foist, see." Tony slid our combined bankroll toward him. "It's all we got. We're flat-ass broke 'til pay day; I'll show youz." Tony made elephant ears, turning his pockets inside-out to prove it. "Wanna see his trunk?" Tony grinned, reaching for his zipper.

"Save it; you'll only attract flies." Howie groaned, but opened his wallet. "I should have known there'd be a catch with you two sidewinders. You were too damned quick to spring for that round."

"Hey, don't I always make da milkman wait for his dough so's I can take care o' youz foist— *Dad*?"

"Oh brother, here it comes," Frazer said, rolling his eyes. "You know what it's like with you, Mosconi? You have a monthly ritual.

You get paid; pay back; spend 'til broke; borrow; get paid; pay back; and your *weasel*-wheel keeps on spinning. But one day, Mosconi, all your friends will lean back on their stools like deaf, dumb, and blind monkeys. Then what'll you do, huh?"

"Simple. Come see dad just like now, cuz youz just said 'pay back' *twice*, and 'borrow' *once*. That means I paid back double, so now, ya owes me a borrow, see?"

"Ah, Jesus— I owes *you* a borrow. Ha, you always have a crazy answer for everything, don't ya?" Frazer laughed. "Don't ever argue with this guy, Nick; nobody ever wins. Okay, I know you're good for it, but it's gonna cost you another drink, wise guy. A brandy, Nick. No wait, how about that fancy lookin' bottle above it, right there? Is that your most expensive one?"

Frazer was a saint, and we thanked the lord he came in. His mature and caring manner had proved valuable many times before, but he likely saved us from serious discipline at the Whistle Stop. Aside from funding our follies, he hustled us out and guided our stumbling back to the station with little time to spare.

COs wasted no time ordering units to fall in for head counts, and God help any who left holes in the ranks. After roll call, platoon leaders ordered us aboard, re-read the do's and don'ts, and disclosed our final destination; Fort Hamilton in New York.

Tony passed out the moment he flopped in his seat. I leaned back into as comfortable a position as possible, but focused on avoiding the spinners before daring to doze off. I smirked, rembering the first time I got polluted.

I was a senior in high school celebrating with a few teammates after trouncing Medford. We lassoed a few gals and drove to Revere Beach for a clambake, singing and drinking by a bonfire. I got bombed mixing vodka and gin with beer. When they dropped me off about one in the morning, they rolled me from the bed of a pick-up and left me sitting on the sidewalk in front of my house. I couldn't walk, and literally crawled on my hands and knees up the stairs and into our den, trying not to wake the folks. I sprawled onto the sofa thinking I was home free, but was I ever wrong.

Spinners whirled the room into a maelstrom and I heaved just as my father entered the room. He went berserk, grabbed me by the neck, and pushed me through the kitchen. He made a racket, paying no mind to banging me against the table or knocking a chair over getting me to the sink just as I let go again. He held me firmly by the neck and kneed me hard in the ass.

"*Puzzare* bevuto!" he yelled, calling me a stinking drunk. "When something round and hairy reaches you tonsils, you can quit puking because it'll be my knee coming through your rectum," he screamed, only he used a string of *factory* vernaculars mixed with Italian.

This was the only time I had ever heard Papa cuss at home. In a way, it seemed like poetic justice as I don't know who was the more apologetic; me, or him when he turned and saw Mama standing there hearing every word. I've since learned to handle booze, but mixing shots was asking for trouble.

I eventually dozed off and didn't stir again until a smorgasbord of delectable aromas tugged at my nostrils, pulling me from my stupor. *My, oh my— the mouth-watering smells.*

Since leaving Baxter, we had nothing but Army-issued baloney and cheese sandwiches to eat. I was famished. After hours cooped up in a humid, musty old coach reeking of body odors, I inhaled slowly and deeply, savoring such tantalizing teasers as fresh roasted peanuts, rich coffees, juicy steamed hot dogs, tangy garlic, spicy curry, and assorted culinary delights filling the train.

I opened my eyes before I embarrassed myself with drool. No one noticed, not even my snoring drew a look as dozens of heads were bobbing at every window, ogling views of the metropolitan skyline. When the tracks ran close to apartment units, I was amazed how many people were leaning out windows, cheering and blowing us kisses.

Most country boys had never been to a big city, pointing and gazing at the New Jersey and New York skylines. They marveled at the sheer size and number of interesting buildings and landmarks, that until now, they had only heard about or seen on postcards. I was raised in a big city and was content to let them have their thrill. I laid back, closed my eyes, and let my *nose* do my sightseeing as the train lazily rolled into Manhattan, crossed the East River, and turned south toward Fort Hamilton on Brooklyn's waterfront.

Fort Hamilton was a massive military complex replete with elegant colonial brick and stone buildings predating the Civil War. The garrison once protected sister forts on Staten Island against Confederate raiders, now a staging area for convoys. Eighty years later, the fort was still heavily armed, yet it seemed strange to see so many camouflaged gun emplacements along the waterfront of a bustling American city. While shuttled from the train, we were amazed at the unimaginable number of different vessels in one place; loading and unloading, round the clock from rows of block-long warehouses teeming with cargo.

Once inside the Fort, we immediately moved into long, three-story quarters arranged in quadrangles around small central squares. Our first few days were busy with several orientation lectures, organizing APO addresses, insurance, and falling in for what seemed an endless string of inspections.

The medical hassles soon followed as countless men stood in line for giving blood or getting shots for typhoid, tetanus, small pox, and lord knows what else as medics flanking either side stuck us with needles. Periodic checks for allergic and feverish reactions were a nuisance, but better than surprise "short arm inspections."

Before reveille, outfits were rousted from bunks and ordered to stand in the middle of the quadrangle wearing nothing but a towel. Medics worked their way through the ranks checking everyone for crabs, lice, and venereal disease. The more bashful ones complained of unjust humiliation, but we reckoned it was probably worse for the corpsmen.

"Ha, ha; too bad we can't make 'em all stand at attention," someone yelled.

"Yeah, with Hitler's mug tattooed under each *helmet*."

The two jokesters drew laughter, but they were not the first to think of the idea; we heard it actually happened. According to a corpsman, a GI stationed at a sister POE up the Hudson was yanked from formation and severely punished by an enraged medic when he saw: *Kiss Me, Doc,* tattooed under the foreskin.

Aside from optional orientation movies, Intelligence Ops held mandatory security sessions. During each lecture, the slogan: "silence means security" was broadcast at regular intervals over loud speakers;

stressing the need to keep our mouths shut. Posters of a drowning sailor shouting the caption: 'Someone Talked', were all over the base, effectively making the reality that spawned the precept: "Loose Lips Sinks Ships", crystal clear.

Mail at Fort Hamilton was subject to more stringent censorship than at Baxter. At the risk of severe disciplines, including court martial and prison time, we were forbidden to write home about *anything* of a military nature.

No one knew how long we'd be at Hamilton, but whether two days or two months, most days were boring. Three main activities occupied our time: falling in for inspections; marching around the mammoth compound for no apparent reason; or watching *other* Companies march in formation for no apparent reason, including Battalions of Canadians and Aussies no one seemed to know why they were here.

GIs spent idle time gambling at dice and poker, playing chess, watching movies, or gathered around singing cowboys with guitars. A chance meeting inspired me and Chase to concoct our own goofy way of passing time.

We met a cheery fellow from Pennsylvania playing a lovely old squeeze-box; a family heirloom brought over by grandparents from Latvia. We were admiring its beauty; the intricate inlaid mother-of-pearl motifs spawned an idea. The three of us huddled, and after a few rehearsals, we worked out hilarious routines for entertaining scores of GIs.

Chase donned an old fedora, pulled his trousers up as high around his belly as he could, and sang silly verses to tunes played on the squeeze-box; I, the organ-grinder monkey, begging for coins at the end of my tether.

I drew my neck into hunched shoulders, pursed my lips, and flailed hands over my face, waddling and bouncing on my toes like a chimp. GIs roared and pointed at my jaw and lower lip jutting out, saying I looked like a pompous Mussolini as I squatted and lumbered toward guys I'd singled out for teasing, or picking lint from their uniforms.

All went well until a pair of unrelated events caught up with me— I was long on laundry and short on clothes when pulling on a pair of threadbare trousers that morning. Mix that with kidney beans and sausage served at mess the night before, and the combination triggered a fitting finale to our act.

Crowds gathered, the fun mounted, and coins clinked into my cup. Near the end of my rope, I leapt at a GI taunting me, landing heavily in a squat. The moment my thighs hit my abdomen, my ass bounced off my ankles and busted loose a robust breakage of wind; my trousers splitting from zipper to belt loop with my shorts ballooning out like a kernel of popcorn. Chase choked and couldn't sing another note as the squeeze box mimicked a braying mule.

On the brighter side, I had panhandled enough coinage to pay a fellow platoon mate more adept with a needle and thread than I, yet *still* had enough to buy us a case of beer. The monkey business ended, but in days that followed, I broke down and unpacked my horn. I teamed with a fellow playing a big Cajun accordion, and we entertained cheering fans with several lively Dixieland numbers.

I hadn't slept well since our arrival at Hamilton and the food got worse. Drained of energy, I felt cranky and unable to handle another disgusting breakfast. Lately, morning mess consisted of a sloppy yellow soup laced with burnt chunks of meat Hamilton cooks called scrambled eggs and ham.

The weekend had come and Captain Estes approved passes, but first, we had another medical checkup for fever. Fearing mandatory confinement, I held the thermometer loosely in my teeth sneaking cool air past my lips, making sure I was released with the others for exploring the Big Apple where *real* chow could be found.

In da 'Hood

Thank God it was Saturday, but not just *any* Saturday. To a country that loved its horse racing, the first Saturday in May meant Derby Day.

All spring, speculation centered on when and where we'd be sent to Europe, but placing a close second was which talented three-year-old would likely win the Run for the Roses. A hot topic for show wondered if we'd witness a back-to-back rare Triple Crown Champion like last year's Count Fleet. He electrified fans when he destroyed the competition at Belmont; winning the Triple's final leg by a whopping twenty-three lengths.

Once in lower Manhattan, the squad split into personal day trips but agreed to reconvene later at a place called *The Curb*. MPs said it would likely be teeming with dames, and was a good spot for catching the Derby broadcast.

Frazer passed on touristy treks since he was from Philadelphia and had been to New York many times. Instead, he joined Tony and me for a surprise visit to Tony's home in Newark. We boarded a commuter across the Hudson and took a bus to a somewhat shoddy neighborhood where Tony's family rented a second floor apartment.

"What d'ya know, you're in da '*hood* now, fellas; where—"

"Yeah, yeah, we know; where sheep are nervous," I beat Tony to his punch line.

"Hey, youz two been here before?"

Tony tried masking it, but I sensed a tinge of anxiety as we got closer to his home. It vanished the instant his mother opened the door. She gasped, her face beaming like a North Church beacon; overjoyed at seeing her son in uniform.

"Papa, lascilo introdurre Vince Zecca, un Siciliano. Eh, il mio amico migliore." Tony introduced me as his best friend, but finished in English to include Frazer. "He's da big galoot from Boston I wrote youz about."

"Buon giorno." My greeting impressed his father, who gave my hand a vigorous shake. Having met his parents, I could see where good looks came from in the family.

Frazer and I took special notice meeting Tony's seventeen-year-old sister, Alessa. She was beyond pretty; she was *stunning*— more like a glamorous magazine model. She was tall and slender, with strikingly perfect features; her alluring eyes and flawless complexion flanked by wavy black hair had me reeling when our eyes met.

Un angelo da cielo, the angel from heaven made my heart flutter. Alessa lowered her eyes and blushed in modest shyness, but chanced a coy smile when glancing at her admiring mother. Mr. Mosconi motioned us toward the kitchen table.

"Venuto. Eh, you come. Please, sit. We eat, have e'some vino."

Though poor, and further affected by rationing, his parents not only opened their home and their hearts, but now their cupboards. Alessa set the table as her mother prepared long sticks of bread, an antipasto, and seasoned olive oil for dipping.

"And now, the vino." Mr. Mosconi added the crowning grace, insisting on decanting his last two bottles of a sentimental Chianti he had been saving for a momentous occasion.

"Eh, what could be more e'special than having my boy home; and with his best e'friends, eh?" Mr. Mosconi handed me the bottle. "Provengono da Siena," he said, pointing to its label with stalwart pride. "Vigna del mio zio."

Alessa translated for Frazer. "Papa said it's from his uncle's vineyard high in the hills of Siena; a little hamlet in Tuscany where my father was born."

She glanced at me and smiled, assuming I understood her father. I could listen to her talk all day. The mood grew festive and relaxed as we worked our way through delicious treats and a superb, fruity wine. Casual chatter picked up as we shared stories of training and people we'd met. Mrs. Mosconi sliced another stick of bread, and then slipped out of the kitchen unnoticed.

"Ah, Jeeze, Ma," Tony cringed, seeing his mother returning with three photo albums. "Don't bring them out here, you'll bore everybody to death."

"Mom, nobody wants to look at photos," Alessa said, smiling in support of her brother. Mrs. Mosconi was hesitant, but I encouraged her forward.

"Oh, no, Mrs. Mosconi; pay them no mind. Please, set them down over here; we *gotta* see these."

Her uncertainty was overshadowed by Frazer's engaging smile as he made room between us at the table.

"What are you worried about, Tony," Frazer asked. "You got wanted posters in here?"

Mr. Mosconi slid his chair closer, anxious to describe numerous pictures of the old country where he was raised. Alessa had likewise moved closer to Frazer, enjoying the old photos of her father's roots. Tony grinned, and yielding to the fun, leaned forward for a better view. A second album contained more recent snapshots of Tony and Alessa growing up.

"Ha, look at this one, Frazer. Don't tell me this is leetle Tony?" I teased. "Aw, look at him; all spiffy in his little alpine outfit, and pageboy haircut. Oh, ain't he so cute?"

"Ugh," Tony groaned. "You had to find that one, didn't ya?"

"He was e'three," his mother said, doting over the photo. Tony was wearing a second-hand, traditional outfit from northern Italy; a gift from a neighbor when they lived in the Bronx. His white, silk stockings were tucked neatly into plaid knickers just below the knee, with wide embroidered suspenders fastened by big buttons at the front. His blouse was white and fluffy, adorned with a rounded frilly collar, a string bowtie, and a small matching cap like a beret with a tiny loop twist on top.

Mr. Mosconi smiled, admiring the old sepia print. "Tony was always a good e'boy. Never any trouble, eh, Felisa?" Mrs. Mosconi agreed with her husband.

"No he wasn't, Mama." Alessa scrunched her nose at Tony, making a playful face in refute of her parents' beliefs. "Don't let Tony fool you; he was a devil, and just never got caught. That's why his school chums called him 'the lucky one'— after you, Mama, remember?" Alessa smiled, telling Frazer: "his pals always teased him he was a Mama's boy because her name means '*lucky*' in old Roman."

"I'll buy that," Frazer said. "He was the same way at Baxter— *lucky*, and *still* a Mama's boy," he joshed, pointing to another photo. "Aw, and what have we here; Tony in the buff, flashing his cute little bum?"

Frazer referred to a nude baby lying on its belly and pushing up from the table, showing off its apple-round buns.

"No, that one's of me," Alessa smiled.

"What are youz gazin' at, Zecca? I know what ya thinking," Tony ribbed.

"*What*? I wasn't thinking anything; just looking at the pictures." I was innocent, but felt embarrassingly trapped.

"Ah, huh; sure ya was. Youz was wishin' that picture was taken yesterday— same pose."

Alessa giggled as a grinning Mr. Mosconi pointed to my cheek.

"Eh, no more vino for you, Vincent. It's up to there, already."

No use. I could feel the heat radiating from my face, my cheeks likely matching the color of the chianti.

The afternoon was one of the most pleasant I had ever enjoyed. The time to leave came all too quickly as Frazer hinted we should be on our way. We said goodbyes and thanked Tony's family for their generous hospitality.

"We'll wait up at the corner pub, Tony, and take your time," I said, affording him a private moment with his family.

Alessa hailed me as I stepped onto the porch of their two-story walkup. Her chin quivered and tears filled her eyes. I felt awkward as she stood on the stair above me, looking deeply into my eyes. *What could be wrong?*

"Tony wrote us how much he worships you, Vincent; how wise and strong you are. He said you're like his big brother; always looking out for him. *Please*, Vincent. Do watch over him. Please bring our Tony back home to us," she pleaded, unabashed by tears. "He's all we have, and my family promises to pray for you, too. *Benedicali*," she blessed me.

My big mitts fumbled at her tiny waist as her hands rested on my shoulders. Over her shoulder, I glanced at her mother looking on from the doorway, her brow crinkled and fingertips pressed lightly against her lips, fighting back tears. Before I could respond, Alessa kissed my cheek, whirled, and ran back into the apartment.

So few words from trepid lips, yet so much said by an expectant face— *both* their faces. I was speechless, and choked up descending the stairs. Alessa's shameless dark eyes appealing to me for Tony's protection had woven a thread around my heart— an image that will never leave me. At that moment, I witnessed the supernal depth to which families must go to reconcile their fears when loved ones are in harm's way. It was a somber walk down the block.

"Good grief, Vince; will ya look at all the flags? It looks like the whole neighborhood has someone in the war." Frazer noted the number of handkerchief-size banners in tenement windows, each meant one or more residents were in the Armed Forces.

"It ain't the *flags* that bother me, Frazer. Did you see how many had gold stars? *Bunches* of 'em— and *all* on this block."

Our pace slowed, eyes scanning both sides of the street aware each gold star symbolized someone *killed* in action. Two tenements farther down, I nearly stopped; my heart sank as the glands tightened in my throat. I lowered my eyes and moved on.

"*Four* of 'em," I whispered, blinking back empathetic tears. "I've seen enough, Frazer. Let's go, this place gives me the creeps. I don't like it. Not one damned bit. How come so many, and why all *here*— on *Tony's* block?" I feared a dreaded omen, and Frazer read my face.

"Don't even think about it, Vince. It ain't worth getting bogged down in all that superstition stuff. '*It is what it is,*' I always tell my little woman— it is what it is. Just a bunch of bad luck is all. So don't worry about nuthin'. We're gonna be fine. After all, how can we miss, Vinnie boy. Ain't we rubbing shoulders with the 'lucky one'?" He flashed a reassuring smile and ushered me into Durso's.

We passed on beer, both opting for a stronger whiskey over ice. We sipped in silence, my mind returning to Alessa and all those gold stars she must see every day. I was unaware Tony had written home about me the way he had; his *big* brother. I was touched, and until now, hadn't realized I felt *exactly* that way toward him. I was an only child, and sometimes missed not having siblings. *How would my parents take it if I got killed,* my thoughts diverting to home.

I envisioned Mama collapsing, clutching the War Department's telegram. Pop would do his best to console her, trying to give her strength to cope with her son's demise with honor and dignity, all the while masking the pain in his own heart.

I suddenly missed my parents. I thought about how Pop worked his butt off in a sweltering shoe factory. He never complained and religiously handed Mama what little money he earned to provide us a home, never spending a dime on himself. I thought of the many times I had shared aspirations of being a history teacher. I hadn't realized it then, but now understand the helpless disappointment in their eyes, aware our poverty meant college was out of the question. When the Army filled the void, they accepted my enlistment with support, and never a discouraging word.

They too must lie awake at night, secretly rueful of the same fears I had just witnessed. Until this moment, I hadn't realized how much I loved and appreciated them. *Honor thy Father and Mother,* a commandment said, triggering another enigma. *How does God fit into all this madness?* I looked up as the last bits of ice melted in my glass.

"Did you see the one with four stars, Frazer? Pitiful. Absolutely pitiful. Probably wiped out the whole damned family."

Frazer didn't say a word, only nodded to an empty glass cupped between his hands while I cynically remembered my catechism.

"We were always taught that God is one, Frazer; for *everybody* on the planet. Humph, an all-seeing and *merciful* God, they said. How do you 'spose the Chinese God let the Japs do what they did to them? Or the *German* God turning a monster loose like Hitler, then sit back and watch a gang of Nazi thugs destroy Europe, murdering millions?" *Questions, questions, questions raced through my mind.*

"I hear ya, Zecca. Look what God is letting Hitler do to the Jews; his so-called chosen people— *my* people. Wish I had answers for ya, Zeck, but I'm only a dumb-ass ghetto Jew from Philly. When it comes to stuff like this, my mystic turban went out the door along with my old man when I was eight. But I do know one thing, pal— we're gonna get our licks in beatin' on the bastards who started it all." We clinked glasses the moment Tony came through the door.

"Hey, look who's here," a patron yelled. "It's that Mosconi kid from up the street." Tony drew surprised looks from those who recognized him from the neighborhood. Some hoisted glasses in hello as others complimented how spiffy and manly he looked in uniform. All the while I studied their faces, suspecting a few could likely claim some of those gold stars, but no one let on.

An elderly lady with thick gray hair tied in a bun approached from playing dominos at a rear table. She spread her arms and kissed him on both cheeks. Tony returned her hug and introduced Mrs. D'Agastino, a close friend of the family who lived two tenements from his parents.

"Ah— il mio Antonio. Voi diavolo grazioso," she said, pinching Tony's cheek. She held both his hands and stood back to inspect her handsome devil. "Look at you. And your friends— ah, so young, but so brave. I pray God protects you." Her expression saddened as she searched Tony's face with loving, yet mournful eyes. "We lose too many from here already, Antonio. Too, too many."

Durso interrupted with another round for the table. "Come on, Rosalie. Let the boys enjoy their drinks. Next thing y'know, you'll be eloping with Tony and he'll end up AWOL."

"Ah, hush Joey. I should be so lucky," she joshed. She clasped each of our hands and kissed them. "I pray for safe return; *no* more stars." She shook her finger, sighed, and went back to her dominos without looking up.

"So Tony, where's all them sheep I been hearin' about?" I asked to buoy the mood.

"I tol' youz already; they be noivous, and must be hidin' out with the likes o' youz two roamin' da 'hood."

"Ah, Christ. Is he using that tired, old line on youz boys, too?" Mr. Durso laughed, all too familiar with Tony's antics.

"Fellas, this is Joey Durso. He's known me from when I used to come in here and shine his customer's shoes, eh Joey."

"Si, not so long ago, eh? But look at youz now; all grown up." Durso leaned in close and kept his voice low. "Tony, youz be careful. Rosalie's right, there's been many a sad time in here. But hey, kick some Nazi ass for me and for da 'hood, okay? I gotta get back to the bar, but how about a backup on the house?"

"Can't, Joey, but thanks. Half the squad's waitin' for us in Manhattan and we're runnin' short of time. Next time— when I get back, I promise, Joey. Youz can *count* on it."

"Ah, capisce." Durso smiled and exchanged manly hugs with Tony, shook our hands, and went back to his bar. We hurried our drinks and caught the next bus from the corner.

Derby Day at "The Curb"

The MPs were right about The Curb. The place was a large multi-sectional bar crowded with civilians and uniforms from every branch of the Service. By the time we arrived, Derby Day gaiety was manifest.

Woofie and Little Mac were saving a pair of tables near the rear. Frazer and I joined them while Tony meandered through the crowd. We hadn't been seated thirty minutes before Tony returned with a petite, gorgeous redhead clinging to his arm and three WACS in tow. Tony engaged in a quick-witted exchange with his feisty companion as I secretly tried to discern which of the others might be willing to settle for ol' Plug.

"So, y'name is Natalie Fox. That means youz must be a *red* fox," Tony teased, alluding to her rich, auburn hair.

"No, silly. I'd be a vixen. *You'd* be a fox."

"No I ain't. I'm a machine gunner. Ain't that right boss?" Tony looked at me as Natalie sidled closer and gently turned his chin with the tip of her index finger. She looked straight into his eyes and, with a spicy grin, leaned closer until their noses nearly touched.

"That's okay, handsome. You can be a machine gunner all day long and *still* be a fox."

Tony took the cue and stole a kiss as her arm curled around his biceps. Little Mac had been watching, and perhaps with a tinge of envy, razzed Tony.

"Get a load of handsome Hank over there, boys. I can already see who the boss is. You had better watch yourself, Mosconi. You'll be putty in her hands before the night's out."

Tony smiled and pecked another kiss as we turned attention to handicapping the Derby. The field was a formidable one: sixteen talented three-year olds were entered; the largest group since War Admiral won the Triple Crown in '37. Serious study was needed if we were to single out a prospect for our pooled wager.

"I like the name Pensive; it sounds romantic," Natalie cooed.

"Ah, picking with your heart, Natalie? You'd best be careful," I teased. "That's how people end up with *losers*."

"Oh, no, Vincent; not *this* time," she giggled. "I know when my heart speaks loud and true." She winked, and squeezed Tony's arm a tad tighter.

"Since the vixen had her say, how about you, Mosconi," Mac asked. "Who you like? You goin' with Stir Up, the favorite?"

"Nope. Gotta go with Pensive to bring Natalie *luck*. Without *me* on her side, her heart won't *woik*, will it?"

I turned to Woofie, asking who he liked.

"Shoot, boss. Why you askin' me? I don't know nuthin' 'bout hosses; 'cept one end bites and the other end kicks, and I ain't never bin *bit*, if that tells ya anything. But, here's twenty-five for the pool. You decide; put me in for twenty and five for Cathy, here."

"Okay, Woof, you're down with whoever we decide." I turned to our secret weapon. "You got the floor, Chase. What's the wizard from Kentucky say? Do we bet on Stir Up with Eddie Arcaro up, or what?"

"He won the Wood Memorial, so there's no question both he and the Arkansas Derby winner, Challenge Me, will be plenty tough. But, I'm thinking it's a big field, and there's a lot of front end speed in the race that could push Stir Up early; maybe run out of gas in the stretch. With all things being considered, Vince, I'm leaning toward a closer, so my vote would be with the sly foxes over there."

"So, you like Pensive, too, huh? Hmm."

"Yeah, I think so. I admit, he hasn't shown a hell of a lot yet, but I think he's coming into his own. He's the best bred horse in the race that Calumet had decided to keep. He likes to come from off the pace, and Ben Jones is a master at training for that game. I think Jones will have him in peak condition for a big stretch run."

"Ha, Pensive's a redhead, too boys," Tony added. "Here's my dough. I vote for Pensive; it's an omen, boss."

"What about Broadcloth, Chase?" Mac asked. "I kind o' like him with Woolf up. Name reminds me of my family's tartan colors: aye, ye McKenzie Seaforth Highlanders," Mac enunciated his brogue.

"He's a long shot, Mac, but you've picked a damned good one for the money. With George Woolf in the irons, you can't rule him out no matter *what* the odds." Chase recounted Woolf's genius when riding Seabiscuit to victory over War Admiral in '38's nationally broadcast match race. "If I had to pick a dark horse for the big upset, he'd be the one, Mac, but I still like Pensive."

Having been a fan of horseracing in high school, I've read charts and understood Chase's analysis of pace and closing speed, but when he handed me sixty for the pool, I was convinced we had our pick.

"I was thinking Stir Up before, boys, but I'm switching my vote, especially given Pensive's better odds. All agreed?"

"I still like Broadcloth, but I'm with the group, Vince," Mac said, "so here's my thirty; plus, here's ten more if that Hymie fella will take a place bet on Broadcloth."

We had planned to pool our money and cover wagers against other GIs, but a well-made Curbette serving our table introduced me to a penny-ante bookmaker working the crowd. Hymie, a small, middle-aged Jewish chap agreed to cover our pooled $180 bet on Pensive's nose, as well as Mac's ten dollar place bet on Broadcloth.

Several patrons moved closer to our table, chanting '*encore*' after hearing Chase sing the traditional Derby song: Stephen Foster's "My Old Kentucky Home." Chase obliged and silenced the gin-mill with a popular, but emotional Irish tune, but still they refused to let him sit. Chase blushed, but agreed to one more. To enliven the crowd, he led the beer-swinging lyrics of "MacNamara's Band":

> "Oh me name is MacNamara,
> I'm the leader of the band..."

and then he roused the crowd to sing the chorus' upbeat lines—

> "oh, the drums go bang and the cymbals clang
> and the horns they blaze away;
> McCarthy pumps the old bassoon while I the pipes do play,
> And Henessee Tennessee tootles the flute
> and the music is somethin' grand;
> A credit to Old Ireland, is MacNamara's band..."

Noise levels of an already charged atmosphere seemed to vibrate the building. Management sent two complimentary pitchers of beer to the table. A pair of Irish immigrants followed with a trayful of

Mint Juleps. They insisted on shaking Chase's hand and offered the Juleps in gratitude for singing a tear-jerking "Danny Boy".

"What's in these?" Woofie wrinkled his nose.

"Boibon. Just drink it, doofus," Tony teased. "Prob'ly made in your back yard, f'crissake."

"Tain't nuthin' from *my* back yard," he sniffed, still hesitant. "This stuff is brown; not clear like Poppa's, and smells sweeter, too— lot like my lil' Cathy here." Woofie squeezed a lovely, dark brunette WAC nuzzling his side.

The magic moment came when the broadcast aired the words: "they're all in, the flag is up, a-a-and— they're off!"

Cheering erupted, and we could barely hear the sportscaster calling the action.

"Stir Up and Comenow quickly charge away from the gate and race for the early lead; sprinting clear of a wall of horses entering the first turn.

"As expected, Arcaro's Stir Up retains command racing down the backstretch. Broadcloth moves up into second by a head over Gay Bit running third on the outside. There's a gap of three lengths back to Brief Sigh alongside Skytracer and Shut Up. A tighter pack of horses trails the early pace another five lengths back."

The girls were bouncing on their toes screaming for Pensive. Other than a single call in the backstretch placing him far back in the field, Pensive never got a mention as the horses came out of the final turn and headed for home.

I shook my head, my eyes meeting Chase's as my expression said: *we're done for.*

Chase winked and mouthed a single word— *wait.*

The broadcast intensified. "And *down* the stretch they come! Woolf slips Broadcloth to the inside and steals the lead from Stir Up. Brief Sigh and Shut Up move up to close the gap beside Gay Bit. It's a *five* horse free-for-all with a quarter mile to go. Arcaro's Stir Up challenges Broadcloth; they're battling head to head. Arcaro has gone to the whip! But Broadcloth refuses to yield!"

My heart was pounding. The broadcaster's raspy voice screamed hope as the action unfolded in the final furlong.

"Here comes Pen-siv-v-e! Conn McCreary is charging his colt up the rail! My God, look at that horse fly; he's passing everything in sight! Pensive has caught the two leaders with only a half furlong to go! He matches stride with Broadcloth; now draws out by a length—now two! And *under* the wire they go!

"Pensive has won the Kentucky Derby by about four lengths. Broadcloth hangs on for a game second a neck in front of Arcaro's Stir Up in third. It'll be a photo between Brief Sigh and Shut Up for fourth and fifth, two lengths back."

A squealing Natalie all but strangled Tony she hugged him so tight. I too was ranting wildly, but with no one at *my* side, I grabbed Chase and wrapped him in a Sicilian bear hug.

Woofie gulped his Julep and bowled through the crowd like a half-crazed linebacker. He headed straight for Hymie, likely inspired by memories of a rigged Monte game. He startled the slender man, catching him unawares as he seized him and hoisted him above his head. Hymie wriggled, his face awash with indignant surprise as Woofie held him nearly eight feet in the air. But he was going nowhere in that dude's grip. Though annoyed, Hymie tolerated Woofie's good-natured fun as he set him down atop the nearest table.

"Hoo hah, y'all. This here Hymie fella is my best buddy in the whole dang tootin' place!"

The crowd chanted: "Hymie! Hymie! Hymie!"

"We're rich!" I shouted, delirious after hearing the broadcast announce Pensive's final odds at 7-to-1; a healthy $16.20 to win. We had over fourteen hundred dollars to split among us.

"What a *fantastic* race!" Chase jubilantly recounted. "I *thought* it might take a closer; Pensive was brilliant coming from so far back."

"Gotta hand it to ya, Chase; you had it pegged."

"Ah, it worked out is all; we got lucky. Pensive reminds me a lot of Calumet's first Triple Crown winner, Whirlaway, though I don't think he quite measures up to that world-beater. He was a freak, and set a track record in his Derby. But don't get me wrong, boys, Pensive still showed something special to put both Arcaro and Woolf away like he did."

Rehashing the exciting head-bobbing duel between Arcaro and Woolf inspired Chase to share coincidences he thought strange.

"Back in '41, it was Arcaro who rode Whirlaway for Calumet, and in that Derby, Woolf ran second. Arcaro's probably livid he wasn't on their winner today. It's got to be maddening for him: to be beaten as the favorite and not only losing to a mount he should have had, but finishing behind Woolf's longshot was *all* in reverse. Mark my words, Arcaro will be seeking revenge in next week's Preakness."

Horse talk dwindled and our group was breaking up, some guys scattering to different bars, USO dances, or going back to Hamilton. In celebration, Chase and Mac wanted to see the new smash musical, *Oklahoma!* They invited Frazer, but he declined; expecting it would be a near impossibility to get tickets. Frazer suggested a *Rockets Review* instead, but in the end, still opted to stay with me and Tony.

Natalie spotted a girlfriend she knew from work and asked if she cared to tag along. Our well-tipped Curbette touted a Broadway nightclub as a fabulous joint to try later on, but in the meantime, I was famished and needed some vittles to soak up the suds. We left the Curb to explore uptown Manhattan eateries.

The Gatsby Room

Frazer's insatiable passion for dancing bested him and he needed an outlet to turn his rubber legs loose. He was in the mood, and warmed up using the sidewalk as his stage to mimic Fred Astaire all the way to the subway. We shared his merriment— all except the new gal who introduced herself as De-bore-ah: "not Debbie, not Deb, but De-bore-ah," she insisted.

I thought she was a lonely mope. She had an attitude, and it got tedious listening to her flout ho-hum derision of Frazer as if he were a simpleton twirling, two-stepping, or tap dancing around any object he came across— including corralling unsuspecting pedestrians into following his lead for a laughable spin or two.

"Geeze, *enough* already," I said. "Let the guy be; he's just having fun. What's your problem, anyway?"

She shrugged indifference, blaming the war for her coldness. "I'm *tired* of it. Tired of our government, and tired of everyone else connected to it— *including* you foolish GIs for getting mixed up in the whole damned thing."

I let it go and tried changing the subject asking about her roots. She told me she was Jewish and lived with her parents who struggled with making ends meet operating a little candy store in Greenwich Village.

"You don't say. I'm Jewish, too."

"What did you say your name was again, Vincent? Doesn't sound Jewish to me."

"Yeah, well, it's a long story. You see, I was named after my great-great Grandfather. He was a Vatican rogue masquerading as the Pope for years, but got caught when he tried banning ham for Easter."

Everyone but stoneface laughed. She burst into another tirade, this time blaming the war for its crippling rationing and for stripping her neighborhood of so many young boys. The arrogant witch tested my patience; lecturing me for being a militant, and sucking up to a lame government she claimed got us into the war.

"Hey toots. I'm trying to be nice. So how about you lighten up with the heavy stuff. Geesh. Let's just have some fun and enjoy the war for Christ's sake."

"You naive GIs really slay me. Here you are headed for some God forsaken hell-hole, liable to get your heads blown off and all you can say is— *let's enjoy the War*," she jeered.

She had to be the most radical person I had ever met. It's been almost three years since Pearl Harbor and I couldn't believe she still belabored protests for American isolationism. She was atypical of everyone we had ever run into. Sure, our boys were getting killed— every day. But they also met the military needs of the country without reservation. Many laid down their lives for peace-loving people *everywhere* in the world, trying to rid the planet of vermin like Hitler and Mussolini. The only way to deal with those Teutonic monsters was on the battlefield, and not in debate forums. Yet she claimed if everyone went on strike and our boys simply deserted the ranks, 'there *would be* no war.'

"Yeah, sure. Open your eyes, Pollyanna. Who's the naive one? There ain't no rainbow spanning the Atlantic."

"Oh, shut up! And its Dee-borah, fatso."

Ah, I see; it's fatso now, huh? I cursed myself for getting sucked into her twisted views, but I was irritated, and felt compelled to confront the ice princess.

"Whatever you say, toots. But how about we kiss and make up? Then we'll save the world together; just you and me, capisce? You give Hirohito a ring and I'll buzz up my old buddy, Adolph. We'll tell 'em to meet us on neutral turf— I know, make it your ol' man's candy store. Momsie can cook up some matzah-ball soup and I'll bring the egg-rolls and beer. Hitler will *really* like that. We'll have a *swell* time. Between the two of us, we'll set them *both* straight; get them to drop everything and go along with *your* plan. Okay with you, little lady?"

Tony smirked, but avoided involvement playing kissy-face with Natalie. Deborah was hot, but so was I. I had a hard time believing she was unaware of the new Refugee Board, created by Roosevelt in response to the mass extermination of Jews and other Nazi crimes against humanity. This brat made no sense. Her family could have had kinfolk in slave labor camps, *assuming* they hadn't already been exterminated like attic rats. How could she be so deadened? To tell the truth, she scared me a little. *I wonder if she's an enemy sympathizer of some kind; a domestic saboteur?*

I tried putting my arm around her to see if her skin felt like scales beneath her clothing, but she pushed me off.

"Listen, Buster Brown. The whole world has gone *nuts*," she barked, "and-so-have-*you*," her stiff finger jabbing my chest with each syllable. "You jerks are just anxious to go over there and blow up people's houses, and *kill* their kids. And you seem happy about it too, you big fat lughead. You're *nuts!*"

"Whoa-ho, little lady. Now what's all this business about my nuts? Is that what this is all about? You want a go at my nuts— *Debbie?*" I goaded her sensitivity further by grabbing my crotch. "All you gotta do is treat me sweetly, and you can come to Papa all you want, baby cakes."

Deborah erupted. Beet-red with fury, she whirled on me. "Ugh! You— you fat, disgusting, offensive, grease-ball, war-mongering *pig!*" plus unleashed a string of profanities I hadn't heard since the cops raided the Social Club back home. She put a hex on me, condemning my *nuts* to be the first things shot off, and then stormed from the subway platform moments before our train arrived.

"Geesh," Tony spouted. "What's eatin' her? Talk about Mt. Vesuvius; va va— *BOOM!*"

"Shush, Tony." Natalie poked him in the ribs. "Be nice. She's having a tough time of it. She lost both her husband and brother at sea; their ship was torpedoed."

"That's too bad, Natalie," I said. "Seriously, that's rough, and I truly am sorry for her loss. But she ain't alone and needs to wake up. War *is* hell. Nobody wants it, and there's plenty of families got big time heartaches— *believe* me they do. I was in a neighborhood earlier today with more than their share of 'em; one family suffering *double* her losses. But let me tell you something. I could see the pain in their eyes, but not a *one* of 'em blamed us, *or* the government. This war *had* to be fought. I believe we're a country united in this thing, and that's why me and lover-boy there are willing to jump in with both feet and put our own asses on the line to put a stop to all this killing and conquering nonsense."

"Calm down, Vince. F'get about it." Tony blew her off. "We kicked ass in the Doiby today, right? So bless us Father, for we're about to sin. Dominic's for biscuits," he mocked parochial Latin. "What d'ya say we spend some of them Doiby dollars and get on with the cruisin' and boozin'?"

"Amen to that, Brother Tony. One, two, I'm an ex old Jew," Frazer blessed, making the sign of the cross.

Natalie giggled and linked her arm through Tony's. We left the subway, and with plenty of time to kill before going to the Gatsby Room, we entered a bar and grill called the Rusty Nail. Only this time, it was my stomach that blessed me; *Dominic's for biscuits.*

The place was lively; a cosmopolitan joint catering to quite an integrated mix of patrons. I found the confluence refreshing though a lot of guys in the Company would shun this joint, not used to seeing so many Negroes and Latinos eating and drinking together with whites. To me, such racial attitudes seemed a blatant shame, and contrary to the very democratic principles we were asked to fight and die for in this war. Maybe one day the country will straighten itself out, but that aside in the Rusty Nail, it wasn't long before we were all comrades-in-arms.

Everyone— whites, blacks, or latinos could not be more cordial. Negroes seated next to us introduced themselves as local band musicians booked to play at a nearby club later on. One produced a horn after learning I could toot the hooter, too. I made his brass beauty squeal and squawk the "wah-wah." People cheered, but it was Frazer pairing opposite a fun-loving rival that brought the house down.

He and a limber black dude laughed their fool heads off dueling it out— each trying to out-tap, -boogie, and -jitterbug the other. Both were phenomenal. Driven by alternating applause, each routine became more elaborate than the one before as they pounced on tables or chairs, rousing every patron in the place. *Why pay for entertainment when we had this?*

We ended up staying longer than planned, and had to parse out excess complimentary drinks if we expected to stay sober for our final destination.

"I think you boys will love the Gatsby Room," Natalie said. "It's a bit posh, but a zippy cabaret in the theater district. It's only a half block off Broadway, so it's not unusual to see celebrities relaxing there after performances. The head usher is my best friend's sister, so if all goes well, maybe she'll be able to take care of us special."

I was shanghaied by the Gatsby's size and swank decor, even if I *did* consider myself citified. The ambiance was tastefully balanced, offering an intriguing mix of traditional English and vibrant Art Deco.

The walls were paneled in exotic flamed mahogany, enriched with intricate crown moldings. Two story recessed windows were framed by heavy tapestries with ornate tie-backs. Dozens of huge crystal chandeliers glistened high overhead and dimly lit, casting a seductive chic atmosphere. The place was certainly elegant, but *far* from stodgy.

Upon entering, we were greeted by a graceful Maitre d' wearing an exquisite red bugle-beaded dress. She expressed pleasant surprise to see Natalie, and embraced as close girlfriends do. Natalie introduced us to Dee Zacari. *Hmm, the second dark-haired Italian beauty today.*

I sometimes question my sanity for wanting to go overseas and leave all these glamour girls by their lonesome. Who knows; they say 'three times a charm', and with two down, maybe a mystery maiden will show up for ol' *Plug* yet tonight.

Natalie hinted she would like to show her charming escorts an especially good time. Dee understood, and flashing a brow-raising smile approving of Natalie's amazing find, she led us to terrific seats adjacent to the dance floor.

"Will these do, Natalie? First round of drinks are on the house, too."

"Divine, Dee, and thank you for everything."

Before taking our seats, I surprised Dee when I took her hand and kissed it with as much Valentino flair as I could muster.

"Ah, la mia bellezza." I called her 'my little beauty', using an over-dramatic Italian accent. "Even my great, great e'Grandfather—

the famous Michael Angelo himself could not capture such radiant beauty in oils; *unless* of course he had the glow of dawn and the silvery sheen of mountain mist on his palette."

In good fun, Dee exaggerated flattery, curtsied, and winked at Natalie before excusing herself to greet new arrivals.

"Oh, brother. Nice try, toikey. If she swallows that crapola, she'll *love* breakfast at Hamilton. She's gotta hear dopey lines like that a million times a week."

I ignored Tony's sarcasm, but felt a slight flush in my cheeks in defense of my hammed chivalry. "Hey, go toikey yourself, paisan. Who cares? She's *gorgeous*. I think I'm in love all over again, today. And besides, Mr. *Vixen*, free drinks and ringside seats in a place like this? Had to say thanks to the dainty damsel *somehow*."

Spirits were high, the music fabulous, and the mood magical. The Gatsby Room was in full swing to Charlie Spivac's band. Frazer was antsy; a hot Cab Calloway tune had him prancing in place like a high-strung racehorse. He was unable to remain idle any longer and pried Natalie loose for a go at the dance floor.

He guided her steps in sync with his timing and balance. Natalie was a good sport, and though having a blast, she seemed intimidated trying to keep pace. Couples moved to the sidelines and cheered them on. The band's rhythm increased in tempo as an overhead spotlight narrowed its beam on Frazer. More people ringed the dance floor to enjoy the flailing Rubber Legs when a female spoke from behind me.

"This is too good to go to waste. Step aside, soldier boys, and let me through." A tall, dark brunette pushed between me and Tony and cut in on Natalie.

A huffing, yet grateful Natalie rejoined us on the sidelines. The crowd roared when her replacement stepped into perfect timing with Frazer— tapping, sliding, and reclining into his trusted arms before he spun the long-legged dynamo out to arms' length, and then reeled her back as she swept a long, perfect leg over the dipping Frazer. The flawless duo inflamed the crowd. I elbowed Tony.

"Don't tell me. Is that who I think it is?"

"Yep. Ann Miller in pois'n."

Holy Christ! Howie's dancing with a movie queen. Unfazed, he never missed a beat— leading or matching that raven-haired starlet step for step.

Patrons loved the show. It was impossible to sit still with everybody clapping and tapping to the beat. Some even tossed aside uptown dignity and stood on chairs for better views over the heads of reveling fans; the pair equaling anything seen in movies.

Ann Miller was in her prime, only twenty-one and already a seasoned Hollywood performer. A bystander next to me said she had been coming in the last few nights; that she was in town doing a B-Musical for Columbia Pictures. The music ended to whistles and wild applause. Frazer traded hugs and chatted with Ann at the edge of the dance floor as we took our seats.

Ann sent two bottles of champagne to our table. I spotted a camera girl, and intended to divert some of Pensive's winnings from booze to photographs, including one of me seated with Ann and her entourage at their table. I found her charming. Aside from posing for pictures, she favored me with a slow dance. She said she knew Spivac quite well, and after Natalie convinced her I really could play the horn, Ann asked Charlie to give a soldier boy a memorable fling with the band.

I admit I was a bit skittish at first, but the tingles vanished the instant the horn touched my lips. I teased the crowd faking a few nervous-Nellie notes and then smoothed that baby to life with a jazzy rendition of "Boogie Woogie Bugle Boy". The rhythm section joined in and away we went.

The trumpet's owner nodded surprised approval, and welcomed an encore. I accepted and followed up with a foot-stomping version of a Mexican hat-dance, drawing hoots and applause led by two thumbs up from a beaming Ann. I couldn't wait to send photos home. Pop plays the accordion and introduced me to music with a toy bugle when I was six. He'll drop his teeth when I send him pictures of me playing with Spivac's Orchestra, let alone of the one with Ann Miller's arms draped around my neck.

Ann and Frazer spent time chatting, once interrupted by a group of fans pleading for another revue. Frazer shared parts of his life, revealing his passion for dancing came from his parents' failed dreams of Vaudeville stardom. I never knew as much about Frazer's past until overhearing portions of their conversation.

Frazer was raised in a broken home, growing up a troubled youth from a dilapidated area of Philadelphia. Broke and frustrated, his father became increasingly abusive toward his mother until he eventually abandoned them when Howie was in second grade.

His mother was an accomplished dancer, but work during the depression was scarce. She earned what she could sewing costumes, working odd stagehand jobs, or performing bit parts and chorus line numbers to keep them going. Despite the difficulties, she never stopped tutoring Frazer, and as he grew older, she'd coach him as he danced with theater groupies and talents hired for local shows.

I better understood Frazer's caring, fatherly attitude toward us younger rogues in the outfit, as well as why he cherished his wife and mother so much. Ann was moved, too. She asked for his APO and gave Frazer her Hollywood address and private phone number in return. It was an incredible happenstance for the guy.

Ann explained her support when relating her own story, citing her break into show business came as a courtesy of Lucille Ball; one reason she felt compelled to offer Howie a similar opportunity after sampling his professional skills. She guaranteed endorsement with key people in California and made him promise to call her the moment he returned from duty. Frazer was near tears with joy.

"Man, oh, man. Can you believe this is happening to me, Zeck? I can't wait to tell my mother and the little woman. Barb's due in about two months but she'll probably calve on the spot when she hears *this* news," Frazer joked.

"I bet she will, but nobody deserves it more than you, Frazer. You have a big heart, and what goes 'round, comes around," I said, patting him on the back.

"All my life, I've dreamed of one day moving them out of the ghettos, Vince— getting a big house somewhere with a nice yard so Mom can live with us in comfort; maybe tend a little garden and help me and Barb raise a family. She's sacrificed so much giving me every chance. Now, it's my turn to take care of her. If all works out when we get back, I'd be doing something I love, and all the while making dreams come true."

"We're truly happy for youz," Tony said. Natalie agreed, kissed his cheek and gave him a warm, congratulatory hug. Our enchanted evening ticked closer to midnight. We expressed regrets for having to leave, but given reduced subway schedules, we had to be sure of making curfew.

Frazer exchanged hugs with Ann; she reiterating her promise to stay in touch. Tony on the other hand was a little drunk and insisted on playing with fire. I tried to ignite his sanity.

"Smarten up, boy. There ain't no Burma Road into Hamilton. Now come on, we gotta go." Tony brushed me off.

"F'get about it. Youz two go ahead. I'll be fine and can still make it." The red-headed siren's suggestive need for an escort home was too strong a lure. Tony shooed me toward the subway. I looked to Natalie for support, but she avoided eye contact and nuzzled deeper into his neck. I understood, but then again, she was not the one risking a year in the slammer.

I threw my hands in the air. "I give up. You're on your own this time, Mosconi. Let's go, Frazer." We ducked into the subway leaving Tony's baited butt to its own fate.

"The lucky one, my foot. It'll be even tougher titties for Tony when he gets back to Hamilton *this* time," Frazer said.

"Well, he is right about one thing; he does have a little leeway, though his margin for error is about as tight as a hare's patootie."

"You mean a *vixen's*, doncha?"

"Ha, ha. You're on a roll, Howie. But you're right: Tony's got two heads, one brain, and *none* of 'em woiks." We roared.

"You heard the dumb bastard, *f'get* about it. What can we do? *Nothing*, but I'd give a year's furlough to see how he wiggles out of this mess."

"Don't worry, Frazer. My guess is, by about noon tomorrow, something tells me you'll get your chance. Meanwhile, what a great day, huh?" We laughed and relived every moment all the way back to Fort Hamilton.

Doogan's

Frazer and I made it through checkpoint shortly after one in the morning, well shy of 02:00 curfew.

I had a mild hang-over when getting up, but a not-so-mild stomach. No way could I look at a Hamilton breakfast, and looked for Tony instead.

His bunk had not been slept in. I figured there were only two possibilities: either he was absurdly foolish and still at Natalie's, or, already in custody facing charges. I went to see Captain Estes and learned of yet a third option.

"You'll find him in D House cleaning toilets 'til we leave Hamilton. He got challenged on the way in, but I was able to get him off since he was less than a half hour late. The cocky bastard waltzed up to the guardhouse like he owned the daggon place. 'Sure hope Uncle Sam didn't pay the ransom, cuz I escaped,' he said, and handed three cigars to the MPs. He claimed he stole 'em from his captors to teach 'em a lesson," C.B. smirked. "The crazy rascal told the MPs he felt sorry for them working terrible hours. All heart, ain't he? It's funny now, but I was fire-breathing furious at the time."

Estes said Natalie borrowed a neighbor's car and dropped Tony off after groping goodbyes. Tony entered the guardhouse a rumpled mess with lipstick smudged on his collar, neck, and ear lobes. By that time of morning, activities had slowed and the MPs were likely bored, milling around, and relaxed. Tony was lucky he caught them in a good mood. We'd heard stories of guys being crucified for being less than five minutes overdue. C.B. said they found Tony's excuse amusing but cuffed him, and threatened formal proceedings if C.B. failed to claim him within thirty minutes.

"Ah, I was about to be gittin' out of the sack anyway," C.B. continued. "But I gotta admit, it crossed my mind to roll over and let them toast his marshmallows one time. It might teach that slickster a lesson, but then I'd run out of bourbon, now wouldn't I?"

C.B. said he reamed Tony a new orifice as the MPs looked on with righteous satisfaction. That's our Tony: *lucky*— lucky it's *all* he got for *getting* lucky, despite cleaning shithouses for the duration of our stay at Hamilton. He also got lucky in an offsetting way, because after finishing a day's latrine duty, it came with an automatic rest of the day off, including an abandon-ship drill. ASDs may be necessary evils, but I *hated* the damned things.

Navy boys conducted the vital practices and sometimes leaned a little heavy on the cross-service zeal. They wasted no time with manuals and quickly put us through our paces. To simulate ocean conditions, they'd line us up at a mock ship railing fixed to a platform forty feet above a rocking dummy craft, a drill instructor blew a whistle, and over the side we went.

I pitied the boys beneath me. I hated heights to begin with, but drained of energy and fighting a sensitive stomach, I'd be lucky to keep from getting seasick just *looking* down at the dummy craft.

Once atop the platform, I ignored weak knees, but felt the color drain from my face. When my turn came, I took a deep breath, clenched my teeth, picked a spot on the horizon, and flipped myself over the railing; telling myself not to look down. Second Lieutenant Durrum, a big, no-nonsense macho-type in charge of 1st Platoon was assigned as Army monitor with the same Navy Petty Officer as before; both below, hollering instructions through megaphones.

If I moved too fast I clobbered the guy beneath me. Too slow, and it was my head and hands crunched under heavy field boots. Only a few rungs down, panic overrode a string of directives, feeding my acrophobia. My foot slipped and I fumbled with the flimsy rope lattice; hands going one way, feet another. I ended up dangling like a giant Christmas bobble as the Navy's Rodgers bellowed orders.

"Get your fat ass moving, private. You're holding up the line. You'd get everyone killed if this were real. Now move it tub-o-lard or you'll do it again and again until you get it right." Snickers from above fueled my defiant, but ill-timed courage.

"Lard floats, sir. So how about I wait for the damned ship to go under and then just step off? Another GI can sit on my chest and row us *both* to Europe. That way, I'll *save* a life— sir!"

I was frustrated and certainly held no warm and fuzzy feelings for a smarmy Naval Officer while I tried to regain my footing. Guys made half-hearted attempts to stifle laughter, but Rodgers was in no mood to accept sarcasm from a ground-pounder. I managed to inch my way down, only to slam both shins against the rocking barge.

"*Damn* it to hell!" Sharp pain fired through both legs. My knees buckled and I rolled into the barge like a sack of flour. *Son-of-a-bitch, that hurt!*

Rodgers showed no sympathy and gloated more when Lt. Durrum promptly got in my face.

"At attention, Zecca. You want jokes? Here's one for *you*: two days mess KP commencing right after you complete two successful runs in a row. You're lucky this wasn't real, or better still, that it wasn't *me* standing on a burning deck waitin' on yer lard ass. Since you float so damned good, Zecca, I'd have thrown your butt over the side like a bucket of swill. And that's how *I'd* save a life, mister— maybe a *bunch* of lives. You got that, soldier?" he yelled.

"Yes, sir!" I stood at rigid attention.

"Good. Now get your *lard*-ass back up there before I chase your hind end *up* those ropes faster than you came down. *Now!*"

"Yes, sir!" I snapped a salute and scurried to the ladder stairs. *Ugh! This is not my day.*

How's that for irony, proving that where Tony goes, I go too. Within hours of each other, we both end up disciplined. I suppose it had to happen eventually, yet for me, KP turned out more of a welcome reprieve than punishment.

The work didn't bother me. I took my time scrubbing piles of pans in deep sinks, all the while delighted with the unforeseen bonus of having access to food items seldom seen by anyone but officers. A couple days saddled with KP kept me well fed and on base. I used the time to rest, stomp another Maytag mash, and write home.

Woofie came by late afternoon and asked if I'd help him draft another letter to his family. I learned of his limited literacy early on at Fort Baxter; finding him off by himself struggling with an *Army Reader*, a primer to help illiterates learn simple words and sentences.

I assured Woofie his secret was safe with me, though he had no reason to feel awkward or ashamed. Woofie was shocked to learn he was far from alone. When thinking of being a history teacher, I cited statistics my school counselor had showed me in a Census report. Over ten million American adults had an education no higher than fourth grade, and that one out eight males was *completely* illiterate.

Woofie felt less embarrassed and more confident. Given his genuine desire to improve, I offered to tutor him.

"Well I'll be hogtied and whupped. You'd do that for me as dumb as I am? How about that, my own teacher. You won't hafta start from scratch, cuz I'm better off 'n some of them other fellas. I bin t'sixth grade, and kin read 'n write a little bit."

Woofie never had the chance to complete a formal education. He was a big family and had to work in the quarry alongside his father during the depression.

Since Baxter, we took it slow but steady, and I was proud of Woofie for sticking to his lessons. He improved, but at times, he still sought my help with letters home. The only rule: I had to write as close as possible to his diction. I suggested alternative wording, but he refused and insisted I transcribe verbatim.

"Nope. It's like I tol' ya before, boss. The folks cain't read a lick, worse than me. Preacher Justin has t'come by n' read to 'em."

Woofie reasoned if I wrote as he articulated, his letters would sound more personal— as though coming straight from him. "They'd feel right proud of me, and not like it was comin' from some fancy schoolmaster a talkin' high 'n mighty to 'em."

If it made sense to him, it made sense to me and I wrote as he said. *Besides, who's gonna argue with Paul Bunyan?*

I scribbled words as best I heard them, and to paraphrase closing comments, he wrote: 'now you be sure'n kiss the young'ns for me, Momma. Tell 'em not to worry dickey-doo 'bout me none. I'm fine and got me a best friend always watchin' over me real good. And I sees t'his hide, too Momma. You kin betcha bloomers tain't nuthin' I won't do for him. Heck, Poppa don't watch over that old still o' his'n near as good.

'He's a real smart fella and is helping me learn a whole bunch. He may be a yank from a big city up north, but y'all cain't hold that agin 'im. I swears, you'd take to 'im like real kinfolk, you would. Well, that's about all I kin say. We're not s'posed to talk about nuthin' here. So God bless and I'll sees y'all when I gits back t'home. Love, Rufus James.'

I read it back to be sure I had it right; his generous smile said it all. *You should be flattered, fatso*; a mischievous phantom suddenly poofed onto my left shoulder. *Yee haw, you done bin adopted. But look on the bright side, you'll be the only dang tootin' Wop in all o' Dogpatch.*

The little hellion snickered as a second thought-kin popped onto my other shoulder. *Don't listen to that insensitive ingrate, Vince. Woofie's your buddy.* I smiled, still overtired I guess, but shooed the pesky pixies into vanishing before I ended up *deceased* kin.

"What are you smirking at, Vince?" Frazer asked.

"Aw, nothing. Just thinking about my, um— my relatives."

"From the size of that banana grin, I take it everything's okay in Beantown. Anyway, I thought you might like to join me and Woofie to see the Statue of Liberty. I promised to take him."

"Nah, you guys go ahead."

"Oh, come on. It'll do you good; we'll have some fun. You've been up to your eyeballs in pots and pans too long, buddy. Why not say hello to the Grand Old Lady before we leave Hamilton? Maybe sip a few brews afterwards. What d'ya say?"

"Nah, not today. I think I'll wait and save my hellos for on the way back in."

Frazer gave up, teasing I let silly superstitions get in the way again. He and Woofie wandered off and left me to my chores. After mess, Tony passed out, exhausted from lack of sleep. I was bored and decided on a leisurely stroll.

I corralled Chase into joining me on a Brooklyn safari, staying close by Hamilton. We chatted, casually probing interesting little nooks along the waterfront. We stumbled upon a quaint little tavern that looked like a setting out of a Dickens' tale. One look at each other and in we went— hooked.

Doogan's was a narrow, weather-beaten little hole-in-the-wall tucked in between two large warehouses. It was darker than Cooter's Cave inside, like a dank dungeon smelling of stale smoke and beer.

Once my eyes adjusted, a chalky-haired bartender appeared to be the most ancient thing in the place, although three patrons looked like they could be older than New York City itself. They barely moved, hunched over drinks as if sipping a ration of formaldehyde before going back to coffins. But the beer was cold, and that's all that mattered.

Chase and I nursed our drinks, saying few words in hushed tones fearing we'd disturb the mummified atmosphere. An old geezer seated at a corner barstool suddenly spoke.

"What's a four-letter word for an Alpine sleigh?" he asked of no one in particular; his face buried in a crossword.

"Sled," I blurted.

"Nope. Starts with an "L", sonny. Gotta be something starts with an "L".

"Shit," I reacted, unable to think, my mind going blank.

"Wrong again, sonny. Said an 'L', an '*L*' I says."

His expressionless focus remained inches from the puzzle. For some reason: my silly mood, atmosphere, the old man's timing, voice inflection— heaven *knows* what, but his glib response started me giggling. I felt stupid, but couldn't stop. The harder I tried, the worse it got, and the more the old man glanced at me. My titters escalated into a giddy cycle until tears ran from both our eyes. Even the bartender, whom Chase and I quietly dubbed Methuselah, smiled at the daffy exchange.

I ordered drinks for all as the old man introduced himself. Cyrus Clemens said he had never married, and except for his years in the service, had lived and worked on the Brooklyn docks all his life.

A veteran of the Spanish American conflict, he again saw action in the Great War; rank of Captain, wounded twice in action, and retro-awarded two Silver Stars. He claimed his age as sixty-eight, but blamed his grizzled appearance on hellish conditions brought home as the only souvenir from the battle front.

"Kept my head down and my ass even lower; you two would be wise to do the same. 'Course, Old Knickerbocker and good Irish whiskey keeps the doctor where he belongs, too. Ain't that right Murph?" Cy winked and introduced the bartender, Sean Murphy, as his lifelong friend. We shook hands; *they were warm, thank God.*

Cyrus didn't get much further on his crossword, but did manage to back into the word *L-U-G-E* before setting it aside. He was an interesting character who piqued my curiosity who didn't seem to mind me peppering him with questions. Maybe he felt forgotten and merely grateful for a young audience giving a lonely veteran a chance to relive old glory days.

He noticed our infantry insignias, triggering a few anecdotes. The more he spoke, the more questions popped into my head. I ordered each of us a shot of Irish whiskey, anxious to hear more of his European exploits. Cy obliged, figuring we were at Hamilton for only one reason.

"Yeah, I reckon you fellas will be going soon enough. I s'pose you could be headed for Italy since we're still knocking the b'jesus out the Huns up the boot. But if I had to guess, I'd say you boys will likely go to England first, then ship on from there."

Cy still fostered bitter feelings toward Germans, especially when relating battlefield stories. "Let me tell you boys something. Make no mistake about German soldiers. As much as I hated them, I had to respect them. They're a tough bunch, brave and well trained, and led by officers who were masters at making war."

He detailed examples of German tactics, such as how they preset coordinates for placing strategic cannon fire into the second and third lines. "The bastards had us zeroed in waiting for us doughboys to try reinforcing the front."

Cy described the horrors of trench warfare, open field battles, village combat, and the repugnant effects of caustic mustard gas. He also recounted gritty details of the ordinary, but necessary personal stuff we never think of, or talk about— like the down and dirty nuances of living for weeks in cold, water-filled and filthy foxholes, or "funk holes" as he called them in World War I.

A strange foreboding suddenly overcame me. I felt something more was happening in this place than rehashing old war stories. Instincts told me to listen, and to listen hard. Of all the intense training we had been through, I had never heard such vivid details as what Cy implied we could expect in combat.

"How's your CO lad; he a good Joe? Knows his shit, and you respect him and get along okay?"

"Yes, sir. He ain't the most diplomatic guy in the world, but overall he's an honest, no-nonsense leader. One of the quiet types you don't mess with. He won't take crap off anyone and has the muscles to back it up."

"That's C.B. alright," Chase added. "Like Vince says, he can be a little tough at times, but he's always fair-minded and seems to have an uncanny sense for a situation; like he knows exactly what to do, and what we're thinking."

"Damned sure are lucky then," Cyrus approved. "Can't say enough about a good CO. Mark my words, boys. He's the guy you gotta be able to rely on when the goin' gets rough. Trust him and work together as a team. If he's a real leader, he'll know when to be aggressive, and when to sit back on his ass and *think*. Never forget that, Vince. Could mean life or death, and not just for you, but the whole damned lot o' ya's."

Cy paused, and I noticed his facial expression change as he fingered the rim of his shot glass. I figured it was not a good time to interrupt and gave him a moment with his memories; I reflecting on a few thoughts of my own.

Things Cy had said about the importance of a good CO got me to thinking about C.B. An odd fact dawned on me: I don't think anyone really knew what "C.B." stood for, or if he even *had* a first name. I knew one thing for sure, he had a name for me and Tony: 'a coupla good-for-nothin' nawthun peelgrims.'

Captain Estes was all business and hated inefficient nonsense. To me, he was a standout; decisive, respected, and trusted by his troops as well as the brass. One difference I personally respected was his distaste for hardcore profanity.

He was no Bible thumper and would use milder expletives, but never bombarded his troops with crude vulgarities. Even though I'm no prude, and from a big city, I side with C.B.'s sensitive restraints. It's how I was brought up. Some COs wouldn't care if a circle of nuns were standing near. 'Better get used to it, Mother Matilda, it's a way of life in the Army,' they'd jeer. But C.B. said otherwise.

'That's a bunch of bullshit— a lame excuse for all thunder and no lightning.' He knew some COs felt a need to sprinkle speech with crude vulgarities for effect now and then; 'sort of like puttin' a dab of mustard on a hotdog, but those foul-mouthed bushwhackers smother it like gravy on Sunday mornin' biscuits.' He said it could be intimidating if blastin' fellas from good Christian homes; 'specially if they come from the Bible belt. They don't like it, it ain't needed, and gets you nowhere.'

C.B. never had any trouble getting his point across. He was about Tony's height and said his chiseled physique stemmed from years of stacking tons of hay and tobacco on a quarter section of land in Winchester, Kentucky. 'Nine years in the Army humpin' miles with whiny little sissies like y'all keeps it that-a-way, too.'

He was flabbergasted when he first learned who Chase was. Estes said he knew of Chase's family for years, but they had never met prior to Fort Baxter.

'They be rich race hoss folk about a dozen miles from me on the east side o' Lexington. Some place they got, too. Big mansion with a bunch of barns surrounded by fancy white fences. Got more money than God, they do.'

Mutual respect swept aside social barriers, and with hometowns in common, they nurtured a good friendship beyond C.B.'s official capacity as CO. As an appreciative gesture of C.B.'s worthy tutelage, Chase invited him to breed thoroughbreds after the war. Chase offered his help selecting a mare, as well as provide complimentary breeding rights to farm stallions. C.B. was moved, and accepted Chase's gracious civility. He agreed thoroughbreds would blend well with a small herd of black angus to help boost farm income.

'Always wanted me one of them race hosses. But 'til now, never thought I'd ever git me the chance.' C.B. beamed, and promised good nutrition and farm management. 'I won't let ya down, son; and dang sure will raise me a good one. Yeah, I s'pose it's about time I paid more attention to m'Willa Mae now. Maybe settle down and raise me some jockeys to go along with them hosses,' he'd wink.

C.B. said the Army had been good to him, but looked forward to going home in November. 'Don't be whoopin' it up cuz I ain't left yet, boys. Until I do, I intend to be houndin' yer sissified behinds to keep y'all fit and in one piece.'

I downed the last of my drink when Cy looked up and caught me studying his somber expression. Our eyes met, and I smiled respectfully.

"Ah, and another thing, Vincent," Cy said, returning to the present. "Murphy, give me a slip of paper."

Cy began sketching. "You're a good size boy, Vincent. These ought to fit you perfect. Now when you get overseas, first thing you do is find yourself an old bicycle inner tube. Cut it into strips about a half-inch wide by about a yard long, and then find a tack shop to cut a leather patch about so big and shaped like this."

Cy formed an oval with his hands. "Have them bind it to the tube strips like so," he finished, and slid me the paper.

"What is it?" Chase asked, looking over my shoulder. Cy eyed Chase's stature.

"You're a stout lad, sergeant. Ever play baseball?"

"Of course."

"How far you reckon you can throw a ball; two hundred feet maybe?"

"I guess so."

"From your knees, or sitting on your ass?" Cy saw we were clueless, and to help with perspective, he alluded to vicious fighting in villages and hedgerows.

"The Germans like to set up their defenses to create deadly crossfire. The bastards will lay and wait for you to show yourselves— then *WHAM!* Sharpshooters will blow your brains out before you see a puff of smoke. After all hell breaks loose, you still gotta get in close to toss grenades, right? That means if you need distance, you'll have to stand and throw— exposing yourself.

"We got grenade launchers," I said.

"Okay, so things have changed some since my day, but what if you don't have one next to you? What then? Slip these off, latch 'em to a couple men bracing rifles, or between two small trees, and— "

"A sling shot!" I blurted.

"Not just *any* sling shot, junior, but one big son-of-a-*bitchin'* sling shot. With them, you can sit on your butt *behind* cover and lob grenades twice as far as anyone can throw one. And they don't weigh spit, either. So no one can bitch about more shit to carry. You wear 'em over a uniform like a waist belt or suspenders. And if you don't use 'em to blow a machine gun to hell, they come in mighty handy for flinging ammo clips or medical packs to guys pinned down across open ground. We used 'em for tossing explosives high up onto roof tops, or into blown out windows where snipers and machine gunners thought they was *safe.* They were itchin' for us to show ourselves, but we fooled the rotten bastards, we did. You just do as I say, young fella," he said, tapping the paper. "Them things might get your ass out of a jam and save some lives."

Cy went on to describe front line warfare as the dirtiest, most barbaric kind of murder man could inflict upon fellow man; "the aftermath even more ghastly than the battle," he said. He reiterated the need for good COs, comparing them to surrogate parents for keeping us focused, teaching us, and trying to *protect* us.

"Then, they gotta know how to bring out the absolute best in you when leading your sorry asses through the gates of hell." The old man was fascinating; everything he said made sense. I had thought the Gatsby Room was immeasurable, but of all the places I'd been, Doogan's was among the most memorable.

"You two seem like real nice fellas. Smart, too. Ain't that right, Murph?" I matched Murphy's grin, and before parting, waved for refills. Cy raised his glass.

"God bless you boys, and thanks for the drinks. Remember— keep your heads down and your asses even lower."

Chase and I downed our shots and snapped formal salutes. I could see in his eyes the old warrior was moved by the respectful gesture as he stood, clicked his heels, and returned a Captain's salute. We waved goodbyes to Murphy and the other living corpses and returned to Hamilton.

Tramonto Rosso

Next morning, C.B. ordered early roll-call and gave strict orders to remain on base. He suggested we pack our gear and tie bedrolls.

We've had dry runs before, but this time, the *bedroll* thing said it all— that we'd likely be in new quarters before the hour hand swept full circle. We peppered Chase for more details, but all he could confirm was what C.B. had relayed from HQ.

The time for shipping out had always been a mystery lingering in our minds, but the nearing reality made my stomach flutter. Days of chasing skirts, closing bars, sightseeing, training, drills— *all* of it stateside was ending.

Packing triggered more thoughts of Cy's eye-openers. 'At some point, you and your buddies will be having a swell time in a pub when someone in the gang will say: 'hey guys, let's all get together for a reunion when the war's over? The saddest part is, while you're all game for the coming picnic, you'll secretly wonder which of those smiling mugs will never get hugged at that reunion. Might even be yours, son.'

I'll never forget his doleful expression; it sent shivers down my spine. I could fathom someone in the outfit saying: 'wouldn't it be great if Vince were here with us? Yeah, too bad he got it in Rome, Paris, Berlin, or wherever. Yup; good ol' Zecca. But hey, did I tell you me and Sally bought a little house in Maine?'

Cy said nobody could blame them. It's not an insensitivity issue but a soldier's way of getting on with life, of trying to bury horrific memories, even guilt for going home knowing many friends were not so lucky.

'Let me tell ya, Vincent. You'll have a hard time getting rid of haunting flashbacks, like stepping over a buddy lying in a pool of blood, and left to rot in the field like cow shit. *Hideous* memories, Vince.' By that time, Cy was fighting back tears.

I stopped packing and closed my eyes in empathy; Cy's chilling words echoed in my head. 'You can't imagine the butchery, the stench, the suffering and gut-retching gore you'll see and taste. It'll clog your throat 'til you damned near stop breathing. During the heat of battle, you'll have no time to stop and vent sympathetic drivel for a close mate. One more thing and then I'll shut up.'

He looked deep into my eyes, and said: 'there's *one* feeling you *can't* ignore— a soldier's *espirit-de-corps*. It's a powerful feeling that exists no place else but on the battlefield; a kind of love for your fellow comrade-in-arms that's never talked about, but you'll sure as hell know it when it happens.'

I pushed Cy to the back of my mind, finished packing, and joined the others waiting to fall in for the most important formation since arriving at Hamilton; the one sending us out of here. We were about to meet the war face-to-face.

Overnight, Fort Hamilton transformed from an orderly human storage bin into something akin to a ravaged anthill. Thousands of troops were on the move. Battalions marched across parade grounds and assembled at piers on the far side of the base. We did likewise, wrestling with backpacks and duffel bags stuffed with everything we owned.

It was near dark by the time we boarded light crafts that ferried us up the Bay, past the Statue of Liberty, and toward Brooklyn's Pier 32. The skipper slowed while passing cargo vessels before he abruptly swung the launch hard to starboard, cut back its engines, and planed in beside what was to be our transport vessel.

Several GIs ogled the multi-decked liner, their mouths agape in awe at having never seen anything much bigger than a swamp pram before. Tony elbowed me as we reached its stern.

"Vince; get a load o' the name. *Tramonto Rosso;* tell me *that* ain't no omen, paisan. E mi diletto!" Tony yelled, and blew her a kiss. "It looks like we're in for a smooth cruise, boys."

I explained Tony's exuberance to guys packed around us. "She's called the Red Sunset in Italian, so Tony expects we're in for a safe crossing because of an old mariner's rhyme that goes something like: 'red sky at night, sailors' delight.'"

Several outfits were already assembled along the wharf, many consuming coffee and sweets courtesy of the Red Cross. After we disembarked, we were given Red Cross overseas bags but ordered to stay assembled within designated spots on the pier.

We chatted with a crewman who said the liner once flew the Italian flag and sailed the Mediterranean and Atlantic along the west coast of Africa. About three football fields long, he said she was designed to carry about twenty-five hundred, but since seizure by the Allies, she'd been retrofitted as a troop ship, crammed to nearly quadruple her original capacity.

Waiting to board, my stomach tingled, but not in anticipation of donuts. More of Cy's comments fanned the embers of long buried questions that challenged my convictions for making such a big effort to enlist in the first place. Perhaps I was delusional; a naive street punk thinking battles were nothing more than glorified alley rumbles, only using bigger tools than switchblades and tire irons.

Maybe there *was* a way I could have stayed in school, pursued a history major, or taken a draft deferment job at Boston's Navy yard. Then one day, I'd be teaching the war from historical documents and not from eye witness accounts.

Or was I guilty of wanderlust? Had I fantasized about going to exotic places on Uncle Sam's nickel; of seeing the country, even the world? Suburban jaunts around Boston on the MTA were about the extent of my travels except for the rare day trip with school chums into New Hampshire for trout fishing, mountain hiking, or carnival fun at Hampton Beach. *But what about duty to my country?*

An overwhelming sense of patriotism wedged its way between my ears. I thought of Papa, and of how angry he got listening to radio broadcasts of the intensive fighting in Italy. Papa was truly proud of his American citizenship, yet blood-ties to the old country still flowed warm within his veins. He had family in Sicily and his homeland had been under violent siege.

Though Italy had formally surrendered last September, crack Nazi divisions were still offering stiff resistance in the mountains northeast of Rome. Papa despised Mussolini with fervid passion, livid of how the tyrant had desecrated the old country.

He'd shake a fist. "If they let me, Vincent, I swear on Mama's grave, I go. Send me, Mr. President. I cut off his head myself. I swear I do it— il maiale *sporco* otterra suo!" he'd curse from deep within his gut, vowing the filthy pig would get his.

I shared Papa's vile hatred of Hitler and Mussolini; feeling an arduous need to flex moral-muscles. I was convinced I helped carry the Sicilian sword of justice, poised and ready to purge the world of the barbaric bastards.

I was convinced I had done the right thing to enlist. From here on, I promised myself: no more doubts, my thoughts replaced by more noble satisfactions. Duty had called and I was ready. *Whatever happens; happens, Vinnie boy.*

I studied the length and height of the massive liner, thinking she'd make a hell of a trophy for a German U-boat. My neck prickled recalling Deborah's wrath; her mighty curse. Maybe the ghosts of her husband and brother waited for me, to seal my fate with theirs. But given the *Tramonto's* size, I felt *some* relief figuring it would take more than a single torpedo to put her under. The tingles disappeared. I believed Tony's omen; the *Red Sunset* would make it.

I was on my third donut when an Ensign announced boarding details. Troops were aligned into rows and funneled up a gangway through a gaping hole in the side of the liner. I looked up and was amazed at how far it was to the top railing, with an equal distance to the water line.

Each soldier followed the one in front as we tramped through watertight hatchways and corridors peeling off into assigned areas. There were endless compartments, many of them former luxurious nightclubs, or dining salons transformed into makeshift quarters. Cots were stacked four deep in places, suspended on chains from ceiling mounts.

We were sent to E-Deck below the waterline, and fully forward of stowage for motorized equipment. *So much for luck; we probably got the worst quarters aboard ship.*

Berths were aligned on either side of a narrow storage hold at the tapered tip of the bow. The compartment was once used for keeping small ship's stores, now crammed with two-by-six foot strips of canvas strung as hammocks stacked three high, each tier two feet from the one above. The top guy's face was inches from a bulkhead, and those below had to contend with natural body contours with little clearance.

"Uh-uh; you get the bottom, big boy," Tony said, yanking at my shoulder. He insisted the middle hammock had his name on it, and ordered the diminutive Mac to the top. "Ain't no way your ass is gonna make music in *my* face, paisan."

About three in the morning, the engine noise changed; the ship pitched and gained momentum. I reasoned we must be out in the open Atlantic. Our compartment was hot and stuffy, and though uncomfortable for sleeping, I thought I was the only one awake. It turned out to be the opposite— few were asleep. Some were getting seasick, heaving into their helmets. A nervous voice broke the silence.

"What if we get hit by a torpedo?"

"Yeah, we could be blown to smithereens down here."

"We'll never get out; we'll drown like rats."

"Well, don't worry about it, handsome," Tony chided. "Most of youz *are* rats. So f'get about it. Besides, if we do get zapped, I'll stuff Zecca's big ass in the hole and that'll be the end of it. Why do youz toikeys think they call him Plug back at home, anyhow?"

Mac anted his two cents. "Hey, Vince. While your ass is hangin' out there in the deep, you can dangle your wedding tackle and troll for sharks. Catch us some fresh meat for supper."

"Better be a great white or bigger then, or the son-of-a-bitch will choke on it."

"What if it's a *nurse* shark, Zeck, and feels like nursing?" Chase countered.

"Then in that case ladies, *I'll* get dessert, and the rest of you jokers will go without dinner all the way to Europe." I ducked a helmet and two pillow rolls as Woofie led a chorus of groans.

By next afternoon, it was our turn for a shift topside. Though the *Tramonto* had been stripped of lavish amenities, sailing aboard the former ocean liner was like putting us in a museum. We were anxious to get out of those stifling quarters and explore the ship. Some visited the intact theater rooms to watch Movietones, others went straight to weather decks to soak in sea views and fresh air.

On our way topside, we detoured into what was once an elegant main dining hall for first-class passengers, now lined head-to-toe with rows of cots.

It was massive. My eyes measured it to be about half a football field long. Three sets of twenty-foot high doors were positioned forward, aft, and middle; each adorned with bronze medallions depicting famed Italian architecture.

The walls were stripped of once elegant wood paneling and painted ship's gray. The lighting system was left in place since the original design prevented natural light from entering. Illuminated, frosted glass pilasters lined the walls, the tops of alternating columns flared soft red, yellow, and purple lighting giving the appearance of sunset hues; hence the liner's name.

We gazed at the decor as we slowly wove our way through the crowded room. A small-sized private from Charlie Company halted Woofie by the arm.

"Hey you mugs, listen up! If anything starts in here, I'm on *this* guy's side. Got it?" He hammed it up for a few laughs. "So, how's the weather up there, big fella?"

Without warning, Woofie snatched the surprised GI and flipped him over his shoulder with the ease of a bath towel, his big hand holding the dude by the ankles.

"Well, I'll be a blue-eyed coonhound. That's mighty neighborly of you, lil' fella. Cuz if I hafta whup a bunch o' these soldier boys, I'm gonna need a real good club, now won't I? So you be it, sweet cheeks." Woofie patted the private's ass, and looking like Alley Oop, he walked off with an embarrassed GI draped over his shoulder.

Everyone howled as he set him down about four bunks away. They shook hands in good-natured fun as we mingled with his buddies in C Company.

Music from the ship's intercom enlivened the atmosphere. Bronx cheers introduced the classical tunes; shouts and whistles welcomed each change to swing. Glenn Miller's smash hit, *In the Mood*, began playing and drove Frazer's rubber legs into action.

One of their boys produced a pair of drumsticks and turned his talents loose on a book, cookie tins, and a couple helmets as an improvised percussion section. Four others put their heads together, cupped their hands and harmonized *bwah-doo-wah* as a horn section. I led them with a rolled up Stars and Stripes in lieu of going below to unpack my horn.

A horde of GIs encircled our jerry-rigged band, snapping fingers and tapping toes to rhythm when the coup-d'etat suddenly squealed from halfway across the room. Someone had uncased a clarinet and had that baby talking. He and two others with guitars joined the group and brought the *Tramonto* to a semblance of its former self.

Miller's tune ended with demands for more. Though expecting Bach, cheers erupted when another B, as in *Benny* Goodman was next on the spindle. The jink-n-jiving resumed until a message from the bridge interrupted the gaiety. Growls were soon replaced with howls when it was announced the captain had approved channeling a shortwave broadcast of the Preakness Stakes over the intercom.

"My God," Chase said, "is it Saturday already?" Living within the bowels of the ship had distorted our sense of time. But, we had a problem— no Hymie on this tub if we expected to capitalize on the Preakness.

I had it drummed into my head there was only one way to win a horse race, but I had a plan worth trying if Chase's predictions held true. I huddled the boys and shared a psychological ploy often used by bookmakers at the Social Club.

"It's simple. If we're to cash a bet, Pensive must win no matter what, or we lose anyway, right? I may have a way to tempt players away from Pensive, *and* get us better odds in the process."

"How you gonna do that?" Mac interrupted.

"Well that's what I was about to tell you, dipshit. We don't have much time, so how's about you zip the lip and listen. Okay, here's what we do. We give them the entire field against our one— Pensive. That's six to one in their favor, right? So we tell them to make it fair, if they want the whole field, we'll do it, but only if they give us just a little two-to-one edge versus six. That means for every dollar they bet, we put up fifty cents. Get it?"

Mac unzipped his lip. "I think so, but don't understand *why* they'd do it." He re-zipped, absorbing my backhand to his shoulder.

"Because like you, they're stupid; it's a sucker bet. We dangle the six-horse carrot and they'll bet with their greedy little hearts and not their heads. If Chase is right, it might as well be a *hundred* horses out to beat Pensive, but they *still* can't win. They only *think* they can. And if we cover bets at fifty cents on the dollar, we'll get better odds then at Pimlico as a bonus."

"Gotcha," Chase said. "The boss is right, boys." He handed me an eye-popping two-hundred, parlaying half his Derby winnings in our pool. Chase's bet spelled *confidence* with a capital *C* as everyone dug for dollars. Woofie's final two twenty's raised the pool to nearly four-hundred. "Boys, we're on a ship full of fish, so let's reel 'em in."

Our first target was an active dice game in the middle of the hall. I approached a gruff corporal at their center.

"What are you selling?" he barked. "This here's a private game."

"Sorry, Corporal. Saw the game and thought you boys might like a little side action on the Preakness. Didn't mean to interrupt. Go back to your bones, boys." I started toward a different group playing poker.

"Hold on a sec, soldier; not so fast. I thought you boys were trying to bust in and make trouble. Jimmy Johnson, C Company."

"Vince Zecca, B Company."

He tested my grip as we shook hands. "So what was it ya had in mind?"

I explained the bet, including why I demanded two-to-one odds versus their six. One of Johnson's cronies butt in.

"Go ahead, Jimmy. Take the fool up on it. Pensive was lucky as shit in the Derby. Stir Up burned himself out and had nuthin' left for the stretch. But not this time, and if for some reason he doesn't get the job done, Platter's a sure thing, Jimmy. Here, Zecca, put me down for a dime's worth: Ron King, ten bucks." King slid two fives from a fistful of crumpled dice money.

"So lemme get this straight," Johnson said, still dubious as his eyes shifted between me and Woofie towering behind me. "You're saying I get all six horses against your one, huh? That means if Stir Up, Platter, or if any one of them other nags wins, you lose, right?"

"Yup, and like King said; call me a sentimental fool, but that's *my* problem, ain't it. Let's face it, Pensive ain't no Man o' War by any stretch. That's why I can't give you six horses unless you cut a little slack. For every two bucks you bet, I put up one so you get back three no matter who kicks my ass. Understand?"

"Okay— *fool*. Put me down for a twenty," Johnson bellowed. "King was right about one thing, Bucko. Pensive was damned lucky to catch Stir Up in the Derby. But he ain't gonna cost me this time. Arcaro won't let him get away with it in a shorter Preakness. He'll eat Pensive for lunch. Ain't that right fellas?" Johnson's blustering drew his cronies into covering a lot of our action.

Word spread. Three crewmen also bet half-a-hondo on the field despite Navy regulations barring sailors from gambling for money aboard ship. I never had to mosey a hundred feet in the dining hall before depleting our bankroll. The play was too great to resist.

Though we had every confidence in Pensive, he was not a sure thing; it could still be a gloomy night in the bow. But no matter what happened, one thing was a sure thing— this section of the dining hall would be a howling free-for-all pulling for *any* horse, hoping we'd get dunked in a monetary bath.

Guys huddled around intercoms. Pimlico's crowd noise rose as the band played *Maryland, My Maryland*. The horses were called to post and the field of entrants announced. The room echoed with boo's when Pensive was named, and at less odds than I figured.

"Ben Jones has the even-money chestnut looking fit for today's second leg of the Triple Crown," the commentator announced. As the horses were warming up, three track pundits were interviewed, their picks divided between Platter and Stir Up as Pensive's toughest rivals. Two of the three felt certain Platter, last year's Champion two-year-old, was fresh and would emerge the victor, inducing more taunts and raspberries from C Company boys milling around us.

"He's good," Chase conceded, "but the one we *really* have to worry about is Stir Up."

"You don't say; two hundred make your knees weak?" I said.

"Nah, but we can't forget he was the Derby favorite and Arcaro is always dangerous. As much as I hate to admit, I think Johnson's right. Arcaro will be determined to make amends with a better pace this time."

"If you wanna side with them and make a loan of your money in the pool, I'll take your action if you want out."

"Nope. I said *worry* about him, not that he'd *do* it. Nope, in for a penny, in for a pound, goombah; I'm in."

The horses were entering stalls as the din aboard ship softened in anticipation of hearing those famous words: "they're all in, the flag is up, an-n-n-d they're off!"

A roar erupted from every deck, everyone yelling for individual favorites. Each time a position was called, GIs cheered no matter who it was, as long as Pensive was not among the leaders.

"Alorter and Platter duel for the early lead. Arcaro moves Stir Up to the outside and slips in behind the leaders. Stymie falls in a length farther back and keeps pace with Stir Up. Arcaro has given his colt more rein and urges the speedy bay to a head in front, and still with an easy stride, stops the first quarter in twenty-three-and-three."

Chase looked at me as if to say: *I told you so*, suggesting Arcaro had set a comfortable pace with plenty of horse left for the closing rush. Horses shifted positions ticking off furlongs as the announcer swept through the field moving down the backstretch. This time, the call ended with: "and trailing the field many lengths back is Pensive."

The approval was deafening. The tension mounted as the field left the final turn and raced into the home stretch.

"Arcaro accelerates Stir Up and widens his lead to two."

Chase grimaced. I mirrored his sentiments; Arcaro having saved his horse for a prolonged sprint to the wire. Just as I was about to toss in the towel, my defeatist dreads got a sudden boost.

"Here comes Pensive, now on the move and gaining ground on the leaders. He passes Platter at the quarter pole and sets his sights on Stir Up still in the lead. Pensive pulls alongside and looks Arcaro's colt in the eye. But wait!"

"Platter accelerates and rejoins the leaders— all three sprinting head-to-head for the wire!

"Platter now moves a neck in front!"

Johnson's boys exploded, screaming for Platter with less than a furlong to go. *Damn it!* My jaw muscles clenched.

"But Pensive is having none of it! He changes leads, shifts gears, and nabs Platter only yards from the wire! The Derby winner has done it again! Pensive wins the Preakness by about three-quarters of a length, Platter takes second with a gap of two lengths back to a leg-weary Stir Up in third."

Platter's fan club changed from shouting holy venerations to foul blasphemies. But whatever the expletives, it was music to my ears as Chase and I were embraced in a bear hug.

"Unbelievable!" Chase wowed. "I thought sure we were beat."

"Me, too. That was too damned close for comfort. I don't know if I can handle another one, but the question now is, Chase: can he win the Belmont for the Triple Crown?"

"I'm convinced. My God, Zeck. Look how he explodes in final furlongs no matter what the early pace. He toyed with those guys. He's a classic come-from-behind horse and the Belmont's mile-and-a-half sets up perfect for him. Mark my words, Vince. Come the first week of June, he'll clobber 'em. I don't think there's a horse in the country that can beat him. But, I suppose nothing's a lock. I've seen crazy things happen in this game. You never know, there could be a fresh up-and-comer we haven't heard about yet."

"Ah, horse feathers," Tony said. "They said the same thing about Platter being fresh; last year's champion, but he got beat. Pensive's got the Triple in the bag."

"Maybe," Chase cautioned, raising a finger. "But only one stable in history has ever won *two* Triple Crowns, Tony— only one. Sunny Fitzsimmons trained Gallant Fox for Belair Stud in, um, 1930 I think it was. Yeah, I remember now, because it was Gallant Fox's own son who won five years later. And he was a chestnut, too; a horse called Omaha. So if Pensive *does* win, Calumet will have their second Triple Crown since they got their first with Whirlaway. Hmm, Vince. Could be there's no better time to jump all over one of your omens. It might be our *biggest* score yet."

"How about them apples?" Tony cut in and pirouetted. "Like the man says, it's *gotta* be an omen, boss. Cuz Natalie says *I'm* her gallant fox, so Pensive is a sure-fire shoe-in."

"What do you mean— *biggest* score yet?" I said, ignoring Tony.

"Well *one* thing for sure, it's not Natalie's Italian stallion here. You skated many times, Mosconi, but remember this: *foxes* get their asses caught in traps and end up wrapped around some gal's neck for life. How you like *them* apples?" Chase teased.

"Not that slippery weasel," Mac said. "Some *vixen* will sure as hell cut him loose after draggin' his ass home to make puppies."

"Kittens!" Tony corrected.

"Whatever, joik, you *still* get lucky." They were trading phony punches when Chase interrupted their clowning.

"What I meant to say is, Whirlaway was Calumet's first come-from-behind horse to win the Triple in '41, *or*, the year we *entered* this war. You follow?"

"Yeah, so?"

"Well, maybe it's divine providence; Pensive is *meant* to win. You know, Calumet's *second* Triple that not only ends Belair's reign, *but*, Pensive's win will mean the *end* of the war. Whirlaway kicks it off in '41— Pensive ends it in '44. Think about it.

"Holy cannolies; sure *does* make a fella think." Goose bumps dotted my forearms.

"We'll find out soon enough, Vince. The last leg is only weeks away in June. If I'm right, maybe the world won't be at war by the time the Triple Crown rolls around again next year. We'll be going home soon, and the world can get back to normal."

"Horseshit omens or not, gents, I like the sound o' that tune," Frazer said. "You haven't let us down yet, Brother Chase, so you got my vote. Sounds like we'll be in for a short job in Europe and be home for next summer's fun. Then Hollywood here I come."

Tony waved us on toward the mess lines. "Frazer said it all boys. Let's get some chow before da boss toins into a cloud and goes poof."

Atlantic Showers

The Atlantic was as mild as a New England pond. Except for a little roughness the first night leaving New York, sailing conditions had been kind for the latter half of May. Despite a stopover in Nova Scotia, and the convoy's defensive zigzagging, we were nearly across the Atlantic after two weeks at sea.

Sunny skies with only a whisper of a breeze drew more than the normal crowds to weather decks. Wrapped in bulky, but mandatory life vests, we looked like a colony of sea lions basking in the balmy, summer-like weather. Cameras were clicking everywhere; capturing smiling GIs against a backdrop of a spectacular convoy steaming through placid seas.

Chase finished a letter and joined Tony and me at the railing, gawking at the humongous convoy. From what we could tell, the *Tramonto* must be positioned near its southern edge since we're flanked by Navy frigates and destroyers running back and forth like sheepdogs guarding a flock.

To the north, and as far as the eye could see, both forward and aft, were hundreds of ships of every size and type; the sheer number of servicemen and supplies steaming for Europe was staggering.

"Those destroyers might account for all the depth charges we heard going off last night," Chase reasoned.

"Better them than a whoppin' *ka-boom* in our face," Tony said. "I didn't sleep a wink."

"I didn't, either," I agreed. "Did you fellas notice how many showed up at rosary services this morning? It was packed too tight to fart; I didn't know we had so many Catholics on board."

"Yeah, sure. What d'ya wanna bet half of them toikeys suddenly found religion overnight?"

Tony was right, it had been a long and troublesome night for everyone. I was unnerved each time the ship lurched and accelerated through abrupt changes in course. I wasn't the only one wearing a life vest in my hammock, nerves strained and every muscle tensed, listening for the slightest indication we needed to scramble topside—*assuming* we'd be given the chance. I prayed like never before, not knowing if we were taking evasive action, or dodging torpedoes.

Tony blew the destroyers a kiss. "God bless our Navy boys. I hope youz got the bastards, Dominic's for biscuits."

"Amen, Brother T," Chase said. Aside from comforting, it was interesting to watch the various warships signaling and maneuvering through courses when Chief Petty Officer Graham approached from behind.

"Afternoon, boys. Sorry for the choppy going last night, but the Captain has no choice but to nix the stabilizing gyros or they'd rip through the hull from inertial forces. But, better rough going than swimming in burning oil, eh?"

"Did we almost get whacked last night?" I had to ask.

"Dunno; I wasn't on duty. But I do know we had to travel no more than ten minutes in a straight line to keep the Jerries from getting a bead on us."

C.B. soon joined us at the rail. "Sorry to spoil your fun in the sun, boys, but it's the unit's turn at the showers. I suggest you git your nasty behinds below and enjoy the Atlantic from down there. Pass the word, Sergeant Fairchild."

Personal hygiene aboard this overcrowded ship was a chore, but showering was a tug-of-war between courage and cleanliness. Lower ranks were assigned showers with frigid seawater pumped in at ocean temperatures. To make matters worse, we were issued rock-hard blocks of soap that never lathered; but more useful for scraping off layers of skin. After drying, our bodies were coated with a scaly residue that left us feeling itchy and dirtier than before.

It was exasperating knowing there was a hot freshwater facility a deck above the main dining hall. Word spread to stay clear, warning it was reserved for officers, with an MP posted within its dressing area. Nevertheless, Tony had enough.

"I don't give a rat's ass. I'm sick and tired of this seawater crap." Several *amens* and groans supported Tony's sentiment. "What in hell do they think we are, a bunch o' *seagulls*, or somethin'?"

"Hey, I'll fix it for ya," Mac razzed, lying in his top hammock. "How about I go tell the Captain they got it all wrong— that you ain't no seagull, but a *toikey* from *Joisey*. Will that woik?" Everyone laughed, but he only inflamed Tony's ire.

"Go ahead and cackle all ya want, but I've had enough of this shit." Tony threw his shirt at Mac's head, infuriated by Mac's taunts and gobbles. And as for youz, ya little squirt, how's about putting ya money where that beak is? A tenner says I get a hot shower; MP, or no MP. How you like them apples, Mac-a-doodle-doo?"

"You're on if you let me get my money, Mosconi." Mac was busy parrying Tony's attempts to pinch Mac's nose. Judging from the bantering, odds of Tony's success seemed about evenly spread between backers and naysayers when all eyes suddenly fell upon me, as if I alone held the measure of partiality.

"Well? How about it, Zeck?" Mac probed. "You sticking by wonder-boy or not?

"I dunno. Betting on horses was one thing, but messing with officer perks was something else," I said, weighing options. I had no clue how he expected to pull it off, but gut instincts told me to go with the lucky one. "Okay, motor mouth. Piss on your ten-spot. How about a *fifty* says he does it?"

Mac whistled. "Fifty smackers, huh? Are you sure you wanna bleed that much, big shot? You might care to save some of that cabbage for tissues."

"Hey boss, I'll take ten of that fifty," JJ blurted from a few bunks away. "I say Tony gets his ass busted."

Woofie quickly matched it. "Stay put, Junior. I'll cover your mistake; I'm with the boss."

Playful bickering and insults were flying in both camps. More confident, Mac dropped from his hammock and used my own precept against me.

"What was it you said before, bossman? Somethin' about *losers* always bettin' with their hearts and not their heads? Okay, chump. I'm in, but only for ten of your *whoop*-d-do fifty." Mac pulled a sawbuck from his wallet, but held it to his chest. "Not so fast, Zecca. I got a condition first." The ruckus quieted to hear what Mac had in mind before making more bets.

"Here's the deal. I get to go with him as a witness and we *both* get a hot shower without going to the brig, or he loses the bet."

Many backing Tony protested, claiming Mac's presence posed too great a risk. Knowing the little jokester as they did, they thought he might hatch a devious scheme to undermine Tony's game plan.

"Keep ya britches on, children." Tony strut the aisle and played down the moans. "No worries. I'll go along with the little turd, *but*, I have a condition of my own, too." He stuck a finger at Mac's face. "*Youz*, gotta do exactly as I says at all times, and I mean *exactly.*"

Tony caught Mac off guard, and like a praying mantis, plucked Little Mac's nose between his fingers and shook him gently. "Ya little twerp, if youz so much as get one hair cockeyed da wrong way, all bets are off, capisce?" Tony tweaked the tip of Mac's nose and let him go.

"Okay," Mac said, rubbing away the sting. "But Father Frazer is the judge, jury, and banker. If there's any bullshit dispute, he decides who gets what— agreed?"

"You got a deal, Macarooni."

The game was afoot as they shook hands. Tony stripped and wrapped a towel around his waist, and ordered Mac to do likewise.

"Why do I have to strip now?" Mac resisted. "We're half-a-ship away from the showers, idiot."

"Do as I say, McKenzie, or the bet's off, remember?"

Mac shrugged, but tossed a second towel over his shoulder per Tony's instruction.

"Now get your travel case and put these in it, then follow me." Tony retrieved a razor and three cigars from his own ditty bag and put them into Mac's case.

On the way topside, Tony was unfazed by side glances and laughter as he sauntered past startled GIs as if nothing were out of the ordinary. Mac flushed feeling stupid, but kept pace with Tony's perky stride. We followed the near-naked pair like a yard full of school kids egging on a playground fight, picking up a few curious stragglers caught up in the fun.

Off the dining hall, Tony detoured into a large ship's head, and saturated his hair and upper body with enough water that a shower seemed pointless. Mac copied and the pair renewed their trek to the far end of the hall. Tony halted the trailing fanfare before entering the stairwell to their destination, demanding everyone stay and wait for them to return.

"Now pay attention, y'little pipsqueak. From this point on, act natural, but follow my lead at all times." Tony retrieved a cigar and razor from Mac's travel bag. "Now turn around and let's see you walk backwards, like this."

"What are you gonna do with that razor? Are you setting me up for something?" Mac grinned, wary of Tony's motives.

"I ain't gonna do nothin'. What d'ya take me for, anyway? D'ya want a shower, or what? Now, do as I say. Come on, turn around and try it." Tony spun him into position and showed him what to do. "And don't youz dare look back at me, either. Leastwise, not 'til I says to; y'got that?"

Satisfied Mac had the unnatural gait down, Tony shoved a cigar into Mac's mouth. "Now when I says stop, youz stop, and don't say a woid. Just keep yer yap clamped 'round that cigar with yer eyes glued on me. Act real interested in what I'm saying, capisce?"

We watched in amusement as the two dripping crazies climbed the short flight of stairs, reversed on Tony's signal, and resumed walking backwards toward a half-alert MP a few feet inside the dressing room.

Tony pivoted Mac and got in his face. "Ah, Jeeze. Now look what youz went and did, lieutenant. Youz got me so woiked up over the Preakness, I forgot to shave." Tony twirled his razor in Mac's face. "Come on, keep me company 'til I finish."

Tony's eyes remained riveted inches from Mac's as he derided Arcaro for twice failing to pace Stir Up, all the while guiding Mac past a curious, but silent sentry. Tony stopped at the threshold.

"Uh, what's y'name, corporal?" Tony asked, and handed the wary, but grinning sentry a cigar before he could answer.

"Ah, Corporal Lynch, sir. Bobby Lynch," he replied, drawing the cigar beneath his nostrils.

"Well, Lynch. Today's your lucky day. It's a fine Cuban and too good a smoke to be takin' back in there. It'll only unravel, so enjoy." Tony flashed a half-salute and pushed a dumbfounded Mac into the shower room.

"Ha, haaa! Way t'go Tony." I whooped and punched a jubilant Woofie in the arm the moment we spotted Tony coming toward us. He and Mac were puffing on cigars, but it was Mac's playful pout that painted the best picture.

"He thinks he won a bet, but I fooled him— and you too, you big wop-a-looza. I would have paid *twenty* clams to get a hot shower. So I figure I got off for half price, *and* got one of Mosconi's big-shot cigars to boot. How you toikeys like them apples?" Mac grinned, pinning the smoke between his teeth.

Tony's turn for needling came a day later after risking another attempt with Woofie. The same MP stopped them on the way out.

"Ah, hold on, you two." Tony's face paled more than Woofie's, both aware of consequences for impersonating an officer. "Uh, just wanted to say thanks for the smokes— *private.*"

Corporal Lynch smirked at Tony's crimson cheeks. "Don't go reelin' in your trouser trout, junior. You guys ain't goin' to the brig. I just wanted you and your flunky pals to know I ain't nobody's fool. I was onto your game from the git go. You're just damned lucky my gig isn't for real, but I do admire your craziness. What's your name?"

"Mosconi, and this big mutt is Mullins. And what d'ya mean by, 'not for real?'

Lynch glanced around and drew them closer, swearing them to secrecy. "These showers are open to anyone; always have been. This whole biz about 'officers only' is all bullshit. As you can see, they're small and out of the way. Few aboard even knows they're here."

Lynch again made sure he could not be overheard. "This fat-ass Major gets his cronies together and had us spread rumors of Article 17 discipline if anyone lower than a looey tried using 'em. They stuck me in here to make it look like off limits so they could keep it freed up for themselves. I get a big steak and beer everyday if I keep my trap shut. So what the hell, why not? I traded a little sunshine for decent grub and suds. Then you fellas showed up with that backward walk of yours. I about busted a gut after you wooshed that little guy through the hatch. You're a funny guy, Mosconi. I actually looked forward to seeing your crazy ass again; you broke up the boredom."

Lynch chuckled, rolling the cigar between pursed lips. "I had more fun duping you out of these cigars. Woulda waited for another, but didn't have the heart. Was more fun watchin' your chins hit the bulkhead— funnier 'n hell." Lynch smirked, lighting all three cigars.

Guys laughed at Tony's presumptuous attitude when hearing of the ruse. He took the loss of pride along with good cigars in stride, but thumbed his nose at Mac's backers when reminding them the bet.

"I said, toikeys. It wasn't *why*, but rather that I *would* get a hot shower without ending up in the pokey. So bless youz for the dough, boys; Dominics for biscuits."

Land Ho!

"Land ho!" a sailor shouted.

By now, we'd had enough of the big pond; ready for a change. Two weeks living like cellar rats in a hot and smelly cubbyhole had tested my patience. Food aboard ship wasn't anything to write home about, either. No matter *what* the cooks prepared, it was boiled to death. If that wasn't bad enough, we had to down each serving while slowly moving through a chow line like a conveyor belt.

From our vantage point, we could see land on the horizon. The massive convoy had split into segments, steaming northeasterly in single file up the Celtic Sea between Ireland and England. We were gawking at the rugged coastline in the distance when CPO Graham stopped to say hello.

"Yes, that's land fellas," he joked. "By now, you Army brats probably thought the earth had run out of dirt, eh? The cliffs over yonder are in Wales, St. David's Peninsula. The next jut of land will be Anglesey at Holyhead. Soon after that, we'll turn eastward into Liverpool Bay, so it won't be much longer before you'll get your land-legs back."

I leaned against the rail, and as the others chatted, my thoughts studied the ship's size and layout trying to grasp an image Graham had painted, when by chance, we had met our third day at sea.

Woofie and I had finished a private reading lesson, and leaving our secret nook one deck below and well aft of our quarters, we came up behind three guys roughing up a naval officer.

I grabbed the guy nearest Graham, spun him, and drove my fist into his solar plexus. He collapsed to his knees, gasping to regain his breath. Woofie had snatched the other two jerks by their necks and cracked their heads together.

"It ain't *nice* to be thumpin' on Navy fellas fer doin' their jobs," he snarled.

"The guy was shaking us down for money and cigarettes!" one of them yelled.

"Bullshit! you lyin' sow bellies." Woofie shoved their faces at a large 'NO SMOKING' sign. "Cain't you fellas read a lick? I'll be an egg-eatin' coonhound 'fore I let the likes of you two slop-hogs blow us t'hell. Now git before I make you *eat* them Camels 'til you shit a cee-gar." Woofie sent them stumbling toward the same hatchway their buddy had staggered through.

"You alright?" I asked Graham.

"Yeah, I'm okay," he said, rubbing his head. "Banged my noggin pretty good when that idiot slammed me up against the wall. Bloody bastards insisted on smoking, so I tried putting out their cigarettes."

"I know, we heard."

"Why do you think Navy Regs and those signs are pounded into your heads at orientation? You damned GIs don't realize that one loose cig, and we could *all* be blown to kingdom come."

"Hey, don't be damning us, we're on *your* side."

"Ah, you know what I mean. I appreciate you stepping in, fellas, but I wasn't about to back off from those jerks."

We exchanged introductions, and as we walked, Graham put things in a perspective we could relate to.

"Touching off an explosion is one thing, Vince, but try this one on for size. What if we were hit by a torpedo, and that dude caused a fire preventing rescuers from getting to you and your buddies up in the bow? Imagine it as an oven; and what it would be like if you were left to bake like a Christmas goose— *alive?*"

He got my attention, and I remember thanking him, grateful he stood up to those mindless idiots. *Good God, what a grisly image; the screaming, skin blistering— cooking to death. Ugh! I wish I had broken every bone in that bastard's face.*

"Hey, Vince. *Yo!* Wake up!" Tony's sharp elbow brought me back to the present.

"Graham had to run, but said he'd catch up later. Where in hell did ya mind go, goombah?"

"Um, a Christmas dinner you wouldn't much like, so never mind. Come on, let's get us some boiled shit on a shingle, instead."

By the time we finished chow, the *Tramonto* had pointed her nose due east toward Liverpool at the mouth of the Mersey River. The liner slowed and announced her presence with repeated blasts of her sea horn. Small vessels moved around us like goslings.

The top deck afforded wonderful views of shorelines dotted with commercial buildings and seaside homes. Some were old and stately with beautifully manicured lawns of a deep emerald-green. Row-houses lined the narrow streets away from the waterfront. The rustic brick accented by white shutters and trim reminded me a lot of Tremont Square, but then, a great deal of Boston's Back Bay reflected early English architecture.

"Too many ships to count," Graham said, off duty and paying us a visit. "Open water between Birkenhead and Liverpool is littered with vessels. This is my third crossing, boys, and I've never seen it jammed like this before. Moorings are assigned all the way up the Mersey as far inland as Runcorn. They must be right about you, Mosconi; word from the bridge is you boys are gonna get lucky."

He explained Liverpool had limited deep-draft slips, and such moorings were at a premium reserved for merchant ships laden with heavy war machinery. Lighter troop transports had to drop anchor in open water.

"Those boys will have to climb down cargo nets and be ferried dockside. I've heard a story of a guy who missed his timing and slipped in between the boats; crushed like a gnat."

I savored my blessings. GIs would be burdened with rifles and hundred-pound packs risking far more than banged-up shins trying to time footing with tenders bobbing hither-fro over deep water. *Better them than me, Dominic's for biscuits.*

We made final approach and watched in awe as the captain, with the aid of a few small tugs gently nudging, maneuvered our seafaring behemoth into place at the wharf. It was if an unseen hand had slipped a mammoth puzzle tile into position, stern to stern only feet from a British vessel loading the wounded destined for the States.

Dock workers hustled everywhere. The scene looked chaotic but apparently efficient. A toy-like steam engine caught our eye— belching smoke and tooting like an little cartoon character moving cargo-laden boxcars and flatbeds around the pier.

Two ships ahead of us were offloading P-38's. Chase and I marveled at the sleek, twin-fuselage fighter planes. Sometimes I wished I were a fly-boy whizzing around in one of those babies rather than back-packing through mud and rain-soaked forests.

"Not so much now," Graham said, "but in the early stages of the war, Germans used to bomb hell out of this place. Thousands died; many still entombed in collapsed bomb shelters up there," he nodded toward the shore. "Women and children had to be evacuated to safer spots inland. You guys gotta remember, this ain't no hometown Prissyville like folks are used to in the States. We're in the middle of a war here, boys. German airfields are only twenty-five miles away across the channel."

Twenty-five miles?

I tried to imagine such a paltry distance separating my home from an enemy dealing death and destruction from Nantucket Island off Boston's coast. Graham was right. Up to now, folks at home had been spared the horrors of what Europeans had experienced.

Aside from rationing, Americans still enjoyed freedoms and civil stability. They hadn't seen the war up close; it was always *other* people— *foreigners* who were left starving and wandering homeless with only the clothes on their backs, living in burned-out villages. Americans didn't know what it was like to have homes ransacked, neighborhoods shelled, or loved ones shot in the head before their eyes by smug, luger-wielding executioners.

"The blitzkrieg united the English, and endeared them to the royal family," Graham said. "King George refused to hightail it for safer havens even though the Brits expected them to. He insisted on staying with his people. Once, when an entire wing of Buckingham Palace was destroyed, tabloids showed pictures of the royals working elbow-to-elbow beside locals, clearing debris."

During opening salvos of the war, I read that U-boats attacked merchant shipping hoping to starve England into submission rather than challenge her formidable Navy. With such heavy dependence on imports, she was brought to her knees, struggling for survival, yet shook a defiant fist at the Fuhrer.

I admired our unshakeable English cousins: standing alone and determined to defend their small island nation as the only bastion left to face the Nazi barbarians. Their cupboards may be bare, homes bombed, and their kids away fighting, but they stood united with an indomitable spirit. A yell distracted my thoughts.

"Welcome to England, yanks!" Several more "cheerio's" rose from the wharf below. The Brits were warm and engaging; they had a way of making us feel appreciated as newly arriving allies.

Officers instructed us not to toss money or cigarettes, but the urge was too great to resist. Most items on our person were free from the Red Cross anyway, so we saw nothing wrong with being good ambassadors. We began tossing chocolate bars, lifesavers, soap, gum, and cigarette packs. The little things we took for granted were severely rationed in England. One agile fellow leapt a small stack of cargo while plucking an errant pack of Chesterfields out of the air.

Graham said the English were especially fond of U.S. cigarettes, citing the local version as grossly inferior, yet costing two-and-six-pence; double the quarter we paid at home.

"If you dudes think *you're* broke half the time, think of the English. Believe it or not, what you consider lousy Army pay is more than what most people make here."

Tony made an immediate friend. A dock worker removed his cap and swept a wide nobleman's bow in appreciation for one of his Montecristo's, his co-workers scurrying over to savor its scent. Tony couldn't resist and threw his last three cigars to surprised, yet grateful recipients.

C.B. and Chase joined us, passing the word we were to go below and pack. "And no dilly-dallyin'! Git yer gear together and be sure 'n hit the sac early for a good night's sleep. Yer gonna need it. We have an *early* departure, then a long march to a train depot."

Timing and destinations were secret, but C.B. hinted we would ultimately be stationed at a large military compound a few hours southwest of London. Crossing the Atlantic had been a long and tedious voyage, and with weariness and last minute packing to do, we were eager to go below for the night.

C.B. wasn't kidding about *early*. My watch read 03:00 when he raked us from hammocks. Most had spent a restless night grappling with pent up anxieties, yet in our numbed stupor, we still managed to gather our gear and disembarked in total darkness. Army trucks with headlights rigged for blackout shuttled us a few miles inland to rendezvous with other units; from there, we marched to a train depot. Stations were closer, but schedules and boarding locations were staggered to avoid attack should knowledge of mass troop movements fall into enemy hands.

Before boarding, a cordial brakeman explained we could expect about an eight hour journey across England's interior. Unlike the shoddy troop train into Fort Hamilton, we were surprised at how cozy English passenger cars were appointed. Each coach offered private compartments with cushioned leather seats, yet spacious enough to comfortably seat four. Blackout curtains were strictly enforced.

"It feels like we're in a foxhole on wheels, for crissake," Tony quipped, though it didn't matter. Once settled, we were all dozing within minutes.

I was jostled awake as the train passed through a switchyard. My eyes opened to a hazy dawn, and once through the terminal, Mother England revealed her countryside.

Endless acres were crosshatched with rock fences and low hedges. Small herds of cattle and sheep grazed in lush pastures cleaved by shallow streams, and sprinkled with wildflowers. My eyes followed narrow carriage lanes lined with stately moss-covered trees, leading to stone farm buildings or large manors with spacious courtyards. Villages were quaint, with old and settled buildings constructed of heavy stone, brick, and Tudor-style stucco.

I was captivated by lovely cottages covered with thatched roofing about two-feet thick. Layers of reeds were neatly trimmed around deep-set doorways and shuttered windows. We half-expected to see a big gingerbread man pop into a doorway and wave as we passed.

After hours in the rail system, we rolled into a marshaling yard somewhere in the southern County of Wiltshire. Army trucks carried us to a huge compound teeming with troops and equipment of every kind. The entire complex was split into two encampments, each flanking the quaint village of Amesbury, and connected by a single, overburdened road running through the center of town.

Several platoons were assigned to Quonset Huts while others slept in pyramid-shaped tents camouflaged within nearby groves of mature oak and beech. We had heard that hundreds more were billeted among private residences from northern Wales to southern coastal towns. We were shocked when arriving at our quarters.

Hague Hall was an elegant stone manor, its three-stories covered with clinging ivy. It was once a girl's boarding school, but its former occupants had been conscripted to work in ammunition plants elsewhere in England. The groundskeeper stopped working near the entrance to welcome us.

"Cheerio, lads. Welcome to England. Name's Matt Hogsden, and anything I can do for you yanks, just 'oller. I've been working these grounds for nigh on thirty years. I'll keep ye warm in winter, and ye'll 'ave all the 'ot water ye want."

Unlike many English families, the school had plenty of hot water and fuel for heat. Due to severe rationing, several homes went through winters with only enough coal to heat a single room, with little or no hot water whatsoever.

"Beats the livin' hell out of what we just left," I said.

Our rooms were large, and left comfortably furnished with four beds, a highboy dresser, desks, and large wall mirror. I was getting settled when Woofie called from the hallway.

"Well I'll be dipped in shit. Hey boss, come lookie here! A gen-u-ine tub you could wash a cow in. *Lawd* have mercy."

Mac poked his head around Woofie and whistled. "Sure is a *big* son-of-a-bitch. I could do laps in that thing; even big enough for your bones, Woof." The four of us stood staring in silence as if gazing upon a porcelain shrine, all thinking the same thing—*a hot soak, and soak some more.*

The corporal in charge of quarters passed word we were to report for morning field exercises at 06:00 sharp, followed by a series of command inspections to make sure we'd been issued everything we needed. We were still tired and retreated early, and looked forward to the comfort of a real bed.

We didn't know exactly where Amesbury was in southern England, nor had any idea of how long we'd be there, but were soon reminded as to *why* we were there.

Germans hit during the night, and probably from airfields only twenty minutes away. We awoke to the drone of aircraft and not-so-distant *whumps* of exploding bombs rattling our windows. Tony got up and pushed aside a heavy blackout curtain. He was soon joined by the rest of us peering out the window, mesmerized by search lights crisscrossing the skies, tracers shooting skyward. We didn't know if it was London or some other hapless city near the coast. It didn't matter; we were close, and innocent people were dying out there.

No one spoke. We watched in silent disbelief as more explosions fed the growing reddish hue on the horizon. My heart went out to the luckless victims I suspected were trapped beneath tons of burning rubble. Photos Graham had described flashed through my mind: people left homeless rummaging through debris, relishing something as simple as single photograph to salvage. Others were of little kids huddled together, shocked and crying— orphans overnight.

My jaw muscles clenched. I was seething, my neck red with rage; the sight and sound of civilian bombing unfathomable.

Blessed Jesus, this is war.

Here and Now

Reveille came too soon given we had little sleep. The morning was pleasant, promising a balmy first day of June to help erase the appalling night. Exercises were less rigorous than anticipated, thank God; mostly light calisthenics to get our land legs back.

After orientations, we marched two miles into the village where C.B. released us for a noon break. GIs were already packed in a pub called The Red Lion, but we squeezed in.

The Lion was a cozy Tudor-style tavern with thick plastered walls and low ceilings. Massive hand-hewn beams stretched overhead, bowed with age. Elegant millwork enriched the windows and doors; broad stained-glass windows filtered light through little diamond-shaped panels in leaded frames. Frazer fell in love with the place. He named it our new off-base HQ, its quaint, yet lively atmosphere second only to its food and drink.

The Lion's menu offered a tasty traditional dish called *shepherd's pie;* a baked mix of minced lamb, potatoes, and seasonings. Another oddly-named casserole was *toad-in-the-hole*, made with *bangers*, or sausages similar to our bratwurst; so named because they tended to explode when cooking. The bangers were baked in a thick doughy batter called *Yorkshire pudding*. Served steaming hot with a slab of strong cheddar and a pint of rich English ale— *oh my*; the delectable combo couldn't be beat.

C.B. rarely joined us, but advantaged the occasion and enjoyed sampling British beer and mixed drinks. He tried a *shandygaff*, or half lager and half ginger ale. Though guys wrinkled their noses when hearing the mix, he let me taste it. It was different, but I liked it. The mood was relaxed as C.B. disclosed daily agendas.

"Mornings will be dedicated to field training," he said, "and afternoons set aside for classroom work."

Once back on base, our first class was a session on radio-directed air and artillery barrages coordinated with advancing ground troops. I found the topic intriguing, it paralleling many of Cy's comments of how Germans were said to position men and equipment during the First World War. I raised my hand.

"Excuse me captain. Can you elaborate on German defensive tactics? I've been told they tend to establish preset shelling patterns where troops are likely to bunch up or seek cover. Oh yeah, and of how they tend to set up machine guns and mobile field cannons for blanketing wide swathes in French hedgerow country."

Captain Watterson ordered me to stand. "What's your name, private?"

"PFC Vincent Zecca, sir."

"Well Private Zecca. I believe I've covered that subject and fail to see what I've left out. Why would hedges in *France* be any different from what we see around here?"

I was nervous not expecting a combative instructor. "Uh, I'm not sure, sir. But I met this old guy in New York— uh, I mean while we were at Fort Hamilton. This guy had been there and done that. He told me about different things to—"

"*Who?*" he cut me off. "*Who* had been there and done that? We haven't any troops in France, or have you been living under a rock, soldier?"

"No sir. He's a retired dock worker. Uh, I mean he was a highly decorated captain in the thick of things back in World War I. He was saying that—"

"World War *One?*" Captain Watterson's smug swagger played to a few snickers. "That was *when*, Zecca— thirty years ago?" He stepped forward from his easel. "Men and machines have come a long way since then. This is here and now— *not* 1918. Why in hell would you want to rely on some old wharf rat reliving past glory days over a warm beer?"

Watterson went back to his board maps, slapping them with his pointer. "I've spent four years studying maneuvers at West Point, mister. And that's why *I* have this rank, and *you* don't. That's why the Army has assigned *me* to instruct tin-horns like *you* on field strategies. *Today*, the first week of June— 1944— *not* yesteryear."

Whoop-d-doo. Aren't you the impressive one, Captain Watterson.

The smarmy bastard flexed rank muscles, gloating over dressing me down in front of the class. I quashed rising anger and chanced another attempt to share what instincts told me the class may need to know.

"Of course, sir, and no disrespect meant, but this guy was saying—"

"No more *buts,* private. You've already wasted enough time. If I want any more *buts* from you, I'll order yours front and center to kick some sense into it. Do I make myself clear? Now sit down!"

"Yes sir." I saluted, fuming. My eyes darted to Tony and Chase, but both faces told me to shut up and stay seated. *Kick my butt, will he?* What I wouldn't give to get that pompous ass in a steam room. No brass, no insignias; nothing but Watterson's bullocky bare ass void of rank.

He wants my butt? Done! I'd make that ferret-faced pansy kiss my ass from here to Sunday. He's the type Cy said every enlisted man dreads; the type who get soldiers killed— ninety-day-wonders fresh out of Officer Candidate School, full of academy pomp and ceremony with an inflexible rock for a brain.

I thought of Cy's sobering words: 'You guys are combat soldiers Vince, so forget about being a bunch of nice, clean-cut, school kids. You don't fight the Nazis by Queensberry rules. Instead, you shoot them in the *back.* You sneak up on 'em, and cut their miserable throats. Blow 'em to hell and back. You do whatever it takes to kill the bastards the quickest way you can— *before* they do you. Never take your eyes off 'em, Vincent, because they'll sure as hell try and trick you. They'll lie in wait and bushwhack you. So if you don't beat the Huns at their own game, I *promise* you, son, you won't retire that uniform you're so damned proud of wearing.'

I calmed down. I supported education and had faith in the Army's system, but there's a hell of lot to be learned from having been there and done that. Cy said it was tunnel-vision jerks with attitudes like Watterson's who were destined to repeat flawed tactics.

He said his doughboys had not the luxury of history for learning modern field strategies, or had the latest communication and mechanized equipment. They had to learn lessons the hard way.

Watterson probably didn't know what it was like to get his hands dirty, much less having to dive into fetid foxholes to keep real bullets from dinging buttons off his uniform. He may know military theory, but proven or not, I didn't see the harm sharing knowledge gained from a seasoned veteran; knowledge gleaned at the expense of men's lives.

War is still war. Artillery shells still explode, bullets fly, and man is just as hell-bent on killing his fellow man. I suppose I could be wrong, but it seemed to me, Cy's first-hand battlefield accounts had a lot more meat on the bone than mere morsels to be washed down with a warm beer, and forgotten.

She's a Doozie

Our second day at Hague Hall opened with a different regimen than jumping jacks; *real* exertion would be needed now. C.B. roused the squad at first light with special orders commencing immediately after breakfast. Division HQ ordered every Company to perform temporary work details in support of the massive influx of troops, equipment, and supplies pouring into southern England.

C.B. put me in charge of a six-man detail to move prefabricated building joists from a supply depot in Salisbury, a town about thirty miles south. We were to deliver them to a construction site within our sister encampment on the other side of Amesbury.

Chase escaped the heavy work ordered to report to Command HQ later in the day. That left me with the obvious ox, Woofie as first pick, and four others for the task. First step: secure a truck.

None of us had a chance to buy a bicycle yet, but two packs of Camels bought us a lift from a passing deuce-and-a-half that saved a two-mile hike to the motor pool. I was greeted by a Corporal Wash, a surly slob shuffling papers at a makeshift desk of crates. He snatched my requisition slip and barked orders to a lot jockey.

"Orders say here you're to get a flatbed, mack. This old farmer's stake-side is all I got left, so take it or leave it," he growled, rolling a soggy cigar stub in his mouth. His assistant left the heap chugging and hustled off to get other vehicles for waiting drivers. He read my dubious face, and smirked.

"Don't worry, mack, she runs good. We use it all the time for hauling parts around this dump."

I sighed. "Well, it ain't a Duesenberg, but I guess it'll have to do then, huh?" He ignored my sarcasm in lieu of gloating over my feeble bargaining position. I was in no mood to get into a pissing match with that bum, so I let it slide.

"She's a *doozie*, alright," Tony added; "only spelled with a *zee*. Maybe it's a good name for the old gal, y'think?" Tony's jest seemed fitting, and thus, we christened her *Doozie* for good luck.

We inherited a '34 English Commer: both fenders banged in or rusted through, a cracked windshield, and the driver's seat split open with exposed springs covered by an oil-stained square of plywood.

Her wooden bed was sturdy, and though relatively short, it seemed to extend longer than normal beyond the rear axle. She was probably jerry-rigged and used for hauling hay bales from the fields.

I signed out as driver. "Tony; McKenzie: up front with me, the rest of you in the back."

Tony took the passenger seat with Little Mac wedged between us on a make-do jump seat; his knees straddling the gear shift. The others climbed into the back and leaned against the cab or side rails.

"What a stinking shit-heap," Mac said with disgust.

The cab was filthy, reeking of old grease and diesel fuel, likely from hauling parts and lubricants around the motor pool. I gave the arrogant corporal another reason to smirk as I made a mess of shifting, lurching and grinding gears when leaving the yard. Once on the road, I improved, but had to focus driving on the left.

We made it through Amesbury, but about six miles beyond we came upon a *round-a-bout*; a center island like the hub of a wheel where several roads converged. I've seen a few around Boston, but never had to manage one lefty-louie. I started downshifting madly—pounding gears into place when Tony started roaring.

"What are you laughing at, Mosconi; think this is easy? Christ, I've knocked guys out with less effort than this."

Tony pointed to Little Mac. Every time I rammed the gear lever backwards, Mac winced, squirmed, and twisted his torso trying to keep his manhood from getting tangled with the flimsy shifter. Sweat beaded his brow and his facial expressions got me to laughing as I made the turn toward Wilton, with Salisbury beyond.

Mac's contortions distracted me, and I habitually steered over to the right. A horn blared, and Tony's laughter changed to a blood-curdling screech.

"*Lef-f-ft!*" Tony slammed his feet against the floorboards, arched his back, bracing himself near ramrod straight.

"Sh-i-i-i-t," Mac squealed, and stiff-armed the dash seconds before a head-on collision.

I jerked hard left, missing the oncoming auto by only feet, and then had to sharply yank her back right before we plowed into a stone wall. The old Commer's weary springs were truly tested as she leaned heavily from side to side.

My heart was pounding. We didn't flip, but I must have scraped another solid layer off an already bald set of tires. Woofie hooted, seemingly entertained by the ordeal, but I was pummeled with expletives from those sent tumbling around the flatbed. From then on, I took my time and guided the old jalopy along the narrow English roads without further incident.

We finally arrived at Salisbury's mammoth distribution yard. Everyone leapt from Doozie, grateful to feel solid ground. The supply depot was abuzz with activity. The diversity of military material was mind-boggling. Hundreds of GIs were moving supplies and equipment to and from stockpiles. Huge dust clouds roiled in the air, thickened by a constant stream of Army trucks and English lorries rolling in and out of the compound. Crews milled around waiting to load or unload, many having been stuck there for hours.

I corralled a harried sergeant and showed him my orders. Since these roofing joists were rated high priority, he directed me to where I could back Doozie into a supply lane for loading. I pointed to her bed and suggested it might be better if we swapped loads with a longer truck, like a lorry. I offered to haul doors, wall panels, squares of shingles, lumber, or just about anything in place of those lengthy joists. Sergeant Brewer was in a frenzy dealing with chaotic traffic, now quite agitated as he shoved a fistful of loose papers in my face.

"Listen, Zecca. Look around ya. I got a shit-load of orders here. So *one*— I don't have time *or* the authority to be changing *anyone's* manifest. And two— you got priority for specific materials needed for construction. Who knows where command will want *you* or any one of them other motor jocks next? Are you willing to take that responsibility, *private*?"

"No, sir. My mistake, sergeant."

"Good. *Now*, we'll get along just fine." He hurriedly endorsed requisition slips and pointed to a nearby shed where tie-downs and chains could be found if needed. "I suggest you get a move on before I forget about this priority rating. You understand me?"

"Loud and clear, sir." I snapped a respectful salute. Maybe I was numb from wrangling with Doozie for the past hour, but that was still no excuse for my idiocy. I felt like a first-day rookie, though I did grasp something of merit as I walked away: *Estes is one sly son-of-a-gun.*

I admired C.B.'s visionary knack. Every platoon in camp had been running around England's countryside on these projects, yet C.B. knew this load ranked top priority over other materials. While other crews were stuck with endless delays, he finagled us a gravy detail knowing we'd be in and out of here and back in time for evening chow.

"What are ya grinnin' at, toikey? That lout just crawled up y'nose."

"Maybe so. But every one of you boneheads are gonna chip in for at least two bottles of England's finest whiskey when we get back. That I promise." I could feel the puzzled looks pelting the back of my head. "Don't worry, ladies, I'll explain later. For right now, I want outta here, so let's get the show on the road."

Cargo lanes were narrow, and I wasn't used to backing up looking over my left shoulder. I ordered everyone off the flatbed so I could see clearly as I slowly reversed Doozie up a tight passageway. About two-thirds back, a large crate protruded a foot into the aisle, preventing me from slipping by. The boys eyeballed the blockage, perplexed at what to do; cussing the thought of having to lug the awkward, heavy frames any distance to the truck.

The crate measured about three-foot-square by five high, and had "stove" and coded numbers stenciled on its sides. A narrow gap at either side prompted Frazer and Tony to try shouldering it backward and out of the way, but couldn't budge it. A crew working the other side of that row had been loading similar crates into a British lorry parked in their lane. They paused to watch, curious as to how we intended to handle our weighty dilemma.

Woofie stooped and managed to squeeze his arms along each side, tried it, but no room prevented him from sliding it back as well. He spotted an open space in a stock row on the opposite side of Doozie, about even with her motor.

"If'n you pull 'er ahead a tad, boss, I'll put this here box over yonder and out of the way."

I moved the truck forward as Woofie again slid his arms around the crate. A middle-aged captain had seen enough and interrupted.

"And just what in tah-nation do you think you're doing, fella?" he challenged in a heavy New England accent. "I don't care *how* big you are; you'll rip your insides apart trying to lift that thing. Those are cast-iron Quonset stoves. It takes four of my boys to load them."

Woofie let go, and stood looking over at a half dozen of the captain's crew. "Well I'll kiss a mama pig smack dab on the snout if you ain't right, sir?"

A few smirked, though we weren't sure if amused at Woofie's diction, or smugness, but he changed their expressions. "Why they sure is a bunch o' dang tootin' *boys*, now ain't they— sir."

"Who the hell do you think you're talking to, private? Forget about my rank for now, you backwoods ingrate. But I'm also a doctor trying to keep your fool ass from coming apart at the seams. Humph. Go ahead; pop a compound hernia or break your damned back for all I give a hoot." The indignant captain motioned his crew back to work.

"No hard feelings captain," McKenzie said. "He didn't mean nothing by it, but care to put a fiver on him lifting it?" Mac licked a five-pound note and stuck it to his forehead.

The crew lingered, and smiled at Little Mac's antics. The mood lightened, and they eagerly reached for billfolds. The only rule was for Woofie to lift the crate off the pallet and stand upright for a count of three before setting it down.

All bets covered, Woofie closed a tight grip around its lower girth. One grunt and he lifted first attempt. Not only did he satisfy the wager, but he backed the huge carton out of its slot, and though strained, he didn't drop it as a bevy of gaping jaws expected. Instead, he walked his hands lower for a better grip under its bottom, bent his knees, and with a weightlifter's motion, hoisted the heavy beast atop a shoulder. He then carried it across the aisle and set it down exactly where he said he would.

Woofie stretched and shook off the strain, but played overly bashful as we cheered and slapped our champion on the back. The captain grinned and shook his head, studying Woofie in disbelief.

"Well aren't you a humdingah. I've doctored lumberjack brutes for years, but I ain't *nevah* seen anything like this before." The captain looked at his clipboard, and motioned for Woofie to come closer. "How much you think that crate weighs, son?"

"Oh, I dunno, it was dang-tooin' heavy," he chuckled, "but I'd say, oh, 'tween two-fifty and three hundred pounds, I reckon?"

"Humph," the captain grinned and showed us the clipboard. "You're a ways off, big fella. According to this manifest, crated with accessories, it tares out at three-forty-two."

"Shoot, wasn't that far off. Less than this little squirt weighs." He grabbed Mac in a playful headlock. "It weren't no banty chicken, that's fer sure. But tain't as heavy as a couple limestone slabs Poppa made me move. Now they'd make yer bunghole snort a bunch; lemme tell ya." Everyone laughed at his colorful modesty.

"Sorry about the money, sir," I said, reaching for the captain's hand. I liked the man and sensed he was a fair and friendly chap. Aside from his being miffed at Woofie's initial remark, he never once threatened, or even hinted differences of rank.

"Ah, don't mention it. A bet's a bet, boys. To tell the truth, it was worth every shilling. I'll have a heck of a story to tell my grand kids one day. I'm Ernie Bouchard from a little logging town in New Hampshah called Fremont. Bet you nevah heard of it?"

"Ah, I knew you were from New England, pilgrim. But don't bet anotha fivah I don't know where Fremont is." I exaggerated my own accent. "Vincent Zecca from Malden, Mass, sir. When I was a kid, a schoolmate's family took me on a picnic at a place called Cluff Bridge on the Exeter River. Know where that is?"

"Shuah. Damned good spot for fly fishin' rainbows. Caught me a four 'n haff poundah there, once, ay-yah." We laughed. "Looks like you boys got stuck carting stuff around, too, huh? We're from the 45th evac hospital unit. Lately, we've been patching up airmen; lot of 'em flown in from Italy. Now with this massive troop buildup, the brass has us moving stuff all over hell's kitchen. I'm not supposed to say where, but we have to deliver these stoves to the coast. Then we have to stay and help set up a row of hospital units just completed. Are you guys hearing anything your way?"

"Nah, just a lot of speculation, doc. Nothing definitive. But I wonder why all the medical buildings on the coast? You'd think they'd be at risk from bombing raids, wouldn't ya?"

"Ay-yuh. Gaul-dang Nazi's don't give a shit about red crosses. Lost a good friend when they sank the St. David off Anzio. It was a British hospital ship, and lit up like a Christmas tree with markings plain as day, too. The murdering bastards bombed it right in the middle of taking casualties aboard.

"Damn! All the more reason why it don't make sense. Move 'em more inland, for crissake."

"Yup. And what's more, these buildings will be equipped to treat a heck of lot more than paper cuts and bruised egos. But don't get me wrong, Vince, I ain't bitching. I'd rather be here than sent to Anzio's 'hell's half acre'. Now, as for what's going on around here is anyone's guess. But if you ask me, I think something's up, ay-yuh."

We shared a few more hometown familiarities and exchanged APO addresses before we agreed on one more thing in common— we'd better get back to work if we wanted out of this supply dump.

I backed Doozie into position and ordered the boys to begin loading. As they stacked, I became increasingly concerned of the heavy spans protruding beyond the bed. I first thought about making turns fearing I'd knock hell out of anything or anybody on the road. But the higher the stack, the more the overhang bowed under the weight. I was afraid the joists would snap if many more were loaded, but before stopping the crew, Doozie made the decision for me as to when she was ready to go.

Frames were stacked nearly to the top of the cab window when the craziest thing happened that had us falling over in laughter. The front of the truck slowly rose, balanced on the rear axle with the frame-tips touching the ground.

There the old Commer poised; her nose angled toward the heavens like an RAF fighter. Woofie walked over and pushed on the fender. He held the truck horizontal while moving around to its front and grabbed Doozie beneath her bumper.

"Hey boss! Watch this. If the captain thought a dumb ol' stove was a story, they'd lock 'im in the loony bin before he gits someone t'swallow this'un."

He faked inordinate exertion and lifted the front of the truck. We exploded into belly-laughs after he held the truck with one hand, flattened his face like Stan Laurel, and fluffed his hair to mimic the comedian's confused dummy look. A passing yard worker locating materials for two truckers heard the laughter.

"What's going on over there?" He spotted Woofie, and his jaw dropped. "What tha— Jesus! Put that down 'fore you kill yourself, you idiot!"

"Aw shit. This aint nothin', see?" Woofie curled the truck three times. "I do this all the time on the farm t'keep in shape," and slowly lowered Doozie to rest. He leaned against the fender, and casually flexed his arm. "Makes Papa's big ol' bull scared t'death o' me, too. Want I should pick you up and whiz you 'round my head a coupla times like I do him t'show ya?"

"What are you morons laughing at?" a trucker yelled.

"Oh, nothin', sarge. Just like you said; *we're* a bunch of morons is all." I hustled into the cab to keep the weight on the front wheels and told the boys to sit atop the frames close to the cab. I slipped her into low, and eased Doozie down the aisle. I couldn't resist stopping opposite the medics on the way out.

"Hey, Ernie! Any one of you guys have a camera by chance?"

"Harold does, a brand new one. We use it for taking pictures of everywhere we go in England. Why?"

"Well if you want a picture to go with that story to tell the grand kids, better get it. Woofie's gonna show you just how strong he really is."

I told Mac to slide over into Tony's seat as soon as he vacated it. I ordered everyone else off the truck and posed us in a tight portrait about the rear axle. Woofie couldn't stop his mountain giggles as he ambled to the front.

"Okay, get the camera ready. Woofie's gonna lift the truck— load 'n all."

"Now hold on, Vincent," Ernie objected. "A stove is one thing, but this is ridiculous. King Kong couldn't pick that up."

"Ridiculous? You can say *that* again, but you just get the camera ready like I said."

Little Mac's hundred-twelve pounds was all Woofie had to lift. Ernie's face was a picture of puzzlement, but did as he was told. His crew came closer or stood on pallets for a better look. Once more,

Woofie exaggerated grunts and groans, but lifted the front of Doozie with little effort.

A medic burst into laughter, pointing to the counterbalancing joists touching the ground. Little Mac stuck his head out the window, his leprechaun grin spanning ear-to-ear hamming for the camera. Ernie chuckled at the scene in the viewfinder, and while snapping photographs, he nearly dropped the camera when Woofie released one hand to again mimic Stan Laurel.

"Well I'll be son-of-a-gun." Ernie slapped his thigh. "If that don't beat all. Why if that ain't the funniest damned-fool thing I ever saw, nothing is. Good lord, it's a classic."

I ordered everyone back onto the truck. Ernie was confident he composed each shot to crop the boys from showing any frames beyond the truck bed.

"What a gag. I'll win me a lot of beer bets with these pictures." Captain Bouchard promised to send us copies. We shook hands and left. After stopping to sign for the joists, we were still laughing two miles down the road.

"Say, ain't it about lunchtime yet?"

"About an hour past due if you ask me."

"Well, since we got thirty more quid than when we started out, what d'ya say we stop and buy the big oaf some bangers 'n ale?"

"You got my vote. I'm starved."

"Hey," Mac interrupted. "Who's gonna sit in the truck to keep it down while we eat?"

"What d'ya mean— while *we* eat, Mac?" Tony chided. Tony and I grinned, satisfied at having solved *that* problem.

"Somethin's Up"

During the delivery leg of our trip, Doozie shifted far more smoothly and ran with less sputter, needing only a little weight on her old frame to prove her worth; unwilling to be converted into ammo boxes just yet. We were out of the freight hauling business by evening, though driving back took full concentration to keep our oversized load from becoming a roadside disaster.

Only our first week in England, there had been no easing of training; each day becoming more crammed than the day before. We were also given French language booklets and lectured on odd topics like: "How to Use Morphine" and, "What to Do if Captured".

'Somethin's up' seemed to be on everyone's lips; GIs gabbing about mass troop and equipment movements, unusual increases in religious services, and the most recent work detail likely the clincher.

Every Company got orders to waterproof trucks, halftracks, jeeps, tanks, and every other type of military vehicle. We were up to our elbows in thick gook applied to sparkplugs, distributor caps, and batteries. Speculation centered on the one thing the world had been expecting for a long time: the invasion of Continental Europe was at hand.

Rumors were not solely reserved for servicemen, but were fodder for civilian gossip as well. During an afternoon cram session, my brain became muddled from memorizing French villages and rivers; my thoughts wandering to a congenial farmer we had met at the Red Lion the night before.

Upon arrival, the place was packed. There were few places to set a pint, much less our butts. I scanned the room and noticed an old, wispy-haired chap sitting alone at a corner table. He was dressed in deeply stained coveralls tucked into dirty wellies. When our eyes met, he smiled and motioned we were welcome to share his table. I took him up on the gesture.

"Set yer arses down, lads. Me name is Willie, Willie Napp. Ye'll 'ave t'scuse the barnyard air about me. I'm a bit rammy just finishin' me bleedin' chores, but got me a powerful thirst for a whiskey mac. Ay, but look on the bright side. 'Tis the only bloody reason there's a nigh empty table in 'ere, ay-up."

He was a cheerful old coot. About mid-sixties, said he was born and raised in Yorkshire, but manages a small farming estate nearby.

"Ah, f'get about it," Tony said. "You're a breath of fresh air compared to these bums. Try livin' two weeks stuffed in the bow of a ship with guys stacked up like poker chips."

"And speaking of bums," Mac said, "I was the top chip on that poker stack with my nose stuck against the ceiling above those two methane factories."

"Hee, hee," Napp chuckled, slapping his knee and looking at me. "So you boys been floatin' the lil' fella some air biscuits, 'av ya?"

Tony laughed and offered to buy the old man a freshened drink in gratitude for the invitation. "What's a whiskey-mac, anyway?"

"Aye, good for what ails yer. A shot o' scotch and ginger wine. Y'ought try one. It'll warm the cockles of yer 'art."

Tony returned from the bar with drinks for all, and we raised glasses to yet another warm and grateful welcome to England. The conversation soon reverted to recent military activities. Napp's eyes widened as he huddled over the table to share bits of a conversation he had overheard.

"Ay, if you ask me, I reckon you yanks'll be leaving 'ere soon. There's somethin' bloody up, I says. Sure as me sheep is shorn, I do. It was only yesterday, four ranger blokes were chin-waggin' about some 'undred foot cliffs they 'ad to climb. Said it was a bloody suicide mission, they did. Wot you yanks 'spose they was belly-achin' about?"

We looked at each other and shrugged. No one could proffer concrete answers of course, but we didn't lack for a bagful of maybes. Any number of qualified structures existed all along the French coast. If they were rangers, *cliffs* could mean anywhere.

My daydream vanished, grateful the class had ended. I stretched, unable to absorb another Ville-de-*somethin'* or other, when C.B. entered the room and reclaimed the podium.

"Ten-hut!"

"Awright, cut the chatter and listen up, ladies. Some squads may be splittin' up."

C.B. said HQ planned to integrate specialists to help balance platoon effectiveness. The news evoked several side glances, many curious which fraternal groups might be affected. A moment later, C.B. shed light on at least *one* mystery; our squad did not escape the knife.

We were losing half a good mortar team and the platoon's song-boy, Chase. As a trade off, we were to inherit five new guys. PFC Johnny Presto and Corporal David Kirk were ordered to stand for eyeballing. C.B. said Corporal Kirk was from Toledo and a specialist at communications, codes, and map coordinates. Presto was a dairy farmer from Wisconsin who spoke fluent German. C.B. also added that two field medics and a bazooka marksman were scheduled to arrive later in the evening. C.B. ran through his list of changes, slapping the podium to restore order.

"I said cut the pissy-moanin'. Fairchild, Zecca; front and center." I couldn't imagine what I had done, but joined Chase at the front of the room.

"At ease, gentlemen." C.B. saluted and faced the class. "Meet *First* Lieutenant Fairchild and your new platoon leader, *Sergeant* Zecca."

What? Promoted?

I couldn't believe it, but did like the sound of *sergeant* better than catcalls circulating the room. C.B. said he *persuaded* brass to bypass corporal and make me sergeant if they insisted on claiming Chase and his best mortar man from the platoon. Chase had not only been bumped to first looie, but was to report to a supply sector of General Bradley's operations within four hours.

"Hey! C.B. yelled. "I said ta shut up. You can quit with yer whinin' right now! I don't wanna hear any more bullshit about Chase getting' a candy ride." Before dismissing the unit, C.B. put a quick stop to cynical undertones thinking Chase's family had landed him a cushy assignment. Orders came from Corps HQ who culled Chase on the strength of his Princeton education; desperate for guys with strong logistics skills.

"Ooh la la," Tony cooed, approaching Chase. "A first looie now. How about them apples, and *Bradley's* command no less. I'm happy for ya, Chase. We're sure gonna miss ya, so do us proud."

Tony looked at me. "And what we got here, a *sergeant*? I guess you're *officially* da boss man, now." Tony placed a hand on my shoulder. "But, y'know what this means, doncha? It means your foist order is to march our tails to the Lion where ya promised to buy us a pint. Ain't that right, fellas?" I glanced at Chase hoping he could join us, but he read my mind.

"Sorry, Vince. Wish I could, big boy, but you heard my orders. I have packing to do and need to be leaving within an hour. But tell you what." Chase reached for his billfold and slipped a ten-pound note into Tony's hand. "No, I insist, and that's an order, private. Since I outrank all of you, I'd consider it a privilege if you let me buy a couple rounds— especially in honor of the boss's promotion. All kidding aside fellas, it's the least I can do. I have to admit that I'll miss the lot of you, but duty calls."

Chase gave me a bear hug with an unsaid, yet heartfelt emotion knowing we would not likely have a chance to visit anytime soon— *if ever*. He shook hands with members of the squad before leaving. Woofie and Frazer had already introduced themselves to the new guys and left for town.

I approached Kirk and Presto who were mixing with the rest of the unit. They seemed like good Joes, and I especially warmed to Presto after learning he spoke Italian in addition to German. Mac had already invited them into joining us at the Lion.

"You guys go ahead," I said. "Tony and I will catch up." We were playing with land mines and booby traps all morning, and my fatigues were splotched with dried mud.

About an hour passed before Tony and I could join the boys at the Lion. Tony noted their near empty glasses and offered to spend some of Chase's money. He returned with two large tankards of ale and a week-old section of the *New York Times* he found unclaimed at the corner of the bar. Tony glanced at the paper as we refilled glasses and renewed casual conversations.

Kirk and Presto elaborated on their talents, and I was impressed, feeling they'd fit the squad well. Kirk was the more laid back of the two, all business, but really knew his stuff when it came to high tech radio equipment. I grew more curious of the outgoing Presto.

"Your name is Presto— Italian, but you speak fluent German, too. How's that?" I asked.

"Call me *Quick* if you like, sarge. A lot of my buddies do since obstacle training. I was always fastest up the rope tower; and won a bunch o' bets never touching it with my feet," he laughed. "I mastered the art scurrying up the hay loft rope on the farm. As for speaking Italian, it's my dad's side of the family; he and bunch of relatives living near us all spoke Italian. But mom was from Bavaria on the other side of the Alps from Dad's hometown in Italy, so we spoke mostly German at home." Presto said it was where he was born, too; in Trento, a northern-most province in Italy. His parents followed a clan of previously emigrated relatives to the States when he was two.

"My folks became citizens and built a four hundred acre dairy farm just outside of Madison, Wisconsin. It's okay; pretty country, good trout fishing, but colder 'n a well-digger's ass in winter."

Tony interrupted our enjoyable chat. "Hey Boss. There's a story in here about the Belmont Stakes."

"Damn! I forgot about the Belmont. What day is it?" I asked, trying to align my mind with a calendar. "Christ, he's right. Any of you guys know where we can catch the broadcast around here?"

No one had a clue, but Kirk thought he might be able to help. "If you like, sarge, I can try rigging a shortwave broadcast with help from some buddies in Radio Ops."

"Nah, too much trouble, Kirk, but thanks anyway. Damn, of all years to miss it."

"Yep," Tony agreed, paraphrasing the *Times*. "Says here Pensive looks to be an unbeatable favorite for the Triple. Chase was right, Zeck, Pensive is a sure thing. I *tol'* youz so; he can't miss, boss. Look." Tony slid me the paper.

"How in hell are we gonna get any action around here?" Mac asked, glancing about the pub.

"Ah, why even bother?" Frazer said. "We made a good lick on the Derby and the Preakness; no sense in complicating things with another crazy betting scheme. Ain't nobody gonna bet against Pensive this time around, anyway; *nobody*."

"Well, what are we gonna do then? Can't just blow it off."

"Why not just keep it warm and fuzzy between ourselves, Mac?" Frazer countered with a suggestion. "What we *could* do, is have a blind draw for shits and giggles. It'll be fun; each of us toss in five quid, winner takes all. What d'ya think?"

"Okay by me," Tony said. The others shrugged and nodded approval.

"Good idea, Frazer; let's do it." I sent Presto to the bar to fetch a pencil. While waiting, I tore a thin strip from the paper's margin, and again into seven smaller squares. Presto returned with a pencil and another tray of ales. The mood was upbeat.

"I can feel it in me bones, Tony, you're mine this time," Mac teased, wringing his hands like a greedy little miser.

Frazer agreed to be banker and slipped our fold of bills into his breast pocket. I scribbled numbers corresponding to horses listed, offering Woofie first draw. He plucked a square from my cap with the zeal of a five-year-old stealing gumdrops from a candy jar.

"What's it say, boss? Who'd I git?" He leaned over the table anxious to learn of the name of its matching entry.

"Let's see, you pulled number six." I traced the list. "Well done, big boy; you got Platter. He's a damned good horse rated at three-to-one, Woof, and likely the one to beat Pensive. Platter was the heart-stopper who nearly whipped our ass in the Preakness, remember?"

"Yee haw," Woofie howled. His nose was nearly in the cap as Kirk plucked the wishful sixty-to-one longshot, Free Lance. Presto drew next, unfolding the number for Who Goes There.

"Halt! Wer geht dort!" Presto barked the horse's name in guttural German. We laughed, and though joking, his commanding voice startled several patrons into thinking the Lion was under siege.

"He's okay, I'll take him," Presto said, satisfied with Platter's stable mate. "He has as good a shot as any. If you think about it, fellas, he won the Withers and should be fresh for Belmont's distance since he skipped the first two legs of the Triple."

"I'm impressed, Quick," Mac said. "Sounds like you know the ponies. Chase did say there could be an untested horse lurking in the shadows. Maybe he's the sleeper; the press seems to like him."

"Could be," Frazer said, peeking at his number. "But not this year, ladies." He ignored the groans and dramatically revealed the coveted number three. Frazer snapped his fingers. "Pensive done came home to Papa, boys."

Mac leaned back in his chair, and laughed. "I told ya's so. Maybe I didn't get him, but the *lucky* one has finally spit the bit;" the cap now sans the sure thing.

"Youz got nuttin' to crow about, toikey. I'll tell youz what. I got me a fiver says whatever horse I pick tosses doit in your horse's mug at the wire. What d'ya say to them apples, Mac-a-doodle-doo?"

Mac accepted the side-bet and kissed another five-pound note for good luck before giving it to Frazer. He waived first pick to Tony who pulled the seven— a new entry named Bounding Home, forecast at twenty-to-one. Tony was unfazed by the long odds.

"There ya go, Brother Mac. It's an omen cuz *seven* is my lucky number, and da name says it all. My ass'll be *bounding home* ten lengths ahead of *your* ploddin' patootie."

"Sure, sure. Listen to you. At those odds, you'll be lucky to get close enough to *kiss* my ass." Mac then drew the number four.

"Oh-oh," I read the roster. "Four is Bull Dandy, Mac. And you ain't gonna like this, but he's by far the longest shot in the field at ninety-to-one. Ouch."

"Heh, heh. What'd I tell youz, paisan? Might as well make it thoity lengths, Mac." Tony grabbed the paper from me. "Lemme hear them cackles now, Mac-A-Doodle-*Dandy.* Your mule ain't got a snowball's chance in hell to get the Belmont's mile-and-a-half. Listen to this. It says here Bull Dandy's a pure sprinter, and he ain't won shit yet. The touts can't believe the trainer even put him in the race. Christ, Mac," Tony snickered, "it's a pipedream. The *war* will be over by the time that *Bull*-shit nag hits the wire."

"Can you guys believe this?" Mac shook his head, certain he had a headlock on Tony's uncanny luck this one time. Tony gloated over Mac's frustration as I inherited the last number; thirty-to-one shot, Boy Knight.

"Good grief," I grumbled. "I got a hopeless wanna-be, too."

"Don't let those odds fool ya," Presto said. "He ain't so bad. He was third to my horse in the Withers, and was a hell of a two-year-old taking second in last year's Hopeful. He's fresh, maybe more mature and in peak form, now. Boy Knight could be that surprise horse you guys were talking about."

"Hmm. Are you sayin' he's *quick*, Quick?" I smiled, unable to resist the pun. My hopes brightened. I was impressed with Presto's knowledge of horse racing, and felt better thinking we had another Chase in the group. *I wonder if he can sing.*

"You can deep six your nag, too, paisan. The bum should be called *Good* Night, cuz its lights out for youz too— *Boy*."

"I wouldn't bluster too hard, Tony," Frazer said. "Your dough is down the toilet right along with the rest of you fellas. But not to worry, I'm a good sport. First round's on me after the race."

"I'll drink to them apples," Tony said, hoisting his glass. "Cuz thanks to Mac-a-doodle-*dandy*, the woist I can do is break even."

Our merriment was interrupted by an officer entering the Lion, ordering every GI under his command back to base. A second officer followed with similar orders. C.B. came in next.

"This is it, boys," he whispered. "We're goin' in. Orders are we're on seal-down as of midnight. Now keep yer traps shut, finish up, and have your butts back at Hague Hall no later than 23:00."

C.B. explained to me he was due for SOPS briefings— Standard Operating Procedures for Short Sea Voyages. "You got a little time yet sergeant, but when you leave, recheck the other pubs on the street and round up any stragglers. When you git back to barracks, make daggon sure everyone's accounted for. *No one* is to leave quarters for any reason, and if someone's missin' by the time I git back, they'll be in shackles within the hour. Is that clear, Sergeant Zecca?"

"Yes sir."

"As you were." C.B. saluted and left; the Lion's mood changing from jubilance to murmurs.

Presto was first to break the lull. "Ah, I'm new and don't want to intrude on your past, but after listening to you fellas talk about *omens* and stuff, you got *me* to thinking about weird things, now."

"Hey, first off, paisan; no more of this *new* guy shit," Tony said. "The minute your ass parked itself in that chair, youz was in like Flynn, capisce?"

"Tony's right, Presto. You're as much a part of the squad as any of us, so what's got you so spooked?"

"Okay, but as I speak, *think* about what we just did: like picking horses; the *Belmont* Stakes; and what Estes just dropped in our laps."

Presto's solemn tone corralled our attention. "When I was a kid, I was a big fan of horseracing. I kept a scrapbook and read a lot about my favorite horse, Man o' War; the *best* that ever lived. Here's where it gets weird— for me, anyway. Back then, August Belmont was a big shot in the horse game; he bred Man o' War. But strangely enough, he *sold* him as a yearling, something he *never* did before."

"Why sell him then, especially if the horse was a legend?" Mac asked. "It don't make sense."

"*Exactly*, Mac. But that year, the War Department had made Belmont a Major, so he sold all his yearlings in order to stay focused on helping overseas doughboys defeat the Krauts."

"So are youz sayin'—

"Hang on, Tony, it gets better. You boys have been jabbering about your *omens*— try this one. When Man o' War was ready to race, he came straight out of training and broke his maiden in his first start— on *June* 6th. Now don't you think that's a little spooky?"

"What is? I still don't get the connection," Mac said.

"*Think*, Mac. We just picked horses on the eve of this year's *Belmont* Stakes, and here *we* are: in a World War, overseas, *against* the Germans, fresh out of training, about to make *our first* start, and on June 6th— breaking *our* maidens by becoming *men* o' war."

"Ho-lee Jesus! That is spooky," Mac said, whistling. He gulped the last of his ale and checked his watch. "We still have time for one more, on ol' Mac-a-doodle-dandy this time. Okay with you, Zeck?"

"After Presto's eerie bombshell, I *need* a drink." I pulled rank and ordered Mac to use my tenner; their *new* sergeant was buying.

Mac-a-doodle-doo returned the place to normal when tucking his thumbs under his armpits, flapping his elbows, and clucking like a crazed chicken while head-bobbing to the bar. He returned with ales and jiggers of a single-malt Scotch. *I always did like Mac's style.*

"You said nuttin' about shots, *sergeant,* and it looks like we're gonna need them parly-voo-francie books real soon. So all kidding aside, fellas, here's to you." Mac raised his glass. "Now hear me out, because I'm not joking this time— I'm dead serious."

"Hey, don't use them woids."

"Oops, sorry, Tony, heh heh. What I wanted to say is, despite the many times I've been trumped by Tony, I feel it's me who's really the lucky one of the outfit. I could have been sent anywhere, but got this one. You not only helped me make the grade, but you made me feel at home. You have no idea what that meant to me, so at this moment, I hereby pledge my heart and soul to you all."

"Here, here," we raised glasses. "To Little Mac."

Mac inhaled his scotch, and then raised his ale as a chaser. "One more thing, fellas; here's to all of us as a squad. May we all get together afterwards to pick up where we left off." He clinked glasses, except for one.

"What's the matter, Zeck, your dog die?"

"Sorry, Mac. It's nothing; just thinking about what someone once said, is all. F'get about it. Here's to all you mugs— saluto."

I managed a weak smile when raising my glass and quickly downed my shot, not realizing I had avoided looking at any faces.

Time to be a Man

Late afternoon, C.B. sent for me to review roll calls, equipment, ammo supplies, and other assorted details. He then excused himself and returned with a pistol and holster.

"This is for you, Zeck. You're in charge of your unit and this is serious business. Take dang good care of that thing; could be yer best buddy one day. It's a standard issue Colt M1911, a .45 caliber seven-shot automatic."

C.B. extolled its durability and stopping power as he watched me caress the weapon with solemn interest. He said they were issued only to officers, demolition and vehicle crews, and NCOs.

"That means you, buster. Won't be long before we'll be lockin' horns with Germans, so you'd best git yer gear together. Dismissed."

I spent the afternoon feeling awkward with a powerful sidearm strapped to my hip. I glanced about the room making sure I was still alone before pulling it from its holster. It was a beautifully made weapon with sleek lines, terrific balance, and knurled grips that fit comfortably in my palm. I slid the clip out; it was unthinkable what damage such heavy slugs could do to a body. I snapped the magazine back in place and made sure the safety was on.

I caught a glimpse of myself in the wall mirror and walked over to it. I could hear my heart beating as it seemed an eternity I stood there— staring. I imagined the fat bastard staring back was a man; a *man* named Schmidt, and only ten feet away.

The heat rose in my neck as I leveled the bead even with Schmidt's heart and wondered: *could I do it? Could I really do it?*

"What in hell are youz doing?" Tony walked in from his bath and casually discarded the damp towel around his torso. "Heh, heh. I know you're a homely mutt, paisan, but why blame the mirror?"

I ignored him, my dead-panned expression remained fixed on Schmidt. I slowly lowered the pistol to my side. Tony saw that I was tense, maybe guessed what was on my mind and dressed in silence.

"Let me ask you something, Tony. Can you look a person dead-square in the eye, and then, you know, just up and *kill* him— take a man's life?"

Tony didn't respond at first, his face impassive as he slowly pulled on his socks. Our eyes met in the mirror.

"I know what y'thinking. I suppose it depends on the situation, Vince. Sure, I've bragged about being tough. Even been in a couple knife fights, but never actually tried to kill the bastard. Oh, I could have cut a dude's liver in half once— but didn't. I *can* tell ya this, though: where we're goin', ain't no Joisey alley dukin' it out with some loser pissed over a straying girlfriend. We'll *all* find out what we're made of. So as far as I'm concerned, when the lead begins to fly at this pretty face, them Krouts is dead meat."

Tony left me staring at Schmidt as he donned a shirt. "Another thing, paisan. For now, the Army says C.B. owns us, right? There ain't no better and we're lucky to have him. But as for *me?* My life is in *your* hands. There ain't nobody I trust more; not even C.B." He returned to my side and poked a finger at my temple.

"If that means ya hafta stick that thing right up against a dude's head like this to save my ass, or for *any* of us— you *will* do what it takes. Your juices will kick in. So don't youz *evah*— evah again have doubts, capisce? That's all I'm gonna say. So put that thing away before you shoot that fat bastard and ruin a poifectly good mirror."

I tried envisioning Schmidt about to shoot my Tony. I sensed deep-down maybe he was right, and pushed thoughts of killing out of my mind. *Time to f'get about it.*

We spent the rest of the afternoon preparing for departure. My field pack was stretched to capacity with an additional two pounds of high explosives, ammo clips, grenades, knives, compass, poncho, self-heating cans of soup, three pairs of slingshot suspenders, Hershey bars, bouillon cubes, escape-and-survival kits— *Christ, everything's here but trap-door flannels and a Sears catalog.*

"We're mounting up, boys!" C.B. ordered everyone to fall in and march to a convoy of trucks idling within the compound.

"Ye-e-e-haw," a GI yelled.

C.B. whirled like a hooded cobra, grabbed the startled soldier, and pulled the private's panic-stricken face to the tip of his nose— and screamed: "Shut yer goddam yap, you dim-witted schmuck! This ain't no Georgia lynchin' yer goin' to, shithead! In a few hours from now, you may be *dead!*"

C.B. was fuming; the veins in his neck bulging. I had never seen him so furious; his words echoed with a prophetic ring as he shoved the trembling GI back into line.

Speculation as to *when* had just been answered— questions now were: where and *what* could we be facing given his sobering reaction? Our destination was still secret, but we were told to be patient; that we'd learn more upon reaching staging areas.

Our packs averaged more than eighty pounds, making it awkward to climb aboard Army trucks. Little Mac fell backwards twice, and would have made it a triple had Woofie not grabbed him under the ass and tossed him aboard like a bale of hay. Everyone applauded as Mac's feet cleared the tailgate by a foot. Woofie ignored the whistles and wa'hoo's.

"Ah, hell, that t'wern't nuthin'. I got boots weigh more n' that little turd— pack n' all."

A dull, ominous haze had formed though it was still light out; the setting sun shrouded by thickening storm clouds. The convoy began moving at about nine in the evening. MPs blew whistles and directed traffic as we rumbled through Amesbury. The sight was incredible; as if the entire nation were in motion. We were surprised to see the number of civilians lining the streets at this hour.

What a wonderful people. Despite hardships and shortages, the Brits were gracious hosts, and seemed to know what was happening. Some were crying, others cheering and waving little flags.

"Good luck, yanks," and, "give them bloody Heinies a wake-up-kiss from the queen," could be heard above the roar of trucks packed with troops in full battle gear. They feared the worst but hoped for the best, every life precious and every smile dear; the Brits rallying around us with a beaming message: *we're all in this together.*

We waved and cheered, and of course, saluted the Red Lion in passing. Considering the massive flow of traffic, we were moving along rather smoothly as if we were the biggest parade in the history of mankind; everything here except a marching band.

It wasn't long before we learned where the trail ended. Portland Harbor in Weymouth was a mind-boggling mass of men, equipment, and supplies converging upon a scene with an equally staggering number of vessels of every type. MPs were busy guiding endless columns of personnel carriers, half-tracks, tanks, and other heavy equipment into assigned staging areas.

What looked to be utter chaos was actually an orderly, well-oiled plan. My thoughts drifted to Chase for a moment, wondering if he had anything to do with this incredible undertaking. We thought New York's harbors were huge, but there was no describing the spectacle. Our transports pulled over and parked with others to await further directives.

"We'll be stagnant awhile, men. After briefings, I suggest you try stealing whatever shuteye you can. You'll be glad you did before we get to where we're goin'."

Until now, few of us had thought of what the landings would be like; much less of getting wounded— or *killed*. I don't know if we were simply young and naive, or just too damned stupid to know any better. Perhaps it was nature's way of dulling neurotic fear, but whatever the reason, the adrenaline flowed. Every nerve and muscle fiber twitched. The air crackled with nervous energy; our destinies teetering on the edge of the coming action. *Sleep? Easier said than done, C.B.; easier said than done.*

"Okay, you boneheads. Git yer behinds over here and pay attention." It had been raining awhile, and he opened a set of maps under a tarp. Kirk held a flashlight as C.B pointed to a sector labeled FOX RED.

"We'll be landing here," he said, pointing to a specific zone at the eastern flank of a five-mile-long beachhead marked: 'OMAHA'.

We stood silent, digesting the reality of the landings; it being the first time we'd heard such code words. A nearby officer whistled for C.B.'s attention to coordinate loading details with other outfits. While waiting for him to return, we studied the maps until Tony's finger started tapping squarely on the beach we'd been assigned.

"Hey, wait just a sec, boss. Fox Red— *Omaha*, remember? Ain't that the bangtail Chase said was the other Triple Crown winner with me— y'know, Gallant Fox's son? I *knew* it was a big-ass omen; I *knew* it! Chase was right, Pensive is a *shoe-in*. We should be going home soon, Zeck. Too bad we couldn't have put a bundle on him— *damn*."

"Yeah, that's the one, but why can't you be satisfied we kept it friendly among ourselves? You're forgetting: Presto said because of the war, ol' man Belmont lost *his* sure-thing— and a chestnut, too; just like Pensive."

"So what! Whirlaway was a chestnut, and *he* romped in the triple for Calumet, so why not Pensive?"

"Okay smartass, you gained a length on that one, but I'm still a *furlong* ahead of you cuz he also said there ain't *never* been but one stable in history to win two Triples. Remember *that*? So *don't* be so cock-sure it's a lock!"

Tony started to press the issue, but I cut him off. "Look! I don't wanna hear another word, *capisce*? I got a bad feeling about this one. I don't like it. Not this time. No dice. *Enough* said, so drop it!" and sliced my fingers across my throat for him to end the conversation.

"Ease up, Zeck," Frazer butted in. "You made your point. Why you chompin' on his ass so hard? Jealous 'cause I pulled Pensive?"

I didn't say a word, but my glare told Frazer he'd best shut his yap as well. I was testy; my jaw muscles working overtime. I must have a bad case of pre-battle willies and didn't realize it. *Humph— Pensive. Hell of a name for horse at a time like this.*

Frazer hesitated, but spouted defiance anyway. "There you go with that foolish omen shit again. Well, here's one I got for you. Someone once said '*fools* and their money were soon parted,' so you might as well stick your omens up your ass. You're *both* a couple of superstitious fools believing in all that mojo stuff, because *I* got your money, and *Pensive* is gonna spank your tails right where it hurts, boys— on your *wallets*."

"Oh, yeah? Well da boss said to can it, so youz can stick the money where da sun don't shine, too. In fact, I got another fin says you'll end up pukin' on my 20-to-1 *gallon* of ale when we get back."

"Ha! With your hopeless wanna be— Bounding Home? Fat chance." Frazer laughed. "Keep your fiver, but bless you, my son; Dominic's for biscuits. You're all mouth, Mosconi. Like Little Mac said: your *luck* has run out this time. Admit it; your money is as good as gone. Drinks'll be on *me*."

Mac squeezed between them and fired them a stern look. "You two windbags can both go pack your panties and go to hell. Think you're *winners*, don't ya? Well, I hope you drink yourselves *pink* on my money."

Mac seemed strange. I had never seen his natural grin disappear like that before; or his body coiled, rife with an eerie energy as he swept his finger about the group.

"You all laughed when I pulled the longest shot in the field; a pure-ass sprinter who don't even belong in the race, you said. Well you twits just watch. When that gate flings open at Belmont the same time as it opens on our landing craft, those horses won't be the only ones cuttin' loose. We will *too*— *won't* we? Then all you're gonna see is my ass and elbows, 'cuz there ain't a horse or man alive on this planet that will out-sprint Mac-a-doodle-*Dandy* up them beaches of Belmont over yonder!" He glared, jerking his thumb toward the Channel.

Mac looked Frazer in the eye. "It was you who said the sure thing came home to Papa, wasn't it? Well you had better not stumble out that gate, rubber legs. Cuz I'm gonna be pullin' on that bit like a horse possessed! And as for you, pretty boy," poking Tony hard in the chest. "Ninety-to-one shot; ain't won shit, you said, huh? Well you'd better be on your game, too, Mosconi; cuz we'll see who eats *doit* this time."

"Shaddup! All you numbskulls!" C.B. rejoined us and disclosed boarding instructions. He crammed us with a final volley of details and landing tactics he insisted we memorize.

"Make sure you move yer tails as quickly as possible, and don't be bunchin' up. Stagger yer paths, zig-zag between any cover you can find, and above all: do *not* cluster in or near any old mortar craters; the bastards already know where they are— understand?"

Once inland, we were to focus on bridge locations, roads, and villages with names like Pointe Du Hoc, Colleville, Sainte-Mere-Eglise, Ste-Laurent, and Cherbourg, a strategic port at the northern end of the Cotentin Peninsula.

I watched C.B. closely. I had always admired the man, but never more so than at this moment. His entire being was totally devoted to our welfare; his mind preoccupied with details giving us every edge possible. He studied our landing crafts and depth of freeboard, their armaments and caliber of guns. He examined sea conditions, studied more topographical maps, and factored in the worsening weather. Satisfied with final briefings, he dismissed the outfit but motioned for me to follow him off to one side. I had never seen his face as serious as when he searched mine.

"Now you listen to me, soldier, and you listen real good." C.B.'s steely eyes narrowed like the tip of a cutting torch, about to sear a hole through my soul. "It was no accident I made dang sure you skipped rank. If anything should happen to me, don't you dare let my boys down; or so help me, Zecca, I'll come back and haunt you 'til you git tired o' pissin' the bed at night. Are we clear on that, sergeant?"

"Yes sir. You can count on me, sir." I snapped to attention and saluted. Houdini failed, but this country cracker would probably do *exactly* what he said.

"At ease, Zecca. I know you're tense; we all are." He paused. "There's never been a doubt in my mind. Y'know, you ain't such a bad egg 'cept for bein' a damned Yankee. Seriously, I'm scared as hell, too, Zeck. But this is where we cut bait and fish. These kids are gonna need us— and need us bad. You hear me?"

"Yes sir."

C.B. looked straight into my eyes. "In some ways, you remind me a lot of me. It's that sixth sense you got. I seen it for a long time now, and it's a gift. You need to trust it and use it wisely. Believe me, Zeck, squad leaders come and go, but you're one of the best I've trained in a long time. Do you remember when you had the guts to step out and stick up for Woofie with Major Baldwin at Baxter?"

"Major Baldwin? Sure. A solid officer, I thought."

"Yes he is; and he had some solid things to say about you, too— like you're a natural born leader with genuine concern for his men. I knew all along he was right. That's why I asked Baldwin for a special favor: to use his rank wherever he could to keep the outfit together. Those boys *trust* you, and look to you for answers."

C.B. nodded toward the platoon. "Take that peelgrim sidekick o'yourn. They keeps t'sayin' he's the lucky one, don't they? Well let me tell ya somethin' boy, he ain't the only one— *all* of 'em are lucky." His deadpan face moved closer. "Know why? Because they had me wipin' their behinds to this point, and now they got you to help out when the shit hits the fan; and believe me Zecca, it's gonna. In a few hours from now, all hell is gonna break loose, and it ain't gonna be *nothin'* like you seen at Baxter. This is for keeps. Good luck sergeant, and may God bless us all." He extended his hand and walked off as briskly as his salute. His expression left a funny feeling in the pit of my stomach.

May God bless us— all?

I pondered his comment for several minutes, my eyes fixed on the black horizon beyond the giant turrets of a battleship prepping for departure. *Which prayers will God be listening to in the coming savagery; American or German?*

I looked at my platoon huddled in smaller, closer friendships; chatting, munching on Red Cross donuts, and smoking. I knew their enthusiastic faces were a ruse, their bodies hardened, and the light of battle glowing in their eyes. But they were nervous at best; most scared witless standing on feeble legs barely supporting the body's sense of dread.

Portland Harbor teamed with thousands of them— boys herded aboard transport vessels like cattle. I wondered how many of them entered the Army thinking the service was about a chest full of ribbons, snappy girl-getting uniforms, or wallets packed with photos for swapping bullshit with new buddies outside of Hometown, USA.

Now, I'd like to have a quarter for every one of them clutching amulets hung about their necks; praying like hell such trinkets will be enough to ward off the hooded cloak of death. Thinking back, who would have thought world affairs would have collapsed into such a global conflict, putting us here, only a Sunday's jaunt from an entrenched infantry no different than us— a country's youth forced to come of age learning how to kill.

Hmm, infantry; from the old Italian word: *infanteria*, meaning young boys. How appropriate, I thought— *kids*; hurling themselves into the coming brutality at the command of fanatical maniacs in Berlin. Yet they must be special to someone in Hamburg, Munich, and every little hamlet in between. The only difference between us was allegiance; each side obeying orders in defense of different ideals.

My eyes returned to the sea. It's likely that in fifty years from now, both armies would meet again, but instead of squaring off with bayonets, they'll embrace with hugs; a band of repentant, snowy-haired old men crying in each other's arms on the same ground both had left littered with the mangled bodies of *brethren*.

Each generation seems to merely go from one war to another. The young maturing in battle at the direction of their older, *wiser* generation; those who had just condemned the very lunacies *they* had wrought. And the cycle continues; only the dead ever getting to see the end of wars. *Same tunes, different dance, but I'll be damned if I can figure it out.*

Again I looked at my unit, one platoon among the hundreds: America's latest gladiators only weeks out of training, and our first *mission*— the biggest invasion in history; order-makers and order-takers each praying the other was ready.

Presto was right. In a matter of hours, we'll break our maidens as *men* o' war one way or other— our youth left behind forever.

What was it Frazer kept telling his young bride; *it is what it is?* Yeah, that was it. In some strange way, his words seemed as soothing as the rhythm of rain pattering my helmet. Sometimes the waiting and worrying seemed worse than actually getting on with it. "It is what it is," I mumbled— my final moment of solemnity.

I filled my lungs with cool sea-air, watching the countless vessels sliding through pitch-dark waters. Our time had come. The acid test of our training, courage, speed, and stamina hung in the balance— our transformation to manhood about to be turned loose on Little Mac's 'beaches of Belmont'. *Yes, we were all in—the flag is up, and... time to be a man.*

* * *

Bounding Home

Twenty-three days have passed since we stormed Omaha Beach; twenty-three days of brutal combat before we're finally relieved from the front, yet proud of having accomplished every mission without giving up a yard of ground since pushing inland.

A regimental command post had been set up amid the ruins of Ste-Laurent, the same village we helped liberate during opening days of the invasion. As our transport squeals to a halt, Woofie is first to spring from the truck— *hungry* as hell, I'm grinning; watching the big bastard charging for chow lines second only to the one he made taking out a fortified pillbox. *I pity any mess cook who tries denying him extra portions.*

Our duffle bags were waiting for us, though sadly, many will go unclaimed. Reeking of sweat and diarrhea that has plagued most of the outfit, some begin rifling through them, eager to be rid of raunchy uniforms. Though we're all famished, several have put a hot shower and clean clothes ahead of chow.

Feverish and nauseated from a festering bullet wound crippling my left hand, I put off seeing the docs expecting to be debriefed at any minute. A field medic said I needed one of the new intravenous penicillin drips, though I'd rather get some shut-eye; feeling more fatigued than wounded.

Sleep is next to impossible on the battlefield; many would have traded their souls for even a few hours' nap. The men are exhausted, dropping wherever they find space within the crumpled remains of a small shop complex in the village center. Word from HQ has it we'll be in Ste-Laurent for only a couple days. Delirious with anticipation of much deserved R & R, they're afraid if passing out now, they'll miss the shuttle back to England, even *if* in two days hence.

"Ten-hut!" A major enters the room.

"At ease, gentlemen. Which of you is Zecca?"

"Here, Sir." I smell horrid and look worse, but try smoothing my encrusted beard to appear somewhat presentable.

"I'm Major Whitt." He ignores my slovenly appearance, but does order me to remove the disgusting, stained bandage covering my hand. The Major gently eases the rotation to better study the damage, cringing at the rancid, foul-smelling pus draining from a fetid hole in my hand. The knuckle is broken and the hand is bloated to twice normal size.

"Jesus, son, that's nasty. I think you have blood poisoning. Just as soon as we're through, you get that seen to, and I *do* mean pronto, lieutenant."

"Sergeant, sir." I wince, and gingerly rewrap the filthy gauze.

"No, I had it right the first time. You're a lieutenant now." He smiles and turns to face the troops. "Men, I know you're anxious to shower and get a hot meal, so I won't keep you. For now, I want to personally greet your arrival and see to your needs. My command is extremely proud of this outfit. You men did one *hell* of a job, and I assure you such exploits have not gone unnoticed all the way up to Ike. Thanks to such unparalleled courage and tenacity of soldiers like you, we have the Jerries on the run." Major Whitt's sincere morale boost is met with cheers and handshakes.

"A briefing can wait, Zecca. I'll check back after you've seen to that wound. Until then, I'll leave these with you." His aide passes mail pouches and merit citations to Presto standing next to me. "As for your new rank, Zecca, I'd consider it a personal honor if you'd allow me to pin the insignia at HQ when you're in better shape."

"Yes sir," I salute, respecting the ceremonious gesture.

"Uh, one more thing." Major Whitt retrieves a letter and two cigars from a breast pocket. "Captain Fairchild asked me to deliver this to you. He said it was his way of assuring I'd find you, uh— let's just say in good form. And which of you is Mosconi; the *lucky* one?" I point to Tony and the major hands him the cigars.

"Chase said these are for you; to celebrate getting lucky in love." He grins at Tony's quizzical expression. "Word at HQ says you're going to be a Da-a-a-a-dy," he mimicked a bleating ewe. "Chase said you'd understand."

"Hey, Tony! I betcha them sheep ain't the *only* one's noivous, now," someone razzes. Tony ignores the ribbing and accepts the cigars with silence.

"That's it for now gentlemen. Showers and hot meals are ready when you are. Get some rest and plenty of it. My staff has orders to see to your every need or they'll have hell to pay, so speak up. I'll let you know when you're to depart for England."

The major faces me. "I'll give you a moment to unwind with your men, but you had better be in medical within the hour. That's an order, Zecca; are we clear on that?"

"Yes, sir."

"Good, I'll be back later. As you were, gentlemen."

Ah, England in two days. I sigh and lean back, propping my elbows atop a wall shelf as Presto sorts the mail. Closing my eyes, I envision an English meadow covered by a blanket of dense yellow rapeflowers under a warm summer sun. I see gingerbread houses in a quaint little village, its center square teeming with pleasant faces; giggling, rosy-cheeked youngsters munching on Hershey treats.

Things are different in Normandy— serene daydreams vanish, replaced by a more disparate scene of once-thriving towns reduced to smoldering rubble. Hectares of rich farmland are strewn with the bloated bodies of soldiers and farm animals amidst the charred and twisted remains of war machinery.

I've seen emaciated elderly and children left homeless, living like field mice within the ruins; their only meals a scavenged potato or K-rations pilfered from the dead.

Besieged villagers may have greeted us with joy at being freed, but as corks popped from stashed bottles of wine and champagne, it was a bittersweet celebration; their gaunt, despairing faces numbed from four years of Nazi occupation.

I suppose the Normandy invasion means we'll be memorialized as liberators— the redemption for a Nazi-free Europe. For me, it felt more like a personal payback. I'll never forget my first night in England, seething with rage as innocent civilians were bombed. For my English cousins, perhaps D-Day will mean more than vengeance for the Blitzkrieg; maybe it will help erase memories like Dunkirk, or the ill-fated political decisions and blind apathies that led to such atrocities in the first place.

A funny thing— *fate*. To think of all the planning and logistical nightmares kept secret for so long, only to have the invasion teeter on the brink of disaster after a freakish mother nature nearly scuttled the biggest military armada in history. The first night at sea, severe weather forced the fleet to turn back. A British Coxswain said it was the roughest channel he'd seen in over twenty years at sea.

The following day, we got underway, but poor weather and faulty planning still caused massive losses of critical support armor and supplies. I saw fully-manned landing crafts capsize in deep water, and the poor slobs who did manage to stay afloat were passed by, left to drown like jettisoned vermin.

When it was our turn to hit the beaches, thirty of us trembling greenhorns were huddled together in a small LCA; scared shitless, fighting either sea sickness or abject fear before the ramp dropped.

We were part of a second assault wave steering toward assigned sectors on Omaha. Previous landings along the five-mile strand ran headlong into fierce German resistance. Obscured by haze and thick, acrid smoke, our skipper turned the craft parallel to the shoreline and cruised for several hundred yards, looking for a gap between mined obstacles. He finally eyed a suitable spot, but a larger LCI gunned her engines and cut us off, racing for the same opening. We could easily have beaten it, but C.B. ordered the skipper to back off.

'Let them go,' he said, 'but cruise in close behind and wait 'til they lower their ramp, then gun your engines and peel away from her flank.'

The moment that LCI hit the beach, artillery and mortars opened up. We watched in horror as pinpointed shelling exploded amongst the wading men. Three more direct hits disintegrated the LCI's bow and mid-sections. We never saw any of those doomed soldiers again. Under C.B.'s instinctive leadership, fate dealt us yet another fortunate hand. He had kept his wits about him when others hadn't, letting the LCI draw fire and expose preset coordinates so we could make it in.

The beaches were awash in the blood and bodies of dead and terribly wounded, many writhing in agony as soldiers scurried past, desperately seeking cover. The number of casualties was appalling. It was sickening; the most grotesque carnage I could not have imagined. I saw boots with partial legs still in them, organs and lengths of intestines hanging from landing obstacles. Big strapping men near Woofie's size were so terror-stricken, they leaned against a sandy berm unable to move, convulsing and crying open-mouthed like month-old babies. Scores of landing crafts, field artillery, and tanks were sunk or burning. We lost about a third of our company during the first forty-eight hours.

Though feeling unsteady, I decide to read Chase's letter while standing, when without warning, I'm overcome with emotion. My eyes fill with tears as I can't believe what I'm reading. *Ah, for the wondrous resilience of youth.*

"Men! Listen up." I hold Chase's letter high. "I have *great* news about Little Mac— he's alive!"

I continue reading Chase's letter aloud: 'I've been checking in on him, and though still in guarded condition, he's going to make it. My CO was kind to relay Kirk's radio message that Mac was on his way in, but warned he was not expected to live. Doctors said the field medics should be given a medal just for keeping him alive. Except for the weakest pulse, Mac truly was all but dead. But the strangest thing happened when I held his hand on the way to OR. It was like a miracle, Vince. Mac could barely open his eyes, but seemed to recognize me, and though faint, he gave me his impish grin that brought me to tears.

'After several operations and blood transfusions, he's propped up in bed with the Medal of Honor pinned to his pajamas by Bradley himself. He's regained enough of his old spunk to keep the nurses in stitches, too. In fact, I think he's in love. The little rascal has a lovely British nurse fussing over him every day. She has an unusual first name of "*Sterling*", and he jokes with everybody in the ward: "she's a keeper, and ya can take that to the bank."'

"Hallelujah!" and "God bless our Little Mackie," spout the men; many of us owe our lives to him. I decide to read the rest of Chase's letter alone so they can get back to their own mail.

Chase wrote: 'I got good news and bad news— first the bad. I lost a C-note on the Belmont, and the good news is, you boys weren't here or you'd have kissed your money goodbye, too. Pensive failed to win the Triple Crown. Yes, our sure thing was beaten a half length by a long-shot called Bounding Home.

'Talk about long shots, this one will really floor you. Bull Dandy ran third at a whopping 120-to-1. He's a nobody; a pure sprinter that defied all reason he was even in the race. Turf writers said that when the gate opened, he ran like a horse possessed. Can you believe it? Well, so long for now and take care of yourself. Chase.'

Bounding Home takes the Belmont— Mac's Bull Dandy third; at over 100-to-1?

Chase said crazy things can happen, but this was *beyond* crazy— more like supernatural. Tony's luck is uncanny; pulling the winning longshot after the '*sure thing*' or any likely spoiler was taken. I shake my head in wry disbelief, and glance at Tony sprawled on his back, head atop a helmet and sucking on a cigar while reading his mail. *I wonder if it's from the vixen?*

Scrunching my eyes fending off a sudden flush of dizziness, my nausea seems to be getting worse. I feel unsteady, and had better plop my ass down and lean against the wall. *Kiss our money goodbye? If you only knew, Chase.*

Another shiver rattles me, but doesn't stop my eyes from filling with tears, fighting images of Frazer's head, half an arm, and chunks of tattered uniform scattered all over Mac's 'beaches of Belmont'. The poor bastard never heard the fluttering sound of the mortar that followed my friend into an old shell hole. I dunno, maybe it was best he held our betting pool; a little bit of us all to forever remain at the side of our fallen comrade.

All Frazer ever wanted was to entertain, to make people happy with his talents. A Cinderella chance awaited him in Hollywood, a future, a chance to fulfill dreams of a better life for his family as well as vindicate his mother's sacrifices. Her only testament now: a gold star pinned to a flag in some rundown row-house in Philly. I can picture his wife holding their baby when the doorbell rings, and the dreaded telegram is placed into her trembling, denying hand.

Presto interrupts my thoughts, handing me two letters from home and a third from Alessa. My heart swells. Letters from home are more than news; they're like medicine to help erase the insanities of war. Yet to some, mail can be a double-edged sword— *death* letters we call them in the field. I've seen 'Dear John' letters tear the heart out of the toughest men in the Army, even endanger the lives of buddies if crucial focus is torn from anything but the tasks at hand.

I'm dying to know what Alessa has to say, but decide to wait and read hers later. I again glance at Tony, and for the first time since Picauville, he's grinning. My emotions soar. I can't imagine losing him, of failing my promise to Alessa. *There's no denying it, I love my Tony— my little brother, my best friend.*

Lately, I've been worried about him. He's been distant, barely saying two words to anyone— a listless, sullen soul far removed from the glib *Joisey* rascal I'm so fond of. Though Mac earned the Medal of Honor at Picauville, Tony is unaware I'm holding a Silver Star and Purple Heart for him. I've heard it said, 'hell knows no fury like a woman scorned', but I witnessed a personal rage I'd never thought possible in human beings.

After crossing the Elle River, we approached a tiny village with few buildings. Normally, we could have walked through town in five minutes, but a pocket of Germans waiting in ambush pinned us down. We had little cover, and only the river to our backs.

Mac was at the point and had been hit. Though wounded, he refused evacuation and waved us back. Firing his machine gun, he single-handedly repelled more than one assault, giving us a chance to seek cover and regroup. During a brief lull, Mac spotted a downed man exposed to sniper fire and crawled to his aid. Fending off yet another assault, he managed to apply a tourniquet and morphine, saving the soldier's life. Severely wounded and weak from loss of blood, he struggled with dragging someone twice his size to safety. Two German riflemen flanking a light machine gun shot Mac twice more in the lower back; his body snapping with the impact.

Tony exploded with satanic fury. He rushed the Krauts, darting from building to building, dodging bullets, and tossing grenades into windows while blazing his BAR at anything that moved. I had been shot in the hand and could only use my .45, but followed Presto mopping up after Tony's onslaught; unfeeling when at point blank, I plugged every son-of-a-bitch I found still alive.

Giltner's bazooka silenced snipers hiding in the church steeple, and then he angled across the street, scoring a bull's-eye on the light machine gun position Tony was charging, killing all who remained except two riflemen who had turned and fled.

Filled with demonic rage and raw adrenalin, Tony ran in an all out sprint, and despite the Browning's heavy weight, he caught the fleeing bastards who had shot Mac, cutting them in half before they could even *think* surrender. He stood over the mangled bodies, wild-eyed and uttering only guttural sounds through clenched teeth like a crazed fiend from hell; and then walked away without a word.

After making sure Little Mac and the other wounded were evacuated, I spotted Tony sitting on a chunk of broken concrete, shaking as though squatting in an icebox. His eyes were blank, fixed on the horizon. I noticed a sleeve and both pant legs were perforated, but his only injuries were a superficial graze to his neck and a deep gash on his forearm. After applying sulfa powder and a pressure bandage, I held him until he stopped shaking. He's been different ever since—withdrawn; a lifeless humanoid possessed by a frenzied hatred for Germans.

Like him, many of the men seem driven beyond emotion— a bevy of blank faces with sunken eyes, and minds drained of every ounce of human spirit. They're my responsibility now— *my* men; ever since C.B. was killed.

His death was a terrible shock. Fear and confusion were hard to overcome, but somehow I kept true to my promise and managed to maintain cohesion and morale. Recalling the value Cy had placed on good COs, I pray I'm at least half as good as C.B.; *and what a godsend you turned out to be, Cyrus Clemens.*

I can picture him sitting on a barstool at Doogans, stuck on yet another word, and mumbling to a mute Murphy with no idea how many lives are in his debt. *Thank God I listened to him.*

I learned more in that morgue-of-a-bar than in all the lectures proffered by that puffed-up peacock from West Point. Cy taught me to pay keen attention to physical clues in the battlefield, like the differences in tracks made by local farm machinery versus military.

Heavy rains prior to the landings had softened the ground, and as we crept along hedgerows near the coastal village of Colleville, I spotted a number of broken branch ends, trodden grass clumps, and an odd width of wheel tracks running parallel to old wagon ruts.

I showed C.B., and we followed until they veered off across a small paddock toward a dense grove of apple trees. C.B. ordered us to retreat and to lay rock-still under brushy cover until after dark. During the gloom of night, Kirk radioed for a rolling barrage of huge fourteen-inch naval guns.

We were lucky to have Kirk. Aside from his talents, I admired his guts and unfailing stamina for keeping up with seventy pounds of radio equipment strapped to his body. To the enemy, radiomen with their give-away antennae meant *officers* attached; making them prime targets for concentrated machine gun and mortar fire.

Kirk's radioed artillery placements were brilliant. C.B. had us following salvos so close I could feel the heat flashes from shell bursts silhouetting our movement. We scurried across the glade and found a battery of nine murderous 88s unattended under camouflage. As the Jerries cowered pending a cease fire, we slipped in, planted noiseless thermite grenades that welded breech and traversing mechanisms useless, and then got out undetected. C.B. saved his best '*Kilroy-was-here*' kiss for last.

He had Kirk radio a cease fire, but told the Navy to stand by with exact coordinates. C.B. had us dig in; waiting and counting the minutes. When he figured the Krauts were convinced the naval guns had stopped, and emerged to check on their precious artillery, C.B. ordered the Navy to 'light 'em up'; we picking off stragglers trying to flee.

During the remaining hours of darkness, we hunkered down along a hedgerow to rest. The bombardment had ceased, but to say it had been a quiet night would have been to ignore the relentless moans from German casualties begging for relief that never came.

Destroying unmanned artillery was one thing, but taking out a heavily fortified pillbox was yet another; the one earning C.B. a posthumous DSC. Driven by pure guts and his cool and collected calm during the heat of battle, C.B. led our human mule, Woofie, and four others hefting fifty-pound beehive charges and gallons of gasoline up an embankment while under fire.

After setting the fuses against the bunker, C.B. braced to cover his men until they could scramble to safety. It was then he caught a machine gun burst in the face. Moments later, the pillbox went up like Mt. Etna. When the flames dissipated, it was charred but still intact with no sign of damage to the concrete.

We cursed failure, but Woofie was manic seeing C.B.'s headless body in the distance. He chanced a second run at it alone, spraying the structure with machine gun fire, but received none in return. We followed, and after Giltner blasted an opening, we encountered a ghastly scene inside. An entire German squad was literally cooked to death; lying in twisted, rigid shapes, their eyes and mouths frozen open in silent screams. Reliving the scene and the retched stench is making me gag; *just like Cy had said it would.*

You tried, Cy, but there *are* no words to prepare a soldier for what I've witnessed. How does one describe the gruesome insanity? *It's impossible.*

There was never a sense of glory, no emotional rush of victory, no remorse— only death and destruction as mutilated bodies piled up around us, and nothing else ahead except more of the same gore. Numbed indifference took over as we wove our way through dying men crying for their mothers, the dead left in our wake like shapeless road kills.

Words, you say?

Cold, unfeeling *words* can be erased, but a soldier will never forget the vile coating war leaves on the palate after bodies are left for days beneath a blazing sun.

What words could possibly recount what it's like crawling over a half-dead human, hearing his futile plea as he holds his innards in blood-soaked hands to keep his organs from slopping into the dirt? Can words convey the heart-stopping jolt of a bullet pinging the side of a helmet; an inch from going through an eye?

What *words* can describe the bowel-loosening terror of lying in a foxhole trying to curl a six-foot body into a six-inch ball; bouncing with the heaving earth as horrendous concussions rain closer to our four-foot patch of real estate? *There are no words, Cy.*

I shuddered, the wooziness and hot flashes increasing as I look at the men— *my* comrades-in-arms; damned good buddies with whom I'd laughed, partied, ate, and drank. I remember their once bright young faces, aged three decades in as many weeks; their furrowed brows the mark of having been pushed to the limits of human endurance.

My family; a frazzled, battle-weary bunch of siblings I've come to love. I now understand the soulful look in Cy's eyes when he impressed upon me the unique feeling of a battlefield love he said is never talked about.

If I do manage to make it home alive, I can see myself a fat and forgotten old veteran, sitting in a rat-hole tavern likely doing a crossword, too. Some smart-ass kid in uniform will barge in with a familiar, naive perk on *his* face. He'll buy me a beer and prod me to open my bagful of war stories, and I'll oblige— but I pray to God the little bastard will have enough sense to listen to us, Cy. Another chill rattles my body. *Are you going nuts, Vinnie boy, or, am I dying, I wonder?*

By now, my perspiring forehead and face are smeared with a slimy mud; I gave up trying to stop the tears from flowing. Maybe it's the nausea, but I keep seeing faces of the Schmidt's I snuffed— and retch, feeling a need to vomit, but I can't; my throat's clogged with false bile.

Pulling my knees to my chin, I openly weep, my soul reeling from disgust and shame. I *hate* myself! What kind of *animal* have I become? *Oh, God— please forgive me; save me from this madness!*

I'm trembling, and though having trouble breathing, I sob and curl tighter against my knees to muffle the noise, not wanting the others to think I'm falling apart. But it's no use. Another sob squeaks out when I feel an arm slide across my shoulders, and a familiar voice softly intones in my ear.

"It's okay, paisan," Tony whispers, pulling my head closer to his chest. "Go ahead, let it out— let it all out, boss. Youz got nuttin' to be ashamed of. Y'never failed us; *especially* me ever since Grand Central."

Reaching up with my good hand, I squeeze Tony's arm with all the affection I can muster as he cradles my head against his bosom.

"Jesus, ya boinin' up." Tony pulls my arm across his shoulder. "Come on, ya big galoot. Y'gotta get up. That's it, easy does it."

Presto helps support my other side, careful not to jar my hand. I'm dizzy on my feet, and my vision's distorted from tears and nausea. Tony's face is a blur, but I think he's smiling. *Is my Tony back?*

"Come on, one step at a time." Tony whistles to Giltner as he's guiding me through a maze of bodies. "Go find a jeep, and on the double, even if youz have t'pull da driver from behind da wheel."

Filthy and unfed, Giltner is one of the few still awake. He's on his feet and out the door before I take another step. I'm smirking, knowing the gruff and rugged Giltner would likely take pleasure in that chore; he'd wait for an occupied jeep in a parking lot of empties.

"What are y'grinnin' at now, ya big slug? Jesus, will ya look at that puss? Looks like y'been eatin' mud pies for Christ's sake." Tony's smile widens. "Easy boss, we're almost there. We gotta get that hand taken care of or my kid won't have an uncle and my ass'll be fried with Alessa's next batch o' meatballs."

Crossing the threshold, he steadies me, the spiking fever clashing with the sudden flash of sunshine makes me shudder. I close my eyes, savoring the fresh scent of the sea carried inland from the channel. While waiting for the jeep, a column of transports packed with new replacements are leaving the village. *They'll be breaking their maidens next, the poor slobs.*

"Jeep's here."

Against my weakened protest, I'm hoisted atop a litter across the back. I can't believe how drained my body feels, every bit of energy gone. The sun's rays feel good on my face, evoking a dream: I'm lying back in a lush English meadow, spring flowers wavering in the breeze all around me. My muscles droop, and I'm nearing sleep when suddenly, an intense, fiery pain jars me alert.

"Oops, sorry, paisan; had to tuck ya hand in."

The instant our eyes met, I *knew*. When closing my eyes again, a *wondrous* sense of peace floods my body. I know now, at some point, I'll be *'bounding home* myself: *'cause where my Tony goes, I goes too.*

EPILOGUE

BEACHES OF BELMONT is a fresh look at an old subject; only this time, the Normandy invasion is retold with an uncannily eerie, but true parallel to the Triple Crown of 1944.

As America's boys train for combat, their "equine youth" counterparts prepare for the classic Triple Crown. Whether horse or human, *all* will test their maturity, fitness, speed, stamina, and heart.

During both World War eras, horse racing was more popular than today. Thus, fewer people will likely have intimate knowledge of the Triple Crown, let alone be familiar with famous historical facts, horses, jockeys, or of racing events now six decades past.

The first leg is the Kentucky Derby at 1 ¼ miles, always the first Saturday in May. The second leg is the Preakness Stakes, a sixteenth-mile shorter at Maryland's Pimlico. During WWII, it was run a week after the Derby versus two weeks today. The final leg is the Belmont Stakes at New York's Belmont Park. Run the first weekend in June, it's a manly, 1½ mile true test of heart, stamina, pace, and speed.

While our characters are fictional, their story is centered on true military events of World War II— such that in sync with historically accurate references to the 1944 Triple Crown, ie: names of horses, jockeys, past racing events, and respective orders of finish; the story unveils an entertaining, yet haunting parity between the two events.

When thinking back on Beaches of Belmont, envision a nation energized in anticipation of an exciting back-to-back sweep of the rare Triple Crown, resting squarely on the shoulders of Pensive. Yet, at the same time, an even more intense energy had Battalions of America's youth within its grip. Four thousand miles may have separated entrants, but when each starting gate sprung them free at nearly the identical moment in history, one set of trainees scrambled for the record books; fame and glory— the other set, for their lives.

A Worst-Way Wee

by D.R.Smith

Aye, water, water ev'rywhere,
When worst way have to pee.
Yon flowing fountains in the square,
Not now I care to see.

With knock-knees pinned, I drag my feet,
My teeth afloat my jaw.
But grabbing groin in public street
Is pooh-poohed by the law.

Stooped and cramped, I shuffle on
Nay, bladder will not last.
Must fight the urge to pinch my *Juan*,
And find a place, but fast!

I scan the busy thoroughfare
For alley, bush, or tree.
I'd pay a fortune, I declare,
For any nook to pee.

Ah, 'cross the way near cafe booth
'Tis hole in alley fence.
I'll stick it thru and turn it loose,
But Bobbie spots offence.

"Oy, you, a whistlin' there discreet—
Up leaning 'gainst that rail.
'Ow dare you do that on my beat;
I'm taking you to jail."

He grabbed my neck and spun me 'round,
As steady stream effused.
I doused his pants from belt to ground,
And filled up both his shoes.

My plea to judge, "was worst-way wee,
Don't throw me in the clink."
Ten quid, two days, he sentenced me,
But not for what you think.

Tho' crime was due to trouser trout
Let loose near coffee shop.
T'was not for whipping willie out,
But peeing on a cop.

The penal system seems unfair,
I'd rather sup with wine.
But bread and water ev'rywhere
Goes well with beans just fine.

Hogs n Hens
by Jerry Powell

"Poor Aunt Edna," June Thayer said as she let water from a glass trickle onto the front of her thin white cotton dress. June raised a bare leg in the air from her position on the sofa, alternately examining it and Jim King. This caused Jim further discomfort since the bright December day was uncommonly warm.

"I know it's been a ways back, but Willie Pierce ought not to have done what he did," she pouted. "He left her all alone and little Hot Shot never had no daddy because of it."

Had he not been distracted by the glistening body before him, the comment would have taken Jim completely by surprise. June, who turned thirty last month, never once offered a sympathetic view regarding anyone, particularly children.

Jim did remember that Willie Pierce, a farmer's son from Morrilton, left Edna Clemons pregnant and unmarried a long time ago. Their offspring, Edward, whom everyone knew as "Hot Shot" for unknown but often speculated upon reasons, ran wild from the time he was three. Willie created other obligations for himself, probably of the same nature and just never returned. June was Edna's niece, but never seemed bothered by that sort of history before.

Recalling this, Jim responded, "Willie's never even been around 'em as far as I can recollect. Besides, I hear Edna's caught the eye of some farmer out of Kansas, now."

June dismissed the remark and chided Jim. "You men are all just alike. Willie ought to make amends to poor Aunt Edna and little Hot." June slowly eased from the couch and approached Jim. Her dark-eyed stare didn't waver. The contrast of those eyes against ivory skin and her small, perfectly shaped nose usually weakened him.

Though he remained at a loss as to why the conversation turned to a subject long forgotten, Jim licked his lips and said, "Hot Shot ain't so little anymore. Well, maybe he is at that, but he's meaner than a diamondback I've heard it said. And besides, it's been ten years I expect, since Edna's even seen 'ol Willie. Closest he ever gets to Plum Bayou is the general store in Redfield." Sharing such information with June was a mistake.

"It's near to Christmas time Jim King and if you're of any account at all, you'll find Willie Pierce and deal severely with him. It ought to be easy since you say he gets to Redfield so often." The last few words were not spoken but breathed less than an inch from Jim's ear. But then she twirled away and with a backward glance, curls falling to forehead, she folded her arms, clearly intending to allow no further advances.

Jim and June built their relationship on regularity, about twice a week, in fact. They rarely discussed much and preferred to accelerate right to the processes involved to the satisfaction of both. The sudden departure of their usual routine, especially since the watered down cotton dress now revealed charms of a shape that Jim intensely admired, forced his voice to pitch higher than his usual baritone.

"I'll have to just about set up camp there at the store. I don't think my wife will take much cotton to that, what with the way things lie between us right now."

"It ain't my fault you let her catch you and Delfina Brown in the cornfield. Why, Delfina's the daughter of one of your best friends. And on the very day you paid me a visit, too. Ollie King is a sweet soul, but she was right to take a switch to you both. I should have whipped you myself. Besides, if you're not of a mind to discuss matters with Willie, it'll give me the excuse I need to ease on up to that tall, rich stranger in town. I'll bet he deals with such problems seriously. What's his name?"

"Winston, and he ain't that tall." Jim winced inside at the thought of Roger Winston, one of many big-city businessmen who took advantage of depressed land prices around the Arkansas River.

The visit to June brought Jim none of the usual relief he enjoyed. In the end and in the interest of preventing further frustration at the hands of June Thayer, he increased his visits to the general store. Folks saw Jim at the tables there often, so the additional visits went unnoticed and without comment. After a few days Willie appeared, seeking shelter from the blue northerner that burst through town that morning. Jim coaxed Willie into a game of checkers with ease.

Roger Winston walked through the door of the store almost to the second Jim finished giving Willie his whipping at checkers. Jim reminded himself to have a few words with Roger - who carried something interesting - after he scolded Willie for not bringing enough money with him.

Willie didn't take it well. "Why, Jim, I don't know why you'd say such a thing. You just took my last four bits."

"That's just what I thought. You ought to be more responsible than that, wasting away the last of your bread money while Edna and Hot Shot sit at home starving. The Depression may be ending for the rest of the country, but it ain't for Redfield, Arkansas."

Willie seemed startled and started to speak, but Jim raised a hand to cut him off.

"You just need to catch the ferry on over to Plum Bayou and see about them two. A man's got to own up to things after awhile."

"But, I ain't seen neither one for nigh on ten years, I reckon. There ain't no call to go and see 'em now. It would only cause a big to-do. Old man Clemons would just shoot me, I'd guess. Besides, I got my wife and kids over at Morrilton I drop in on from time to time and then there's that bunch up Memphis way and..."

"Oh, shush Willie," Jim said, shaking his head, "It was forced on me to even mention such a thing. I wish I hadn't now. Just go on and git. And bring more money next time."

As Willie eased out the door, Jim turned his attention to Roger Winston. To his surprise, he found Winston glaring at him.

"King, your remarks to that young man were highly inappropriate. I find it remarkable you could preach to him at all, given your own reputation."

Winston's features, a set and noticeable jaw line surrounded by a full head of dark hair irritated Jim. In particular was Roger's lack of gray. Both men had edged past fifty and Jim's own hair, though it remained thick and wavy, lost its battle to the changes of color several years back. Most would still vote Jim on the right side of handsome, and Jim himself had long been convinced he was the most dashing man in the county; at least, until the arrival of Roger Winston. This may have colored his response.

"Well Winston, now that you've stuck your nose in the matter, I'll explain so things will be clear. I didn't like Willie Pierce much before, and now I like him even less. He ought not to go poking them young girls like that if he doesn't plan on settling down with one."

"I don't disagree," replied Winston, "but I find it hard to imagine you are the one casting the stone."

"It ain't the first one he's had throwed at him. Besides, none of them rake and rambling types like Willie Pierce ever pay attention to the kind of wisdom folks like me toss out. But thanks for the compliment just the same, Winston."

Winston turned away with a shake of the head and placed an object on the counter near the checkout box.

A brand new Philco radio.

Jim admired it with great concentration. To assist in such focus, Jim removed a flask from inside one of the extra pockets Ollie had sewn into his overalls. It contained a certain tincture made from fermented corn and muscadines by Jake Johnson from over at Humphrey. What it lacked in pleasant flavor, it made up for in solace.

Jim watched and listened as Roger demonstrated and talked about the radio, a fancy portable Jim had heard much about and had seen in the newspapers placed in the various outhouses he might have cause to use. Dark blue in color, it possessed a handle so you could tote it. Its fresh, new appearance offered a striking contrast to the worn wooden counter upon which Roger set it.

Although Roger actually bragged to no one in the store, Jim figured he would before long, considering the way the radio was being admired. Normally, this would not have affected Jim, but several factors contributed to his state of irritation; the biggest part being Jake's white lightning and muscadine wine mixture. Second, there was that lost poke from June, thanks to Willie Pierce's stubborn hide. Finally, when things were about to come into balance after Jim beat Willie at checkers, Winston, the newest would-be-farmer from out of state had to show up with that radio and proceed to talk about it.

"They call it a TH-16," Roger explained to Hattie Jo, the owner of Hattie Jo's General Store.

Hattie Jo, for some reason only harrumphed, but Jim decided he had to have it.

"You look awful proud of that Philco, Roger," Jim said. "You ought to see what you can get out of it. Why not stack it up as a wager on a game of checkers and let's see what kind of man you be?"

This brought a hush to the crowd around the counter. A challenge to Roger Winston, a rich northerner, from Jim King, also known as King Jim, was something that would generate a lot of talk along the back roads.

But Winston had an answer. "I wouldn't presume to be so foolish," he said. "Undoubtedly, you have nothing with which to place such a wager. The entire exercise would be pointless."

"Now, see, you're doing right there what rich, city-folk I've met in my life are wont to do. I figured for a long time it must've been a bad habit y'all picked up from living in them big cities. But now, I've seen so many of you do it, I reckon you're just born with it." Jim flashed a grin so charming Roger appeared confused, as if he wondered about it, unsure if the insult was intended.

"Whatever are you talking about, King?"

"Assuming you're better than your betters. Of course I know you can't help it, so I'll just set you straight," Jim pulled a chair at the table invitingly, but Winston pretended to pay no heed.

"I got things of value I can risk," Jim explained. "I got me three fat sow-hogs and a passel of hens. Them's the kind that lay those big brown eggs that's so good at breakfast time. Since you're buying up all that bottom land, you'll be needing the livestock."

The only thing Roger did in response was to place the dry goods he had retrieved from a nearby aisle on the counter. He also handed Hattie Jo a list of the rest of his needs. This was Hattie Jo Hooker, the grocer who was some kind of kin to Jim's wife, Ollie. She was not the Hattie Jo from over at Humphrey who was a painter and a heavy drinker. That Hattie Jo was somewhat younger than the Redfield Hattie Jo.

Roger had yet to become comfortable around King Jim. Jim knew this and knew as well Roger held a high level of interest in those hogs and hens.

He watched Winston out of the corner of his eye, looking for a sign of weakness, be it an expression or a gesture. The more he observed the man, the more Jim wanted to take his measure. He would prefer to beat him good at checkers and win that fine radio, but he considered for a moment to just walk up and punch his smart mouth. But Jim saw Hattie Jo return and immediately dismissed all thought of violence. Hattie Jo was massive and took no guff. Also, Jim heard she'd broken the bones of a male trustee while serving a two year sentence at Tucker for manslaughter; an act which occurred immediately after she discovered her lover and some fellow from Chicago doing strange, unnatural things in a boat out on Crooked Creek. Jim suddenly realized the reason Hattie Jo showed no interest in a radio owned by someone from Illinois.

Besides, Jim thought, he could sell the Philco for a good price; at least a third of its store-bought cost. He felt it best, as a result, to just win the radio fair and square by cheating Roger at a game of checkers.

Jim reckoned Roger suspected the hogs and hens were stolen. Actually, they weren't, since they still needed to be obtained, but

Jim decided to ignore any problems caused if Roger won. He knew how to deal with such contingencies anyway.

When those who never took cotton to Jim or his ways laid comment regarding him, along with "scoundrel" and "lying cheat", they used words like "cagey" and "wily" and such. This confidence in Jim's abilities was well founded. He suddenly hit upon an idea which might just guarantee Roger's participation, and would not let the opinion of his peers slip one bit.

"All right Winston," he said. "I got one other valuable I can offer, but I can't mention it in mixed company. It just wouldn't be proper." He motioned Winston over.

Reluctantly, Winston complied. Jim leaned forward and whispered, "I know you know June Thayer, I seen you looking at her quite a bit when she sashays to town."

To his credit, Winston displayed no expression, but the mention of June Thayer brought a clear change in attitude, one Jim recognized easily.

While Roger considered his next move, Jim continued, "If by some miracle you win and I lose, I got several pokes saved up with her. I'd be of a mind to pass those on to you along with the hogs and hens."

Winston outwardly expressed shock and dismay. His face actually turned red. He used big words like sordid and disgraceful. But Jim, wise to the ways of men, waited patiently for the tirade to end.

Later, about the time Hattie Jo finished filling Roger's order, he joined Jim at the checker table. Hattie Jo snickered and then turned her attention to the Reverend Thorne, as he and his wife walked through the door. Jim stifled a smile as the tall and imposing Reverend Thorne, dressed in his usual black and his taller and even more imposing wife thrust stern glances at Winston, then pulled up a couple of chairs to join the gathering crowd. Hattie Jo gave candy to the children and sold jerky to the adults. She added a couple of logs to the stove since the wind kept sneaking in with a whine each time the door was used. The old store seemed to jump from dreary and colorless to lively, warm and fresh in only an instant. The aisles of dry goods extended outward from the checker tables and the old wooden counter. These were placed very naturally near the front door. The aisles were always clean and neat and now filled with those who could not crowd around the table.

Winston chose to set the rules. "Alright, King, let's eliminate luck. The first to win three games will be declared the winner."

Jim nodded and responded by announcing to everyone gathered around. "Fine with me. That means that we could play as many as five games. I look forward to it."

Redfield's network of gossip worked quickly to spread the word. The fact that more games than usual were played allowed half the town to show up before the match ended. June Thayer even found the time to make an appearance.

Of course, she could not have realized the role she played in such an important event, but she seemed awfully disappointed that Roger Winston lost the fifth and final game and thus the entire match. Sometime later, she revealed to a friend she had become taken with the pretty blue radio set with the fancy handle. She also didn't want that scoundrel Jim King to win. All he would do is sell the darn thing. She told her confidant, had Roger won and retained the radio, she'd planned to let him know the Philco was worth a good twenty pokes, maybe more.

* * *

Roger Winston passed the Philco radio to King Jim in a manner that could only be considered as one lacking ceremony.

He said, "Well, at least you've come by this radio honestly, King. Take it as a sign and stay on the same road."

Jim thought Roger might be a decent sort after all. He did, in fact, hand over the radio without complaint; so although Roger was incorrect in his final assessment regarding how the match was won, Jim saw no reason to argue the point. He chuckled to himself and replied, "You know you're right Roger, I plan to do just that."

Even as he said the words, another thought came to him, and by the time Roger departed, Jim decided to develop the concept to its fullest extent.

The particular hogs and hens Jim had in mind when he made the bet with Roger belonged to Oscar Figtoe, who owned that spread on the way to Whitehall. Jim figured that since he was dealing with a newcomer like Winston and one who bragged too much at that, he was well within his rights to offer up Oscar's hogs and hens. After all, it was checkers, and with checkers Jim never planned to lose. Jim didn't lose, so the remote chance he might have to make off with Oscar Figtoe's hogs and hens had passed.

But in a way, the hogs and hens could be considered Jim's until the chance of losing had passed. Jim thought about that another moment or two as he emptied his flask of Jake's latest with a shake of his head and a loud sigh.

Since he established ownership to himself of Oscar's livestock in such a logical manner, he might as well maintain it along those same lines and take possession of the hogs and hens. Further, in pursuing the same logic, Jim knew it would be less than a good idea to discuss the issue with Oscar Figtoe. Oscar might just see it another way and object to the entire effort. Therefore, Jim concluded, it would be better to collect his hogs and hens while Oscar was asleep.

Jim had no small argument with himself over this as he stepped outside the store to his wagon, found a hidden bottle and refilled his flask. He even looked at the issue from Oscar's point of view momentarily. Then he decided that was a waste of time since Oscar was clearly biased and might even conclude that Jim was stealing the livestock. Besides, Oscar also happened to be a bad checker player.

Jim's logic won out: sneak quietly in the dead of night and grab them, thus establishing rightful, legal possession of the hogs and hens that Jim now realized probably never belonged to Oscar Figtoe in the first place.

Jim owned two mules and a rubber tire wagon that didn't squeak. At great effort and aggravation, he trained his mules to be quiet as mice, a fact which he often proclaimed to many at the checker tables with pride. This, because many knew Jim had long encountered difficulty in addressing the mules.

Once, he thought about naming the mules during a lively discussion with June Thayer's father Odell. The conversation was held at the dice hall by the railroad tracks, a caboose converted to a building used previously for offices before they shut it down right after the Depression began. Ricky Joiner kept the keys after the railroad laid him off, but he only charged admission on Friday nights and all day Saturday. While the heavy-set and gregarious Ricky smoked ribs and chickens or blackened catfish, men rolled dice, tasted Jake Johnson's latest brew, cussed, smoked and engaged in heated debate.

During the enjoyment of such pleasures, Jim finally decided to not name his mules.

"When are you gonna get around to naming them mules of yours?" Odell had asked. "I get tired of hearing you just yell 'Mule' at 'em."

"Why, I don't know that I am. I can't tell them apart, so how would I know which was which?"

"I named mine and now they seem better able to give a listen."

Jim considered a moment and swallowed more of Jake's Juice from his flask. "I reckon I could just give 'em the same name. I figure if I can't tell 'em apart, they sure can't themselves, unless they're smarter than the bunch of us."

"Nah," said Rickey Joiner as he passed out some smoked ribs he'd looked up. "Them mules of yours King Jim, is about the stupidest I ever saw. Why, right this moment they's just standing in the middle of the tracks."

"Oh, I put 'em there. I noticed that when they get between the tracks, they're afraid to move. They're better at the crossing, but get 'em on the tracks and they freeze up. That way, I don't have to hitch them to that post. It's always so damned crowded."

Odell, a short, usually unbathed gray-bearded fellow who often appeared confused, once again appeared confused and asked, "Well, how do you get 'em going when you leave?"

"I ain't for sure because I usually never remember when it is that I leave here or what I do after." Jim gave Odell a stare and continued, "Anyways, I figure that when they look at each other, they may just think that they're one and the same. And if that's true, and I give 'em the same name, why, then it wouldn't matter to 'em."

Odell scratched himself across a dirty undershirt that failed to entirely cover his potbelly and yawned. "That don't sound too bad, Jim. Hell, they might just become less stubborn."

Jim had about decided to do just that: give the mules the same name, but then he had another thought. He realized that if he took to calling both mules the same name and folks heard him do it, they might think he'd lost a screw. And Jim wouldn't put it past some to petition then and there to send him off to the loony bin. No, Jim finally concluded as he laid a bet and sipped a drink, it'd be best to give them no name at all, especially considering there were folks that might just be waiting for him to make such a mistake.

Among those folk, Jim included Oscar Figtoe, whose barn he now approached. Before the thought caused Jim to utter a curse on Oscar, he noticed that Oscar and his whole clan were gone. Jim later learned they had traveled all the way to Hazen for a family reunion. Jim immediately set aside all contingency points he'd planned to make should the unfortunate occur and Oscar happen to show up with his shotgun, a device he was famous for wielding often, since he had six daughters.

Jim, with his quiet mules and wagon, made off with two of the hogs and most of the hens into the silent night.

He didn't take them all.

After all, it was the night before Christmas Eve.

* * *

The next day, Jim reluctantly began the trip back to Redfield from Little Rock. Earlier that morning, he'd hitched his wagon to his old Model-T since the mules would dawdle way too long for a trip twenty miles away.

He'd done some successful trading. He and Ollie had three little girls and he carried three gifts apiece for them. He also bought a dress for Ollie. He was really happy about the dress. He hoped it might help her to feel better.

Once, this past summer, that big-breasted Delfina Brown came to town with her daddy. Rufus, a fine fellow, who always did right by Delfina, had helped out on Jim's farm in the past. Conversations held at length while they worked led Jim to believe that friends didn't get much better than Rufus Brown. And Rufus loved his daughter.

Delfina had to be one of the prettiest girls in the state, but not the brightest. So even though she was almost twenty-five, she stayed at home with Rufus. She'd run off every now and then, but she'd always come back, dropped off usually by a frustrated beau who'd given up on getting her to understand anything.

Now, as far as Jim was concerned, Delfina could choose to understand as little as she wished. Actually, to Jim's way of thinking, Delfina understood more than she let on. That was why on that day last summer when Delfina came to town; Jim took her under his wing after Rufus got to drinking.

"Delfina, you sure look pretty in that dress. It even looks store-bought. One of your beaus get that for you?" Jim asked, not even bothering to look up into her brown eyes. Jim was not a short man, but Delfina was taller and this afforded a great view of the dress and other things.

"Why, thank you, Mr. Jim," she said. "I picked it out my ownself up at Little Rock."

"That so, honey? You know, your daddy's doing a right smart of drinking. Looks like he's gonna be awhile. Remember the last time we went to the cornfield over behind the church?"

"Yessir, I does. Them stalks wasn't tall enough for us to get much done, was they?"

"No they weren't, but they are now. They're even taller than your daddy. Want to go on over?"

"I reckon that'd be alright."

Somehow, and Jim was never sure exactly how, Ollie showed up in the cornfield during the few minutes Jim was showing Delfina the growing ears of corn. This unfortunate circumstance caused in Ollie a rapid deterioration of a normally pleasant manner. She was so affected that she took a switch to the both of them. Jim barely had a chance to get his clothes. Later that night, Ollie woke him up twice with that switch.

But now he had gotten Ollie that nice new dress. It was frilly and mostly blue, which Jim thought to be her favorite color, though he wasn't sure. He hoped that the dress would adjust matters between them in some way. He felt at least, she should become less prone to random attacks with the switch.

Back in Little Rock, Jim had picked up enough supplies and meal to last the winter in exchange for the hogs and hens.

Never in a hurry to leave the largest city in Arkansas, Jim lingered and said to his livestock broker, "Have a look at this here Philco radio I won at a checker game yesterday."

"Nice unit," the broker commented and he looked at it closely. "You ain't trying to sell it are you?"

"Why, I sure am. What's your offer?"

I got one just like it already. Bought it at that new Sears & Roebuck store right down the street. Take a look at that little bronze tag on the back of it. It tells you that it came from the same store, as well."

"Well, I'll be," said Jim. "I never thought to look."

"You know they'll refund you full price on it if you just take it back and tell 'em you don't like it."

"Now that's the best idea I've heard since Prohibition ended. That'll be three times as much as I was hoping to get."

Jim exchanged it for the dress and the gifts. He even got a box of King Edward cigars and two bits above a dollar in the bargain.

There was no denying Jim was happy, but he felt a little dry. He found the time and fifty cents to stop and buy a couple of bottles of good drinking whiskey. His supply of Jake's Own became low due to the steady sips he had given it lately. Swigging the store bought rye was a pleasure, particularly in taste. This caused Jim to nip on it a little too often and the resulting soporific effect led him to nod off to sleep while still driving his Model-T.

"Well, now. Ain't you just a sight to see."

At that, Jim awoke with a start and chanced to notice someone sitting beside him, someone who was no taller than a toddler, but whose face glowed with a knowing. Jim felt those little tingly things on the nape of his neck, something that happened when he encountered situations that were somewhat strange. Jim also realized his error when he recalled that he had mixed Jake's home-cookings with real whiskey once before and mistaking a cranky mule for an outhouse, received a vicious kick. Apparently, the mixture produced another dire effect.

"It ain't the hooch," said the tiny fellow.

"You say something, midget?"

"I said it ain't none of that booze and I'm not a midget."

"Well, I don't care. I think it's the hooch, else you wouldn't even be here a talking to me."

"Ain't the hooch," the visitor repeated. *"Ain't your lucky day none, neither."*

"What say?" Jim asked.

"You're fixing to break down. Then you're gonna get set upon by a gang of no good cutthroats out of Perdition's sump and robbed naked."

The small man disappeared.

Jim thought to ignore this strange twist of events realizing he must have been hallucinating.

The hallucination suddenly reappeared, this time leaning with his back against the passenger door, his hands folded behind his head, his legs crossed. He said, *"Won't do no good to ignore this strange twist of events, Jim."*

Jim said thickly and with a slur, "Hey, you're awful short, even for a midget."

"Like I said, I ain't a midget. I'm one of your angels, a cherub. We all drew straws to see who would come, and I lost."

"That so? Well what'd you have to come for then?"

"Not that we think you'll take heed, but we're obligated to remind you of your responsibilities as fair warning of what might happen right around that bend over yonder way." The tiny man pointed in an ambiguous direction and when he did Jim thought he glimpsed something feathery behind his back, just under the pointing arm.

"I ain't sure what you're talking about. I look to my responsibilities."

"Do you now? What about your family, your girls?"

"Well, they's girls. Ollie tends to 'em the most. Besides, the dad-blamed farm ain't hardly feeding us, so I got to think of other things to put in the pot."

"And a commendable job you do, Jim King, but you also run and hide behind your vices. Them girls don't need that, not after what happened."

"That's something I don't figure on discussing with the likes of you. You ain't real, no how. And besides, I'm just their grand-pappy."

"They call you Papa."

"Their real daddy run off after my daughter Ruth left us."

"That he did," said the angel. *"He went back to Belgium out of duty and he won't be coming back. Hitler's done seen to that."*

Jim recalled the letter addressed to Ollie six weeks ago. Since the United States was not yet involved in the war, Belgium soldiers had assisted in the evacuation of an enormous amount of Americans. An American Colonel had met the girls' father who was fighting for Belgium, his country of birth. Lawrence Bonet had asked that the Colonel get word to his children that he was okay. In May, the Nazis overran the tiny nation. The Colonel's contacts in Brussels reported Lawrence missing. The Colonel waited, but after a few months decided to send the letter. Ollie and Jim chose not to mention it to the girls, since only the eldest of the three remembered their father.

"This is stuff I try not to think on very hard," said Jim.

"You try not to think on it at all, Jim King. That's the problem. With their mother Ruth gone and their daddy not coming back, they need both Ollie and you. You, Jim King. They need you. They don't get you and your guidance, such as it is even when you're sober, then you ain't no use to nobody."

"What's that mean?"

"Means just that. And you might as well be removed from the picture. Then Ollie can find a man who pays attention, somebody like Roger Winston. That's why them thieves is laying in wait down the road with knives and clubs. They might not strike today and if they don't you still got time to change your ways. But if you don't, strike they will."

The cherub disappeared with a pop, but his voice hovered a moment longer. *"Choice is yours King Jim. Choice is yours..."*

* * *

Jim awoke and noticed the darkness. He quickly took stock; his clothes, his money, his gifts remained. He'd been dreaming. Apparently, no highwaymen skulked nearby. Oddly, he found no bottles or flasks. He reasoned he tossed them, probably in anger after discovering they were empty. Still, he wasn't so sure.

He had been out for hours. He dug his watch out of his pocket. It was almost nine. He strained to think, and concluded it was probably around noon when he struck the tree with his car. He understood also, that he was sober, though his head ached and his stomach hurt. He noticed the steering wheel of the car had cracked, as did the windshield. He felt for damage and found a couple of small knots on his forehead.

Jim reflected, it felt nice to be clear minded. It had been some months since his thoughts came so logically. Hardly an hour went by that he didn't swill moonshine. He'd wake three or four times a night to maintain the relief. He had never been a drunk. In fact, before things went bad, he didn't drink at all. He'd always worked hard and made his Sunday meetings on time. The Reverend Thorne even asked him to be a deacon. But when Ruth left, he went to see Jake and hadn't been without the special brew since.

He checked himself further for cuts and bruises and broken bones and found none. He noticed a nasty dent in the front of the Model-T and missing bark from the tree, a strange double-trunk Live Oak.

Miraculously, the old car started and he was soon on his way, thinking mostly about the dream. The words of the little fellow disturbed him, but Jim found the courage to dwell upon the meaning, to attempt to understand the message. In so doing, it took him back two years to the time when his daughter Ruth left them.

The White Plague, known also as Tuberculosis by the doctors, took its toll only a week after the quarantine. Watching her taken away as Helen and Elaine – Bobbi was an infant - screamed and cried was his most difficult day, his darkest hour. He knew, like most all the others, she would not return.

The Model-T clacked and clicked, squeaked and squawked in the cold December night until Jim recognized the silhouette of the two Maple trees his great-grandfather planted on each side of the dirt road that led to the family farm. With relief he made the turn, suddenly feeling uplifted that he was finally sober, that his mind was fresh and that he was almost home, bearing unexpected gifts.

* * *

A short time later, food inside him, Jim stood in his country bungalow. He felt warm and clean, the radio produced soft tones of a Christmas melody. The fire needed wood and Jim needed a cigar. He wrapped himself to go outside as he looked at Ollie. She'd been reading her Bible, probably the Christmas Story from Luke, her favorite. Bobbi played on the rug in a pajama robe with bright green booties. She batted at her new teddy bear. Elaine sat in Ollie's lap in a red Christmas gown, her hair in pigtails tied with purple ribbons. Helen stood beside the chair in her Christmas pajamas, too. She handed Ollie a hymnal and then smiled at Jim with sparkling green eyes.

Ollie and the girls had cut a tree yesterday and now it wore scant but bright decorations. As soon as Jim arrived home, Ollie forced him into the attic to retrieve them. There, mementos of Ruth confronted him. Her things, even her scent inhabited the area as if she'd only just left to go on a hayride with a favorite beau. The power of those moments, as he stood alone in melancholy reflection left him weak in body; he instinctively looked for some hidden stock supplied by Jake, but Ollie had long since used it as firestarter.

Jim pulled a fresh cigar from the King Edward box. He grabbed a match, but Ollie gave a look, waved a hand and pointed outside.

Elaine noticed and pouted, "Papa, please come back soon."

"Don't worry sweetheart, I'm just gonna have a smoke."

"Can you hear us if we sing?" she asked.

"I reckon I can. I like my girls to sing."

He stepped outside onto the porch. He smiled at the snow. The last it snowed on Christmas Eve into Christmas Day, Ruth was only ten years old. He recalled they stood together to watch it; Ruth raised her face to the sky, to the falling flakes, and blessed their approach with her wondrous beauty. His mind's eye presented him the image of his girls around the fire, just before he had walked outside. In each he saw their mother. Each held a part of a look that belonged to Ruth. Each had some of her gestures, her expressions; each reminded him of Ruth in her own, unique way.

It had been two years. At times, it was two long years. Tonight, it was only two years. And tonight was one of those rarely given, a night where the heart could be heavy, but joyful, too. Jim stepped off the porch and into the falling snow. The old Model-T was completely covered. A soft white blanket grew quietly across his land. He heard Ollie and the girls begin to sing:

"Oh, holy night, the stars are brightly shining. It is the night of our dear Savior's birth"

Jim looked up to see the stars, but couldn't. He felt only the wispy passing of snowflakes falling. He closed his eyes. They touched him with grace.

He thought again of Ruth, his daughter gone, as the song and sounds of the loving, living gifts she left behind surrounded him.

He wished he knew how to grieve. All he did, it seemed, was run to June, to Jake, to the dice-hall, to the hogs and hens and away from his responsibilities, away from Ruth. But now, he realized that on this night, he could feel again the closeness of their past.

He prayed for the return of memories, long pushed aside. Now, he needed once again to see how she looked, to feel how she was. Christmas Eve ticked over to Christmas morning as he recalled the days of his only daughter.

"Here comes my heart, Daddy," she would always say.

Here comes my heart, Ruth, Jim King told her silently.

"Please touch it once again," said he, aloud.

Ollie and the girls sang on:

"Fall on your knees, Oh, hear the angel's voices. Oh, night divine. Oh, night that Christ was born."

He fell to his knees in the night and he listened. They listened, he and Ruth, to their angels' voices sing:

"Oh, night divine. Oh, night that Christ was born."

It was Christmas, 1940 and King Jim, he who was wily as a fox, he who had the look of the wolf, forever ceased his run. With precious memories restored, he began to cry.

To finally cry.

* * *

"Papa why does that man talk so funny to Miss Hattie Jo?"

"Why, darlin' he comes from another place. He comes from up north." King Jim smiled at Elaine. She sat in the chair next to him and counted the black checkers Jim had removed from Oscar Figtoe's side of the board.

"You mean he's a Yankee? I never seen a Yankee before."

"Yeah, I guess Roger is at that, but he ain't so bad a feller."

"Hattie Jo don't like him."

"She'll get used to him. It just takes awhile for us back-roads folk to cotton to new faces is all."

The door of the general store swung open, not an unusual event at Hattie Jo's, but on this occasion an unusual visitor stood in the light of the sunny winter's day.

"Well if ain't the High Sheriff himself," said Jim as he nodded in the direction of the visitor, an extremely tall, uniformed man with a shiny badge and an even shinier gold tooth.

"King Jim, I might have guessed you'd be here at the checker tables," said the Sheriff of Pulaski County, the largest county in Arkansas and a man that had known Jim since their days together during the Great War.

Jim stood and with a smile grasped the hand of his old friend, "Gene Garrison, I guess it's been more than a handful of years since you been to Redfield. What on earth brings you this way?"

"I come to fetch Hattie Jo to court."

Jim lost his smile and glanced at Hattie Jo, who without expression put on a shawl.

Sheriff Garrison reassured everyone in the store. "Hattie was on her way to Little Rock right about noon on Christmas Eve. Had to visit her parole officer one last time. She ran into four of the most vile creatures you ever saw out on Double Oak Bend. Why, they actually thought that the four of them with knives and clubs could do her in. Had to be strangers, thinkin' something like that.

Couldn't a known her. She laid 'em out one by one. Now, they's out of the hospital, so it's time to get on with the trial. I reckon Hattie Jo remembers what they look like, so they'll be down at the prison farm by nightfall."

For once, Jim had nothing to say. He glanced at Hattie Jo, who busied herself with one last wipe of the counter. She remained expressionless.

Elaine tugged at Jim's sleeve, "Papa, Mr. Oscar just jumped your last checker."

Jim pretended to regain his focus on the game, a focus that, in reality, was never diverted. He looked at the board in feigned surprise.

"Why he sure did. I'll be. Oscar done won a game from me."

Oscar motioned for everyone to come over and have a look. He said, "I told you I'd get one in on you one of these days, King Jim. And it couldn't come at a better time. Now, where's them mules of yours? I guess I've won 'em fair and square."

"Ain't mine anymore, Oscar. They're hitched right outside."

"What're their names, Jim?"

Jim chuckled, took Elaine by the hand, nodded at Sheriff Garrison and walked out the door. As he eased the door shut, he looked back at Hattie Jo who provided him a rare and beaming smile.

✄

A Freckled Face of Fear

by D.R. Smith

Most everyone in Orin Falls, a sleepy little village in southern Maine drudged through the sultry summer afternoon as towering thunder clouds on the horizon promised relief from the heat.

Young Derek was an exception. Despite the stifling humidity, the high-spirited seven-year-old was charged with energy, anxious to go exploring after lunch. Daily safekeeping was entrusted to Grampa as both parents worked at a nearby egg farm; today, he tested the old gent's patience.

"Me and Davy can whup anything." Derek fancied himself as Crockett's sidekick, and parried Grampa's cautions of venturing too far into the forest beyond the marsh.

"Don't worry, Grampa, I'm a *real* trailblazer now that I got me a coonskin cap." He was immensely proud of his ring-tailed hat; a treasured find scavenged from a trash bin no matter how scruffy its condition.

Derek gulped the last of his milk and was ready for action. He grabbed trusty Ol' Betsy, once the shaft of Grampa's broken hoe, and was off to the marshland bordering their bungalow.

Since early summer, he had spent days in the slow-moving flowage, probing it foot by foot, learning passageways around rotting stumps, dead trees, mud bogs, and pockets of deeper water among islands of brush and razor-edged sword grasses.

A skinny, yet athletic lad shy of fifty pounds, he mastered the art of hopping atop floating grass clumps before sinking beneath tannin-stained waters— like a frog uses lily pads to avoid hungry bass lying in ambush below. Ol' Betsy came in handy for vaulting wider gaps between perches, as well as for dislodging five-foot black snakes or bad-tempered water adders coiled atop his landing areas.

He eventually blazed a serpentine trail across its breadth to solid ground where he had discovered a mammoth boulder left by glaciers eons ago. The rock was enormous to him, but erosion had notched a vertical crack enabling him to scale its height. He anointed the giant granite his throne— a towering citadel from where he could survey his kingdom, and from where he could always see his home above the cat-o-nine tails flanking the heath.

He had never ventured beyond this area before, though many times tempted by an alluring, dense wall of evergreens beyond the brushwood leading away from the swamp. But today was the day for adventure, and gaining nerve, he was ready to pioneer new territory.

Ol' Betsy did her job of parting brambles and clusters of young broadleaves sliding past his face. He trudged on, snaking his way through the undergrowth until breaking through and standing in awe of a vast grove of mature hardwoods and pines. A thick canopy prevented much sunlight from penetrating, allowing only scattered vegetation to sprout above its cushy layer of pine needles.

Derek hesitated; daring only to peer into the shaded interior. Wooed by wonderment, his curiosity fanned the embers of courage that drew him forth, despite recalling sinister storybook images he'd seen in *Hansel and Gretel* and *Alice in Wonderland*.

He crept deeper and deeper into the wood, every few yards glancing over his shoulder to confirm his bearing. The further he trekked, the more he imagined the huge conifers were watching him; scowling upon this strange little intruder.

The stillness seemed unearthly. There was no sound. No wind. No birds; not even a playful squirrel or chipmunk scampered about. A wood devoid of life, and noise muted by scores of bristled pine trees, seemed eerily strange.

It was scary enough standing within the spooky shadows of such imposing giants, but when heavy thunderclouds billowed closer, the sunlight was blocked, rendering the forest as near nightfall. Dark and dreary, the woods seemed to close in on him. He was convinced gnarled and scraggy oaks were inching closer, their crusty barks animated by evil faces secretly conspiring to snatch him up among twisted, boney branches.

His mettle stretched to its limit, he stopped; opting to challenge his bravado another day. But the moment he was about to retreat, a most unnerving wail iced the blood in his veins.

GREE-YOWLL! An earsplitting scream shattered the stillness. The deep-throated cry of a wild bobcat can castrate the burliest of men's moxie, *let alone* invade a young mind with terrifying images of becoming a meal. Forcing riveted feet to move, he dove for the shelter of an uprooted pine, cowering amongst its clod-covered roots like a captive hare.

GREE-YOWLL! A second bestial wail echoed from somewhere within the sunless wood. Its piercing howl sounded a *hundred* times more formidable than any mountain lions heard on TV westerns. His body trembled, not knowing if the soul-chilling growl came from over a mile away— or an adjacent tree. Adrenalin fueled his throbbing heart, his mind racing.

Should I run, or yell out? he wondered. *Maybe I could just will myself invisible;* he juggled options, real or imagined.

He squeezed Ol' Betsy tight, his rising fear thrusting him into momentary reality; regretting she was no longer a lethal flintlock, but only a stick. His eyes darted from tree to tree, desperate to detect any outline or movement. Worse, his heart pounded at the thought of locking onto a pair of slanted yellow eyes radiating from within the shadows.

Where he squatted, he felt more and more vulnerable; it was time to scoot. He focused on an entry point and bolted like a sprung greyhound toward the brush. His chest out and little legs a blur, Jessie Owens had nothing on this sliver of seven-year-old sprinting for the undergrowth. A few yards from the perimeter, he chanced a peek over his shoulder, fearing gnashing jaws were about to savage his butt before he could disappear into the foliage.

His head turned, the momentary blindness caused him to miss his target by a few feet, and charged headlong into a tangled growth of wild blackberries. Needle-sharp thorns snagged his clothing and gouged several wounds, but failed to slow him down. He thrashed through the brambles until spotting an escape hole, and dropping to his belly, slithered like a flattened mole under boughs of thorny vines to freedom.

He jumped to his feet and resumed his dash, seeking the safety of his rock. Only steps free of the briars, he ran face-first into a huge communal spider web; its sticky mass swallowed his face. He ran on, scooping gobs of clinging web from his eyes, paying no heed to half-dollar sized spiders skittering beneath his shirt.

Once atop his fortress, he scanned the path from which he came. Satisfied he was alone, he collapsed; exhausted from fright and overheating in the high humidity. He lay on his back, his tiny chest heaving as beads of sweat trickled over his face and body.

Ominous clouds rumbled. He'll need to head for shelter soon and sat up to assess damages. He nonchalantly flicked a bloodsucking tic from burrowing into his skin, and dabbed at coagulating blood covering several scratches. It was then he noticed his torn and soiled shirt, its condition spawning new fears of being punished praying it was still salvageable.

Oh yeah! He wriggled from eight-legged creatures crawling up and down his spine, trapped by sweaty fabric sticking to his back. He removed his shirt and set them free, giggling at the bulbous black-and-yellows scurrying across the granite. But, his entertainment soon vanished; panic once again gripped his freckled-face with fear.

My coonskin!

He patted his tussled hair, praying as if by magic it would suddenly reappear, but it was gone. He at first reasoned it had to be in the briar patch, or got knocked off at the spider web. Yet another, more dreaded possibility entered his mind— *maybe it fell off in that big bad wood.*

Fighting tears, he feared the loss of his most prized possession. He knew it was unlikely to ever find another, let alone expect his family's poverty to budget its replacement. A loud crack of thunder interrupted his thoughts. His cap must wait. He had no choice but to risk another expedition first chance he got, hoping he'd recover his fallen comrade no matter *where* it lay.

Heavy spits of rain felt cool against his skin. He looked homeward for reassurance and spotted Grampa on the stoop, yelling for him. A wave of Ol' Betsy sent the old gent back indoors, confident his "little whippersnapper" would beat the storm home.

Derek smiled, knowing only fifty yards as the crow flies were all that separated him from domestic comforts, though it required careful maneuvering through a snake-infested, mud-sucking quagmire filled with leeches, mosquitoes, and bone-crushing snapping turtles the size of wash tubs.

A flash of not too distant lightning brightened the sky as he leapt atop a floating tussock, and then tippy-toed the length of a fallen branch to where he could vault across a smelly mud hole in his sprightly trip across the mire.

A cool gust of wind leaned on the reed grasses as another jagged streak zapped an ill-fated target close by. But it didn't faze him; *nothing* did— now that he was back in his murky swamp where he felt comfortably safe.

Rhubarb Wine

by Harold Orville Kempka

Everett stepped through the kitchen door and kicked off his boots. He picked at the perspiration soaked tee shirt clinging to his muscular chest and back as he strode toward the refrigerator for a cold Corona. After spending the day mending fences on the eastern border of his twenty-acre, Temecula Valley ranch, he felt bone tired and energy drained.

He opened his beer, and took long drink, letting its tart blend of malt, hops, and lime soothe his parched throat. After pressing the blinking message light on the wall phone, he sorted several days of unopened mail piled up on the counter.

"Hey Ev, Jesse here," the first recording said. "Call me. There's a new band playing at the Rusty Horseshoe tonight, and Edie's got a friend who wants to meet you."

Aw Jesus, Jesse, give me a break, he thought. While Jesse had good intentions, Everett's blind date radar sensed an evening entertaining either an intelligent yet homely and shapeless woman, or a brain-dead bimbo with huge hooters and a great smile.

He'd dated little in the five years since Maria, his third wife, divorced him. She was a good woman, and he'd truly loved her, but her constant nagging and inability to put up with his hardened ways proved more than he could handle. Finding a woman to match her beauty and brains as well as put up with him had dropped to the bottom of his wish list.

Everett skipped through messages from a nearby Baptist church soliciting his attendance, and a wrong number spoken in some Asian tongue. The next message drew his attention.

"Everett, This is Ellen."

He smiled upon his hearing sister's voice. Ellen had moved to Minneapolis after graduating from high school, and married some hotshot insurance salesman Everett didn't like. Since then, they'd been so busy with their own lives they kept in touch but once or twice a year.

"Daddy's dying of cancer," she continued, "and the doctors don't think he'll live past the weekend. I know you two have had your differences, but you need to come home and make your peace with him. *Please?*"

The quiet desperation in her voice quelled anger that usually consumed him whenever his father's name was mentioned. His smile faded, and he stared out the window. Thoughts swirled through his mind like the dust devil whirling across the open field next to the house.

He hadn't seen or spoken to Buck, his old man, since Thanksgiving fifteen years earlier. Buck was drunk, a common occurrence then, and pushed Everett's mother over a coffee table. Everett remembered stepping toward his father and hitting him once, breaking his nose.

He stood with clenched fists over his father, who lay sprawled across the floor dazed and bleeding.

He remembered screaming, "You ever touch her again you son-of-a-bitch, and I'll kill you!"

Everett hugged his mother, and walked out. He hadn't been back or spoken to his father since. His only contact with the family besides Ellen was an occasional phone call to his mother.

Reluctantly, Everett called Jesse to cancel the blind date. He caught the three-hour red-eye flight to the Twin Cities, Minneapolis-St. Paul. For most of the flight he wrestled with the idea of reconciling the years of contempt he felt toward his father.

He stared through the plane's window, mesmerized by the jet's wing lights flashing against the darkened sky. By the time the plane touched down on the icy runway at seven-thirty the next morning, his eyes felt gritty, and his mouth dry and sticky.

He slung his overnight bag over his shoulder, and hurried across the parking lot to a waiting rental car shuttle. The temperature hovered just above zero with the wind chill notching fifteen below. The bitter cold burning his nostrils and numbing his ears was one more reminder of why he opted to settle in southern California.

A dreary, gunmetal sky hovered low over the city as Everett crossed the bridge spanning the Mississippi River. Ashen snowdrifts flanked the river road he followed into St. Paul before turning onto Summit Avenue, the one-time bastion of old money in the Twin Cities.

He slowly drove past the massive brick and stone mansions, eyeing their long and neatly plowed driveways and vast lawns dotted with Pine trees, Oaks, and Maples. He recalled how, in high school, he'd envied the Jewish kids living along the wide, tree-shaded boulevard whose fathers were doctors, bankers, or lawyers.

While his family wasn't poor, Buck worked construction, and they lived in a predominately Catholic, working class neighborhood near the railroad tracks linking the two cities.

Everett broke his thoughts and turned north until the street and buildings of his old neighborhood took on the familiar comfort of home. After all this time, nothing appeared to have changed and a twinge of nostalgia tumbled in his gut.

After leaving home, Everett joined the Navy and spent the next four years on submarine duty. Four years spent stationed at the naval shipyards in New England as well as San Diego had given him an entirely different perspective on the pursuit of wealth and respect.

After his discharge, he settled in Southern California, and became a surf bum for a couple of years. He worked at a head shop in the beach area, selling hippie clothes and drug paraphernalia over the counter and marijuana and peyote smuggled in from Mexico *under* it.

The drug profits proved lucrative, and he eventually bought the store as well as several beachfront, rental bungalows. A narrow escape from a DEA investigation convinced him real estate was a more amenable method for achieving the American dream. He sold the store, and bought the ranch in Temecula, semi-retiring with the income from his rental units.

Everett hadn't eaten since the previous evening. His stomach rumbled, and he turned into an old familiar haunt, the White Castle. With the exception of counter to ceiling bulletproof glass, the place had aged well and looked the same as when he used to stop by after a night of drinking and partying.

He flashed a reminiscent smile at the clerk, and ordered six of the tiny grilled and steamed hamburgers smothered in onions... *gut bombs* as he remembered them. They always tasted great, but would either settle in the stomach like bricks, or would wreak havoc on his intestinal tract for a day afterward.

Everett then drove to his parents' house and pulled alongside the curb. The red brick bungalow resembled most of the others along the tree-shaded street. All were built of either brick or wood siding painted in faded whites, grays, or dusty blues, and had small yards encircled by wire fences. Other than being smaller than he remembered, they looked pretty much the same as when he left.

Stately Elms and Maples, now barren of foliage for the winter, lined the street. Their crooked, skeletal limbs arched over the street. Everett remembered raking carpets of ginger, scarlet, and russet leaves into huge piles once summer surrendered to the mustiness of fall.

After carrying them behind the house, his father would burn them. It was one of the few times Everett remembered working together with the old man, despite his father's bitching about the sloppy raking job.

Everett stepped over the snow piled against the curb. A thin layer of snow and ice covering the slippery sidewalk crunched beneath his feet at each step. He couldn't count the number of times he'd shoveled that walk as a kid, only to have his father complain he hadn't completely scraped away all the snow.

His mom answered the door, stooping slightly and looking pale and drawn. The last time she saw Everett was shortly after his discharge from the Navy, when he had a full beard and shaggy mop of hair down to his shoulders. She didn't recognize him with his hair neatly trimmed and parted to one side.

"May I help you, young man?" she asked matter-of-factly.

"Hi, Mom."

She took a step back, and gasped, "Oh, my god. Everett!"

Then, she hugged him tightly, and an 'everything is going to be okay feeling surged through his body. Her once shining, autumn brown hair had turned mousy gray, but still emitted the same Lilac scent he remembered while he was growing up. He couldn't help but notice how small and fragile she felt in his chiseled arms, almost like she would blow away in the slightest breeze.

"When did you get here?"

"I flew in this morning, and drove straight here from the airport," he said, not wanting to elaborate on his hesitance about coming home.

She shivered, and tugged on his arm. "B-r-r-r, it's freezing out here. Come in before you catch your death. I made some coffee."

"Sounds good, mom."

"Let me get you a little lunch," she said, leading him toward the kitchen table.

"Nah, don't bother. I stopped and got a bite on the way here," he said, knowing her idea of a little lunch was a four-course meal.

He sat at the end of the table, in the same chair from where his father once ruled holiday meals. The kitchen light reflected off the table's polished cherry wood. His mom poured them each a cup and sat across the table from him.

The warm aroma of toast and coffee filled his nostrils. Everett thought of the time he said 'oh hell' after spilling his milk at dinner.

The old man's beefy hand swatted him in the head so hard it knocked him off his chair.

"Are you going to the hospital to see your father? He asked about you."

"Yeah, I'll get around to it," Everett said, figuring the only reason the old man would ask about him was because he wanted something to bitch about. "I wanted to make sure you were all right, first."

"Me? Oh, don't fuss over me. I'm fine," she said. "But, you should really go and see him."

"In a little while. Want to go with me?"

"Not now. I spent most of the night there and need to get some rest."

"Okay, but how about if I come back later and pick you up. We'll get something to eat before we go."

"Oh, we'll see, honey," she said, sounding tired.

It was after five PM when Everett arrived at the Northern Pacific Hospital. The gargantuan brick building had been built at the turn of the century by a philanthropic railroad tycoon, probably feeling remorseful after raping the city of its prime land. When Everett was nine, his dad had brought him here to the emergency room after he broke his wrist falling from a tree.

"You're lucky it was only your wrist and not your neck," his father said. "And dammit, look what you did to the tree."

Something always seemed more important to his old man than Everett, and that time the broken tree branch was more important than his wrist.

Everett stepped off the elevator. His footsteps echoed through the tiled corridor as he walked toward the Intensive Care Unit. He stopped at a large window, and stared down at the parking lot to gather his thoughts.

Night had fallen, yet the snow still sparkled like glitter under the parking lot's street lamps. In the distance, he could see the flickering lights of the state capitol and St. Paul's skyline spotlighted against the darkened December sky. Several cars dotted the lot, tucked beneath a blanket of freshly fallen snow like memories frozen in time.

Why the hell did I even come here, Everett wondered. *The old man probably won't give a damn anyway, despite what Mom said. Hell, he probably didn't even ask for me.*

He corralled his thoughts and continued down the corridor into ICU. A whirring sound and intermittent blips of life support monitors broke an otherwise, eerie silence in the dimly lit room.

A Filipino nurse wearing surgical scrubs sat behind a long counter. She glanced up from her computer monitor, frowning as though Everett had interrupted her.

"May I help you, sir?"

"I'm looking for Buck Baxter's bed."

"Are you family?"

"I'm his son. I just flew in from California."

Everett jaw muscles twitched as he resisted the urge to tell her it was none of her damn business.

"Well, visiting hours are over until seven PM, but since you're here, I'll let you see him, but only for a moment."

"That would be nice. Thanks."

He followed her to a corner cubicle, and gingerly stepped around the privacy curtain. At first glance, Everett momentarily wondered if she'd brought him to the wrong bed. He wasn't sure what he'd expected to see, but his father looked nothing like the man he once remembered. The strapping steelworker, with tanned muscular arms and callused hands square as anvils, was now a shriveled little man tucked neatly beneath the clean, crisp bedding.

The only recognizable feature was the old man's nose, which angled sharply toward one side of his face. His pasty skin resembled a wax candy bottle drained of its colored contents. Thoughts of lashing out to relieve the anger held within for so long vanished, were replaced by the soaring emotions of seeing his father so fragile and helpless.

Everett leaned over, and gently stroked his father's disheveled hair, now thin as wind-blown corn silk.

"Hi, Pop," Everett softly intoned. "How are you feeling?"

Buck groggily opened his eyes, and glanced up at Everett, struggling to focus through the Demerol haze. His eyes, the color of rusted rivets, were sunk deeply within their sockets. They darted side to side like a captive hare upon hearing Everett's voice.

"Everett?" He whispered. "It's good to see you son."

Buck managed a weak smile, and Everett gently squeezed his father's frail hand. His father used to grab his arms with those once-powerful hands and swing him around the back yard like an airplane. When he was eight, he cried after dislocating his shoulder and his dad calmly popped it back into its socket.

"Quit acting like a crybaby, boy," the old man had grumbled as he massaged Everett's shoulder. "Don't be a sissy. It doesn't hurt that bad."

Everett's harsh memories of never measuring up to dad's approval faded. The thoughts of criticism and ridicule seemed moot; like the time he beamed with pride over how well he played after his little league team won the championship. His father merely pulled his ball cap over his eyes, and chastised him for dropping one fly ball that nearly cost his team the game.

Buck moaned intermittently from the pain. Bruises and liver spots dotted his pallid skin like mud splatters. The Prostate cancer had eaten away at him and spread throughout his once rock-solid body.

Wires attached to his father's body sent erratic green lines bouncing across the monitor. A steady hiss emanated from the oxygen tube looped over his ears and under his nose, and an ugly bruise surrounded the intravenous morphine needle taped to the back of his hand.

"Water. Get me some water," Buck whispered through parched lips.

He pointed a shaky finger toward the tray next to his bed. Everett poured water from a pink plastic pitcher into a foam cup, and bent the straw.

"Sure Pop. They taking good care of you here?"

Everett lowered the straw to his father's lips, expecting the old man to moan about how he was neglected. Instead, his father nodded approvingly and sipped from the straw.

Water suddenly spurted from his father's mouth, and trickled down his cheek. Buck began to choke and his body went rigid. Everett lifted his father's head, unsure of how to clear his throat.

"Nurse! Can I get some help here?"

By the time the nurse stepped around the curtain, Buck had managed to clear his throat and was breathing normally. He gave Everett a weak smile, and calmly patted his son's hand. Everett stepped aside to give the nurse room.

As she leaned in closer to check the monitor and adjust the IV, he admired the creamy softness of her skin, and her thick auburn hair coiled in long, crinkly ringlets.

Jesus sweetheart, you look too young to be a nurse, Everett thought.

"How are we doing today, Mr. Baxter?" she asked. Her voice was pleasant and buoyant, yet professionally rhetorical.

"I want to go home," Buck rasped, wincing in pain.

"Well, we'll just have to make you more comfortable then, won't we?"

She adjusted his IV drip, and fluffed Buck's pillow. The nurse glanced up at Everett, and flashed a mischievous smile. Everett noticed the attractive dimples taking shape beneath her sparkling, jade-colored eyes. He glanced at her ring finger, pleased it was barren of any gold, and thought he might risk flirting with her later on.

"You must be Everett. Your father has told me all about you. He says you're a rancher out in California."

Everett's cheeks flushed.

"Well, I'm really just a cowpuncher who spends a lot of time mending fences. Don't believe all the lies he's told you."

"Quite the contrary. He is awfully proud of you," she said.

She disappeared around the curtain, and Everett glanced down at his father. He didn't see him as the same SOB who drank beer, constantly complained, and used to belittle Everett and slap him around.

"The Vikings won again today, pop," Everett said, trying to sound upbeat. "They kicked the hell out of Green Bay... 27-21."

"Ha," his father popped in a shrill voice. "Remember when you were twelve and we went to that game against the Rams? We had a lot of fun, didn't we?"

"Yeah we did, pop," Everett replied, remembering a slightly different version.

His mother used to demand they attend church as a family every Sunday. His father became an church usher to appease her and give the appearance they were a good, Christian family.

Once, a co-usher invited Everett and his father to go to a Vikings game after church. Buck declined at first, using the excuse that Everett probably would not likely sit still that long. The man insisted, and Buck finally relented.

Everett could still see the scowl on his father's face when Buck's friend patiently explained the referee's calls during the game.

Everett's sister, Ellen quietly stepped around the privacy curtain, interrupting his thoughts.

"Hey, big brother, I'm so glad you came," she said quietly, and squeezed his arm.

"Hey sis," Everett said, embracing her.

"How's he doing?"

"He's still feeling a lot of pain, but it looks like they've got him pretty doped up."

Ellen leaned down, and kissed her father's pale cheek.

"Hi, daddy."

The faint aroma of *Old Spice*, the only aftershave Buck had ever worn, emanated from his scratchy white whiskers. When Ellen was little, Buck would lift her in the air after he finished shaving, and nuzzle her neck making her giggle. Then, he'd dance around the bathroom holding her in his arms, and sing the Old Spice jingle.

Buck squeezed Ellen's hand, and motioned for the two of them to come closer.

"When I'm gone, you two take good care of your mother," he whispered.

His father reached up, and lightly stroked Everett's cheek. Everett's throat began to constrict as stabbing pangs of emotion welled up inside him. He cleared his throat, and fought them back.

"Hey pop, you're a tough S-O-B. You've got a long way to go yet."

"When you were little, son, you reminded me so much of me. Didn't want you to make the mistakes I did. I want you to know, I'm sorry I was so hard on you."

Buck's already-drooping eyes closed, and he drifted off to sleep. Ellen looped her arm through Everett's.

"C'mon, let's go grab a smoke."

They walked to the waiting room. Ellen lit a long, slim cigarette, and blew a smoke ring toward the ceiling. She watched it expand and dissolve into a haze.

"Where's mom?"

"At home, resting. I guess she was here most of the night. When I got to the house, she looked pretty exhausted, so I told her I'd pick her up later. Where's that shit-for-brains husband of yours?"

"C'mon be nice," she said, blowing another smoke ring toward the ceiling. "He had company bigwigs in town for a meeting. He said he might come over this weekend."

"Oh, lucky us," Everett scoffed.

Ellen elbowed Everett in the ribs, and he flinched.

"C'mon Ev, Barry's good to me. You should be happy for me."

"I am, sis. I'm just yanking your chain. But, Barry's always been such an arrogant bastard and it irritates me."

"Ev, He's not arrogant. He works hard, and is proud to be successful in a difficult business."

Everett shrugged. "If you say so."

Ellen tamped out her cigarette, and lit another.

"Hey," she said. "Remember the night we stole a couple bottles of rhubarb wine dad used to make during the summer?"

Everett stared out the window, smiling slightly.

"Yeah, I remember. I was what, fifteen? And you twelve?"

"Yep, and we puked our guts out," Ellen continued. "I haven't tasted rhubarb wine since."

"Me neither." Everett said, remembering its pinkish hue and bittersweet taste. "But, the old man sure could make good wine, couldn't he?"

For the next hour they reflected on their childhood, and caught up on each other's lives. Ellen and Barry had recently moved into a new home along the shore of White Bear Lake. Everett described the improvements made to the ranch.

"Hey, why not dump shithead for a week, and come out and visit?" Everett baited, knowing he'd get a rise out of Ellen.

"Everett, Barry's not a shithead. Give him a chance. If you got to know him you'd like him."

"I doubt it," Everett said. "But to please you, he can come to. How about that? And I promise not to call him a shithead to his face." Ellen smirked, and playfully pushed Everett into the wall.

"You're such an ass sometimes Everett, you know that?"

"That's what big brothers are for," he replied, laughing.

"C'mon, let's go back and see daddy."

She put her arm around him, and led him back toward ICU.

"He really does love you, you know."

Everett shrugged uneasily, not quite sure how to respond. Here he was, forty years old, and unable to remember his father ever telling him he loved him... or was proud of him. His throat tightened again, and his lower lip quivered slightly.

"Just a sec," I've got to take a leak."

Everett stepped into the corridor bathroom, and shut the door. He fought back tears that seemed to flow from nowhere. "Dammit, Everett," he mumbled.

You need to be strong. That's what the old man has always wanted. He took several deep breaths, and rinsed his eyes and face before rejoining Ellen.

Midway between the waiting room and ICU, a voice on the hall intercom announced, "Code Blue in ICU. I repeat, Code blue in ICU." Several nurses and doctors rushed past.

"Shit, I wonder if it's daddy," Ellen said.

They hurried down the hall. The Auburn-haired nurse Everett spoke to earlier met them at the door.

"What's going on?" Everett asked.

"Your father has had some complications. The doctors are tending to him."

Ellen gripped Everett's arm tightly.

"Is he all right?" Ellen asked with trepidation in her voice.

The nurse smiled reassuringly, and touched Ellen's arm.

"I'm sure everything will be fine. We're doing all we can. Why don't you go back to the waiting room and wait for the doctor?"

Ellen leaned on Everett as they slowly walked back to the waiting room. She curled up in an overstuffed chair, and began to cry. She buried her face in the cushion. Everett let her be, lit a cigarette, and stared out the window.

You can't die pop. Not yet, he thought. He knew he'd have to go get their mom, but decided to wait until he spoke to the doctor. An hour later, his father's doctor entered the waiting room accompanied by the hospital priest.

"I'm sorry," the doctor said. "We did all we could, but your father's body couldn't take the pain anymore."

Everett hugged Ellen, fighting back his own tears. She buried her face in his chest, and sobbed.

"Can we go in and see him?" Ellen said after several minutes.

"As soon as we move him to an empty room," the doctor said, "you can spend as much time as you feel you need."

Everett turned to the priest. "Father, I have to leave, and pick up our mom. Would you stay with Ellen until I get back?"

"Certainly, son. But first, why don't we say a prayer for your father," the priest said.

Everett stood with his hands folded as the priest and his sister prayed. He hadn't even been inside a church in the last twenty years, let alone pray. *What good would prayer do me now?*

As Everett drove to pick up their mom, he began sobbing, and pulled over. When he was ready to drive on, he felt as though an incredibly heavy weight had lifted from his shoulders.

Everett broke the news to his mother, and held her while she wept. She felt small and helpless in his arms, and he wondered how she put up with his father for all those years. She wiped her tears, and nervously laughed.

"I thought I was prepared for this."

Everett stroked his mother's hair.

"Why don't you get ready, mom, and I'll take you to the hospital."

The wooden stairs creaked as she made her way upstairs. Everett walked into the darkened living room, and sat in the old man's favorite chair. It smelled of *Cherry Blend*, his father's favorite pipe tobacco. The living room looked the same as the day Everett had left; knick-knacks, books, and his mother's usual clutter of magazines gave it a warm, homey atmosphere.

As he gazed around the room, Everett could almost hear his father's raucous laugh that used to fill the house whenever he won playing cribbage at Christmas.

Jesus, Everett thought. *Even when he isn't here, he's here.*

Shadows cast an eerie pall across the hospital entrance by the time Everett and his mom returned to the hospital. Ellen was asleep, curled up in the overstuffed chair sleeping when he and his mother entered the waiting room. They woke her, and she led them to the somber, dimly lit standby room.

Buck lay tucked into a freshly made bed, and appeared to be in a deep sleep. His head was tilted back and his jaw slacked open. He seemed so at peace, Everett almost expected him to begin snoring.

Everett stood beside the bed, while Ellen and his mother were at its foot. He gently lifted his father's thin lifeless hand. It felt soft, yet cold and waxy.

He held the grip for a moment as if waiting for his Father to squeeze back. He then removed his father's wedding band, and handing it to his mother.

"I don't think he'd mind if you took this back. He always bitched about catching it on something, and I'd hate for him to bitch about catching it on the pearly gates."

Ellen and her mom smiled in acceptance of Everett making light of the moment. They remained at Buck's bedside for nearly an hour, making small talk about some of the silly things their father used to do. Everett remained behind after Ellen and his mother returned to the waiting room.

Everett lightly stroked his father's cheek. "Well pop, we've certainly had our problems. I know I've hated you for some of the things you said and did."

His lower lip quivered rapidly and tears streaked his cheeks, "But, I guess I've always loved you too. I'm glad you're not suffering any longer."

Later that night, after their mother had gone to bed, Everett and Ellen sat in the living room discussing funeral arrangements. Ellen suddenly excused herself, and left the room. She returned moments later holding a dusty bottle and two glasses. She waved the bottle high as if it were a trophy.

"Look what I found in the cellar."

"Ah, geez," Everett rolled his eyes. "Don't tell me. That dreaded rhubarb wine, right?"

She smiled and shook her head approvingly.

"I should have known he'd have some hidden somewhere. Probably for an occasion just like this."

Ellen poured them each a glass, singing, "Chug-a-lug, chug-a-lug," mimicking Roger Miller.

Everett raised his glass, and joined in, "Makes you want to holler hi-di-ho."

He touched her glass against his and they harmonized, "burns your tummy don'tcha know, chug-a-lug chug-a-lug."

They burst into laughter and hugged each other. After a few minutes, Ellen raised her glass.

"Here's to Dad, except this time, we don't get sick, right?"

Everett smiled lovingly at Ellen, and replied, "To Dad."

They toasted, and he took a long, slow drink, engulfed by warmth he hadn't felt in years.

&⌀

A Kiss from Alex

by D.R.Smith

Anita was rinsing the last of her dinner dishes when a strong scent of evergreen wafted through the screened window above her sink. She closed her eyes to savor its richness, when suddenly, *something* spiked her senses— *something* she couldn't quite put her finger on but it made her tummy tingle. *Ah, I'm being silly.*

She smiled and dismissed the sensation as pure complaisance, pleased her husband had enjoyed his favorite meal, trying to comfort Butch since the tragic loss of his lifelong friend the week before.

Alex was killed when overheated brakes failed to slow his old logging truck as it descended a steep downgrade. Heavy with timber, it toppled into a deep ravine near the base of Mt. Washington, the flagship of New Hampshire's White Mountains. It was a sorrowful day in Bretton Woods. Anyone who knew the jovial Alex was touched by his loss, especially Butch who was Alex's inseparable friend for years.

Anita joined him in the den and noticed he seemed restless and unable to get comfortable. On such balmy weekend nights as this, he and Alex used to run their hounds hunting raccoons for pelts. She had been sensitive to his troublesome time grieving Alex's death, but his fidgeting began to annoy her. She sighed, and noted the delightful summer night; its deep violet sky set aglow by the moon about to poke its nose above the rugged horizon.

"It's such a lovely evening, darling; why not take the dogs out? I know it won't be the same without Alex, but it's been a month since you last exercised them. Maybe a little hunting will do you all some good. Pepper could use the experience, too." She appealed to his sentiments for breaking in his new yearling with the older dogs.

Pepper was Butch's pride and joy. The handsome Bluetick was a birthday gift from Alex four months ago, and aptly named for the bountiful markings spattering its coat. Butch warmed to her idea though he vacillated between romping in the woods, or catching the Amos and Andy Show on the Philco. *Maybe Nita's right.*

He kissed her temple and gave her a gentle hug. She smiled and offered to get his boots while he retrieved his pistol and flashlight from a corner cupboard. Anita followed him onto the veranda and watched him cross the yard toward the kennel, happy to see him more perky. Moments later, Butch returned with four tethered hounds eager to burn off pent up energy.

"There's no sense driving anywhere special tonight, hon; plenty o' coon in there." Butch gestured toward wooded acreage bordering a boggy lowland where Anita often strolled to gather hickory nuts and blueberries. He petted the playful youngster's flanks. "Besides, it's mostly for training young Pepper here, anyway; ain't that right, li'l fella."

She bid him luck and watched the troupe cross a two-acre hayfield before Butch turned the hounds loose at the perimeter. Within seconds they vanished, her peace lulled by the bawling hounds growing faint as they ran deeper into the woods.

Anita lingered outside to enjoy the rural solitude in the warm night air. As she swayed on the porch swing, her eyes were drawn to an especially crystalline sky. She marveled at the density of brilliant star clusters, and humbled by the celestial vastness, she sensed the resplendent clarity was somehow— *different* tonight.

Anita returned to her den and settled comfortably in her rocker to crochet. She was enjoying a Red Skelton broadcast when a flicker of motion caught the corner of her eye. Curious, she parted the window sheers and was shocked to see the silhouette of her husband running toward the house.

Anita jumped to her feet. Butch bounded the steps and nearly knocked her aside pushing through the doorway. She followed him into the kitchen.

"What on earth? What's *wrong*, Butch? Where are the dogs— your precious Pepper?"

Butch ignored her, and gasping for breath, stood bracing himself against the kitchen table. Anita placed an arm around his waist to soothe him, concerned as she guided him into a chair.

"What happened out there, Butch?" She picked a couple pine needles from his hair and noticed his muddy clothes, the loosened flap of his holster, its pistol gone.

"And where are your Wellies?" She pointed at his feet absent of green slip-ons; a sock on one foot, the other bare. He looked at her with wide, frenzied eyes.

"Come on, damn it! Say something. Are you alright? Did you surprise a bear or something?" Anita was getting edgy.

"In a minute," he grunted, and drew a sleeve across a sweaty brow. He popped from his chair, fetched a bottle of bourbon from the cupboard, and grabbed a tumbler from the dish basket.

Butch was visibly shaken as he poured a jigger of whiskey, inhaled it, and poured another. Anita slid her chair closer to the corner of the table, and placed her hands atop his forearm.

"*Please*, honey, what the devil is going on? You're scaring me."

"I'm scaring *you*?" He leaned closer and peered into her eyes. "Let me ask *you* something; do you believe in weird stuff like spirits? Well I sure as hell do— *now*," he said, not waiting for an answer. "I ain't never seen nothin' like it."

Seated on the edge of her chair, she listened closely as Butch explained how he and Alex used to have a set routine. After releasing the hounds, they'd follow until the pitch of yowls changed, signaling the dogs had treed a raccoon.

"That's when we'd hustle in for the kill. Since Alex was old and fat, he'd hold back the hounds while I climbed the tree for a clear shot. If we had dead ones already, Alex had this crazy habit of laying 'em out side-by-side instead of just dropping them in a pile; sort of in a neat row— like *this*," he gestured with his hands.

"Well, tonight, I had two coons by the time I reached your blueberry patch. I was feeling pretty tired and was about to call it quits when the hounds treed a third deeper in the bog, so I followed.

"Traipsin' through that spongy, summer-dried swamp was spooky, Nita. It was dead quiet with this dense, ground-hugging fog glowing with an eerie sheen in the moonlight; swirling like you see in them werewolf flicks.

"I snapped the hounds to their leashes and tied them to a sapling out of reach of my kills. The dang coon was up near the top of a big walnut, and hard to spot out on a limb. I climbed, and once in position, shot the coon and watched it tumble through the outer branches. I was so focused on getting down, I didn't notice the dogs weren't barkin'. But when I hit the ground, I glanced toward them and *that's* when I froze."

He raised his hand in oath. "So help me, Nita, th-there they were— one, two, *three* dead coons." Butch described them, stroking his finger on the table.

"All three laid out in a row and only a yard from the dogs— *just* like Alex used to do." He glanced at her face for a sign of belief, his eyes moist with emotion.

"And the dogs just layin' stone-still on their bellies; the back of their necks bristled and tails tucked 'tween their legs just starin' at them coons. Even young Pepper didn't budge. It was like they were trying to tell me *something* was there with us— real close." He tossed down his whiskey and paused to wipe a tear from his eye.

"I sensed it, too; kind of a tenseness— like how a big cat gets about to ambush prey. It gave me the willies. I drew my pistol and listened for a crunch of moss, a twig to snap; *anything*. But there was no sound, not even a cricket chirping."

In reenactment, Butch slowly swept an imagined beam of light around the kitchen as if probing the darkened corners of the swamp. "But I couldn't see a damned thing, hon."

"'Alex?' I whispered, and pointed my flashlight at the shadows. 'Alex? Are you out there?' Still, there was nothin', honey; nothin' but this heavy silence hanging in the air."

Goose-bumps dotted his forearms as he relived the jittery feeling that *something* was lurking in that creepy fog roiling around him. Butch narrowed his focus, and again slowly swung his phantom beam about the kitchen.

"*Alex!*" he barked, jolting Anita upright.

"I gotta tell ya, hon, my knees felt weak and I was losin' it. I couldn't move and just stood there like a dumb fence post. Every nerve in my body was on edge trying to see or hear something— *anything.*" He paused, and looked deep into her eyes; "but it don't end there."

"The dogs still hadn't moved and I got the shakes. I was just about to bolt when I see this wisp of fog slowly rise from the swamp. But it wasn't thick and shiny like the ground fog. It was different; more of a haze— like how a thin column of cigar smoke rises from an ashtray." Anita followed the motion of his hand, slowly rising while twisting before stopping a few inches from his face.

"When it got to about here, it leveled off; and there it hung. I know this is gonna sound crazy, but uh— well, it seemed almost like it was *lookin'* at me. My eyes were glued to it; barely wavering, back and forth, ever so slight." Butch's nostrils flared and once again, hairs prickled his neck and forearms.

"Then all of a sudden, *ba-zoom!*"

He thrust his hand past Anita's ear, nearly bouncing her from her chair.

"It shot past my face and vanished just like that. But I felt no breeze. You're gonna think I'm nuts, but for a split second, I could have sworn I felt a clammy coldness touch my face— like a tiny pressing sensation right here." Butch tapped his cheek as Anita slid her hands over his to console him, mystified by his story.

"That's when I got a full dose of the heebie-jeebies and ran like hell."

On the way out of the swamp, he stumbled into a shallow mud hole that sucked off one of his boots, its sock still inside. Frantic, he kicked off the other to level his step. Once on solid ground, he tripped over a surface root and hit the ground hard. The impact dislodged the gun and broke the flashlight. He ignored the pain, sprung to his feet, and resumed his frenzied charge with only moonlight to guide his path.

"I couldn't help it, Nita. I was scared out of my cotton-pickin' mind," he confessed, leaving the dogs where they were.

"You left the hounds tied to a tree; how *could* you, Butch? You'll have to go back and get them," she admonished. "What if a big moose happens by? They'll be torn to shreds if they can't run away."

"I don't care!" he shouted, his eyes flared with determination. "I ain't goin' near that God-forsaken place 'til daylight, I tell ya. They'll just have to wait. That's all there is to it." He ignored the guilt and downed his whiskey praying they'd be safe until morning.

Anita was confused. Unsure of what to make of his story, she hesitated saying anything. Butch was not easily rattled and never prone to fanciful embellishment. She didn't doubt the sincerity of what he *perceived* had happened given his state of trepidation, but it was another thing to refuse going back for his beloved hounds, *especially* for Pepper. Butch studied her face certain he detected a restrained, but dubious smirk.

"I know damned well what you're thinking. You think I'm a dang lunatic, don't you? I swear, Nita, I ain't made nothing up." The inflection in his voice pleaded for support. "I *saw* what I saw."

"I'm not saying it ain't so, darling. But you've been under a lot of stress lately. You said so yourself, you were overtired. Maybe you rested and nodded off or something. You know, maybe you didn't realize it, but thinking of old times, you copied Alex. Maybe your mind was playing tricks on you in the moonlight."

"Bullshit! I *wasn't* daydreaming. I was on my feet in the middle of a damn swamp. And what about the dogs? Why didn't they howl or tear hell out of the coons only a yard from their mugs? How did the coon I just shot end up with the others? Huh? Answer me that!"

He challenged her sense of reason, but Anita chose only to listen for fear of agitating him further. Butch rose and kicked back his chair. Frustrated, he removed his soiled shirt and threw it into the sink. A medley of emotions grappled with his manhood; unnerved, embarrassed, and confused.

Well, I wasn't there, Anita conceded, though she was bewildered and unable to offer any plausible explanation. She allowed Butch to vent before joining him by the door, staring at the woods through its small window. She slid a reassuring arm around his waist and kissed his shoulder.

Many things didn't make sense at the moment, but she was certain of *one* thing— the dogs needed to be freed and brought home. She nudged his ribs with playful enthusiasm, carefully choosing her words so as not to appear skeptical and risk discouraging him.

"I'll tell you what; how about we get the camping lantern and I'll help you get the dogs. You said they were in my blueberry stomping grounds, so they can't be too hard to find, okay? Come on; maybe between the two of us and that big kerosene lantern, things won't be— um— quite the same."

Pepper is only a pup; Butch knew in his heart it was the right thing to do. He felt ashamed and emasculated that his wife had more courage to go into that dreaded swamp than he did.

"I'll get the lantern," he sighed, giving in. Anita was relieved, his confidence returning as she retreated to the bedroom to get Butch a clean shirt and socks. Grabbing a long-sleeved pullover and hiking shoes, she returned to the kitchen. While tying their boots, a muffled commotion arose from the veranda. They looked at each other and momentarily stared at the door before Butch snatched it open. All four hounds were wagging tails and prancing about. Pepper pawed the outer screen, eager to embrace his master.

Butch stood in the doorway and studied his hounds in amazed disbelief. Relieved they were home safe, Anita watched as he pet the dogs. He looked up and glowered.

"Still think I'm a damned lunatic?"

"Oh for Pete's sake," she flustered. "I never said any such thing." Not entirely convincing, she offered what she deemed a plausible explanation. "I dunno," she shrugged, "maybe when you ran off they got excited and wriggled free somehow."

"Think so? Try again woman." He pointed at the hounds. "Take another look— a *good* look. Where are the leashes, huh? Do you see any? Who in hell do you suppose unsnapped the heavy clasps from these turnbuckles?" Butch slid two fingers under one of their collars to demonstrate.

He left her wrestling with stupefied thoughts as he brushed past her and whistled the dogs into the house. Anita would never have permitted such a thing in the past, but she was stumped; her mind a blank.

"Tonight, they stay in here— with us."

Anita said naught, still spellbound and unable to react as two hounds curled up on the sofa, a third opting for the braided rug in front of the radio. Butch sat in his favorite chair and motioned Pepper to his lap. Anita looked on, trancelike; her eyes focused on its collar. As Butch stroked Pepper's head, the dog turned and nuzzled Butch's chin.

Anita's eyes widened. *Oh-h-h, my God. Is such a thing possible?*

Her emotions soared. She had heard of the paranormal, but had no idea if such phenomena actually existed, let alone of being able to explain it. But feminine intuition told her something very strange had indeed happened in that swamp.

Alex kissed him goodbye, tonight; she was convinced of it.

Tears welled in her eyes. She was overcome with confusing, yet wondrous emotions trying to grasp the depth at which human bonding must be to lift the cosmic veil separating mortals from the supernatural.

Anita smoothed the goose bumps from her arms as she tiptoed into the kitchen. Though an infrequent drinker, she spotted Butch's whiskey and poured herself a shot. She drew a taste to moisten her lips, shuddering at the bourbon's initial bite. Once again, she found herself leaning against the kitchen sink, gazing out her window.

The heavens are more than beautiful tonight— they're mystifying.

Immersed in thought, she smiled, mesmerized by what glorious secrets must lay concealed out there— *way* out there in the Cosmos.

Her tummy suddenly tingled as before, but rather than dismiss the feeling, she encouraged it; her eyes glued to what seemed to be the biggest and the brightest of full moons she had ever seen— now fully risen and seemed to be smiling back, as if to showcase Luna in all her radiant splendor.

∝∝

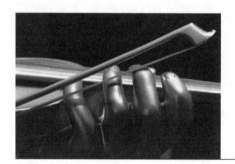

Play on, Maestro
by Deborah L. Kloeppel

A beam of sunlight filtered through the smoky window pane, bathing the elderly gentleman's face in its amber light. The tender kiss of the sun's warmth was better than any alarm; waking him at the perfect moment each morning.

After a restless night, Cas rubbed his eyes, brushing away dreams of the old country. He yawned and slowly stretched, the cracking of his octogenarian joints protesting the new day. Cas shuffled toward the console table and switched on the hotplate.

While he waited, Cas looked around the room; *old and worn out*, he thought, *just like me*. The kettle's whistle was answered by a cricket hiding beneath the radiator in the corner.

"Aw, Babka, *moj muzyk malutki*: my little musician," he said, smiling. "It's time for my morning tea; and your nap, little friend."

Few appreciated the gift of life as much as Cas; he embraced each new day with the reverence such a miracle deserved. To him, it was indeed a miracle to be alive; one of the few to survive five years of slave labor, disease, and starvation at Auschwitz.

Cupping the warm mug between his hands, he subconsciously glanced at the tattooed number on his forearm. His eyes followed the shaft of sunlight inching its way up the wall, spotlighting his name at the bottom of a yellowed theater poster.

"Casimir Szumski, Virtuoso Extaordinaire".

I'm the last of my entire family, he thought. Tears blurred his vision as he stared at the faded placard. Of all the concert posters he had saved, this one was inordinately special, perhaps as precious as the centuries-old violin he played. Though many years had passed, he could still recall every detail of his reception; the silent, emotional ecstasy of his audience; the feeling of being home again; the thrill of playing for his countrymen.

"'Twas the best day of my life, Babka," he whispered, admiring the picture of his younger self.

Sitting on the edge of his chair, he stared blankly out the window, slowly sipping his kosher tea as memories of home flooded his mind: sharing a family breakfast; music lessons and long walks with his father and grandfather; his younger siblings chasing about their home in suburban Krakow.

He sighed heavily, glancing once more at the despicable number which had marred his forearm from the age of fifteen; a grisly reminder of unspeakable horrors.

Cas leaned back in his chair, allowing his thoughts to drift as freely as the steam floating off his second cup of tea. He recalled the sparkle of adventure in his grandfather's eyes while reciting stories of their ancestors, tracing their lineage to a band of gypsies who plied the trade routes across the Alps into Bavaria, where they obtained the Guarneri which had been handed down through generations. The priceless instrument had survived against all odds, one of a mere hundred twenty such master-crafted violins ever created.

With nothing left to keep him in Poland after the liberation, Cas recovered what he could of the family's hidden valuables and made his way to Berlin, escaping to the west. In America, Cas honed his musical talents and earned a prestigious seat with the Philadelphia Orchestra.

His focus returned to the poster. It represented more than a personal honor; it was the billing of a lifetime; the most profound performance he had ever delivered, and at a most unusual, but fitting location.

Two decades had passed since the Philadelphia Orchestra went on European tour, keeping a secret surprise from Cas until their arrival at the Weiliczka Salt Mine, near his former home of Krakow, Poland. At this venue, he was the featured attraction; the concert held in his honor.

For nine centuries, miners had excavated countless tons of rock salt, taking it upon themselves to carve intricate statues, bas-reliefs, and the exquisite Chapel of Saint Kinga, along with some two thousand other chambers six hundred feet below the surface. Even the Chapel's huge, lighted chandeliers are fashioned entirely from salt crystal.

The concert was held in one of the largest chambers; its unique acoustics could make any musical performance an extraordinarily moving experience. The program began with numbers from noted Polish composers before the emcee introduced Casimir to a captive audience filled with dignitaries, including Poland's former President and its Prime Minister.

'Ladies and Gentlemen, it is my great pleasure to introduce Casimir Szumski: not only is he the last of his family of gifted musicians, but he is the last-known holocaust survivor from this part of Poland, born and raised only miles from here. Tonight he returns to his homeland, a virtuoso extraordinaire; to play for his beloved people of Poland.'

The audience stood, applauding in a prolonged, heartfelt ovation that brought him to tears. Cas bowed repeatedly as the thunderous applause echoed through the chamber, taking the moment to regain his composure. The audience grew still as, with dreamlike fluidity, Cas drew deeply upon divine inspiration and expressed one of the world's finest encore pieces: a masterfully executed rendition of Massenet's "Meditation".

The voice of an angel emanated from his priceless instrument; its haunting resonance filling the concert chamber, infusing the air with life as if he had freed the embodied spirits of his family and countrymen; their singing souls emerging from his ancient violin with each extraordinary note of the tender adagio, rife with emotion; full, rich, and vibrant. High notes spiraled to the pinnacles of the arches, floating into silent nothingness like a wisp of morning fog.

His fingers moved with effortless precision, waltzing the full length of the Guarneri's neck, extracting each delicate note, coaxing them out into the open with warm, exquisite vibratos that elongated every tremulous, wavering tone. Cas poured such sentiment into the piece that his audience was overcome with emotion; their concluding ovation lasting considerably longer than the first, with nary a dry eye to be found in the house.

"Chee-churrp," the cricket resounded, interrupting his soulful journey back in time.

"Aw, my little Babka," Cas began, wiping away tears; "you have trouble sleeping, too, I see. We're getting old, *malutki*. Between us, we haven't much time left, do we? But today, how would you like the maestro to serenade you, eh? I shall play for you as I did years ago; at my home."

He removed the candle from atop the old trunk and lifted its lid. Cradling the rare Guarneri as gently as he would a newborn, Cas brought it out and lovingly caressed it, ever mesmerized by the rich translucence of the oil varnish highlighting its exquisite Carpathian tiger maple. Next, he retrieved the remaining flake of rosin; fingering it with sad, but solemn dignity.

"'Tis our last, my dear Babka; like us, it too must come to an end. Once it disappears, I shall play no more."

Tightening the horsehair, he drew the bow a single stroke across the rosin's sticky surface, traveling from the ebony frog to the ivory tip in one graceful, flowing movement. Setting it aside, he turned to the violin, plucking each string with care; his acute sense of tone guiding him to adjust the tautness to precisely the correct measure.

Satisfied, he tucked the priceless violin beneath his grizzled beard, positioned his fingers without thought, and instinctively drew the bow across the strings.

All other sounds in the room ceased and faded into the recesses of his mind. In his reverie, he imagined himself in the magnificent carved chamber; his spellbound audience agape as the conductor emphatically waved his baton at the orchestra, blending their subtle harmonic tones with his more lively melodious rhythms. The old gentleman's breathing matched each delicate bow stroke as his heart kept the tempo like a well-timed metronome. All present thought was lost in the memories of time.

Cas was once more a younger man, his soul at home and at peace among his people. Had the roses on the dingy wallpaper been animate, they would have been weeping when there was a rap at the door; vanquishing the phantom grandeur, whisking him from the music hall back to the dusty boarding room.

He looked toward the door, wondering who it could be. He'd never disturbed anyone with his playing at this time in the morning before. "Ah, perhaps there is new tenant, and not so cultured as you, eh Babka?" he said, smiling.

Cas opened the door. No one was there; neither a sound nor a soul to be found. The hallway was deserted but there, resting on the edge of the threshold was a tiny box. Curious, Casimir picked it up, pausing only to glance at each end of the hallway, but there was no sign of anyone; so quickly had the mysterious source disappeared.

Opening the lid, he found an equally tiny note handwritten in German: "Spiel an, Maestro, spiel an: Play on, Maestro, play on."

A familiar, pungent aroma tickled his nostrils when he lifted the note to find a new cake of the finest rosin, elegantly presented in a velvet pouch tied with satin drawstrings. Tears of gratitude filled his eyes; *the music would play on.*

The Price of Loyalty
by Xin Wang

Despite the heat of late morning, crowds still jostled elbow to elbow in the bustling marketplace. Everywhere, vendors cried their wares in the sing-song of accomplished hawkers while their customers examined the offerings or proposed counter bargains. Harried mothers grabbed at escaping children, their other hand clutching their baskets. Off to the side, a group of tumblers occupied the area between two stalls, their dazzling acrobatics eliciting cheers and gasps of awe. Here and there a small clear space opened up as a nobleman strolled past, his sword at his side, disdainful and amused by the antics around him. Few carriages or horsemen tried to cut through the throng; those who attempted more often than not found themselves mired in the surging masses, drivers and riders cursing at the pedestrians around them.

Taerin Torris alighted from his hired hansom and eyed the scene with a rueful smile. It served as a poignant reminder of his youth in the village of Murrey, when he used to scramble under stalls and dart through the crowds, nimble as a monkey and delirious with the excitement of a market fair. The bazaar before him was larger by far than the one of his childhood, Little Cayenne being the capital of the nation and one of her brightest jewel. As he watched a wide matron drag two screaming toddlers after her, he could not help but grin at the memories it evoked.

"Want I should wait, my lord?" The driver behind him shook his whip impatiently.

"No, I'll be fine, thank you." Taerin tossed the man a coin and waved him away. The wheels rattled on the cobblestones as the hansom turned, and Taerin watched it disappear around the corner, his mood sobering. He was not here for a pleasurable stroll, but on grim business. If he succeeded, he would need more than a cramped hansom on his way back. He grimaced at the thought, distaste twisting his mouth.

He had barely stepped into the fray when he was accosted by the shouts of the merchants. Stamping down the temptation to loiter and put off what he had to do, Taerin gave them a polite but uninterested nod before passing.

"Shiny jewelry for yer lady, my lord!"

"Sir! Use only the purest incense when you pay homage to the gods!"

"M'lord, the finest silks from Carraway! T'would bring out the lovely green o' yer eyes, m'lord!"

Taerin's lips twitched into a reluctant smile at the brazenness of this last crone, who had thrust the material almost right under his nose, but he did not slow. His destination lay on the far side of the marketplace, and he saw its approach with a sigh of mingled relief and regret.

Unlike the other buildings around the market, the single-story stone edifice before him had no stalls set up in front. Instead, a high wooden platform stood to the side, steps leading up to the improvised stage. The gray exterior looked weathered and neglected, planks of wood nailed in the place of a broken window. No sign boasting its wares hung outside and an air of gloom seemed to seep from beneath the sturdy door. The large open area before it lay singularly quiet and abandoned amidst the turmoil all around, as though people found themselves hesitant to step too close. Passers-by eyed the building and its wooden dais with wary glances before hurrying on, their eyes averted. One elderly woman clutched her shawl close and made the sign against evil.

Taerin struggled with himself, chewing on the ends of his mustache, one hand on his hip and the other tapping on the hilt of his sword, unable to take the final few steps forward. For all that he had accomplished so much during the thirty some years of his life, Taerin still sometimes felt young and uncertain. He was almost grateful when a young woman from a nearby stand caught his eye and gave him a shy smile. Half-cursing himself for his sudden weakness, Taerin turned to examine her wares, fingering her trinkets with a preoccupied air. She was probably new to the hawking trade; her large hazel eyes watched him in fascination, and she offered no prices on her goods. When he selected a jeweled pendant, she took his coin with a blush, ducking her head. He smiled when he saw her examine him from beneath her lashes, not coy as most girls would be, but rather with an innocent curiosity.

"My thanks," he said softly, to put her at ease.

She colored again, but her smile lit her face with simple pleasure. "You're welcome, my lord."

Taerin stowed the bauble in his pocket and hesitated. The building beckoned to him out of the corner of his eye, blind windows staring a hole into his back. The urge to linger was almost overwhelming, especially when the girl gave him a concerned frown.

"Is something the matter, my lord?"

"No," he forced a smile. "No, nothing. Thank you again." With an inward sigh, Taerin turned away. Behind him, the girl let out an audible gasp as she discerned his course. She dropped her gaze when he glanced over his shoulder at her, but not before he caught the expression of startled revulsion in her eyes. Her reaction cut at him, but he resisted the urge to justify his actions to her. He had the uncomfortable feeling that he wouldn't succeed in any case, when he could hardly justify them to himself.

The door opened a crack at his impatient knocking and an unfriendly eye peered out at him. "We ain't open yet, come back tomorrow!"

Taerin jammed the door with his foot before it could slam shut. "I have business with Master Sims. Tell him it's private and it will not wait."

For a moment, it looked like the guard would try and close the door anyway, foot or no. Thinking better of the idea, and moved, perhaps, both by the quality of Taerin's dress and the confidence of his voice, he opened the door with a begrudging grunt. "Wait 'ere," he grumbled ungraciously, before stomping through a second door.

Taerin ran his fingers through his sandy brown hair and looked around. The room he found himself in inspired no more confidence than the dilapidated appearance outside. A crude table and three chairs stood next to the door, an overturned flagon leaking a thin stream of some foul-smelling drink onto the floor. The fireplace against the far wall looked like it had not been swept for years, soot and ashes clogging the interior. Broken furniture lay piled in one corner and cracks ran along the walls. The sunlight filtered in through a set of dingy curtains, looking weakened and paled by the ordeal, and with the walls muffling the sounds outside, it was difficult to remember the life and bustle that lay just beyond the door.

Taerin blew his breath out in a snort of exasperation. His fingers were once again drumming against the hilt of his sword, and he forced them to stillness. He carefully set his expression into a bored mask and crossed his arms. To anyone else, he would appear to be no more than an indifferent nobleman, irritated at the wait, but not unduly agitated.

Within, he was shaking. It was not fear; the very notion of being afraid of anyone in this establishment was laughable. It was not excitement; he would rather be facing the full wrath of Parliament then standing in his current spot. It was, he admitted with a wry twist of the mouth, nothing more than downright, stubborn reluctance and the guilty awareness of the fact that though he was only doing what had to be done, that did not make it any more the right thing to do.

Sweet stars in heaven, he thought, sighing. *I can't* believe *I'm thinking about... no, actually* doing *what I'm about to do.* An image of his hardworking parents floated unbidden into his mind, and he pushed it away with a shudder, thankful that they had no notion of what he was up to. *How the son of an honest farmer and his loving wife could end up here, of all places...*

He remembered with a wince the outraged indignation with which they and much of the nation had greeted the royal decree that legalized slavery in Cayenne. At the time, he had fought a covert, losing battle against court politics to halt such a measure. The Queen Mother had proved an invaluable ally, as had the young King, but their power had long been limited by the expanding influence of wealthy nobles grown bold under the rule of a child sovereign. As a last resort, Taerin had mobilized his network of spies and informants to sway public opinion. The task was easily accomplished, since the majority of the common folk were aghast at the notion, but it had not been enough. Unable to move Parliament, Taerin had settled for imposing harsh restrictions on the practice, though he suspected that many such restrictions went ignored.

It was, therefore, a painful irony that he now stood in one of the despised slave trading posts.

The Queen Mother had understood, when he explained in a private audience, though she too detested the necessity. As the King's Spymaster, Taerin could take no chances with his staff; nor could he appear to be anything other than another young nobleman enjoying a life of pleasure at court. He had put off the decision for months, convinced that loyalty could neither be bought at the end of a lash nor shackled by chains, but after discovering one of his footmen pawing through his mail, he could not ignore the need any longer. The man hadn't found anything, but the possibility of it had chilled Taerin's heart. He dismissed the few servants he had, fearing that any or all of them could be in the pay of others, and presented his dilemma to the Queen Mother, along with his solution.

After her initial shock, she had tried to help him; tried to explain the situation to her son. They had had only limited success. Young as he was, King Wilhelm already possessed the same sense of justice that had marked his father. His serious gray eyes had born into Taerin with all the solemnity of a child confronted by adult problems and in their depths were the first glimmerings of disapproval that Taerin could recall. The boy king shrugged and told him to do what he needed, but his tone and the set of his small shoulders as he turned his back on his Spymaster had sent a bittersweet shiver down Taerin's spine. Someday the boy would come of age, and Taerin knew with gut-wrenching certainty that he would be a strong King worthy of service. Whether that King would still consider him acceptable for that service when the time came though, was anyone's guess.

Taerin jumped as the door leading deeper into the building opened with a loud creak, so absorbed was he in his thoughts. He shook himself, trying to clear his head. The King would not reach his majority for several more years. In the meantime, the job of protecting him from ambitious nobles and guarding his interests against those who would exploit them fell on Taerin's shoulders. He would do what was necessary, however disagreeable, and pray that it was enough for the end to justify the means.

The hulking guard that had granted him entrance emerged and pointed back over his shoulder with a grunt, his watery eyes still suspicious. Taerin pasted a smile on his face and headed down the narrow hall. Pushing open the door at the other end, he stopped in his tracks and blinked, surprised at the sight that greeted him.

Instead of being as dim and shabby as the room he had left, this room was clearly designed to impress visitors. Sunlight flooded in through two large windows. An imposing desk stood facing the door, behind it a high-backed leather chair. The cheerful yellow paint on the walls set off a couple of hanging landscapes and a thick carpet covered the floor. Two potted plants held sentry duty on either side of a well-stocked bookcase.

A short, portly man with a balding pate rose as he entered, a wide smile stretching across his face. "Welcome, my lord," he said, the slightest hint of a foreign accent on his tongue. He bowed and gestured to a chair.

Taerin sank into the seat, noticing as he did so that the color had faded from the carpet and the varnish on the desk was cracking. Small tufts of white cotton stuck out of rips in the leather chair and a thick layer of dust lay on the books in the bookshelf. Apparently the trader was more concerned with first impressions than lasting ones. Taerin forced a thin smile. "Master Sims, I presume?"

"The very same." The man puffed out his chest, as though his name were an honorific. His eyes glistened as he took in Taerin's appearance, the rich blue velvet doublet and white silk breeches, the gold buttons and polished boots, and the gold and silver inlaid hilt jutting out of its red leather sheath. Taerin watched the trader's tongue dart out to wet his thick lips, fat fingers twitching as though he could already feel the gold coins about to come his way, and suppressed a shudder of revulsion. "How can I be of service, my lord?"

"I find myself in need of household staff. I would like to see your... what you have to offer."

Master Sims hesitated. "My lord, the auction is on the morrow."

"I want to see them in private," Taerin said, a trace of impatience in his voice. The thought of publicly bidding on human flesh, hearing the auctioneer's callous assessment of each slave, and in the company of a large crowd of spectators made his stomach turn. "I was told that you're willing to... accommodate certain patrons before the public auction." He paused. "As long as they make it worth your while, of course."

Master Sims smiled again, showing off a row of yellow teeth. "I see my lord is a true gentleman, unwilling to subject himself to the scrutiny of the masses. I shall be most pleased indeed to give you a private tour." He bustled to a side door, pulling out a thick ring of keys. "Through here, my lord."

They passed into an open courtyard, surrounded by high walls topped with glass shards. A few guards loitered at one end, tossing dice. "The exercise yard," Master Sims explained. "Sometimes we must hold a shipment for a few days before the next sale, and we mustn't allow them to get sick and weak away from the sun and fresh air. Here we are." They stopped in front of another building while the trader muttered and flipped through his keys. He summoned a couple of guards with a wave "just as a precaution, my lord", and pushed open the door.

Taerin squinted in the dim light, waiting for his eyes to adjust. Thinking of what he knew about the neighborhood's layout, he realized that they were in the backroom of a store. The front, if he recalled correctly, was a cooper's shop. Master Sims was pulling open yet another door. This one led down a set of rickety stairs into a cellar-like space. He apologized as they descended, his voice an aggrieved whine.

"There's never enough room, my lord. I've tried to find other holding places for 'em, but no one seems to want anything to do with slaves. Seems to think it's evil. I had to rent this from that cooper at an outrageous price, and dig out the underground pens with my own money! It's completely backwards, of course, these people's sense of morality; why, in Camden and the Tricity, the slavers even have their own guilds! But we mustn't complain too much. No doubt in ten, twenty years, things will be different and Cayenne will have gotten used to the idea, and the wealth, of the trade."

"Indeed," Taerin managed through gritted teeth, silently adding: *over my dead body.* The air was close and damp underground, and the only illumination came from a couple of lanterns along the walls and a torch that one of the guards lit. Already, he could smell the odor of too many bodies packed into too small a space and hear the murmur of restless movement.

At the bottom, the passage led through another door, which opened with a groan to reveal a long hallway. On either side stood the *pens*, as Master Sims had called them. They were nothing more than caves carved into the walls, with thick iron bars set in front. To one side of the hall stood two large, open rooms, a rough wooden tub and water pump half-visible in each. Heads raised as the trader led the way into the hall, showing haggard eyes staring listlessly out of sunken faces.

Taerin's fists clenched at his sides. The guard with the torch touched fire to sconces along the walls, and the unexpected flares of light made those behind the bars cry out and draw back, shielding their eyes. He suddenly understood what Master Sims had said about the slaves' need for sunlight and fresh air. The stench was unbelievable, sweat from unwashed bodies mixed with human waste. He closed his eyes and took a few shallow breaths, trying to calm his anger and repugnance.

"This way, my lord," said Master Sims, oblivious to Taerin's reaction. "We separate them by age and gender, you know. What did your lordship have in mind?"

Taerin shrugged, not trusting his voice. "I... I'll know it when I see it, I guess," he said after a moment.

The trader gave him a skeptical look, but did not press the matter. He led Taerin down the hall, keeping up a running commentary about the slaves around them.

Taerin's head soon cleared enough for him to pay attention. He stuffed his reluctance and disgust back into a corner of his mind, peering into the cages at their inhabitants. What he saw was not encouraging. Many sat with their heads hung down, dispirited and apathetic. Others glared at him with hatred burning in their eyes, teeth bared like wild animals. Neither kind, Taerin knew, would serve him willingly or keep his secrets. He hadn't been expecting unswerving devotion, but if these were his only options, he might be better off taking his chances with hired servants.

Taerin was about to move on when one man caught his attention. Dark eyes gazed steadily into his own, cold and fearless. The tawny skin and straight black hair, pulled back in a braid, told Taerin he was a native of the deserts to the west. There was something about the way the man sat, one leg folded and arm resting on his knee, that suggested coiled readiness. His muscles rippled when he moved and in the flickering light Taerin could make out the jagged shapes of scars on his bare chest.

"Ah, a fine specimen, is he not, my lord?" Master Sims said, noticing Taerin's interest. "As you no doubt know, most of our slaves come from the deserts these days, but you can hardly do anything with them before you break their spirit. Savages, they are. This one though, he was caught young and trained as a guard in a nobleman's house. Wields a good sword, or so I hear."

"Why is he here then?"

"Well, seems he and his fellow guards failed to protect the young lord they were supposed to serve. He was killed in a planned attack, I think. In a fit of rage, the father sold the young lord's entire household to me, at quite a bargain too. The whole lot's scheduled to be sold tomorrow. He'll fetch a good price on the block, unless my lord is interested?"

"No," Taerin said, tearing his eyes away from the man and shaking his head as though coming out of a trance. "No," he repeated more firmly, ignoring the twinge of regret that plagued him. "I've no need of a warrior. Let's move on." He followed Master Sims' footsteps, but as he walked away, he could feel the man's gaze on his back, silent and assessing.

"This is where we keep the womenfolk and children," Master Sims said as they approached another cell. "If you're looking for a servant, you'll likely find what you need here." He gave Taerin a salacious grin. "Some of these girls can serve in more ways than one, my lord." His ribald chuckle echoed off the walls.

Before Taerin could respond, a loud grating noise shook the metal bars as the outer door opened. A trio of guards came into view, two toting heavy slop buckets and wooden bowls while the third held his naked sword in his hand. One by one, they opened the cell doors and set the food and a stack of bowls inside before retreating and locking the doors again. Taerin wondered what Master Sims fed his slaves that would make them eye the proffered meal with such a complete lack of enthusiasm.

A trickle of sweat ran down his brow, and Taerin wiped at it impatiently. He was weary of the ordeal and eager for it to end. He was about to turn away and examine the women huddled in their cell when a loud clamor broke out and a guard shouted in alarm.

Taerin whirled just in time to see the second guard go down and a figure burst out of his cell. Catching the remaining guard by surprise, the slave wrenched the sword from his grasp and drove it into his side in one smooth motion. The guard screamed as he fell against the open cell door, slamming it shut before he hit the ground with a thump. Pandemonium erupted as slaves on all sides began screaming and yelling, hands thrust through the bars as though pleading for help. The two guards who had accompanied Taerin and the trader rushed to aid their comrades.

Master Sims was right, Taerin thought with bemused interest as they engaged. *The man does wield a good sword.*

Holding his weapon in a double-handed grip, the slave slashed at the guards as they came up. He ignored the howling around him, eyes intense and focused, movements as deliberate as if he were sparring in a fencing salon. The first guard went down quickly, his sword flying from his hands and his eyes rolling up to show their whites as the man dealt him a solid blow to the head. The second, more cautious, tried a few probing strikes that were easily parried. The slave feinted to the left, drawing his opponent off-balance, then spun in a tight circle, his hilt coming down hard on the back of the guard's skull. The man crumpled without a sound.

Taerin had a bare second in which to own himself impressed before the slave lifted his sword and charged with a roar, the first sound Taerin had heard from his throat. Behind him, Master Sims gave a screech of pure terror and stumbled back, but Taerin hardly registered the trader's fear. Reflexes from a lifetime of training took over. His sword rang free of its sheath with a clear, bell-like chime as he stepped up to meet the charge. The other sword came down on his with a clang, jolting his whole arm, but he held firm. For a moment, their eyes met over their locked blades before they both drew back to assume new positions.

Taerin sidestepped the man's thrust, his own weapon darting forward, trying to find a point of weakness. The man parried and fell back a step, a startled expression on his face. His eyes narrowed and a snarl escaped him, but his next attack showed that he would not underestimate his opponent again. For his part, Taerin fought with a deadly calm. He did not want to kill this man, whose only fault lay in trying for his freedom, but neither was he about to let himself be impaled on some stranger's blade. Besides, time was on his side; already he could hear the shouting and commotion from outside as the guards in the courtyard began to realize that something was wrong.

From the look of desperation in the other man's eyes, he could hear it too. His strikes became less calculated, more careless as he took greater risks, leaving himself open and barely able to hold off Taerin's counterattacks. Finally, with a grunt, he took a wild swing.

Taerin evaded the blow, turning so that he was just beyond its reach. The man was overextended and his balance off. At that moment Taerin could have easily run him through, but instead he caught the other's sword on the tang of his own. A subtle twist of the wrist, and it fell with a clatter. Not giving his opponent any time to recover, Taerin followed through, ducking and stepping neatly into the man's guard and planting an elbow squarely into his midriff. The man collapsed to his knees with a groan, arms folded over his torso as he tried to regain his breath.

Taerin lowered his weapon and stepped back. In the heat of the moment, he had had no choice but to defend himself, but now that the fight was over and he saw the two knocked-out guards stirring, a strange regret gripped him. He shifted, but before he could analyze it further, an enraged cry startled him.

Master Sims had retrieved the man's fallen weapon, and now he lunged forward, spittle flying from his lips. "Murderer! Assassin! Try to kill me, will you? I'll show you!" He raised his arm.

Taerin's sword snaked out to intercept the attack just as it fell. For a moment, Master Sims stared at him, eyes still slightly mad, his chest heaving. "Please, Master Sims," Taerin said, amused at the trader's sudden burst of courage now that the threat had abated. "I think he's subdued. T'would be a terrible waste to kill him thus."

The words seemed to bring the trader back to his senses. "True, true," he muttered, dropping the sword and wiping a hand across his brow. At that moment, the two guards fell on the man from behind, wrestling him to the ground and pinning his arms. One added a vicious kick to his ribs for good measure, then hauled him to his feet and punched him in the face. The man grunted at the impact, but made no other sound. A cruel gleam lit the trader's eyes as he watched. "Still, it might be worth it to make an example of him, so no one else gets any bright ideas. You hear that?" he sneered at the slave. "I won't kill you – that would be too easy. I'll have you chained up to the whipping posts and lashed until you've got no back left, and I'll make everyone watch! That'll teach 'em, and you too, I daresay!"

Taerin turned away, disgust twisting his stomach as Master Sims continued to rant and abuse his victim. By now, the guards from outside had arrived to assist their hurt companions and a fearful hush had settled over the other slaves. Taerin sheathed his sword slowly, suddenly tired and wanting nothing more than to escape the confines of this underground dungeon. His eyes wandered aimlessly to the cell where the women were held. Like the other captives, their wide, glazed eyes showed their horror. Someone wailed quietly in a corner while others hugged small children close. One young woman stood pressed against the bars, tears running down her face and a wrapped bundle clutched to her breast.

Taerin looked away from their misery, feeling unaccountably guilty, for all that he had acted in self-defense, and found himself staring at the man held in the guards' grasp. A trickle of blood ran down his face from a cut on his forehead and his lips were bloody. He paid no attention to Master Sims, gloating over his punishment, but stared straight at Taerin. There was no fear in his eyes, but the boundless anguish in its place pierced Taerin's heart. The man was unafraid of his fate, so why was despair written across his features?

Taerin chewed at his mustache, a frown forming across his brow as his Spymaster mind began to work. Now that he thought of it, the man's actions made no sense. He had escaped from his cell and overpowered the guards. There had been nothing barring him from bolting out the door. With a bit of luck, he could have won past the other guards, who would have been startled and unprepared, and Taerin doubted that the wall of the courtyard would have presented too big a challenge. Once outside, an escaped slave could have found refuge among many of the common folks, or lost himself in the market day crowds.

So why had he decided to charge *deeper* into the passage to attack Taerin and the trader? To eliminate witnesses, or prevent them from attacking him from behind? Taerin doubted it. The man had chosen to knock out the guards instead of killing them, and from what the Spymaster had seen, a trained warrior like that would never have given in to a panicked impulse. He had a reason, and a desperate one, for what he had done, and to persist even after it became clear that Taerin's skill surpassed his own.

Then Taerin gasped as the connection formed in his mind, like a flash of lightning illuminating the darkness. His head whipped back to find the man's eyes. They weren't looking at him, he realized. They were looking *beyond* him. And looking back at him was the young mother he had noted earlier, one hand held to her mouth, trying to stifle her sobs.

The guards were dragging the man away, their rough handling making him stumble. Master Sims followed, still muttering dire threats. In the space of a heartbeat, Taerin had made up his mind.

"Hold," he called, his voice clear and commanding. They stopped to look at him in amazement. Master Sims shook himself.

"My lord," he cried, bowing and unctuous once more, "My lord, my deepest apologies! In the fervor of the moment, I had almost forgotten your lordship! Yet how could I, with such a recent demonstration of your bravery and courage? Please, my lord, wait right there, I'll just put this rebellious slave in the stocks, then I'll return to finish our business!"

"Hold, Master Sims," Taerin repeated, softer this time but no less imperious. "Surely a few minutes' delay will make no difference in the end?"

The trader looked confused at the request, but nodded, the memory of Taerin's battle still clear in his head.

Taerin approached the cell and the woman inside in a slow arc, not wanting to startle her by too direct an advance. Even so, she shrank back from the bars, hand lowering to shield her babe. Taerin caught her eyes and held them, silently asking her to trust him, though he knew she had no reason to after watching him help the slavers. Still, he was the Spymaster of Cayenne, and he was used to imposing his will upon others. She did not draw near, but neither did she back further away, though she trembled as he came up. Taerin held her eyes a moment more, then reached one hand through the bars. She gasped, instinctively jerking her babe away, but when he glanced at her, she reluctantly allowed him to peel back the first layer of the swaddling.

A plump, round face crowned by peachy fuzz peered up at Taerin through two curious black eyes. Taerin stroked the soft cheek with one finger and the head turned, looking for a nipple. The babe gurgled, one small fist breaking free of the swaddling and rising to wave aimlessly in the air until he caught it. Tiny fingers curled around his.

Taerin took a careful breath and released it, startled by the emotion that stirred in his chest. He gently pried his finger loose and stepped back, turning his head to look at the man down the hall. The longing he saw confirmed his suspicions, a naked hunger on the man's face that twisted his heart.

Turning away from the cell, Taerin strolled casually to where Master Sims waited, the trader's mouth pressed into an irritated line, careful that his bored expression gave away nothing of his thoughts. It was true what he had told the trader, that he had no need for a warrior, but he had even less use for someone whose loyalty might be swayed. As his old Master once told him, "A man with a family is a man with something to lose." But beyond that, beyond the cold logic of the Spymaster that governed his life, he knew that if he walked away and turned his back on these people in their plight, he would never be able to look his King in the eye again; would never be able to say truthfully that he was worthy of the King's service.

"Is my lord finished?" Master Sims asked, trying and failing to conceal his impatience.

"Mmm, almost," Taerin drawled. He swept his eyes up and down the slave's half-naked body, lips pursed thoughtfully. "Perhaps I was mistaken earlier, Master Sims. Maybe I do need a warrior after all. How much do you want for him?" His lips twitched as slave, trader, and guards alike gaped at him.

Master Sims recovered quickly. "Him? This one? Oh, my lord, surely not! If it's a fighter my lord wants, I have many others, more skilled, more–"

"I don't know that I can survive a more skilled slave," Taerin interrupted, amused. "How much?"

The trader struggled with himself a moment, torn between greed, the reluctance to offend a potential buyer, and a thirst for vengeance. Almost he was on the verge of refusing the sale when the idea struck him. His oily smile bloomed. "Fifteen hundred gold, my lord," he stated.

The guards gasped at the outrageous sum, but Taerin only burst into laughter. "For a slave whose back you were about to have whipped off? I think not. Two hundred."

"'E's got 'fire, my lord, and that's not something that can be bought! Thirteen hundred."

"Yes, and I've seen to what uses he puts that fire of his. Four hundred."

"Four hundred for such a well-trained guard? 'Tis robbery! One thousand."

"A well-trained guard who apparently failed to protect his last lord. Five hundred."

"'E could fetch more 'n that on the auction block! I can't possibly settle for less than eight hundred, at least!"

Taerin rubbed his chin, brushing one finger against his mustache to wipe away his grin. In the heat of bargaining, Master Sims had clearly forgotten his original plan to force him to buy a different slave. "Hrm," he said, as though considering his choices. "'Tis still a high sum. Very well, but I'll want you to include his wife and child as well."

The man's head snapped up as though jerked by a string, his eyes enormous. From down the corridor, Taerin heard the girl gasp. He kept his own gaze fastened on Master Sims' face, eyelids drooping as though bored by the interaction. The trader looked confused for a moment, as though unaware that this particular slave had such things as a wife and child. He had, Taerin remembered, bought the household entire, after all. Realization dawned slowly across the trader's face, then he roared.

"Eight hundred gold for three healthy, able-bodied slaves! Ye must take me fer a fool!" he cried, his accent becoming more pronounced in his passion.

"Oh please," Taerin waved a dismissive hand. "Able-bodied indeed! I grant you that without the babe, you might make a good price off a woman her age, but that child makes the pair of them more of a liability than anything else. It's too young to be separated from its mother and it'll just be another hungry mouth for years to come. What's more, that woman's going to have to spend half her time taking care of it instead of working, so you're really only selling me half the labor of a normal slave, not to mention the extra food and other costs. You'll be lucky to get so much for her at your auction. I suggest you think over my offer."

Master Sims growled, then fell silent as he considered Taerin's words. His visage darkened into a scowl, but even he could not dispute their truth. Still, it galled him to admit it. "Nine hundred," he said, a stubborn set to his jaw.

Taerin eyed the trader just long enough to make him wonder at the wisdom of challenging a nobleman, then shrugged and smiled. "Eight-fifty. *If* you agree to clean them up and arrange for some form of transportation. I'm not about to march them through the city like dogs on a leash." One corner of his mouth curled upwards. "And there might be a little extra in it for you and your guards too, to recompense you for your lost revenge."

Master Sims blinked, taken aback, and even the guards looked surprised to be reminded of their original intentions. Still and all, now that their anger had had a chance to cool, Taerin knew that they would find the prospect of gold much more tempting than slapping around a helpless slave. The guards, at least, were looking at each other and grinning. Master Sims must have noticed as well, and bethought himself of his future relations with his men if he refused. He nodded decisively. "Done!" He rubbed his hands together and beamed at Taerin like they were now the best of friends. "Perhaps my lord would like to wait in my office while my men prepare them? I'll be along directly."

Taerin nodded and pushed open the door. "Oh, and Master Sims," he said right before stepping through onto the stairs. "Do make sure you and your men restrain yourselves during the... preparation. Remember, they're not yours anymore, and I don't pay for damaged goods."

The shadow of hesitation flitted across the trader's face so quickly Taerin would have said he had imagined it if he had not known better. Master Sims bowed. "My lord may rest assured that we will take the utmost care."

Taerin ascended the stairs, taking the last few two at a time and throwing open the backdoor of the shop to emerge into the courtyard. Ignoring the guards, he closed his eyes and breathed in the fresh fall air until he thought his lungs would burst. He grinned, half-surprised to find that the sun still shone overhead. He could hear sounds of the marketplace carried on the air, the merry voice of a street minstrel rising exuberantly overhead. The guards looked at him as though he had lost his mind, but Taerin only laughed at their puzzled faces as he crossed the courtyard.

Once inside the office, he appropriated pen and paper to compose a short note to his factor, then summoned a guard to deliver it. He spied a bottle on the table and helped himself to some of his host's wine. Just as he finished his glass, Master Sims entered, the man behind him, now considerably cleaner. Two guards flanked him and chains shackled his hands and feet, but he did not appear any the worse for wear. Taerin raised an eyebrow at the trader, who shrugged.

"She wanted to wash the babe," he said, correctly guessing Taerin's question. At that moment the door opened again to reveal the surly guard who had admitted Taerin. Behind him came a fussily dressed elder gentleman followed by a uniformed guardsman bearing a heavy, clinking bag.

"Only for you would I do this, Lord Torris," sniffed the notary, ignoring the others in the room. "Frankly, I was very surprised by your request, but if you're sure..." He sounded hopeful that Taerin would reconsider.

"I'm sure, Master Brogan. Do you have the papers?"

"Yes, yes, of course." Master Brogan produced a pair of spectacles and a sheaf of documents. "I do so witness... blah blah blah, that on this day of... and so forth... that Lord Taerin Torris did purchase... from below establishment... at the price of... the following individuals... ah, here we are." He peered over his specs. "I'll need their names before you can sign."

That brought Taerin up short. He blinked, then gave a sheepish chuckle. "I'd almost forgotten. What's your name?" he asked, turning to the man.

A pair of dark eyes met his own green ones. They narrowed with suspicion, but after a moment the man gave in. "Derryk," he admitted with a toss of the head that sent his braid dancing.

"And those of your wife and child?"

The harsh lines of the man's broad face relaxed and softened at the thought of his loved ones. "Adita and..." his mouth twitched into a smile "And little Derryk." He cleared his throat, looking suddenly abashed, and mumbled something that sounded like "...said she wanted to name him after his father."

"Because he is a brave, noble man," spoke a clear voice behind him. Derryk whirled, and the next instant had his arms around his wife and son, crushing them into his embrace despite the chains. She wrapped one arm around his back, her other holding the babe, and buried her face in his chest. Her shoulders shook.

"Ahem, yes, well," Taerin turned away from the sight, embarrassed at having witnessed their joy. A rueful smile tugged at his mouth at the twinge of envy that pricked him. He clapped his hands together briskly. "You heard the man, Master Brogan. Derryk, Adita, and little Derryk."

"Yes, quite." The notary sounded thoughtful. He gave Taerin a penetrating look. "Well, perhaps 'tis not so poorly done after all, my lord." He affixed the names to the paper, then blew on it to dry the ink before presenting it to the young nobleman.

Taerin stared at the contract for a moment, the final step to completing his purchase. For a moment, the thought brought back the old feeling of disgust, but then he glanced at the trio standing together, still lost to everything else around them, and signed his name with a flourish.

"I've arranged for a wagon, my lord," said Master Sims after the transaction was finished. He looked quite cheerful. "It should be waiting outside. It has been such a pleasure!"

"I'm sure," Taerin returned dryly.

"I shall make a fair copy of this document, my lord, and send it to you with all haste," Master Brogan said once they were outside watching Derryk help his wife into the wagon. He shot Taerin a sidelong glance and waggled his eyebrows. "If you don't mind my saying, my lord, while I sincerely hope that there is no next time to this kind of business, should you desire more servants of this... nature, I advise you to call upon me beforehand. As a notary I cannot take sides once a deal has been concluded, but that old rascal in there cheated you quite badly."

Taerin chuckled. "I figured. You can hardly expect a man like him to be honest after all."

"You knew?" Master Brogan's eyebrows shot up. "And didn't call him on it?"

In the back of the wagon, Derryk had pushed some straw into a sort of nest. He led Adita to it and settled down beside her, one arm draped behind her neck, her head resting on his shoulder, the babe nestled safely between their two bodies. Taerin knew that neither one trusted him yet. To them, he was just another owner, and an eccentric one at that. Still, the contented smiles on their faces soothed his heart. There would be time for more later, when they got to know each other better.

"All in all, Master Brogan," Taerin said lightly, heading toward the wagon himself. "I think I got the better deal."

Twelve Labors of Hercules

by D.R.Smith

In days of yore, time honored lore
Of Gods and mortals told.
Fabled stories, grief and glories
Preserved in myths of old.

An epic tale that ne'er goes stale;
Fancied for centuries.
'Tis new rehearse of Ancient verse;
Labors of Hercules.

The tale unfolds when Hera scolds
Hubby's mortal affairs.
Her Zeus aroused, on Earth caroused;
Bristled the Queen upstairs.

One fateful tryst Zeus failed resist
Enraged her jealousies.
Zeus infant born, inflamed her scorn,
Cursed son named Hercules.

When Herc passed out from drinking bout,
Hera took o'er his will.
She addled brain, made temp insane,
Children and wife, he killed.

Awake from fit, saw crimes commit
Collapsed from retching grief.
Beset with shame, himself to blame,
From Gods he sought relief.

For true repent, begged punishment
Devised by deities.
"We Gods propose, that king impose
Twelve labors, Hercules."

Hera conspired that tasks required
Be schemed to make him fail.
His life would end with soul condemned,
If Herc should not prevail.

Outlandish tasks the king would ask;
All twelve Herc must complete.
To sate her spite, true tests of might,
The first of twelve we meet.

The Nemean Lion

"Just for fun, for number one
Of dozen deeds to dread.
Slay killer cat and wear it back
From Nemea Mount," king said.

For his debut Herc must subdue
A beast in mountain den,
A fearsome task, could be his last,
Of days midst Gods and men.

A monster lion with hide of iron
Stood 'fore the Hercules.
Yet razored claws, nor gaping jaws
Gave rise to weakened knees.

To seal its fate, Herc barred escape
And fearless there he stood.
To stun at least, first struck the beast
With club of olive wood.

He dazed his foe with crashing blow
'Tween eyes of feline's head.
Then to expunge, upon it lunged
And strangled lion dead.

Used claws of steel so he could peel
The hide from lion slain.
From tawny coat made handsome cloak
Complete with braided mane.

"Oh, drats!" king wailed, "my plan's derailed,"
The King of Tiryns sneered.
Herc proved the best of vengeful test,
Now brute of brawn, he feared.

In awe of might, the king took flight
Induced by knocking knees.
Mettle deplete, preferred retreat
O'er facing Hercules.

King acted fast, had smithy cast
An o'er-sized brazen jar.
Removed the lid, and in it hid
From hero's strength bizarre.

Since first retired, the king required
Of ten and one yet still:
"For next partake, a dreaded snake;
The Hydra ye must kill."

The Lernan Hydra

To help him win, took nephew kin
On trek near Argus Bay.
Drove Lerna road to find abode
Of Hydra he must slay.

Midst murky mire with venom dire
Lived deadly snake austere.
With heads of nine on scaly spine
No mortal dared go near.

Shot darts aflame to lure his game,
From lair brought Hydra out.
Yet Hera fumed of fight that loomed,
Sent aide to battle bout.

Told monstrous crab, Herc's heel to grab
And hold his ankle taut.
Big battle raged, two foes engaged
One high, one low, they fought.

Must first arrest crustacean pest,
Then deal with venomed nine.
Kicked crab in face, punts into space
Where Cancer stars now shine.

With axe precise, from snake must slice
Nine heads if death be true.
Yet with each chop, from headless spot,
Where once was one, sprouts two.

To nephew shout: "come help me out,
Bring burning torch aglow.
From whence I prune, quick sear the wound,
So ne'er two more can grow."

Tho' weakened snake deprived of eight,
Immortal was the nine.
Herc swept his axe at last attacks,
And ninth one left the spine.

Alive not dead, he buried head
In pit 'side road to town.
The Hydra's doomed and still entombed
'Neath boulder weight for crown.

From corpse he cut its lethal gut,
Drained Hydra's gall so vile.
Each arrow point he did anoint
With daubs of venom bile.

The serpent slain erased the bane,
Two down and ten to square.
To serve the King, alive must bring
A deer with auburn hair.

The Cerynitian Hind

A Hind that year was female deer
But not just any doe.
Diana's pet, her favorite
No mortal dared aim bow.

Had golden horns and hooves of bronze;
Its sacred coat was red.
Herc's job was clear to capture deer,
Bring back alive not dead.

One year he chased, now face to face,
Yet 'tween them flowed a stream.
Weary and spent, an arrow sent
To wound, not kill, his scheme.

His mind had slipped, the arrow tipped
In venom, he forgot.
On piercing skin the Hind fell in,
Dropped dead upon the spot.

Herc's soul at stake, he cursed mistake
And grieved the Hind's demise.
"Hera's riled, Diana's wild,
Now *two* with fire in eyes."

No mortal drug could fix his flub,
His failure must embrace.
The Gods displeased, damned Hercules,
Redeeming deed disgraced.

Courage bolder, o'er the shoulder
The Hind he tossed now cold.
Diana met, for Hind she wept
Before she chose to scold.

Goddess of Hunt was brutal blunt,
Unleashed her wrathful scorn.
Yet truth disclosed, Goddess disposed
Of anger she had borne.

Apprised of deeds, asked Hercules
To place the Hind at feet.
For truthful proof, forgave his goof,
Revived her pet's heart beat.

Misdeed dismissed, her hand he kissed,
Live Hind across his back.
His faith renewed, more feats pursued
With third of twelve intact.

The king set free, and watched it flee
To herd from whence it came.
Ne'er gave him rest 'fore king request
His fourth to banish shame.

The Erymanthian Boar

A fearsome boar was number four,
O'er which king gloated next.
"For fourth contrived, bring back alive,
Most vicious pig when vexed."

People in town feared coming down
Off mount from yonder den.
The deaths increased from wretched beast,
T'was scourge to mortal men.

When e'er it thrust its sharpened tusk,
It gored whom e'er it found.
O'er countryside left wreckage wide,
Wrought havoc all around.

To find the swine, up steep incline
Herc had to go to chase.
But 'fore ascent, to Pholus went
For lonesome friend's embrace.

A horse unique he stopped to greet
His friend of Centaur kind.
Human to waist, torso replaced
By equine rump behind.

By fireside sat to dine and chat
As guest in Centaur's cave.
Filled belly first that triggered thirst,
A taste for hooch he craved.

Pholus declined request for wine;
"All Centaurs owned thy flask."
The snub ignored he drank their hoard,
Near emptied common cask.

The Centaurs fumed o'er booze consumed,
Cursed brute for piggish prank.
With rocks in hand, the first two planned
To heave for mead he drank.

'Tween fireplace bricks took burning sticks,
And threw them at his foes.
Then raised his club, hell bent to drub
Some noggin knots with blows.

Once satisfied they'd scattered wide,
Herc climbed the mount once more.
He knelt to ground, its spore he found,
Resumed the hunt for boar.

Not hard to find, and close behind
He chased it round and round.
An endless race at torrid pace,
Boar's heartbeat begged to pound.

Its run ran out, and snort from snout
Meant shorter stressful stride.
T'was out of breath and fearing death,
In thicket tried to hide.

In tangled bush, Herc poked its tush
With tip of spear held low.
Exhausted boar sped off once more
'Til belly-deep in snow.

Feet firmly set, Herc tossed his net
O'er top of weary boar.
Big pig in sack, he carried back,
Defeated number four.

As Herc came near, king faint with fear
Of both the beast and man.
So scared was he, he chose to flee
Dove back in hiding can.

Sent word forthwith, "for labor fifth,
Get off your derriere.
Must muck feedlots of cattle plops,
So Aug' can breathe the air."

King Augeas Stables

No demon beast to face at least,
Thought easy chore this time.
Yet 'fore his eyes to his surprise
Were massive mounds of grime.

The numbers fed of cattle bred,
No herdsman could outdo.
For stacked in aisles were endless piles
Of cow dung, yuck, and goo.

From herds so vast, cow pies amassed
With droppings piled in drifts.
To his dismay, within one day
Such filth he had to shift.

"No gutters here, yet rivers near,
A clever plan," he thought.
Hacked holes through walls of stable stalls,
Thence payment scheme he sought.

To king proposed: "if waste disposed,
Make bargain pledge with me?
Fair deal I think, if rid your stink,
One head per ten my fee?"

The king said, "sure, when finished chore
Will honor payment pact."
With spade in hand, Herc dredged the land
To alter river tract.

The dirt flew fast, and 'fore day passed
Dug trenches double wide.
Thence dams undone, the surge begun
Flowed fast through water guide.

Two rivers rushed and sewage flushed,
T'was time for getting paid.
The king denied, said, "Herc had lied,"
Reneged on promise made.

Sued king in court with claim of tort,
Spoke 'fore a judge's bench.
"This crook agreed that once I freed
His barns of awful stench;

He gave his word, a tenth of herd;
My fee he must fulfill.
So from this thief I seek relief,
For which he's paid me nil."

"And what defense for this offense
'Tis there 'fore I decide?"
Afraid to shun, king's only son
Came forth and testified.

"T'was valid deal," the son revealed
And vouched for Hercules.
Since son attests, the judge assessed
That king must transfer deeds.

"From son such guff? Ye said enough,
Now go thy dastard dunce!"
The king enraged from sham uncaged,
Banned both from land at once.

"Promises made should be obeyed,
Not broke," said Hercules.
"Your cheatin' kind, like cows' behind:
Both good at slingin' sleaze."

His duty done and court case won
Herc plodded home once more.
The stable cleansed, fifth caper ends,
Now next, his half-way chore.

From nasty herds to morbid birds,
No rest for Hercules.
Stymphalos Lake, a danger waits,
Murd'rous fowl were these.

The Stymphalian Birds

Our hero stood within the wood
Perplexed at what to do.
"The king had asked a grievous task,
Must think of ways to shoo."

Talons of steel and beaks that peel
The flesh from man and beast.
His deed began by hatching plan,
How best to make deceased.

No rule forbade Athena's aid
For help she could provide.
"Make big ding-dongs with hellish gongs,"
T'was wisdom she supplied.

Thus smithy God used brazen rod,
A master at his trade.
Olympus shops had forged the props,
Hence finest craftsman made."

The calm destroyed when gongs deployed,
Roused nesting birds with fright.
Big clapper clops had scared the flocks,
And frenzied birds took flight.

Once in the air, within cross hair
Each arrow aim was true.
His venom darts had found their hearts,
Clear skies they tumbled through.

The chore t'was done, thus five and one
To do before complete.
A savage pet King Minos kept,
T'was fire-breath bull from Crete.

The Cretan Bull

Across the seas went Hercules
To Grecian Isle of Crete.
When reaching shore, 'fore launching chore,
A pompous king must greet.

He ruled the Isle in lavish style,
King Minos was his name.
When taking throne it should be shown
Of how he gained his reign.

As stories stirred, Poseidon heard
Of kingdom realm aspired.
"If I'm to please," said God of Seas,
"A treaty is required."

Minos agreed, then asked of need,
"Of what must I dispose?"
Poseidon's price: "must sacrifice
Whatever gift I chose."

"I do concede, so let's proceed,
What is thou token fare?"
To his lament, Poseidon sent
Divine bovine so rare.

A ghost-white bull, so beautiful
King Minos could not slay.
Yet terms of pitch allowed no switch,
A promise he'd betray.

Poseidon swore to even score,
And shame the king for life.
He got the bull excitable;
To mate with Minos' wife.

For king's offense, in nine months hence,
A Minotaur was born.
T'was horrible, with head of bull
Atop a human form.

This half-man freak with vicious streak
Caused king much grief for days.
Big pen he planned, that beast be banned,
Entrapped in palace maze.

No cud was chewed, but fancied food
From Athens sent to Crete.
To sate the thing, the bloodlust king
Fed youthful maids for meat.

Still incensed, the God dispensed
More havoc with a smile.
He muddled brain, made bull insane,
Turned loose to rampage Isle.

King begged of Herc, "my bull's beserk,
Please make this menace cease."
Herc wrestled round, 'til beast gave ground,
Then rode it back to Greece.

E'er dutiful, presented bull
As soon as he arrived.
Yet king released the brainless beast
Then ordered eighth contrived.

Before excused, Herc quite amused
At king's stupidities.
White bull still crazed, it wrecked and razed
The king's communities.

"To me must bring," said red-faced king,
Mares of Diomedes!"
"For penal eight, lead live to gate,"
He ordered Hercules.

Mares Of Diomedes

Set sail again with sev'ral men
As volunteers on drive.
With men he planned to capture band,
Return with mares alive.

Four vile equine, man-eater kind,
These mares of Thracian clan.
Blood thirsty beasts engaged in feasts;
They gorged on flesh of man.

Clan's stable men were chased from pen
And driven to the shore.
But soldiers there tried taking mares,
On Hercules made war.

So Herc could fight with all his might
'Gainst seasoned men robust.
He need be freed from double deed,
In boy he placed his trust.

Lad gathered reins, and grabbed their manes
Thus tethered mares in hands.
With loyal mind, tight grip entwined,
Held fast to leather strands.

Ferocious beasts desired release,
Charged off with lad still bound.
Mare's sordid ploy to trample boy
'Til stomped to death on ground.

The mare's misdeeds fumed Hercules,
Sought vengeance for his aide.
Herc slew clan's head, then soldiers fled,
Abandoned their crusade.

Once mares re-caught, and still distraught,
"Fresh meat!" yelled Hercules.
Thus mares were tamed with diced remains;
They ate Diomedes.

Now timid pets, in double sets
Brought mares across the sea.
When led them in, to his chagrin,
The king declared them free.

Without a home, mares left to roam
Amidst the Mounts of Greece.
Where valued prize, met sad demise
At claws and jaws of beasts.

The labor score meant hero's chore
Now rests at number nine.
King's next one dealt: "must bring me belt,
A gift for daughter thine."

Hippolyte's Belt

"Oh that?" said king, "mere little thing,"
In making sport of quest.
"A girdle belt from critter's pelt—
It's worn by broad out west.

"A gift of awe from God of War;
He gave to tigress kind.
'Tis weapon sling encircling
Hip-polly-tee's behind."

To find the tribe that king described,
Herc's ninth of dozen chores.
Twelve men aboard his warship oared,
Departed Grecian shores.

Upon the seas sailed Hercules
To Isle of Amazons.
Devoid of males, he'd heard such tales
Of war-like female blondes.

Minus a breast, the right one left,
T'was lopped to favor bows.
Those brutal girls teased men with curls,
Then killed as battle foes.

Lest need for child, these women wild
Of men they had no use.
To service them, select few men
Were sanctioned to seduce.

Thus when the need for mammal seed
If numbers need revive.
Male infants speared, and females reared,
Restored the tribal hive.

The island reached, Herc looked for beach
Where warship could be moored.
Unfurled the sails, set foot on trails,
Then Pontos Isle they toured.

It wasn't long 'fore brutish blonde
Stepped out from back of tree.
And female band with spears in hand
Stood 'hind Hippolyte.

"What brings you here?" she pointed spear
At startled Hercules.
"Ninth labor thine I shall define,
A king I'm bound to please."

Apprised of deed, their Queen agreed
The favor of assist.
To aid his chore, said belt she wore
"I'll give, so deed dismissed."

But first a fete, to celebrate,
Their Queen to pair with him.
While feast wore on, concealed as blonde
A catty knave slipped in.

Hera disguised, spread vulgar lies
That men had vile intent.
The mood intense, tribe took offense,
Now war was imminent.

Since men alarmed that tribe re-armed,
Herc gathered up his crew.
His goal complete, preferred retreat
Lest forced to fight anew.

As men fell back, "expect attack,"
Herc warned as they withdrew.
Soon horseback charge and spear barrage,
Led by their manly shrew.

No warning word, quick drew his sword
And killed Hippolyte.
Beside her knelt, undid her belt,
Then sprinted toward the sea.

Tho' arrows rained as men regained
Positions at the oars.
And pulling hard put distant yards
'Tween them and tribe on shore.

Once on the seas, a steady breeze
Filled sails t'ward mainland Greece.
With belt in hand, neared coastal strand,
Now labor nine deceased.

On bended knees stooped Hercules,
Before the king he knelt.
"For daughter's need, a gift indeed,"
And gave the king the belt.

"Sire, if you please," said Hercules
Weary of pulling oars,
"For number ten, what is thou yen;
Your next of spiteful chores?"

"Since nine complete, next penal feat
To distant Isle," said he.
"Steal herd divine of red bovine,
Return the lot to thee."

The Cattle Of Geryon

The Sun admired Herc's feats retired;
Gave him a special gift.
A goblet boat o'er seas to float
And westward set adrift.

While journeyed forth to end of earth,
Took side treks to explore.
Along the way found beasts to slay
On course to isle of chore.

Discovered strait, Atlantic gate
Where land tried interlock.
From granite stone built massive throne,
'Tis now Gibraltar rock.

Then splitting slate, twin peaks create,
Stands guard to inland seas.
Both mounts he claimed, today still named,
Pillars of Hercules.

A quarter mile to hostile Isle,
Approach with caution planned.
Titans at gate that lie in wait;
Guarding yon pasture land.

Two legs support three headed sort,
Trip torsos joined at waist.
Lo, fierce defends its cattle pens,
From yards all strangers chased.

And at its flank, a hound so rank
Not one, but two heads bite.
Plus giant brute, a roguish mute,
Neither which lacked for might.

First threat inbound was Orthus hound,
Devil dog charged ahead.
Twin trouble clubbed, he double drubbed
Each hellish head 'til dead.

The Titan vexed, his charge was next
And rushed to even score.
Yet mighty club down upon the crown,
And big brute lived no more.

Done with battle, found the cattle
Knee deep in grassy field.
Tho' stealth arranged to lead from range,
His theft was not concealed.

Eyes in village spied the pillage,
Reported herd's hijack.
Beast alerted, theft subverted,
Geryon sprung attack.

Herc aimed his dart straight for the heart,
Coated with Hydra's bile.
The Gorgon beast collapsed deceased,
Now free to leave the Isle.

Relaxed afloat with herd in boat,
Thought easy deed was done.
Yet in repose, more snags arose,
His trammels just begun.

Poseidon's sons made pirate runs,
Sought booty boats to seize.
Two tried to steal the herd in keel,
Both killed by Hercules.

In midst of fight, the bull took flight
And leapt o'er rail of boat.
It swam like hell for quite a spell
'Til reaching isle remote.

Herc found the bull quite comfortable
Munching on feedlot hay.
Poseidon's third had put in herd,
Refused return of stray.

"Before 'tis freed," third son decreed,
"My king and I are team."
Thus wrestling bout the pair worked out,
Three times Herc beat them clean.

Thence slew the king, told son to bring
The bull he won in pact.
Now safe in boat, once more afloat,
Sailed on with herd intact.

Tho' trek near close, more trouble rose
As Hera fumed with spite.
Her grievous grudge refused to budge,
Conceived another plight.

She filled the skies with swarming flies,
A plague for Hercules.
Her sneering snit, sent bugs that bit,
A menace worse than fleas.

To flee the dread, the cattle fled,
Swam seas to Isle of Thrace.
Again must catch, brought back the batch,
Now ticked from second chase.

Herc's need to vent from fly torment,
Caused anger to inflame.
Thus to avenge, he sought revenge
But wrongly placed the blame.

Thought nasty gnats from river flats
Was source that upset trip.
Filled shipping lanes with boulder banes
That peeled the keels from ships.

Survived onslaught, to king herd brought,
Thus tenth one now on ice.
Yet king absurd killed precious herd;
For Hera sacrificed.

Ten labors done, now twelve less one,
Next tough one to produce.
A wedding gift he had to lift;
The golden fruit of Zeus.

Apples of Hesperides

If to proceed with complex deed,
Must search for garden yards.
T'was golden trove in secret grove
That Ladon dragon guards.

The hidden lot of apples sought,
He knew not where to find.
From Spanish strands to Arab sands,
Yon hither journeyed blind.

The Delphic muse revealed some clues:
"A sea god had such lore;
Nereus knew the pathway to
The Garden of thou chore."

Our hero crept as sea god slept,
Then snatched awake in shock.
Transforming shape, god tried escape,
But vice-like grip was locked.

"To sacred ground where gods abound,"
Said lesser god of seas.
"Thence top its crest, is place of quest,"
Showed way to Hercules.

On mountain spine of range divine,
Prometheus he found.
He stole Gods' fire, inflamed their ire;
Condemned to peak be bound.

Thus ev'ry day, flew bird of prey
To execute his fate.
On liver chewed, by night renewed,
For thirty years it ate.

The God restrained was soon unchained,
Relieved by Hercules.
With self as bait, Herc lay in wait
To end Zeus cruelties.

To rid torment, on bird's descent
T'was hero there instead.
When stretching neck for painful peck
Herc lopped off vulture's head.

Since creature slain, no more such pain;
Prometheus was freed.
For kindness showed, on Herc bestowed
Advice to help succeed.

"Must first conceal intent to steal,"
Prometheus decreed.
"Atlas despised supporting skies,
'Tis he thou need mislead."

"His daughters guard the Garden yard,
Hence kin Hesperides.
Can get to fruit to pilfer loot,
Sneak back to Hercules."

Herc's eyes agleam hatched clever scheme,
Put sneaky plan to test.
Since friend from birth was holding earth,
He'd tempt the man with rest.

"I'll give relief and take but brief,
That earthen globe you bear.
But for reprieve, thou shall retrieve
God's fruit in daughter's care."

"A deal you got, I'll fetch the lot,"
Said Atlas making trade.
Then gripped the earth about its girth,
Set 'pon Herc's shoulder blade.

Atlas returned with apple urn,
But change of place refused.
Tho' bargain made, good faith betrayed,
And Herc was not amused.

But thinking quick deployed a trick,
Claimed pain from Earth he bore.
"Not used to weight, need padding break,
Relief for shoulders sore."

"Mere moment please," said Hercules,
Feigning a brief adjust.
Atlas confused, he fell for ruse,
Retook the globe in trust.

Gave Atlas slip, took fruit to ship
And sailed back home to Greece.
With apples won, eleven done,
One labor left 'fore peace.

But sham was panned, told contraband
Zeus property alone.
Thus king gave back the apple sack
Since mortals could not own.

For ten plus two, he had to do
Most grievous task of all.
For final deed, he must proceed
To Hades Judgement Hall.

For last foray, he must waylay
A hellish hound revered.
Such freakish beast awaits deceased,
A fiend the gods all feared.

Kidnap Kerberos

From serpent's womb born beast of doom,
Of strange and horrid kind.
Typhon its sire, had breath of fire,
On human flesh it dined.

From 'long its back, snake heads attack,
Like dragon tail behind.
Atop its bod, three headed dog,
Most brutish beasts canine.

Kerberos berth was depth of Earth
Where souls went after death.
The beast stood guard, kept mortals barred
'Til Man took final breath.

Once life had ceased, thence soul released
For trek to underworld.
Yea heart divine, or cutthroat swine,
All souls to Hades hurled.

Since Pluto's pit might not permit
Return to living land.
Such risky deed inspired a need
For careful thought out plan.

Mortals who tried were crucified
If challenged portal gate.
This trek of dread t'was home to dead,
Herc's toughest task to date.

To conquer chore, need sacred lore
In arcane mysteries.
Divine rites trained by priest ordained,
Now blessed was Hercules.

Our hero brave found deepened cave,
Went down the trail of gloom.
Met ghostly ghouls, midst gods and fools
'Fore entered Hades room.

Of Pluto asked, "give beast of task,
Put end to Hera's spite."
The god agrees if Herc succeeds
To best the beast with might.

No weapon tools were Pluto's rules,
To wit, Herc gave his word.
Pure brutal force his sole resource,
No sling, no club, no sword.

Kerberos found at gate renowned
And painful bout ensued.
As tail teeth bit, three heads he gripped
'Til battle end was ruled.

The beast submits, its struggle quits,
Its will to fight recedes.
In wrestle hold lay beast controlled,
Exhausted, it concedes.

'Cept wounded pride, no harm to hide
Of Hades hellish hound.
Pluto concurred and kept his word;
He honored pact they'd bound.

Herc led the hound from underground,
To King of Tiryns Greece.
Last test confirms his twelfth of terms,
To Hades, hound released.

When life is drained God status gained,
No underworld once dead.
Immortal fame, Herc's rightful claim;
Olympus Mount instead.

Twelve labors beat, repent complete,
Soul cleansed of penalties.
"Control thy will, lest soul shall kill,"
One theme," said Hercules.

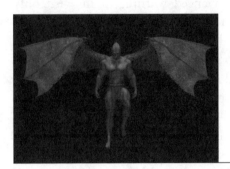

True Name

by Xin Wang

"Rash'kyel..."

I stiffened, gasping, as the smell of warm blood and flesh washed over me. Tension gathered in my shoulders and back, sending a powerful shudder traveling down the length of my spine. My tightly furled wings pressed close to my body. Against my will, I sank to one knee before the man who had materialized. I struggled to keep my eyes on his, but it proved a futile effort; my head bowed, unable to resist his authority. "Master..."

"Even after all this time, Rash?" His voice held a hint of derision; no doubt my brief attempt at rebellion and subsequent surrender amused him. I held my breath. It had been a foolish risk, but he didn't sound angry. Of course, that was no guarantee with my master, but perhaps, if I were lucky, he would overlook it.

"Forgive me, Master."

He dismissed my words with a shrug, one hand rising to call a chair across the room. He settled into the padded cushions and arranged his black robes more to his liking, then crossed his legs and regarded me in silence. Apprehension rose within me as the seconds turned into minutes and still he did not speak. I knew that my fear played right into his hand, but as always I was powerless to resist. Confronted by his relaxed pose and calm stare, I felt wretchedly guilty, though I could not imagine what I might have done wrong. The fact that he had given no advanced warning of his visit only compounded my confusion. His unexpected appearance and closeness had my senses reeling; hunger blazed through me, almost overwhelming in its need. An eternity passed before I wrestled myself under control and the red haze that clouded my vision faded, leaving me drained and empty, a perfect receptacle for the dread that settled in my stomach.

Finally, just as I thought I could not bear the strain an instant longer, he stirred— uncrossed his legs and sighed. I flinched at the sound, at once disappointed and reproving, like a teacher saddened by the failings of a pet pupil. "It seems that there is a child missing from the village."

His words took a moment to make sense, and when they did, I jerked. Fear skittered through my veins as the implications became clear.

"Did you take it?" he asked, his voice hardening.

"No!" I blurted, panicked. "Never, Master, without permission."

"Never?" he asked, mocking disbelief lacing his tone. I could almost see the cool rise of his eyebrow.

"Never ever?"

I realized my blunder. "Not since the last time, Master," I amended.

"Mmm... I see," he said in a lazy purr— a cat toying with a mouse. "You would swear it to me, then, Rash'kyel?"

I breathed in sharply as he invoked my True Name again. My skin heated and felt stretched taut, and I flexed my shoulder blades, a sudden itch developing between them that I could not scratch. My wings rustled at the movement. All in all, though, I was grateful that he had asked it of me. We both knew I could speak nothing less than truth when under the influence of such a powerful geas. "I swear it."

"Humph," he muttered, sounding almost surprised. "Perhaps you do remember some of your lessons after all." He paused, then relented. "Very well, you may rise."

"Thank you, Master." I levered myself upright, relief flooding over me and making my knees weak. The atmosphere eased, and even the bleak sunlight filtering through the narrow window seemed to lighten somewhat. It outlined my master's head in a pale halo, casting his features into partial shadow. Even so, it was not difficult for me to make out the thoughtful look in his dark eyes, the pensive frown on his brow as he rested his stern, pointed face in one hand while the fingers of his other hand tapped on the armrest of the chair.

Almost fifty years had passed since Lucien D'Aetira first bound me, yet no sign betrayed his age. Beneath the flowing black robes of his rank and station, inscribed with a golden lining of protective runes, his muscles were firm and strong. His hair was as thick and black as ever, neat and slicked back in his usual style. If the lines on his face appeared deeper, they only lent an air of stern command to his features. My nostrils flared, detecting the familiar smells of cinnamon and ginger, ashes and smoke that lingered about him, leftover from his spell casting. And, over it all, so strong that I could almost taste it, floated the sweet, tantalizing scent of his mageling blood.

He shifted in his seat. I realized I had been examining him with undue attention, and dropped my eyes. He did not appear vexed, however, his thoughts occupied elsewhere. "You monitor the village at times. Do you know what happened to the child?"

I blinked, then shrugged. "No, Master." Did he expect me to keep track of every farmer's brat or shepherd's whelp? "Wolves, perhaps, or a bear, forced from the mountains by the spring famine."

His lips twitched, as though he heard my unspoken question and sensed my annoyance. His glance swept around the room, noting the books and papers strewn everywhere with a wry grimace. He withheld comment, however. Alone in his tower, this one room was mine. He had granted it to me decades ago, to use as I liked as long as it did not disturb his own designs. Compared to his luxurious study, mine appeared sparse and utilitarian, the dark gray walls barren of decorations and the carpet faded with age. Dust and cobwebs hung from every corner save one on the far side of the room, where I had carved a sigil into the floor. He had been startled, all those years ago, when I demonstrated a talent for magic, for pure demons cannot master the spells of human mages. He never tried to deny me its practice, though, and attributed my abilities to my human heritage. Here, I could practice such small magic as did not require the use of the larger laboratory of my master.

Now, he rose and approached the solid oaken desk in front of the window, reaching out to the tome I had been studying before he came. He squinted at the text; the light was rather too dim for a human to read comfortably by, though more than sufficient for my eyes. He raised an eloquent eyebrow and shot me an amused look. "Planar gates, Rash? Does you demon blood yearn for home then?"

I hissed under my breath, my wings opening and snapping shut again before I could stop myself. It was a sign of irritation, of anger, and I cursed myself for being so easily provoked as Lucien's lips twitched. "My home resides on this plane, as you well know," I retorted, the words perhaps bolder than was entirely wise. The sudden shift in topic made me uneasy; I knew him well enough to recognize it as a cover, a prelude. He wanted something from me, and had chosen this roundabout way to approach it.

Lucien took no notice of my ill temper— a further sign that something was up. He flipped through a few pages of the book, glanced out the window, and finally turned to face me again, apparently done with his charade and ready to tell me what was on his mind. I was prepared for some strange request, but certainly not for what he said next.

"I do not believe that the child is dead. I want you to find her and bring her to me."

I gaped at him, unable, for a moment, to find sufficient words for my astonishment. He wanted me to find a child? A *human* child? "Why?" I demanded, a note of sheer incredulity in my voice.

His eyes narrowed; I was close to overstepping the bounds of his patience. "Don't presume to question me, Rash. I have my own reasons for wanting her here. Alive," he added, as an afterthought.

I stared at him, still unsure whether he was serious or not. He returned me look for look, the beginnings of a scowl on his face. I shook myself out of my stupor. "Of course. As you command, Master."

* * *

The doll was a typical example of the sort of toy human whelps amused themselves with. Curly yellow yarn spilled down its head and its ragged dress fluttered in the breeze. It turned its mismatched button eyes up at the clear, blue sky with a serene gaze, its inane smile fixed upon nothing.

An angry snarl escaped me as I swiped at it, tearing a gash along its body. Cotton spilled out of the opening, fluffy and white and not at all like the blood I wished in its place. My vision hazed red. I sank my claws into it again and again with careless abandon, enraged by its calm smile and lifeless eyes. The air filled with the sound of ripping cloth and floating wisps of stuffing and fabric.

A minute later I halted, mainly because there wasn't a shred left of the doll larger than a small pebble. The need to rend, to feel softness giving way under my claws, had not abated, but I felt somewhat calmer as I gazed, panting, at a button that used to be an eye. I snorted a short laugh. At least *something* was having a worse day than I.

Rising from my crouch, I unfurled my wings and stretched their leathery length as far as they would go, taking care to avoid the trees around me, and sighed, wishing it were later in the year, so that I could bask in the sunlight dappling through the leaves. Full-blooded demons find sunlight uncomfortable at best; it was one of the few blessings of my mixed heritage that allowed me to enjoy its warmth.

Besides the rustling of the wind through the foliage, the woods around me were wrapped in an eerie silence. Not even the earliest bird or most foolhardy squirrel lingered when the smell of sulfur and brimstone touched the air. I had set off an unholy racket from the village dogs three nights ago; for all that I did my best to mask my scent.

It had been a risk, going to the village, but I needed something with the girl's scent on it before I could begin my search. And now the fruit of my labors lay scattered around me, pieces of it drifting away on the wind.

I shrugged and folded my wings. I had no more need of the doll, as I had found the girl, and the men who had taken her. As far as bandit gangs went, this one had done well for itself, and no wonder. Not only did they prey on helpless travelers, they supplemented their income by dealing with the bands of slavers that sometimes passed through the region. Besides the girl Lucien was interested in, they had two small boys. The children were half-drugged and confined inside a dilapidated wagon, no doubt waiting to be sold off.

I cared little about the filth and neglect the children endured, nor about their eventual fates; it was not that which had provoked my temper.

I had tracked the bandits to their temporary camp in an abandoned quarry in the woods. From what I had seen, they were well-armed and most even knew what to do with their swords. They posted sentries around the site and it was not surprising that none had tried to dislodge them, as they showed surprising organization for a bunch of outlaws.

This too, had nothing to do with my simmering anger.

When I had first stolen the doll, it had stirred a vague unease in me. The smell of the girl lingered only faintly about the toy, but something about it had tickled in the back of my mind. I had dismissed my concern; I was impatient to complete this ridiculous quest and get back to my studies. But now...

I had spied on the camp from downwind, to avoid alarming the horses, and as I finished, the wind had brought me my first real whiff of the girl. It had frozen me in my tracks, and for a moment, I had forgotten everything in the lure of that enticing scent. Then the implications had crashed down on me, and my temper flared up in a white blaze of heat.

She was a mage. She was a *mage*, and Lucien had not told me. Her blood carried her birthright as clearly as his did, and just like his, it called to me, to that demon side of me that found mageling blood so irresistibly sweet. The hunger that I kept banked, that was often satisfied with non-magical sustenance, roared and pounded in my head. I wanted to sink my teeth and claws into her, to taste her pain and fear and feast upon her flesh.

But Lucien had forbidden it. He wanted the girl alive, and I was bound to his will. Now I had to rescue her and bring her back to him, all while enduring the exquisite torment of having her heritage so close and yet so untouchable.

I snarled a curse under my breath. Damn Lucien. He knew what this would mean to me, and had ordered it nonetheless. Might have ordered it simply *because* he knew.

Then my eyes narrowed as I looked in the direction of the bandit camp. I could not disobey Lucien, but I *could* do something about the infuriating frustration I still felt. I bared my fangs in a savage grin. Those bandits had taken the girl, and thus, promoted Lucien to force me to retrieve her. By this time tomorrow, I decided, they would never plague this region again.

* * *

I had to plan my attack well. I could not risk harming the girl through carelessness. And so, from the cover of the brush, I watched and waited, while the drifting scent of the girl's blood stoked my burning need to rend and destroy. Finally, as night settled over the camp, the lone woman who cared for the whelps herded the three small figures into the wagon and locked the door.

The calm of inevitability filled me. I rose from my position; no longer caring if the horses should hear or smell me, and stretched to loosen cramped muscles. For a single moment of clarity, I felt my demon side recede, as though taking a step back to gather itself. Then the pent-up fury, the rage, the hunger, exploded out of me with a pressure so painful it bordered on relief.

Bloodlust washed across my vision, a luscious red tide redolent with the taste of wanton slaughter. I felt it flow through me, a sizzling tingle in my fingertips and toes, a shivering in my wings, and I welcomed it. I reveled in it. It had been so long since I had given free rein to my natural instinct for rage and destruction, and now I embraced it with all the fire in my demon soul.

A bestial howl filled the air, a sound of senseless malice and unrestrained cruelty. It froze the humans where they stood; the first never even saw me coming. My claws sank with ease into his soft, yielding flesh, as my teeth sought his neck and the life pulsing just below the surface. Blood flooded my mouth. Hot... Rich... Sweet... A wave of pleasure rolled through me. I savaged the body once more, then turned my attention to the others. Their screams of horror, their panic and mindless terror, their frenzied scramble for weapons, their mad dashing forms in the flickering light of the dying campfire...

I could not say, afterwards, how long the massacre lasted, and massacre it was. For all that they outnumbered me, for all that they were hardened bandits skilled in the use of their weapons, in the end they proved no match for teeth and claws and pure chaotic fury. The wounds they inflicted only fueled my desire for more blood, and when it became clear that their efforts were futile, many threw down their swords and fled. Fools, to think they could escape.

In a small clearing in the middle of the woods, with the full, cold moon as witness, I brought down the last of the fleeing figures. He fell on his back with a cry, throwing up his arms to ward himself, and I felt a savage amusement at the futility of the gesture. So instead of ripping into him as I could have, I sliced a single claw across his belly in a deep, precise line. He gasped and said "Oh!" in the most surprised fashion, his hands growing slick and slippery with blood as he tried desperately to keep his guts from spilling on the ground. The hot tang of his innards filled the air, but the worst of my bloodlust had been sated with the slaughter beforehand. Rather than finishing him off, I prowled on the edges of his vision, growling and relishing his muffled sobbing, hoarse and raw with pain and fear.

It took him a long time to die.

Finally, when his whimpers had ceased forever, and the heat from his entrails had attracted the first of what would soon become a swarm of flies, I shook myself. The last of the bloodlust fell away, leaving a pleasant lethargy behind, a delicious ache in my muscles. I spared the body not another glance as I turned and retraced the way back to the demolished campsite.

At some point during the carnage, the embers had been scattered over half the camp, and it was by some miracle that they failed to ignite any of the dried leaves or grasses. Their reddish glow highlighted the shadowy, unmoving forms on the ground. I kicked the coals back together into a rough pile, and then took a moment to lick my wounds. Most were superficial, but a few cut deep, and now that my demon blood had cooled, they stung.

The silence of the night lay thick and heavy around me, as though a muffling cloak stifled even the chirping insects. I had no problem, therefore, hearing the quiet sniffling coming from the wagon. No doubt the whelps inside had heard the screaming and the sounds of slaughter. They would keep. I was more concerned about the state of the horses.

The beasts had been driven almost mad with terror during my attack, and a few had fled when their panicked riders tried to escape with them. I had let them go; I had little interest in horseflesh, after all, and better prey to concentrate on at the time. The ones left at the camp retreated to the ends of their tethers at my approach, rolling their eyes at the smell of blood and sulfur. Impatient and in no mood to deal with the refractory creatures, I cast a quick charm. They calmed, lulled by the magical reassurance, and I chose the best of the lot. I had been puzzled about how to get the girl back to Lucien's tower; I could cover the distance myself in a couple of days, but then, I could fly. Now, with the girl in tow, I would have to settle for the pace of this horse, as the thought of carrying her myself stirred up such a rush of hunger that I knew it to be useless.

I could see no point in delay. The faster I returned, the faster I could deposit the brat in Lucien's care and distance myself from her scent. The lock on the door presented little challenge; I ripped it away with a jerk and tossed it aside. In the gloom within, I could make out three pairs of terrified eyes.

"Out," I growled. They didn't budge. There was no question of going in after them; the space was cramped even without the addition of my wings, so instead I snarled, and putting my hands under the door jamb, lifted the front of the wagon a couple of inches before letting it fall back again with a splintering rattle. "Now!"

This time, they moved. Scrambling in their haste, they tumbled over each other and out onto the ground. For a moment, they stood still as their eyes adjusted, then they took in the sight of the slaughter around them as though in a trance. Their horror-filled eyes turned to me, to my horns and my sulfurous yellow eyes and my wings.

The boys' shrill screams of terror lanced the air, and they darted under the wagon with the agility of feral rats. The girl, too stunned to follow, simply stared. She looked about four or five. Even in the moonlight, I could see that her eyes were a startling green, and they held a disturbing numbness. For the first time, it occurred to me that overwhelming fear might damage her mind as easily as physical force would damage her body.

It grated, but I forced myself to take a step back and uncross my arms. I pulled my wings tighter to my body and spread my hands, palms outward, hoping she would notice only the placating gesture and not the claws.

She roused at my movement, and I tensed, ready to catch her should she bolt, but whether it was my ludicrous attempt at being less threatening or the drugs that still dulled her senses, she settled again. A strained moment passed, as I wondered what I should do next, then, to my surprise, she spoke, her voice a hoarse whisper.

"Are you a demon?"

Her question startled me and I answered unthinking. "Part demon," I corrected primly. Then I felt like an idiot. What the hell did this brat care whether I possessed a pure pedigree or not?

But she seemed reassured, if only because of my apparent willingness to communicate. She considered me a moment, then said, "My name's Jayleen."

Drugs, I decided. *Definitely drugs.* The irony of the moment was not lost on me, but I replied nonetheless, "You can call me Rash."

She nodded, her expression still dreamy and unfocused. Her eyes strayed to the horse behind me, and I saw my opportunity. "I'm going to take you away from here," I said, my voice slow and careful. "So I'm going to need you to get on the horse, alright?" She looked blank and I ground my teeth. "Alright, Jayleen?"

She reacted to her name, and finally seemed to understand. In any case, she made no protest as I approached. I stamped down on my hunger, easier now after the bloodletting and scooped her up and onto the horse's back in one smooth motion. Then I had to make a grab for her as she teetered and nearly fell off the other side, cursing myself for not thinking of a saddle. When her hands clenched into the beast's mane and I was reasonably certain that she would not fall, I took the rope tether and led the pair out of camp, trying not to show my irritation at the leisurely pace. The trip back would take the better part of a week.

As we left, I wondered what would happen to the two boys, but I had enough problems to deal with. What did it matter, after all, whether those whelps lived or died?

* * *

I peered at the faded spines on the shelves, trying to read the titles of the tomes without stirring up a cloud of dust. My master rarely used this library, and the books stored here smelled of time and neglect. Most of these works dealt with magic only in passing, which explained why they had been relegated to this forgotten corner of the tower. There were a few, though, that delved into magical theory; though they held no spells, I'd often found answers to my researches in their yellowing pages.

A soft noise came from two shelves back, and I suppressed a sigh. It was getting harder to overlook the pair of curious green eyes that followed my every movement, harder to pretend I didn't notice the surreptitious tip-toeing that dogged my steps. Above all, harder to ignore the scent of mageling blood that tickled my nostrils. I gritted my teeth and determinedly began perusing the next shelf, rustling my wings in annoyance.

The next few minutes passed in silence, and I had almost forgotten my unwelcome audience when a most peculiar sound reached my ears. A series of muffled sniffles and gasps... followed by a chain of uncontrollable sneezes. I closed my eyes, not sure if the growl bubbling in my throat was amusement or exasperation or both.

In any case, there seemed no longer any point in the charade. The girl gave a small squeak of startlement when I placed myself in front of her, my wings spread slightly for maximum effect. "What," I rumbled, my words spaced apart to convey my irritation, "do you think you're doing?"

She stared up at me, her green eyes wide, and I ruthlessly squashed the hunger that stirred in me. I was forbidden to harm her, and giving free reign to my demon side would only result in the ache of unsatisfied desire. Even so, my blood grew heated and my senses heightened until every nerve felt fine-tuned and on-edge. I fought it, but I could not deny the whisperings of my bloodlust, the uncurling of the fury that lurked always on the periphery of my consciousness. And I knew, with bone-deep certainty, that the minute the girl bolted, I would no longer be able to control myself, and it would take the full, awful weight of my geas, my True Name, to stop me from ripping her to shreds.

Then she blinked, and though I smelled her fear, she held her ground. Ducking her head, she picked at a loose string on her dress and mumbled "Sorry" to her toes, before sneaking a quick look at me and returning to her contemplation of the floor.

I stared at her, so startled that my rage stuttered and melted away before I even realized it. Laughable, that this tiny figure could have so easily defused my simmering temper; all of a sudden, I felt oddly ridiculous. To cover my confusion, I asked, "Sorry about what?"

"You looked busy. I didn't wanna interrupt."

"Which doesn't tell me what you were doing here in the first place."

If I didn't know better, I would've sworn the look she gave me was abashed instead of fearful. "I was bored..."

I watched her draw patterns in the dusty floor with her big toe, unable for a moment to link her reply to my question. Then I succeeded, and I gaped at the top of her curly head. She was bored? "And stalking a demon sounded like a fun game?"

"*Part* demon," she pointed out, for all the world as though I might not know it already.

I glared. She faltered under my gaze, unsure once more. "Don't you have anything else to do?" I finally asked, meaning, didn't she have anyone besides me to bother?

Her curls bounced as she shook her head. "Master Lucien is busy, and he doesn't like for me to get in his way..."

"Mariam?" I tried, though I knew as soon as I asked what the answer would be, even before I saw the girl's impatient look. The gods alone knew where Lucien had acquired the woman who cleaned the tower and cooked his meals, but I was willing to bet that a duller creature did not exist. While I did not see much of her, for I never suffered her presence in my own quarters, I knew she could neither speak nor respond to any but the simplest commands, though I could not say whether she had always been thus or whether Lucien had altered her with his magic. She had simply appeared one day, and never once since shown more initiative than a golem, and it was to her care that Lucien had entrusted the girl when I first brought her back.

In the ensuing silence, for the girl had not bothered to dignify my inquiry with an answer, I examined the figure before me. She looked well-fed enough, but an air of neglect clung to her. It showed in the way her blond curls lay tangled and unkempt, in the dirty smudges on her face, in the way her dress hung limp and bedraggled on her shoulders. Mariam had kept to the word of Lucien's orders, which was to keep the girl alive, but even I could see that "alive" and "well-cared for" were two different concepts.

I still did not know what Lucien wanted with this whelp, and my hope that bringing her back would end our contact had been in vain. At first, when the drugs wore off, she had been terrified of me. But one day, exploring the tower on her own, she had stumbled upon me in this very room. She had fled with a squeak of fright, but then, two days later, she was back. This covert surveillance had continued for almost a month. I had ignored her, hoping she would leave, my blood heating every time I smelled her scent, but this was the first time we had spoken.

Her interest baffled me. "What do you want of me?" I demanded abruptly.

"Nothing," she protested. "I just... wanted company..."

I huffed a half-sigh, half-snort. I no more needed her in my way than Lucien did, but there was nothing I could do to stop her from staying in the same room. I managed an ungracious "Suit yourself" as I turned away, determined not to let her disrupt any more of my day. She seemed satisfied enough, settling on a dusty chair and

watching me with her legs swinging. At least she forebore to plague
me with questions.

* * *

"So why do you do everything that Master Lucien tells you to?"

I glanced up from my book, startled. Jayleen, her own book
tossed to the side, regarded me with honest curiosity, her face cupped
in her hands, her elbows resting on the table.

"Why do you?" I countered, trying to sidestep the question.

Jayleen frowned, the expression producing a familiar crease
between her eyebrows. "Because... because he's a powerful mage and
he controls this tower."

"And you're scared of him," I said, unable to resist the tease.

She stuck her tongue out at me. "Well, he *is* a powerful mage
and he *does* control this tower," she said. "I'd be a fool not to be."

I snorted, amused, and returned to my book.

"But that doesn't answer my question," she said, unwilling to let
me off the hook so easily. When I did not answer, she rose from her
chair and crossed the study to where I sat. A trace of adolescent
awkwardness still showed in her step, left over from her recent
growth-spurt. Reaching across the desk, she tugged the book from
my hands, ignored my half-hearted snarl, and asked again, "Why do
you obey Master Lucien, Rash? I know his magic is more powerful
than yours, but you're part demon, so that pretty much balances out.
And you're always making fun of me for being scared of him, so it
can't be that. So why do you stay?"

"Because," I snapped. Her eyes widened at my tone, and I
worked to restrain my temper. My anger stemmed not from
bloodlust; over the years, I found it easier to control my hunger,
unless she happened upon me unexpectedly. Rather, she had touched
on a sensitive subject, but I would gain little by avoiding the issue.
After all, Lucien would tell her readily enough if she thought to ask
him. "Because he knows my True Name."

"Your True Name?" I saw her put two and two together and
realize that the name I had given her and by which she had always
addressed me had been less than the full story. For a moment, she
looked hurt, but then she rallied. A thoughtful look came into her

eyes. "I've read of True Names," she said, with the air of someone reciting a lesson. "It's said that long ago, before magic became so scarce in the world, many people knew their True Name. Such a name was held to be sacred, for it was bestowed by the gods, and only to be shared with one's closest, truest friends. Also, though the True Name held no arcane significance for humans, if a person should learn the True Name of a faerie or a demon or a dragon or any other magical being, it would be possible to hold that creature in thrall through its power." She blinked and her eyes refocused on me. "And Master Lucien knows yours?"

I grunted an affirmative. I had never bothered to research True Names myself— living under one was enough for me; and I could not fathom anyone simply telling another being his, no matter how trusted, but Jayleen had gotten the essentials correct at least. It allowed Lucien to control me; what more was there to know?

"But... but how did he find out? I mean, there are ways of divining it, it's true, but it's never a sure bet, and even then—"

"Through my dam," I interrupted, impatient for this conversation to be over.

Jayleen looked surprised at the idea that I had not simply sprung out of the ground fully formed. "Your... but, uh..."

I rolled my eyes at her embarrassed stop. "She was a half-demon." I sighed and rubbed a hand over my forehead. An expression of avid curiosity shone from Jayleen's face, and though she would not force me if I resisted, I knew she would never rest until she had heard the story, which meant that she would be shooting me pleading, sidelong glances for days if I did not tell her now. "I have only vague memories of her," I said, evasive. Then I chanced to glance at her face.

There was a strange expression in her eyes, a pensive stillness that took me aback. She dropped her gaze when she noticed my scrutiny, but not before I recognized the look of wistful longing. In a flash, I realized that she probably did not remember her own family; certainly she never spoke of them. She had been too young when the bandits took her, and though the village lay only a day away from the tower, she could not know that, never having been allowed outside on her own.

I had never pitied anyone in my life, but suddenly, I wanted to tell her this story, to give her some glimmer, however unlikely, of what she had been torn away from at such a young age.

"I remember... I remember the instinctive yearning for her teat as my siblings and I shoved and struggled with each other, the rough rasp of her tongue on the rare occasions when she bestowed a moment on her litter of squirming whelps, the impatient swipe of her paw that sent me tumbling head over heels whenever I squabbled too loudly with my brothers and sisters..."

Jayleen's lips twitched into a smile, and I scowled, knowing that she was picturing me as a newborn whelp. "What of your sire?" she asked when I did not continue.

"I doubt she let him live long past their coupling," I said with a shrug. "Unlike her offspring, she was only half-human, and for all that it showed, she might as well have been pure demon. Like all she-demons, the urge to rut had overcome her innate loathing of males and driven her to mate, probably with the first male human she came across. So paternity is a bit hard to establish, and no doubt as soon as her sexual lust abated, a different sort of lust took over." Jayleen's startled look amused me, as though she did not know whether to be appalled or not. I grinned. "Don't feel too sorry for him. That nameless human had his revenge in the end, by saddling her with a litter of mewling demon spawn."

"But she cared for you."

"Purely instinctual, I assure you. Being what she was, my dam was not tainted by any inkling of maternal feelings."

"Uhm... alright... So, what happened to her?"

"She died. Killed by a zealous knight who'd come upon our nest in the woods. She killed him, but not before he'd slaughtered all of her litter, besides me, and given her a mortal wound." I did not add that I still remembered the terrified sounds of my siblings as they lay dying, and the thick stench of their pooling blood around me. For once, the thought of gory carnage stirred no excitement in me.

"I... I'm sorry, Rash."

Her sympathy surprised me. "Whatever for? It happened a long time ago; no use mourning it now."

Jayleen remained silent only a minute. "What did you do afterward?"

A short laugh escaped me. "What *could* I do? I was a helpless whelp, with no knowledge beyond that he must feed to live. I doubt I would have survived the week, if Lucien hadn't found me."

"Then he rescued you?"

"If you can call it that." My bitterness startled even me, and I hastened to add, "He was a young mage then, and though more powerful than most in his position, he had little to his name save a few simple spells and his burning ambition. When he found me, I was huddled next to my dam's cold body, scared and alternatively crying and pawing at her." That much he had told me, years later. And while he did not go into details, I suspected that the only way I had survived so long was by feeding off of whatever lay closest to hand— that is to say, of cannibalizing the corpses around me. I shook myself to clear that image. "I don't know what spell he cast, to drag my dam's spirit back into the mortal plane..." I trailed off, uncertain how to explain what happened next.

Luckily, Jayleen understood what I meant, for she nodded. "One of the ways of divining a being's True Name— to force the knowledge from someone recently dead. The more powerful the association between the dead and living subject, the more powerful the spell." She paused, then continued gently, "No one could have been closer to you than your dam, and not only that, but she had died by violence to protect you. Those symbols must have lent overwhelming power to Master Lucien's spell, far more than what would normally be available to a new mage. It was a monstrous thing he did."

I gaped at her, speechless. It was not the extent of her knowledge that surprised me; she had often demonstrated an astonishing capacity for learning in the past few years. It was the way her eyes saw right through me, the way her words eased some long-held knot of tension inside that I had not even known existed. Whatever I had pretended to myself, the thought that my dam had betrayed my True Name to Lucien had been an unhealing wound that I had ignored all my life. Now, for the first time, I felt as though a clean bandage had been applied, and I breathed easier. I snorted a chuckle. "I bit him, you know, when he first approached me." Back then, I had been too young to experience the demonic bloodlust that his mageling blood should have evoked. "He didn't stop cursing me for the better part of a day."

That startled a laugh out of Jayleen, and I grinned too. The comfortable silence between us stretched for the space of a minute before she stood. "It's late; I should go." She hesitated on the threshold, looked back and smiled. "Thank you for telling me all this, Rash."

I stared at the worn wood of my study door for a long time after she had gone. "Thank you for listening..."

* * *

"Well done, Rash. Very well done indeed," Lucien murmured, cradling the jewel I had brought him. The light reflected off its facetted surfaces, setting its blood-red core afire. Lucien's long, thin fingers stroked it lovingly as he savored the feel of the magic imbued into its crystalline matrix. After a moment, he drew a deep breath and remembered my presence. "You may go, but stand ready. I may have another task for you ere long."

Once out of his sight, I spread my wings as far apart as they would go, and stretched until my muscles popped. A growl of pleasure rumbled deep in my throat. I was sore and bruised and exhausted, but Lucien was not the only one satisfied with my work today. And while the coven I had destroyed had been brutal in their magic, Lucien's shields had kept the worst of the assault from harming me, as his portal had allowed me to enter unchallenged. Those mages had been fools, to deny him what he sought, and now nothing remained of their hall save a pile of rubble and the blood that stained the broken stones. And Lucien had not minded that, afterwards, I had fed until my hunger grew satiated and retreated like a purring cat to sleep off the feast.

My body desired nothing more than to follow suit, but my mind was still too wound up with the battle and the aftermath to allow for rest. I wanted to share the giddiness of my victory, to recount to someone the savage pleasure that had rushed through me.

The library had changed much over the years; now, a cheerful fire blazed on the grill and the dust that had covered everything had long been banished. I chuckled at the sight of Jayleen next to the window, her eyes distant and unfocused as she gazed outward. She turned at the sound, and rose with a glad cry to greet me, the open book in her lap falling unheeded to the floor.

"Rash! I was worried—" she gasped as she took in my condition: the dried blood, the tears and scratches in my wings and on my arms.

"I'm alright," I assured her with a grin, pleased at her genuine concern. I flapped my wings once, creating a waft of wind that stirred her hair, to show the truth of my words, and her alarm faded. The sunlight streaming in through the window behind her picked out the golden highlights of her curls and framed her figure like a picture. Not for the first time, I found myself thinking that she had grown to become a beautiful young woman whom men might gladly die for.

"What happened?" she asked, oblivious to my thoughts.

It was the opening I had been hoping for, and without further promoting, I launched into my story. The excitement came back with the telling, and I paced with excess energy as I described how I had overcome the coven and wrested the jewel from its ancient resting place beneath their hall.

I did not notice Jayleen's silence until after I had finished. She sat still as a statue, and there was something about the way she perched on the edge of her chair, something in the set of her shoulders, that puzzled me— an unexpected tension that I had not expected, an unreadable expression in her eyes. I stopped my restless movement, uncertain.

She roused at last, but instead of meeting my eyes, only walked to the window and stood with her back to me. "Do you know what the jewel does, Rash?"

I thought it an odd question; both of us knew better than to meddle with whatever Lucien had planned. "No. Its magic is strong; I could feel that the minute I touched it, but I don't have any idea what its purpose might be." I tried to suppress my irritation. "I only fetched it back, as Lucien commanded."

"And killed all those mages? Did he command that too?"

The silence in the room thickened. She glanced at me over her shoulder, and the sadness in her eyes dried up any words I might have had. Finally, "No," I admitted. "He only told me to retrieve the jewel." My shame turned into resentment. "What else could I do, surrounded by so many mages? I've told you of the demonic bloodlust."

"There is more human in you than demon, Rash."

Her quiet words stung. It was an old argument, one that had gone on for the past year or so. I knew what she would say next almost before she said it.

"Why do you deny your human side so, Rash? Why do you embrace only the demonic part of your bloodline?"

I ground my teeth in frustration. "It's who I am, Jayleen!" I growled. "Stop trying to make me into something I'm not!"

"Your demon blood is only a part of who you are!" she shot back, turning to face me at last. "Stop rejecting the choices that your human heritage gives you!"

"Choice?" I taunted. "What *choice?* Lucien knows my True Name! I don't have a choice and I never have!"

"Don't give me that!" she snapped. "Everyone has a choice! Only those who lack the courage to face theirs ever claim otherwise." She paused, her chest rising and falling with emotion. There was a chill in her voice I had never heard before. "I never took you for a coward, Rash."

My already-simmering temper flared, a wash of fury that dyed the room in bright crimson. How *dare* she! By what *right* did she pass judgment on me! I wanted to hurt her, to watch those green eyes widen in fear and pain, to make her regret those words. A deadly snarl blistered the air. It was a sound that struck fear into hardened warriors, and I felt a vicious satisfaction as the color drained from Jayleen's face.

Then her jaw set in a stubborn line, her fists clenched, and her chin went up. She stood her ground, every line of her body screaming defiance. Her courage infuriated me, and in a way that had nothing to do with bloodlust and everything to do with the sudden, unexpected hurt and pain that her words had inflicted.

I didn't even realize I had raised my hand until I saw her crash to the floor. She lay there unmoving, and for a terrifying moment, my heart stuttered and my breath froze. My rage vanished so quickly that it left me cold and shaken, my blood turned to ice. Then she stirred, with a soft moan, and the world started up once more. One hand rose to touch the blossoming bruise on her cheek. Her eyes locked on mine, and the shock and hurt in their green depths went through me like a lance.

"Rash..."

I didn't give her a chance to finish. I turned and fled that room like it was a portal to the last circle of Hell. Back in my own quarters, I placed every magical lock I could think of on my door, then threw myself onto the bed.

It was impossible to think, equally impossible not to. The whirling maelstrom of thoughts and emotions within would not be ignored. At any other time, I would have used my temper to quiet my inner turmoil; breaking things had always managed to calm me before. Now, the mere idea brought to mind the disappointment in Jayleen's eyes and the sick shame that had twisted my heart when she looked at me.

Finally, exhausted by the day's events and the rapid succession of conflicting emotions, I fell into a fitful doze, thankful that at least none of the nightmares that plagued my dreams bore green eyes nor possessed anything beyond teeth and claws with which to wound me.

* * *

I glared at the text before me, telling myself that I was reading even though all I could concentrate on was listening for the sound of footsteps outside my door.

When Jayleen had first found my door sealed against her and obtained no response to her knocking, she had been angry. She had pounded, told me that I was being ridiculous, and threatened to learn portal magic solely in order to break my mage locks. She had accused me of sulking, called me a stubborn fool, and stated that I'd have to emerge from my lair sooner or later. It was petty, but I had taken a childish, malicious pleasure in ignoring her.

By the second day, she was worried, though she tried to conceal it. She had asked me if anything was wrong, with a not-so-subtle undertone of whether it was something she had done. It was shame more than anything else that stopped me from answering her then, but I had regretted it almost immediately. Something in her voice had made me uneasy, an odd note that sounded like fear. But that was silly. Nothing in the tower could harm her; Lucien had seen to that.

In any case, I had decided to answer her today, but, in typical Jayleen fashion, she had not come as I expected.

I gave up on any pretense of studiousness and thrust my book away with an impatient snarl. Did that girl take pleasure in tormenting me? *Well, it won't be the first time I've swallowed my pride,* I thought with a glum snort as I rose to find her myself. *Nor, I expect, will it be the last.*

I sensed footsteps approaching as I reached the door, and pulled it open, ready with a glad greeting. It died on my lips when I saw Lucien on the other side, looking just as surprised as I felt. I fumbled my words and bowed my head. "M-master."

Lucien dismissed my discomfiture with his usual briskness. "I am almost done with my preparations, Rash, but I have need of a few final spell components." He handed me a piece of parchment and made to leave. "I will need them before this evening."

"Wait!" I blurted before I could stop myself. He turned and shot me a look of quelling impatience. I stuttered, wondering if I had really meant to tell him that I needed to see Jayleen before I could run his errand. To buy time, I glanced over the list he had given me. My eyes widened. Virgin's blood, for innocence; breath of wight, for undeath; bloodwyrm fang, for stolen strength. What spell could Lucien be preparing that would require such things? "These components..."

"Are no concern of yours," Lucien said. "Just see that you get them!"

If I had not known him all my life, I would have missed the note of repressed excitement in his voice. I folded the parchment in half with deliberate care, examining him out of the corner of my eye. One hand, almost concealed in his sleeve, clenched, and his nostrils flared as he breathed. His eyes glittered in the dim torchlight of the hall.

Wariness hummed along my veins, whispered suspicions into my mind. In all the years I had known him, Lucien had always maintained the strictest control over his emotions. Even when his experiments met with spectacular success, he never allowed more than a satisfied half-smile to cross his face. I did not know what his volatile mood might mean, whether it might make him more lenient, so over my own misgivings I asked, "May I see Jayleen before I go?"

My request took him aback. He hesitated, then said, "I have need of her tonight, so there is no time. Do as I command, Rash'kyel."

"Of course, Master. As you wish." My reply was pure reflex, and I watched him until his back had turned the corner, considering his words. They puzzled me even as I left the tower to harvest what he had requested.

Other than a fleeting glance when I brought her here as a child, Lucien had never shown the slightest interest in Jayleen. In fact, he ignored her even more completely than he ignored me, for at least he had uses for me from time to time. I had been convinced at first that he meant to take her as his apprentice; instead, as her magical talents grew, I was the one who had asked to be allowed to teach her to use them. Lucien seemed surprised at the idea, as he had when I began to dabble in magic, but had granted permission without further ado, looking amused. And because Jayleen had never gotten over her childish fear of him, and stayed out of his way for weeks at a time, there were times when I believed he had forgotten her existence entirely.

So what manner of business could the two of them have with each other?

Maybe he's finally taking charge of her training. After all, she surpassed me weeks ago, and must be catching up to his own level. The surge of pride inside made me smile.

Then I remembered Lucien's strange excitement and the quaver in Jayleen's voice the day before. A shiver of apprehension ran down my spine. I tried to put it out of my mind, but nonetheless, I could not deny the haste in my steps as I hurried to finish my task.

* * *

The stairs leading to Lucien's study spiraled upwards in a dizzy curve. Normally, a simple cantrip would have whisked me to the top, but it would also have destroyed any chance I had at stealth. Instead, I cloaked myself in every shadow, muffled my steps, and climbed.

Lucien had spared me not a glance when I returned, had taken the bag I handed him and hastened back to... to what?

The sturdy door of his laboratory was closed, and flickers of light shone out from the crack underneath. He had sealed it with magic, of course, but he had granted me exemption long ago, as I could pose no threat, and had not thought to revoke that passage now. I murmured a quiet spell, and felt a faint tingle as I faded through both door and seal.

Within, the air crackled with magic, snapped with power. My skin goose-bumped and I hissed as I pulled my wings as close to my body as I could. Neither torch nor magelight lit the room, yet there was no need, for a white brilliance shone from something in the center of the sigil on the floor. Lucien stood before it, outlined in stark relief, so that all I could see for the moment were the symbols he had chalked unto the stone and the upside-down pentagram inscribed within the circle. Where the light did not reach, shadows danced, turning the edges and corners of the room into places of wild, twisting shapes.

Then Lucien shifted, and I gasped aloud. Jayleen hung suspended, apparently unconscious, in midair, caught in a web of magic whose glittering strands emanated from two posts on either side that curved over her to form an arch. At the apex of that arch, set like some sinister keystone, rested the blood-red jewel I had obtained for Lucien only days before. Even as I watched, Lucien chanted an incantation, and the jewel began to glow with sullen anger, its color bleeding into the strands of the web until the whole structure looked like a gory instrument of torture.

I was so transfixed by the sight before me that for a moment, I forgot about Lucien. His sharp demand made me jump, and I found him glaring at me with cold anger in his eyes.

"Exactly *what* do you think you're doing here, Rash?"

I quailed before the fury in his voice, and had to swallow before I could muster an answer. "M-master... what..." I glanced at Jayleen again and shuddered. Some things, even a demon did not want to know.

Lucien's lips curled in impatience, but then he seemed to reconsider. I realized that he must still be quite early on in his spell, for otherwise he would never have taken the trouble to answer. And, possibly, he was not altogether displeased at having an audience to show off for; this was, after all, his crowning moment. He gazed with fond possessiveness at the arches that held Jayleen and smiled with pride and triumph. "She will be my greatest experiment," he said, almost purring. "A feat that will live forever in history... even as I live forever!" My blood ran cold at the mad glee in his voice. "For so long, I searched for the ultimate secret, until I almost despaired, but then the answer came to me. So simple; so brilliant. For life and death are inextricably intertwined— two faces of the same coin. All I needed, then, was a way to transmute the one into the other."

Stunned comprehension burst upon me. My chest tightened. I felt as though pieces of a puzzle I had not even known existed had suddenly fallen into place to reveal a terrifying landscape to my eyes. "Then, all these years... and even before..."

"Yes, Rash." Lucien sounded patient, as though lecturing a slow child. "I have watched her almost from birth. When I thought her lost, I almost panicked; magical aptitude is hard to come by nowadays. But then you found her and brought her here, and that was even better than leaving her in the village, for now I could be sure that no harm could befall her before she served her purpose. All these years, I have waited and watched, as she grew and her magic matured. And now," he crooned, "now, she is finally ready. With her death, I will become greater than ever before! And after her... well, there will be another lifetime to search for the next sacrifice!"

"Master, please... don't..." My voice sounded small and pleading. Horror clawed at my heart. Fear sucked at my breath.

Lucien's face betrayed his surprise; I think for a moment he had forgotten about me as he contemplated the glorious future only he could see. His eyes raked over me, and whatever he saw apparently amused him a great deal, for he threw back his head and laughed.

"Why, Rash! I do believe you've grown fond of your little playmate!" He chuckled at the idea. "Not to worry. When this is over, you can take another child from the village, if you wish; there are plenty of the brats running around, after all." Then, as quickly as it had come, his humor vanished and he waved a hand in dismissal. "Now, leave me, Rash. I still have work to do."

I stood rooted to the spot as he walked toward the arches once more. Lucien had brushed aside my plea with no more thought than one might give the whimper of a stray dog. Had, in fact, told me to replace Jayleen as calmly as though I was a child who could be placated with a new kitten after my old one ran away. Did he think that she was no more than a pet to me? That I thought so little of her companionship that I would be satisfied with any substitution? *Of course he does.* Bitterness welled up in my throat. *After all, it's how -he- has always thought of -me-.*

That thought galvanized me, and before I knew what I was doing, I had reached out a hand and grabbed Lucien by the arm. He whirled on me, furious. "I am not a patient man, Rash, and when I give an order, I expect to be obeyed." Contempt laced his voice. "Since you obviously didn't hear me the first time, I'll tell you again. Get out of my sight, Rash'kyel! Go and hide in your hole until I have time to deal with your insolence."

The geas of my True Name crashed down on me, forcing my body into motion even as I fought its power. I had the vague impression of Lucien turning away from me, of his voice rising and falling in the familiar sing-song cadence of incantation as his hands gestured, but what he said or did I could not tell. Because as much as my mind screamed at me to stop, I could not resist the force of his command. With sinking despair, I raised my head for one final look at Jayleen.

The tainted, bloody gleam of the web cast a sickly light onto her features, made her hair a dull, rusty color, so different from when I saw her last, with the sunshine playing off those golden curls. And suddenly with that memory came another— her words, spoken with the quiet steel that formed the center of her being.

"There is more human in you than demon, Rash."

"...more human..."

For the first time in my life, I turned inward and reached, not for the bloodlust or the rage or the hunger of the demon within, but for the human, for that part of me which I had always repressed, which I had disregarded, and which I now recognized as having responded so warmly to Jayleen's love and care.

For long, agonizing seconds, I found nothing as the unrelenting pressure of my True Name drove me back toward the door. And then, so faint it might have been nothing but my own breath, something stirred and uncoiled. Though it cost me every ounce of control I had, my steps slowed. The air wheezed in my lungs as I struggled through the crippling pain of two conflicting desires waging battle over my body.

When my vision cleared, I found myself crouched mere inches from the door. Even my teeth hurt. But I had overcome Lucien's command, and as I staggered to my feet, the roaring in my ears faded until I could once again make out his voice raised in spell casting.

I had no idea when his spell would conclude, only that I had to act fast. There was no subtlety to what I did. A moment to gather myself, then I sent a raw blast of magic straight at Lucien.

Had he not been distracted in his task, my attack would never have worked; Lucien was more powerful in magic than I could ever hope to be. Even with the element of surprise, he almost emerged unscathed, for he sensed the hostile power and threw up a shield with a speed I could only envy. Our magic collided in a blinding flash, and the shockwaves sent me stumbling into the wall. Lucien, closer to the explosion, grunted as he fell to his knees.

After the steady drone of his spell and the rumbling backlash of my foiled attack, the silence in the room sounded deafening. Then Lucien straightened with studious calm and turned to face me, and the unbridled rage I saw in his features told me with sick certainty that at least one of us would not be walking out of this room.

"All these years, Rash," he said, his tone so conversational it raised my hackles. "I saved you when you would have starved. I raised you from a sniveling whelp. I allowed you to practice magic in my tower. All these years, and *this* is how you choose to repay me?"

I made no answer, but watched his every movement. Now that we faced each other on equal footing, I was at a disadvantage, and we both knew it. On the other hand, he had been casting a spell on a scale of complication that I could only guess at, one that, though uncompleted, should have drained much of his resources.

My shield flew into place the same instant his hand flicked forward, and only its intervention saved me, because as I bunched my muscles to dodge, Lucien raised his voice in command: "Rash'kyel! Submit!"

My body froze in obedience— only for the slimmest half-second, but long enough for his attack to reach me. My shield shattered under the assault, sending me flying into the wall. I felt a sickening crunch as I landed wrong, then a blazing pain along my broken left wing, but I was still alive. And now I understood how Lucien meant to fight. He could not use all of his energy to kill me, because then he would have nothing left to finish his spell, and so it would be this cat-and-mouse game of reflex and timing, until I became too exhausted or battered to resist any longer. If I wanted to have any chance at all, I would have to go on the offensive, as ludicrous and suicidal as that sounded.

My magic sizzled in my palms as I forced it to my will. I had never taught myself much battle magic, having always relied on my bloodlust. Now, that instinctual weapon was my most deadly enemy, for it lay bound with my one essential weakness. I would have to improvise.

What followed was a hell that would have cowed even a pure-blooded demon. Lucien and I, bound together for so many years we could almost read each other's minds, stalking and striking at one another as the shadows around us capered like deranged imps. Spells and counter-spells bounced off the walls and rattled the windows. Shelves overturned, spilling their jars of specimens across the floor in a wash of liquid and broken glass. Fireballs formed, to be blocked by earth, which dissolved under water, which turned into a storm of icicles, only to be vaporized in a flash of heat.

And bit by bit, ever so slowly, I was losing.

We both knew it, and Lucien's smile held his triumph; he was stronger and more experienced, and it was only a matter of time. And then the solution hit me, as I made a desperate lunge to avoid his next attack and landed with a full view of the arch and Jayleen.

I had mistaken the point of the battle; I had thought that the goal was to survive. Instead, his ultimate aim was to attain immortality, which meant that *my* ultimate aim was simply to stop him. And I didn't need to survive to do that.

Lucien sneered as I gathered the last of my power, as well he might, for he had dealt with my other attempts with contemptible ease. If this did not work, I would be at his mercy. But unlike the other attacks, this one was not directed at him. Instead, I turned it at the last second, and as I released my power, he divined my intent, and a terrible cry rose to his lips.

The blood-red jewel atop the glittering arches pulsed as my magic hit, reminding me of a beating heart torn from someone's chest. Then, in a second that stretched an eternity, fine, hair-line cracks appeared and raced across its surface. Behind me, Lucien screamed, a raw, harsh sound that should never have issued out of a human throat. I had no time for him, though, because the destruction of any magical artifact could unleash an enormous amount of uncontrolled power. Heedless of the pain, I spread my wings and made a single, gliding dive at Jayleen. I caught her as the jewel overhead shattered, and with no other way to protect her, I wrapped her in my arms, closed my wings over us both, and prayed.

The expected explosion hit. The pain proved excruciating. My final thought, before everything turned black, was the knowledge that Lucien would not survive either. No human could scream and scream like that and live.

* * *

"Rash? Rash, c'mon, wake up. Oh, please, *please* Rash..."

The tiny but persistent voice irritated me. I dug in deeper into the comfortable blackness and ignored it.

A hand touched my face, my shoulders, shook me a little.

A low growl rumbled at this new annoyance. I wanted to reach up and swat it away, like someone shooing away a determined housefly, but at my twitch and the indistinct sound I produced, the pestering movement only redoubled.

"Damnit, Rash!" she snapped, "I know you're alive! Wake up!"

It was the exasperation in her voice that did it. I had never heard Jayleen plead, but that ruffled, aggrieved tone could only belong to her. This time, I made an effort to open my eyes.

She yelped in sheer surprise when she glanced at my face and saw me watching her. One hand flew to her chest. "Don't do that! You just cost me ten years of my life!"

A feeble ball of magelight bobbed over her head. By its glow, I could see that she was bruised and battered, no doubt from my falling on top of her. There was a thin trail of blood down one side of her face, and some of it had caked in her hair, most of which hung down in a dirty, limp, defeated fashion. Her eyes looked like she had been crying and her nose was red and puffy. There was no way that the white dress she had been wearing would ever be white again.

I thought she had never looked more lovely, and opened my mouth to tell her so.

"...Ngh..."

"Shh! Don't try to speak." She vanished from my line of vision, only to reappear a moment later with a broken cup half-full of water. "Here."

After an awkward attempt at sipping while lying face down, I grunted and she moved the cup away. I made to sit up, and the pain that had poked at my consciousness turned into hot, slicing knives.

"Hey, take it slow," Jayleen scolded, though she helped prop me up when I listed. "You... you were hurt real bad, Rash. I found some bandages and fixed you up a little, but your wings at least will take months to heal. I... I don't know if you'll be able to fly again." Tears filled her voice. Her concern embarrassed me, and I shrugged, then regretted it as I had to bite back a whimper. She continued, "You saved me." It was not a question. "You saved me, even though it almost killed you. Rash..."

Her words skirted the issue I had been avoiding. Bracing myself, I asked, "Lucien?"

"He... I'm sorry, Rash. He had braided too much of himself into the jewel. When it shattered, most of the backlash followed the paths he had set. It... it isn't pretty."

I couldn't help myself. A convulsive shudder shook me. I was suddenly aware of the overpowering smell of blood, of the half-glimpsed dark blotches that covered walls and floor. Jayleen's words explained why we were still alive, why the explosion hadn't killed us both. It had travelled through Lucien's magic to reach him instead. Now I knew why Jayleen used such a small ball of magelight; I didn't want to see what lay beyond its illumination either.

She shifted to my right. Then, to my surprise and pleasure, settled against my side. Her warmth comforted me, and I draped an arm around her shoulders. Despite the horror that surrounded us, I felt calm and at peace. Jayleen huddled closer.

"It won't last, you know," I said, finally. She tilted her head to look up at me, puzzled. I forced myself to continue. "I... the demon inside. I'm too exhausted for it to manifest, but it'll be back. It's..."

"A part of who you are," Jayleen finished for me. She sat up and gave me a serene smile. "I know. But it's not *all* that you are. And, after all, no one is perfect."

I stared at her, feeling a goofy grin stretch across my face. After a moment, I said, "You smell nice."

She looked startled. "Uh..."

"No, no, not like *that*," I said, guessing her thoughts. "I mean, under your mageling blood, you smell nice. Like... like good books and flowers and spring air."

An odd look came over her face. Without saying a word, she settled back against me. "I never knew you were a poet, Rash."

And suddenly, it seemed silly that she should call me that.

"Jayleen, my name... that is, my True Name..."

Her eyes widened, and even in the pallid light, I could see the green that reminded me of new leaves and hope and life.

"...is Rash'kyel."

❧

The Whispering Stone
by Deborah L. Kloeppel

Hands clasped as though in prayer, the renowned sculptor circles the immense block of white Carrera marble; round and round, day after day, peering into each irregular vein, visually getting to know its pristine surface. His trained eyes study it with the rare intensity of genius searching out the secrets held deep within the stone; receiving a privileged vision from his muse—a vision unseen by the rest of the world until his hands can bring it to life.

Each day he ponders the cold stone in varying degrees of light, from all possible angles as the sun changes position overhead, taking note of the subtle color variations and natural veins, scheming with his muse over how best to incorporate its unique qualities into the finest work of art.

At long last, he touches it; lightly at first, barely skimming the periphery with his finger tips, the cold smoothness of the stone heightening his senses from anxious expectation to exhilaration. His hands continue to explore the marble's surface, searching for the being trapped within, measuring each idiosyncrasy in palm-breadths and finger-lengths; tracing the veins, examining each superficial bump, dimple, and blemish; coming to know every indigenous feature as intimately as a lover.

As daylight yields to nightfall, a candle casts surreal shadows through the studio as he circles the marble block one final time, confirming the precision of his sketches, measurements, and plans.

"Be patient, my reverent one," he whispers, his lips gently brushing the marble. "I shall begin on the morrow; my decisions are made. Speak to me as I work. I am your servant; guide my hand as I search for you."

The tranquil dawn is broken by the footsteps of the artist as he readies his tools. Once prepared, the first chisel is positioned beneath the poised hammer; he strikes it sharply, sending marble chips to gather at his feet. He meticulously removes a bit here, a chunk there; each change met with a pensive grimace, then an approving nod as he labors with deliberate veracity to transform the stone into a tangible representation of his vision.

With each passing day the emerging shape gains refinement; the flowing folds of a garment undulate in an unfelt breeze, the high points brightened by the fresh, white surface. He presses on with unfathomable accuracy to release the imprisoned beauty within, interrupting his meticulous toil only for sustenance and sleep.

Finer tools add intricate detail, smoothing any blemishes that remain; his sensitive hands investigate every surface. Heedless of the marble chips in his hair and beard he continues until he is finally satisfied. Dust billows from his cap and tunic as he drops onto his cot and gazes at the sculpture. Meditation gives way to exhaustion, and he drifts into sleep.

Basking in the morning light, his magnificent creation greets him in his waking moments; he approaches, reaching toward the finger tips of the figure towering above him.

"You are free."

With water and a soft cloth, he prepares to bathe his creation; like an adoring father he tenderly swabs the dusty film from the flawless form, revealing the opalescent sheen of its fine, new marble surface glistening in the morning light. His eyes delineate the ridges of tousled hair, observing how the stone's natural veins accentuate the play of light; his fingers tracing each life-like curl as if trying to coax them into place. Cupping the chin in his deft hands, he cradles it lovingly, pleased at the perfection imparted to the facial features; yet he shudders as his senses register the frigidity of stone rather than the expected warmth of a living being. As he continues downward, he smoothes over the well-defined shoulders, the torso in its flowing garment, the muscular legs, and gracefully extended feet.

His thoughts are interrupted by a knock at the door as he finishes adjusting a drape over his work. Hurriedly, he brushes the dust from his tunic and greets his devoted patron.

"Welcome, your Eminence. Please, do come in," he says. Stepping aside, he respectfully removes his hat and bows in honor of the distinguished visitor from the Vatican.

"Do allow me to see what you have crafted. There is nothing your genius has rendered that I have not as yet admired," his guest exclaims, anxiously awaiting its unveiling.

With a gracious nod, the artist guides his patron forward and maneuvers him into an ideal viewing position. He reaches for the corner of the tarp and gives a sharp tug; the cloth gracefully cascades and puddles at the base of the pedestal.

"Oh!" the Cardinal gasps. "How do you manage to evoke such splendor from lifeless stone?" he asks, awestruck by the arduous detail displayed by the majestic form unveiled before him.

"Truly, it is not of my ability alone. I am but a tool in the hand of a greater artist more skilled than I. It was Michael who kept whispering to me from within the stone, revealing himself as I worked." The artist humbly diverts his eyes as he confesses: "I merely applied his counsels to set the Archangel free."

⁂

54 Excuses
by D.R.Smith

"Come on in, buddy," Bob said, and cheerfully welcomed me to his home. "How delighted I am to see you; so glad you could make it. How the horses treating you?"

"Ah, no complaints. Got a filly running tomorrow at Belmont, in fact. That's why I'm in town."

"Gonna win?"

"Hope so, but it's only her second start. She should have won her debut, but she stumbled out the gate. She went to her knees and had too many lengths to make up, but I like her chances this time."

"Chances, schmances." Bob chuckled, leading me into his den. "Heh, heh, listen to you; and you call yourself a horse owner? The ultimate optimist? If you expect to squeeze a hondo out of this old dude, you're supposed to say: 'heck yeah, Bob. Can't lose. Bet the farm and we'll meet at D'Nato's in the Village for a victory dinner.'"

Bob motioned to a tray of delectable treats as he coaxed the cork from a fine Bordeaux. "'Til then, help yourself. Marianne made us a few hors d'oeuvres before she went to work."

"Don't mind if I do; they look good."

Bob is a noted equine journalist and co-hosts a weekly television show on New York's racing circuits. More than a good friend, he's been a tremendous help guiding me in the racing game. His den is a gallery of awards, photos, and bits of interesting memorabilia. I spotted a framed parchment, its alluring title, **54 EXCUSES** drew me closer. I knew there was only *one* way to win a horse race, but I couldn't hide my guilt-ridden grin when reading the zany document.

"Where in blue blazes did you find this little gem?"

"Oh that; isn't it neat? I found it posted in a trainer's tack room at Aqueduct. I'm sure there's more, but over the years, someone compiled a list of excuses horse owners use after losing a race. Lord knows I've heard 'em all at some point. Don't ya just love it?"

"Say, wasn't it you who once told me bangtails have a way of making monkeys out of owners?"

"Yep, that be me. You remember your lessons well, my friend."

Hmm, 54 Excuses, I paused to reflect, "and over many *years*, you said, huh?" My facetious grin widened. "You know, Bob. This thing reminds me of an event that happened to me and my buddies once."

"No kidding." Bob added another measure of wine to my glass. "Make yourself comfy and tell me about it."

"Okay, but I think I'll change *one* name to protect the guilty," I warned, raising my hand in jest.

"Whatever trips your trigger, amigo." Bob offered his glass in toast and settled into an overstuffed armchair.

"Let's see," I said, composing my thoughts. "About four years ago, a few of us country club cronies pooled our money thinking we'd try our luck at owning a race horse. We hired Terry Pawl to be our agent when buying a yearling."

"Ah, I know Terry well. He's a good horseman."

"Well, at an auction in Saratoga, we failed to score on the first two, but kept at it. Nervousness mounted as the bidding slowed on a third try. It was a chestnut colt, and this time, the price was well within our budget. One partner had his young son along who blurted: 'Are we gonna get diss'un, daddy?'

"A moment later, the hammer fell on Terry's bid, and we were in the game hook, line, and *stinker*; even named him *Dissun Terry*," I said, chuckling.

"The colt ran poorly his first start, but the trainer said not to be discouraged: 'that few horses win their first time out, but with more experience, he'll improve.'

"Weeks later, and pumped with "can't miss" enthusiasm, we went to the track for his second start. Though only a modest race for maiden claimers, to us it seemed like Derby Day.

"We arrived early though our race was ninth on the card. All eight partners came decked out in fancy duds, full of new-owner pomp and energy. Even little Mikey squealed: 'we're gonna see our horsie win today, right Daddy?'

"'You got it, son,' Bobby patted him on the head.

"Though overcast and threatening rain, nothing could dampen our spirits. We were not to be dismayed. After all, we were bona fide racehorse *owners*, flaunting privileged passes and perks.

"We chatted, sipped a few brews, and bided time betting early races while waiting for Charlie Sharp, the colt's trainer. He finally showed, but when I introduced him to partners he hadn't met, he seemed aloof and uneasy.

"'You look perplexed,' I said. 'Is something on your mind?' Charlie thoughtfully sipped his beer before revealing concerns.

"'Actually, there are a few things bothering me.' Our revelry waned and we circled Charlie to hear details.

"Rich blurted, 'Hell's, bells. So what's eatin' ya? Are we gonna run today, or what?'

"Startled, and not knowing his new owners that well, Charlie paused, reading our faces. 'Um, y'all remember Dissun's first start when I said [27] he just didn't run his race that day, right? A blend of mumbled *yeah's*, and *so what's* confirmed his preface. 'Well, I'm worried [25] he ain't the same horse he was earlier when you first hired me to train him; that maybe [26] he was ruined by the hard track he came from.'

"Charlie was referring to the colt's initial breaking and pre-racetrack training with his friend, Kelly, in South Carolina. We were dumfounded, our zeal going down the same drain as earlier beers.

"'But y'all brushed it off and urged me on,' Charlie continued, 'and demanded I keep him in training, remember? [3] **He'll be better next time, he needed the race,**' you guys said. 'So when y'all insisted [47] **he needs his races closer together,** I trained him even harder, but if you ask me, [44] **he left his race on the training track.** In fact, I'd say [45] **he needs a rest.**'

"Thank God someone had the presence of mind to suggest another round of drinks. 'On me,' Bobby volunteered, and started toward the bar.

"'Change mine to whiskey!' Chuck hollered.

"'Yeah— make it a double for me!' Bill added. Bobby flashed thumbs-up and soon returned with whiskies for *everyone*. I again asked Charlie if we were still going to run.

"'Of course we are,' Charlie confirmed. 'It's way too late for a scratch. But there's still another thing that bothers me about last time; I'm pretty certain [19] **it wasn't his distance.**'

"'I knew it. I just knew it,' Bill said, disgustedly. 'I've heard enough of this hedging baloney; the guy's full of excuses. We came here for nothing.'

"Bobby faced the trainer, his expression distorted from a healthy gulp of whiskey. 'Bill's right; what a bunch of hogwash. Just what are you trying to feed us? We all know the *real* reasons he lost his debut: [23] **the track was too deep** and [28] **the turns are too sharp** at this track.'

"Larry interrupted. 'Yeah, I also recall somethin' said about how [15] **he didn't like the track.** So what gives, Sharp?'

"Dubious eyes set upon Charlie, who by now sensed a need to allay mounting apprehension.

"'Like I said, boys, things were different then, and had nothin' to do with the track.' Charlie reminded us that [33] **it was his first time he's been around two turns,** and then sheepishly added, 'um, there's still more.'

"Hearing that, Bill took a menacing step toward the trainer. 'Oh? You say there's more— *more* excuses?'

"Charlie seemed unnerved, and didn't bother looking up from studying the toes of his boots. 'Have you guys forgotten what you said about race conditions as well— like: **[1] the weight was too much** or that **[18] he was giving away too many pounds?**'

"By this time, verbal exchanges were becoming more heated, yet ceased when distributing another round of drinks.

"'Jesus, Mary, and Joseph; is there anything else?' Doc's eyeballs met the top of his head. He turned to Larry and poked him in the shoulder. 'Did you hear all that crap?'

"'Sure did. What have I been saying all along, boys? It's not meant to be,' Larry mumbled.

"Everyone spouted opinions; our way of coming to grips with Dissun Terry's certain demise. David was first to test the waters spouting tin-horn knowledge that comes with rookie ownership.

"'What's Charlie talkin' about? Why should distance bother him just because **[39] his sire was only a sprinter?**'

"'So much for what you know,' Doc countered. 'That was his *broodmare* sire, dummy. **[40] His sire could only win at a mile and a half**,' though neither of them was sure of who knew what, only stared each other down from behind whiskey glasses pressed to their lips. Things were getting testy, and I tried patronizing.

"'Why is everybody so riled? Maybe **[52] he needs blinkers**, for Pete's sake.' But that only spurred a sharp retort from the bulky Chuck standing to my left, who up 'til now, had only been sipping and listening.

"'That's a load a malarkey, schmuck,' Chuck grumbled. 'We all know **[53] he runs better without blinkers.**'

"A little shoving and glaring induced Charlie to referee. 'Boys, boys, calm down. We should go anyhow, it's almost race time.'

"Grateful for the reprieve, and despite the intermittent drizzle, we ambled toward the saddling paddock, but not without stopping for more liquid courage. Crowds gathered round, but we managed to wedge our way in along the paddock railing.

"'Good grief,' Bobby groaned. 'Look at all these people. Why so dang many have to hang around the paddock, for crissake. *We're* the owners; not *them*.'

"'Hey Bobby, look at Dissun Terry,' Rich said, shoving his drink toward the saddling stall, slopping a splat of whiskey on little Mikey's head. 'Looks to me like [5] the crowd scared him.'

"We agreed; it was obvious [14] he was nervous.'

"Dissun Terry appeared antsy, prancing and pawing the ground when 'riders up' was announced above the din of the crowd. People dispersed as jockeys mounted horses for post parade. We continued on through the clubhouse and stood at the outside rail near the wire.

"On the way, Doc pulled at David's arm. 'Saaaaay. Ain't you gonna get a bet down first?'

"'*Hell* no,' David said. 'You heard what the trainer said. Besides, didn't you notice? Don't you know nuthin' about horses, Doc?' David seized a second chance at one-upmanship.

"'What d'ya mean?' Doc blinked, wondering what he'd missed.

"'Look around.' David swept his hand as if blessing the grounds. 'Can't you see it's been raining?' More confident, and armed with nouveau-authority, David continued to educate old Doc. 'Why, any fool can see [35] he wasn't wearing his mud caulks. And another thing, doofus, [43] the jockey didn't fit him, let alone that [2] he had a bad post. No sireee; no bet for me.'

"The horses finished warm up jogs and were nearing the gate. We guzzled recent refills attempting to stave off the rising jitters; our eyes glued to the far side of the track as the horses gathered behind the starting gate. Assistant starters snatched bridles and led horses into their respective stalls. No one spoke, but our faces were nearly audible: *Saints preserve us, our champion is about to get his ass kicked.*

"Larry pointed at Dissun Terry. 'Good Lord, do you guys see what I see?' [46] He was fractious at the gate, wasting precious energy fighting his handlers. Moments later, the intercom came to life: 'they're all in, aaaaaaaaand they're off!'

"Only seconds after the explosive start, Chuck fumed. 'God almighty! [48] The assistant starter held his tail. Damn him,' Chuck cursed, but Larry corrected.

"'Not so, [49] the jockey was asleep when the gate opened. That's why [50] he walked out of the gate.'

"'Damn!' I yelled. '[29] He should have gone to the lead.'

"'Whadja 'spect,' Doc slurred, '[42] the jockey almost fell off when [31] the saddle slipped.'

"But as it turned out, we were all wrong. Two jumps from the starting gate, [34] the jockey lost his irons as [11] he was knocked off stride coming out of the gate. Worse, [24] another horse clipped his heels and [32] he lost a shoe. Yet amidst the jostling and banging of flanks battling for positions, our jockey managed to hold on; his knees pinching the colt's withers with all the strength he could muster.

"David's typical stoneface changed to that of a bug-eyed cartoon character transfixed on the action. He cringed and grabbed both ears. 'Ugh! I think [51] he stepped in a hole.'

"Larry again corrected: 'no he didn't, [6] he jumped over a hole in the track, you twit.'

"David glowered, his bluff exposed, but he resumed watching the race as the horses neared the half mile pole. By now, it seemed obvious [4] the early pace was too much, and Dissun Terry had moved forward in the pack, expending precious energy needed for a closing rush. [9] He was too close to the early pace, likely sealing certain defeat since [8] the jockey didn't rate him. I glanced at Charlie who was watching the action through binoculars.

"Charlie said, 'it looks to me like [16] he was climbing, not running,' and that he'd try using a shadow roll next time. Charlie suddenly became enraged. 'What's that numbskull doing?' Charlie said [36] The jockey hit him left handed when he was specifically told never to hit him on that side. Charlie feared Dissun might bolt to the outside now. Clenching his teeth, Charlie lowered his glasses, seething with contempt for the diminutive Juan Gomez.

"Chuck's face gnarled into knots. '[37] The jockey shouldn't have hit him at all; [38] he needed a stronger hand ride,' f'crissake! Charlie's right, [20] he was trying to bear out all the way, now.'

"To our dismay, [10] he lost too much ground on the outside. *My God*, I prayed, trying to will the jockey into doing *something*— and quickly. I must have conjured too much mojo, because at that moment, [12] the jockey moved too soon. Another ill-fated decision since [41] the jockey had to take him up.

"Chuck was still miffed. 'Dang it! Now **[21] he was trying to get in all the way.** Christ, Gomez! Don't you know where you're going? The blasted idiot should know better that **[17] it was too deep on the rail.**'

"Bobby made the sign of the cross and kicked the chain-link fence between little Mikey's legs. 'Jesus, we're finished.' Rich had already given up as the horses reached the quarter pole. We had no doubt **[13] the jockey moved too late** because **[7] he got pinched back at the turn.**

"Just when we thought we'd seen it all, Dissun Terry had to quicken pace to regain lost ground, and as he tried breaking through a wall of horses, **[22] he was blocked in the stretch,** and with only a furlong to go, all hope fluttered like a spent balloon.

"We had enough; emotionally drained and couldn't bear to watch another stride. Larry and Doc held each other for mutual comfort, tears streaming down their cheeks. Rich and Bobby draped their arms over the fence and stared at the dirt in defeat. I felt dizzy and closed my eyes to steady myself.

"Chuck and Bill were the only two still watching the final furlong disappear, holding their breath until forced to gasp for air as a wall of horses stampeded toward us, nostrils flaring and heads bobbing, charging for the wire. As they reached us, Chuck rocked Bill with a heavy hand to the shoulder, jerking Bill's head around.

"'Look!" Chuck yelled, pointing at the jock. 'Hey, Gomez; are you stupid or what!' Chuck screamed expletives as the field passed in front. 'You used him up, you damned fool. Don't ya know **[30] he spit the bit?**' Chuck turned his back to the track in disgust, threw his drink at the pavement and leaned against the fence, grateful only yards were left of his torment.

"Just as quickly as closing cheers reached a wild crescendo, noise flittered to scattered shouts when the horses passed the finish line. Hundreds tossed torn tickets into the air, cursing. Others were bouncing on their toes, pinching wagers and praying for a favorable photo.

As for us, within the span of a single minute and change, we were reduced to a band of blithering losers; moping in whiskey-numbed stupors as Charlie's cell phone came to life.

"'Hello, Kelly,' Charlie noted the caller ID.

"'So what's your take on Dissun Terry?' Kelly asked.

"Charlie glanced at his crestfallen owners. 'As I see things right *now?* Uh, I guess you could say **[54] he just didn't run his race today**.' Momentary silence seemed to stun the other end as Charlie scrutinized our horse cantering back for unsaddling.

"'What d'ya mean? I caught the race on simulcast,' Kelly said, confused. 'I know those guys can be a bunch of newbie idiots, but I'd o' thought they'd be goin' crazy right about now.'

"Charlie smirked. '*Going*— you say? Yeah, I suppose you could say that. But hey, it's a long story and I gotta run. I'll call you back.' Charlie cut him off and went to help his groom unsaddle a heavily panting Dissun Terry walking in tight circles with four others in front of the grandstand.

"Kelly, still puzzled, studied the replay on the off-track monitor. 'What does he *mean*— he didn't run his race today?' Kelly mumbled. Despite the rough start and racing problems common with green maidens, Kelly's professional eye told him Dissun Terry hung tough; he showed class.

"'Something's really strange up there in River City,' he mused. What do those idiots want? And lookie there,' Kelly pointed to the monitors and burst into laughter. 'He got it by a nostril.'

The photo finish confirmed the results official as the cameras zeroed in on a jubilant Charlie Sharp leading a panting, but feisty chestnut into the winner's circle.

* * *

"Well I'll be a son-of-a-gun," Bob laughed. "That's a heck of a story. My producer would probably like to make a movie out of that one, but the Marx Brothers are dead. Heh, heh, and looking on the flip side, you've just proved my point: in less than two minutes, your horse made a monkey out of *all* of you— *and* those excuses."

"All right, all right," I conceded. "But if you promise to be nice, I got another wacky story for you. It's about a *monkey* who's willing to buy a win ticket for his buddy tomorrow— *providing* the monkey gets to swap more lies with more wine *tonight*."

"I hear ya, but I'm fresh out of Banana Ripple, my friend." Bob chuckled. "He'll have to settle for Chateau Moutin, but I guess he's worth it."

As Bob pulled the cork from another bottle, he paused. "You know, on second thought, I've got an even *better* deal for you."

Bob peeled a c-note from his money clip. "Here, put this on your filly's nose. Now, if you promise not to boost that list to 55 with something like: "she stumbled,' or 'had too many lengths to make up,' then Marianne and I will join you at D'Nato's for dinner tomorrow night no matter *what* happens; *deal?*"

My face flushed as Bob's famed, mischievous grin widened, and we shook hands— "deal."

❧

The Idiot
by D.R.Smith

I'm gonna be rich!

I carried that thought all morning. It was Thanksgiving Day and I scrambled from bed an hour earlier than on normal school days, eager to launch my latest venture. Five inches of wet snow had fallen during the night, not uncommon for central Maine this time of year. Given the holiday, sidewalks would be free of shoppers; I was dying to fire up my new snow blower.

I finished clearing my first set of customers, and before moving off Main Street, I paused to admire the patchwork of clean walks among several snowed-in storefronts. *Let the holdouts take care of their own ice and slush*, I mused. Maybe after a few pedestrian mishaps, I'll win them over; even if I *do* charge a premium versus my pre-season sign-ups.

"Come on, Frank, hurry it up," I yelled, goading my eight-year-old brother to pick up the pace spreading salt behind me. I had to giggle at the frumpy sight.

He looked like a chocolate ice cream cone, trudging along on stumpy little legs. Frank was *beyond* pudgy, weighing about as much as I did though five years my junior. His over-sized snow leggings bunched up at the waist and tapered into galoshes from beneath a rumpled, hand-me-down woolen coat that was way too big. Only his eyes were exposed, blinking from behind a bright red ski mask that topped the lumpy mess like a maraschino cherry.

I waved him on as I guided the massive blower to a side street lined with old tenement buildings. Residential sidewalks and short alley driveways were a cinch for this beast. By noon, I had ninety dollars in invoices, and with a number of customers yet to do, I should have about two-hundred in receivables by day's end; *about what my Dad makes in a whole week.*

I love my dad and mean no disrespect. He's a kind and honest man, but labors hard at a shoe factory for nominal wages. The depression was hard on his family, and he was forced to make a greater sacrifice after his father was seriously injured. The oldest of eight, my dad left school in the seventh grade to till potato fields or stoke brickyard kilns to put food on the table for them all.

I fantasized doing a brisk business given normal Maine winters. Even after allowing for fuel, salt, my employed little brother, and sharing proceeds with Mr. Wilkins as overhead; *oh my*— the numbers were intoxicating. I'll have this blower paid off in no time; *easy,* I puffed with zeal.

Yes, I am gonna be rich!

I swooned from dreams of untold wealth, envisioning a whole fleet of these things. *Yeah*— hire me a bunch of high school kids, and spread them out in neighborhoods all over Farmington. *Yeah!* Set up divisions in Portland and Bangor; maybe get State contracts from Augusta. I was so absorbed with wild expansion plans, a second ear-splitting screech rocked me in my boots.

"Arrggh!" Mrs. Bernstein screamed. "Stop, boy! Vhatch out you damned fool!"

Oh my God, my heart pounded. Her little Chutsie was standing belly-deep in snow, its muzzle snapping only an inch from the rotors.

I had been widening her front walk when her screech halted me a few feet shy of her porch steps. Mrs. Bernstein barged from her doorway and snatched her yapping mutt before it was swallowed by the blower.

I quickly disengaged the blades and reversed the machine about ten feet. She stomped toward me, cursing above muffled yips coming from somewhere beneath a huge breast ballooning her housecoat. I was relieved her pooch wasn't mincemeat, but feared I had botched things up my first day in business. Mrs. Bernstein was more than just a customer; she was our landlady, hiring me to clear driveways and walks of all six of her tenement buildings. I panicked.

"I'm really, really, sorry Mrs. Bernstein! I— uh— I was blinded by the flying snow."

"Oh shut up, you putz!" She thrashed a chubby finger at me. "You should pay more attention to vhat you do."

After lecturing me, she whirled and plodded toward the door. I felt a need to bolster my excuse, and followed to apologize further; *another* mistake.

My eyes held focus of her enormous bottom as imaginary kettle drums sounded in my head— *boom*, boom, *boom*, boom; timed with each cheek thrusting her housecoat from side to side. I likened her to one of Dumbo's aunts and failed to stifle giggles. She heard me, spun on her heels, and stuck her fleshy face to within inches of mine; her intense glare magnified through horn-rimmed glasses.

"So vhat is this? You think making chopped liver from my little Chutsie is so funny, do you? Vell you're a schmuck! A meshuggener! Now you take that yellow monster and get your goniff ass off my property, 'cause I ain't payin' ya." She slammed the door in my face yelling a final word: "Idiot!"

I finished my afternoon work, parked the blower at Wilkins' hardware store, and trudged home in the afterglow of a sunset. I was famished, and looked forward to Thanksgiving dinner.

Sated, and staring at remnants of turkey and a lone carrot blurring from focus on my plate, I drifted deeper into thought. I was thinking of my day, and of how I nearly scuttled my business within hours of infancy— *just as Dad had predicted.*

I fancied my business as the newest darling of Wall Street; a ticker tape spewed stock quotes as I was sitting behind a huge desk, barking orders, and sifting through spreadsheets reflecting gobs of income from hundreds of crews clearing Maine's towns of phantom snowfalls that would shame the Arctic.

"Henry! Snap out of it." Mom jolted me from my stupor. "Pay attention to your Aunt Millie when she's talking to you; now pass her the cranberry sauce."

"Oh, sorry Aunt Millie." I blushed, and ignoring Grandpa's snickering, I attempted to redeem myself by offering her the gravy as well.

I always looked forward to Aunt Millie and Uncle Charlie spending Thanksgiving weekends with us. They usually drove in the night before from a small town in the Aroostook region noted for its potato production. Dad's younger brother, Uncle Charlie, was an impish, fun-loving kind of guy who worked as a mail carrier. Aunt Millie was always sweet to me and Frank— 'a true gem of the earth,' as Mom always said.

"Wake up, boy!" my father bellowed.

"Oh leave him be, Hank," Mom scolded. "He's just tired. He put in a long day today; you should be proud of him." She flashed me a reassuring smile.

"Yes, indeed," Aunt Millie seconded while dousing a spoonful of stuffing with gravy. "I was wondering where you two boys had gone to so early this morning. Why, I never even heard you leave. Mom tells me you're quite an enterprising young man, Henry."

Dad pointed a shredded drumstick at me. "Him? Enterprising, my foot. More like a harebrained *idiot* if you ask me. He busted the daggon window, ya know." Dad jerked his thumb over his shoulder in reference to the large pane behind him. "Made the idiot pay for it, too."

Mom shot Dad a stern look. "I said to leave him be, Hank, and don't call him an idiot anymore. You should be grateful he's a good boy, and not like those dreadful urchins in the neighborhood."

"You mean the wretched little bastards from across the street?"

"Shush, Hank, and behave. We're at the table— with company."

Uncle Charlie pointed a finger at Dad, teasing he should be more careful who he called an idiot, citing how the acorn doesn't fall far from the tree. Frank giggled, infusing Grandpa's cackles that enlivened the playful mood. Mom seized Uncle Charlie's lead and chided Dad further.

"You're only miffed because he made you pay for doing the driveway today. He even finished paying you back for the window too, didn't he?"

"Oh, be quiet yourself, woman. The idiot *should* pay for the stupid things he does."

"Henry was only honoring his deal with Mr. Wilkins, Hank. That's all. And it's *your* fault, too." She playfully poked him in the ribs. "You should be proud he listens, and looks up to you the way he does. You were the one who taught him about integrity— to own up to his responsibilities, remember? So you only have yourself to blame."

Mom's a pro at handling Dad, though by now, everyone was poking fun. Frank shared "winning-battle" nods with me as Uncle Charlie aimed his thumb and forefinger, pretending to shoot Dad; now grinning himself at having instigated lighthearted controversy.

"Well, maybe so, but he's always doing *something* stupid. Ain't that right Pop?" Dad looked to Grandpa as his only ally. "Remember the time he set the den on fire? Or how about when he riled up the neighborhood biddies with that crazy casino scheme of his?"

"Yep," Grandpa said. "Burned a hole in my crotch, too, I did."

"Great balls afire." Uncle Charlie couldn't resist and took an elbow from Aunt Millie. Grandpa Ray started cackling, his twisted body bobbing in his seat. He had lived with us since before I was born; crippled for life and unable to work from his early thirties after a huge maple toppled from a logging truck, and crushed him against a loading dock.

Everyone was laughing at me; Dad referring to one of my dumbest escapades when I had stashed a fold of cigar loads in my locker to protect a classmate.

Our science teacher smoked smelly cigars during soccer practice after school. Somehow, my friend managed to pack one with an exploding load, but gave *me* the packet to hide. He convinced me that *he* would be the prime suspect; the class cut-up. How was I to know a lock-down would ensue, and the principal refused to believe I was only a storage stooge.

My parents were called in, and at one point, were told they were raising a common, good-for-nothing, no-account delinquent. Mom exploded. My Father and I watched in mummified silence as she ripped into my principal, telling him what part of his anatomy *he* could shove the loads. She grabbed the evidence and stormed from his office; my father calling me an idiot for agreeing to hide them in the *first* place.

Things would have remained fine and forgotten had I not stumbled upon the loads months later. During Christmas break, I was looking for wrapping tape and found them stuffed in the back of a drawer. They spawned an idea since Grandpa Ray smoked a pipe.

Although small, cigar loads can deliver a powerful wallop. I figured if I shaved them into granules, they would be more or less harmless; just enough snap and sizzle for a good joke. But after scraping the first one, there didn't seem enough to be worthwhile, so I shaved quite a few. Christmas Eve, I tamped the scrapings between layers of tobacco and placed the ready-to-go pipe on his smoking stand. For some reason, he never used his pipe that night, and before long, Frank and I were shooed off to bed.

Christmas Day, gaiety was manifest as the family convened in the den to unwrap gifts. I forgot all about my prank— that is until Grandpa leaned back in his recliner and lit his pipe. How was I to know he wouldn't smoke the night before— *when* I could have prepared everyone for the joke— *while* the room was free of clutter.

My nose was buried in model biplane instructions when a wisp of Prince Albert tickled my nostrils. I panicked and spun on my tailbone to warn Grandpa, but it was too late. No sooner had my shouts disrupted the merriment than a glowing mass of tobacco blew up, spewing embers in every direction. Grandpa's face looked like that of a barn owl; frozen wide-eyed behind a shower of pops and sparks shooting skyward. His mouth agape, the pipe dropped into his lap, dislodging another burning clump of sizzling tobacco.

We were so busy saving Grandpa's private parts that no one noticed discarded wrapping paper smoldering. No sooner had we relieved Grandpa of his hot seat, when paper flashed into flames in two places. Mom screamed and raced to the kitchen to fetch a dishpan filled with water. Dad and I stomped like warring Indians, sending flaming confetti floating around the den. Grandpa Ray directed Frank hopping about like a chubby Tinkerbell trying to net drifting embers in Dad's new hunting hat.

When it was over, I was a goner. Adding up the drenched gifts, singed clothing, and a few toys trampled to death, I was condemned to my room for a week to contemplate financial ruin. I gave up every dime I made mowing yards all year to pay off that fiasco.

Yet, my Phoenix arose from the ashes, inspired from a summer carnival in town. I became intrigued by the Rotary Club's gambling wheel; watching patrons place money on a number board paying odds to matching numbers on the spin-wheel. *Hmm, easy money.*

I thought I'd make one of my own using parts salvaged from my bike, wrecked after trying to duplicate a stunt seen on TV. I had made a ramp using a plank atop cinder blocks, and after a few trial runs, I spiced the show with live bodies by talking Frank and two of his fourth grade chumps into lying down behind it. I figured if Joey Chitwood could charge admission for *his* thrill show, so could I.

I gathered speed, hit the ramp, and pulled extra hard on the handlebars to insure high lift. I easily cleared the whimpering trio lying prone in the street, but when landing, I stood on the pedals to brace for the impact. My weight sheared a pedal off— my crotch slamming *hard* against the crossbar.

My eyes bounced and teeth rattled. The pain paralyzed me. I felt nauseous slumped over the handlebars as I coasted off the street, only to ram a fire hydrant head on. I didn't care about the bike— or its new oval-shaped wheel; only laid on my side clutching my groin, praying to remain conscious.

My bike was totaled, but that day at the carnival ushered in a new era of prosperity. I removed the bike's good wheel and painted spokes different colors of varying frequency. I hammered spikes through the axle and into an upright two-by-four, fashioned a clicker from the tongue of an old shoe, and *voila*— my new casino wheel.

I colored paper plates paying corresponding odds to the spokes, and tacked them to an old board set atop two waste barrels in the alley. Word spread and business was booming. I took all bets; beginning with buttons, marbles, baseball cards, jelly beans; or anything else a kid had to wager. Cash bets started with pennies and escalated to assorted change and dollar bills. I was making good money— that is, until the police came to the door escorted by two very irate mothers.

How was I to know the wretched little bastards raided piggy banks and cookie jars, and then graduated to stealing from Mommas' purses until one of them got caught?

My mother talked a sympathetic policeman into sparing me from juvenile hall— *provided* I agreed to make restitution no matter how long it took. But the vengeful Moms wouldn't settle for a bag of cats-eyes, or a Brooklyn Dodgers team card, now would they?

After Mom reassured the police and the neighborhood ninnies it wouldn't happen again, I had to give back all cash plus make up any shortages cleaning windows or whatever else they wanted until paid off. But as they say, every storm cloud has its silver lining. All I needed was another senseless episode to fertilize seeds of ingenuity— *and* a dining room window to showcase my colossal screw-up.

Aunt Millie's voice brought me to the present as she turned the conversation to me. "How did you break the window, Henry?"

"Go ahead," Dad said. "*Tell* her. The damned fool nearly put his eye out, too."

I blushed as all eyes focused on me. Maybe Daddy was right— maybe I was a harebrained idiot. I sighed dreading relating that story again, but explained siphoning money from my failed casino to order a water rocket advertised in Frankie's comic book. On the surface it seemed harmless enough, but I managed to bollix things up within an hour of delivery.

The concept was simple. About a foot long, its convex body was made of thick plastic to hold pressure. The instructions said to fill it half full with water, and then seat its tail against a rubber seal on the launching pad. Once locked in place, a plunger device pumped it full of air. Then holding the assembly upright and flicking the retaining latch, the air pressure forced a powerful stream of water through a small venturi, propelling the rocket skyward.

After a few test flights, I was not satisfied with simple up and down NASA launches. No, I had to show off; reinvent the wheel, but *not* without an audience. After all, what good was ingenuity if I couldn't demonstrate my genius to a doting public?

Grandpa was as good a test audience as anyone, so I positioned him in a chair in front of the dining room window to enjoy the show. This time, I intended to sail that thing clear over the building. To insure against losing it in the gutter, I cranked that puppy beyond the instruction's twenty-stroke limit, pumping at least thirty until I could no longer push the plunger.

That time, I'd show the world I was no idiot, and made a mental checklist. I tapped powers of eighth-grade science to calculate an angle of trajectory, and then made sure of no passing traffic during launch. Made in the shade, Wade— all systems go. Squinting, I rifle-sighted the Polaris, and fired. *Whoosh!*

In my cocky, self-proclaimed vein of genius, I forgot about the high-pressured water. The instant the blast hit my eye, I fell on my butt, jerking my aim off target. The pain was immense. Natural instincts caused me to slam both eyes shut, but panic forced me to open my good eye, convinced the other was stuck to the back of my skull. There I sat, helplessly watching a rogue rocket hone in on new coordinates— the center of a picture window.

I saw Grandpa's panic-stricken face pressed against the pane. He tried scrambling his crippled torso from the chair, but only managed to get to his feet before touchdown. The window exploded, sending him tumbling backwards over his chair amidst shards of glass.

"Momma said Grandpa was floppin' around like a beached whale," Frank interrupted, worsening my embarrassment; everyone staring and chuckling at me. I was grateful when the phone rang.

"Henry, it's for you," Mom called me to the kitchen. "It's Mrs. Bernstein."

After hanging up, I rejoined the table expecting Dad to question the reason for her call. He did not disappoint.

"What have you done this time; or dare I ask?"

"Nothin'," I said. "She just wanted to know if I could come by tomorrow and finish cleaning her driveways. I told her not to worry;

that I'd take care of things in the morning." *I figured she'd be calling; my wholesale price to Casey's Gas Station plow was too great to resist.*

"Oh, boy. How much for me, Henry?"

"Um, two-fifty."

"Yippeee!" he squealed, likely contemplating candy and a comic book collection growing by the boxcar load.

"Is Mrs. Bernstein one of your customers?" Aunt Millie asked. I nodded, mindful of manners not to talk with a mouthful of turkey.

"She's our landlady," Dad answered. "Maybe soon to be our *ex,* for all we know."

Aunt Millie smiled. "Well, Uncle Charlie and I think you're quite the clever fellow— especially for just turning thirteen. Momma says you figured out the whole idea all by yourself, too. You'll have to tell me all about it after dinner. Okay?"

I nodded, not bothering to mention *why* I hadn't finished Mrs. Bernstein's driveways. Neither did anyone ask as table talk shifted to an apple pie I spotted on the kitchen counter. Everyone was anxious to sample Aunt Millie's homemade specialty, leaving me to worry about Mrs. Bernstein— *and* the events that nearly caused me to deep six yet another of my endeavors less than a day old. My thoughts drifted, only this time while downing a slice of fresh-baked apple pie with lots of cinnamon.

* * *

I couldn't have known at the time, but breaking the window blossomed into my latest venture. A twist of fate once again saved me from a youth condemned to child labor camps.

After cleaning up the mess and enduring a barrage of verbal assaults from Mom and Grandpa, little time was wasted marching me to Wilkins Hardware. In theory, a prompt replacement would help soften Dad's *certain* irritation when he got home.

Mr. Wilkins gave Mom a generous price break, aware of our family's limited means. In return to help pay for it, she volunteered me if he thought I could be useful as an errand boy after school and on weekends. I didn't have a bike anymore, so a paper route was out; *might as well learn the hardware business.*

Mr. Wilkins turned out to be really nice, and easy to work for. He taught me a lot about business. I learned how wholesale and retail worked; how to do invoicing, plan overhead and inventory control, and so on. I had always been a whiz at math and impressed him with my ability to cipher basic algebraic problems that came in handy for helping customers figure paint and wallpaper quantities.

When a fall shipment of snow blowers came in, I helped set up floor displays. I couldn't take my eyes off the biggest self-propelled model, and even took home its manual to read. I studied snow volume charts, and calculated what it was capable of shifting under varied conditions. My father thought I was nuts spending idle time reading a machine booklet instead of comics or adventure books like other kids.

I had overheard stockroom workers talking about the store's forklift being leased rather than bought outright. That fueled an idea, and it wasn't long before I hatched a plan. I projected incomes based on average snowfalls, and then solicited pre-season commitments from store owners and landlords around Main Street.

Mr. Wilkins was impressed when making my proposal. He said my eagerness and well thought out business plan convinced him of my sincerity. He agreed to give my idea a try, and leased me the blower using snow removal proceeds to buy it at cost.

I agreed the blower would be kept in the stockroom, and in addition, we agreed to split income into equal thirds; one assigned to the lease, a second to Mr. Wilkins to justify his investment until it was paid off, and a final third to me for work effort.

My business logic accounted for a sold unit for Mr. Wilkins, and I'd end up owning an expensive, income-producing machine at some point. I bargained that he throw in a push-spreader so Frank could earn money scattering salt. I was overwhelmed with excitement and shook hands on the deal.

I couldn't wait to share the news. Frank jumped with glee after I explained he was hired to spread salt for fifty cents per customer. Mom was thrilled for us both and rustled my hair, congratulating my entrepreneurial efforts. Dad seemed pleased, but less demonstrative. He was skeptical, and had a hard time accepting how I managed to finagle a respected businessman into such a deal. I tried boosting his mood by suggesting he throw away the heavy coal shovel if I agreed to clear our walk and driveway for free; except for the one-third to honor my deal with Mr. Wilkins.

"I ain't throwing anything away. Somehow, you'll find a way to mess things up. Just wait and see. You always do."

Mom came to my defense. "Oh don't be such a wet blanket, dear. Henry will do just fine. Give him some credit for Lord's sake— and try be more encouraging." She pulled me close and kissed my forehead. "You're so smart, Henry. We're both very proud of you, aren't we, Hank?" Dad smiled and made us laugh asking a ludicrous question; his way of appeasement.

"Is that thing big enough to grind up the wretched little bastards across the street?"

Underneath, I suppose my dad is proud of me, though I wish he'd lighten up now and then. Mom always told me to pay him no mind, relating how often he shared private feelings with her. She said he only wants the best for me, and in some ways, was envious of how smart and creative I could be. She said he picked on me as his way of teaching me to appreciate the value of opportunities— opportunities he never had.

* * *

"*Now* what!" Dad was annoyed at the phone ringing again.

"Henry; for you. It's Mr. Le'Ron, the jeweler. Don't be long, dear. It's impolite." Mom accepted my explanation he was one of the hold outs. I took the call and returned a minute later; smiling at having secured another customer.

"Hope you dinged 'im good, Henry," Dad said. "That Le'Ron character has always been a tough tightwad." Dad was referring to his own futile bargaining efforts when shopping for Mom's birthday last summer.

"No sweat, Dad; got 'im for a fin higher than the other stores. I told him he could take it or leave it, too— *just* like he did to you."

"Good for you, son."

"Whadju expect? You think you're raisin' some kinda *idiot*, or something?" I stabbed an apple wedge with a confident fork.

Dad looked at me and grinned. "Ah hah; that's-a-m'boy," and pulled me closer to deliver a playful noogie. I winced and giggled. When looking up, our eyes locked for a precious instant that would be embedded in my mind for a lifetime— sharing that special look of a deep, mutual love and admiration only a father and son can know.

"Um, I've been doing a lot of thinking, son. Christmas is just around the corner, and uh— I could use a little extra spending cash. Any chance you could use another employee here and there? I'm a hard worker and take orders real good."

My eyes watered. I buried my face in Dad's chest and hugged him as his calloused palm caressed the back of my head.

I heard Mom's chair move as Aunt Millie suggested the table needed clearing. She shoved an empty cranberry bowl into Uncle Charlie's chest, and motioned him toward the kitchen. "Come on Frankie, pick up your plate; you can help your Momma, too. Why, I bet there might be another piece of my famous pie in there."

For the moment, I leaned against my dad, facing the abandoned table with only Grandpa remaining. He slowly rose with the aid of his cane, but never took his eyes off me.

I wiped a trickle from my cheek, and the instant our eyes met, not a word was spoken— yet so much said as Grandpa Ray winked at me, and nodded the approval of a lifetime.

✐✐

Hardly Heathens
by D.R.Smith

The teacher was late. Ricky Doucette leaned back in his chair and folded his arms across his chest, his mind seduced by shimmering dust particles swirling within a shaft of sunlight angling through the window. Slipping deeper into supernal thought, he likened them to billions of stars suspended within a micro-Cosmos.

Why is this *religion* class taught by Mr. Alvarez, he wondered; a *layman* who doubled as the academy's Spanish teacher in a parochial school run by Marist Brothers?

Sainte-Beuve Academe was part of an old and stately Cathedral complex in Quebec City; a prestigious boarding school renowned for its stellar education. Ricky was in his sophomore year of a four-year, residential scholarship. Though grateful, he knew the grant wasn't a charitable gesture offered Quebec's poor, nor was their intent to introduce *his kind* to pious enlightenment.

Rather, his parents were cajoled into enrolling him after it became public knowledge the Montreal Canadiens had secured his future contract, even though only thirteen at the time. No doubt the faculty relished the publicity, as well as having landed this certain superstar for its varsity team.

He missed living at home, and thought of his parents whom he adored and delighted in pleasing. His father was a humble laborer with limited education, yet upheld stalwart pride of having roots tracing to one of the original Acadian settlers. He ignored the social stigmas that came with taking an *injun squaw* for a wife, and married a full-blooded Souriquois revered as a *royenah,* or entrusted matriarch of her clan in northern New Brunswick.

Ricky's reflexive grin disappeared; his daydreaming wandering to resentful memories of his family being maligned as worthless half-breeds, heathens, or snubbed as rural riffraff; people jeering their poverty for living in a four-room shanty overlooking Chaleur Bay in far-eastern Quebec.

Though dealing with ridicule, they were a close-knit family thriving on love, dignity, and self-respect. Like his father, Ricky retained pride of his French Canadian roots, but also identified with his mother's Native heritage.

Growing up, he loved listening to her tribal stories. On many a wintry night, both he and his father sat by the warming hearth, captivated by her solemn face aglow within the softened firelight as she recounted tales of when the first settlers came ashore.

"If not for my peoples' compassion sharing food and shelter, the fledgling invaders would surely have perished during the first winter. The white men came as strangers, yet we welcomed them in peace under *'the tree of the great long leaves';* the sovereign symbol of our vast and powerful confederacy."

She relayed how the Jesuits followed, hell-bent on converting the New World pagans.

"But they did more harm than good. Soon, the white man corrupted tribal customs and ignited several conflicts. My people were used and despised; even murdered as primitive heathens. Our League of Nations may be no more, but our *primitive* wisdom has never faltered. It shall always survive, secreted by the *nemgayo dyan ju*— those of the higher will who keep it silent."

Ricky's genteel grin resumed as he trusted instincts that opened his heart to her words. Though born Catholic by paternal default, he and his father chose to embrace many of her Native allegories as faultless and insightful wisdom.

He was convinced much of her traditional lore mirrored several fundamental constants fostered by ancient creeds to modern world theosophies. He also believed his mother's contention that to achieve piety, one need not convene at a communal place, like a building or a shrine to practice faith.

Mahog ga kootchik na ho tah, he pondered his mother's teachings: that by virtue of birth, Man is *already* a divine being that segregates him from other life-forms; infused with a soul, a sacred will, and an intuitive intellect to know right from wrong. All he need do to attain divine harmony; is *be it*— pure and simple.

Mr. Alvarez rushed into the room, jarring Ricky from his sentient mind-state. He set his brief case atop his desk, and needing a minute to collate loose papers, told everyone to open text books to Chapter Twelve.

"Good afternoon, boys. Sorry I was late, but before we begin today's lesson, let me tell you about a funny thing that happened to me over the weekend. A couple of those nut-case Jehovah Witnesses rang my doorbell and tried preaching how *they* were the only ones to be saved, heh, heh," he embellished his story with false laughter.

"What a bunch of dim-witted fools. You'd think by now they'd get a clue, wouldn't ya? Well I set those misguided pagans straight. You should have seen the look on their faces when I booted their butts down my driveway, heh, heh. How can they be so *dumb*? *Everyone* knows that only Catholics will be saved." All but one approved with adolescent laughter.

Ricky's face remained expressionless watching Mr. Alvarez strut his stuff, dismissing his teacher to be nothing more than a blind-faith buffoon— a Pied Piper plying his own zealot's tune upon student lemmings.

How is he any different than the 'stupid prophetic butts' he sent scurrying down his driveway?

Saved? Ricky challenged. Saved from what; and to the exclusion of the planet's diverse billions— each likely a devotee of some form of "ism" rooted in Gnostic ground they considered just as sacred; many cultivated millenniums before the word *Catholic* was even invented?

Ricky recalled yet another solemn, but simplistic precept his mother had taught him: "ki choonah quahog nah hotay," he mumbled to himself— *there can be no religion higher than truth.*

I guess that must make me a heathen, he scoffed— *hardly!*

Ricky closed his book for the duration of class— and then his mind to Mr. Alvarez forever.

The Magic of Moses

by D.R.Smith

A steady summer rain spattered the plate window next to where Mike Magee was seated at Duffy's Tavern, a popular eatery about a block from Belmont Park. He lazily sipped a lager, pleased his chores were done and no racing scheduled for the afternoon. The clamor of a noonday crowd faded as droplets dotting the glass mesmerized him; an image that took him back fifty years.

"I'll give a dollar for *those* thoughts," Robby teased. "The place is packed; mind if I join you?"

Startled, Mike smiled and motioned his farrier to set his lunch down. "Sorry about that; was lost in space, I guess. Have a seat."

"Thanks, and by the way; congratulations on taking second in last weekend's Belmont Stakes. Tiawah was awesome." Robby cited the colt's impressive rush, nearly beating the even-money favorite. "What a finish; he closed at least a dozen lengths in the stretch, eh."

"Yep. Almost got the job done. Ran out of real estate was all."

Between bites, Robby glanced in the general direction of Mike's interrupted trance but failed to see anything other than ordinary traffic. "What the devil were you staring at outside?"

Mike grinned. "Ah, was nothing *outside*, but the window itself is what had me hooked."

"The *window*? What's so dang special about this window?" he wrinkled his brow, exploring the pane for clues.

Mike finished his drink. "Let me ask you something— and think about it no matter how trivial, okay? But has any event, or perhaps something a person might have said or done, ever had such a strong impression that it influenced you or in some way changed your life?"

Perplexed, Robby paused, sipping his beer as Mike afforded him a moment to search his memory. Robby's face lit up.

"Yeah, as a matter of fact, I do. When I was a kid, I bought a stolen catcher's mitt from a classmate with initials tooled into the wristband. My Little League coach noticed the mismatch and asked where I got it. I eventually 'fessed up to getting a five-fingered discount, but was I ever embarrassed. I respected him for being nice enough, but I'll never forget how *ashamed* he made me feel; that I was no better than a two-bit thief myself, for Christ's sake. The guilt stuck with me all my life, Mike, and I swear— I never bought another stolen thing; ever. I won't even look at hot goods, but what's that got to do with this here window?"

"Well, when I was little kid, my Grandpa used to say people are like a race of raindrops— a bunch of colorless souls, created in the heavens, and born by chance upon a window pane of life; like this one here." Mike pointed to spates of droplets; many of them static, others zigzagging or commingling on down the panel.

"Grandpa said some just sit around and never go anywhere; others plodding every which way, bumping into people and causing chain reactions that affect other peoples' lives forever. Sort of how your coach did to you."

"Hmm, a rather intriguing thought, actually." Robby scanned the glass. "Sounds like your Grandpa was a wise old gentleman."

"More than you can imagine, Robby."

Mike grinned coyly, as if hiding a secret. "Tell you what; while you enjoy lunch, let me tell you a little story." Mike said, and flagged a barmaid for two more beers.

"You may remember my dad, Dermot. Well, he taught me a lot about training horses, but what would you say if I owed everything I am today to an old Negro; the most decrepit, flea-bitten, worthless old codger that no one in the world would have dreamed could affect *anyone's* life, much less mine?"

"It's true," Mike said, amused at Robby's surprised look. "My mother died a year after giving me birth, about two years before Pearl Harbor. Papa got a hardship deferment since he was the only one left to care for me. He was the only child of Irish immigrants who barely survived the depression. They kept him out of gangs and raised him to be a fair and honest man, though he did have a stubborn streak a mile long. Papa seldom deviated from convictions once his mind was made up.

"Papa was always strapped, yet somehow managed to raise me migrating between winter racing in Cajun country and summers at Boston's Suffolk Downs. The travel, living in backstretch shanties, or even camping out in Papa's old Woody didn't bother me. I grew up learning the horse game and loving every minute helping Papa train a half dozen cheap horses. I guess you could say he personified the ultimate optimist," Mike chortled.

"You know the type. A die-hard horseman; always broke but keeps hanging on to a dream of one day plucking his *'Seabiscuit'* from a bunch of also-rans.

"Not long after my mother died, fate happened to where Papa took in a pathetic, dirty old vagrant; literally for a ham sandwich.

"His name was Moses LeBlanc; a busted-up former bush-league jock who at one time had a promising career. Born in 1865, Moses was the second son of Cajun slaves from the Mississippi delta region of Louisiana. But unlike his folks, he never knew the backbreaking work of farming cotton. Instead, an aging blacksmith hired his father as an apprentice after the Civil War, and Moses grew up working with horses.

"A favorite pastime among local colored folk included match racing whatever dreadful steeds could be saddled away from plowing fields, or after patching up giveaways rescued from euthanasia at nearby race meets.

"Moses started real young," Mike recalled. "He was fearless and won his first race when only seven. By the time he was a teenager, he became known as *Meanie Mo* for not hesitating to tattoo passing jocks with his whip. Moses emulated Isaac Murphy, the famed black jockey who won forty percent of his races, including three Kentucky Derbies. Moses even patterned his life after Murphy; known for his integrity and loyalty.

"'Never lose yo intiggerty, young'n,' Mike quoted one of the many times Moses would preach to him. 'Cain't nobawdy take dat away c'ep'n you.' He'd stress it was the most valuable thing a man could possess.

"Moses was small, but had strong, sensitive hands and tireless legs— a natural for a near motionless pilot astride the withers of a charging thoroughbred. His future vanished at the old Fairgrounds in New Orleans; nearly killed in a tragic spill that claimed the life of a fellow jock and three horses. His shattered arm never healed properly and was left disfigured and crippled for the rest of his life. Disabled, uneducated, and with nowhere to go, his life crumbled to bare subsistence. He hung around bush-league racetracks, grateful for the odd handout, or took menial jobs watering horses for whoever would tolerate his slovenly appearance.

"Papa hated to see *any* human being rummaging through garbage barrels for bits of food like a stray cur, or sleeping in empty stalls or wherever he could lay his weary bones without being chased off. Papa felt bad he couldn't help the old geezer, but we were only a sawbuck away from being vagrants ourselves. Yet somehow Moses survived, though many times abused by cruel and aimless riffraff hanging around the ovals.

"One day, Papa was passing through a rear parking lot when a skirmish between horse vans drew his attention. Two lowlifes were pissing on Moses after knocking him down to rifle his pockets for loose change. Papa flew into a rage and gave them a beating, sending one to the infirmary in need of several stitches.

"Times were hard for us, but Papa took Moses in anyway. He cleaned him up and fed him. Moses asked to stay on as a groom despite the lack of normal wages; likely more grateful for Papa's kindness, and no longer homeless than for any pittance Papa could afford from time to time.

Moses' needs were simple and he never complained of anything. He slept on a cot Papa set in the tack room, and had a hot plate for heating meals. Moses eventually became known as a fixture in Papa's barn; always upbeat and never failed to greet passerbys with a congenial, 'mawnin boss,' or a 'howdya do missem.'

"What a boon Moses turned out to be, Robby," Mike reflected. "He not only potty-trained me, but he was a *brilliant* horseman. Papa learned a ton of homespun training talents that dovetailed his own skills. Yeah, Papa really admired that old Negro's extraordinary way with horses," Mike reminisced.

"He'd marvel at Moses' eerie affinity for bonding with them; as if he could touch their equine souls and galvanize the competitive spirit within their hearts.

"Moses would stay with a sore horse for hours after a race— humming old Negro spirituals while massaging swollen joints with his special poultice remedies if he thought it would comfort one of Papa's worn-out nags even the slightest. Moses used to boast he could talk to horses." Mike smiled. "And I believed him, too."

"'You gonna be jess fine,' Mike imitated Moses. 'Doncha go worry none, cuz ol' Moses be workin' his magic, now— fo' sho. Why, he be fix'n you up *reeal* good.'

"Moses seemed to identify with their lot in life as being bred for only one purpose— 'to run yo hawt out for da Massah.'

"No matter how poorly a horse performed, Moses never held losers in contempt; he respected their 'intiggerty' as much as his own.

"'Doncha fret none, Massah D,' Moses attempted to appease Papa's disappointment. 'Why, he done his best. He be jess unlucky t'day. We git 'em nex'un, fo' sho,' and then he'd cackle like a demented old witch, secretly relieved his *baby* was able to walk back to the barn on its own power, let alone run up the track costing him his last deuce for the week.

"The day after my tenth birthday, I was sitting atop a barn rail facing the track. I was sharing a jelly sandwich with Moses; he teaching me how to spot injuries or conformation flaws in horses passing by. A disturbance flared up in a neighboring barn, and peering beneath the eaves, we saw someone battling a rank horse in its stall. Fearing injury to man or beast, Moses hobbled to assist as quickly as eighty-one-year-old legs could manage.

"A stable hand was beating a horse with a muzzle twitch. Moses lunged at the groom, grabbing for the thick club before another vicious blow could be delivered. Moses got whacked in the forehead, but managed to hang on; wrestling the man to the straw bedding at risk of being kicked or trampled by the highly agitated horse.

"Working nearby, a vet and his assistant were drawn to the fracas and dragged the scuffling pair from the stall. Moses and the groom were still cursing and hurling threats at each when the stable's trainer returned from the track. Upon learning of his groom's antics, he fired the man on the spot.

Satisfied justice had been served, and despite a huge, throbbing welt on his noggin, Moses ignored warnings of the horse's mean-spirited ways and re-entered the stall to check on the abused animal. It was then Moses recognized the small mahogany bay as Cohasset, a four-year-old he had been observing on and off the track for weeks.

"Moses calmed the colt, and gently stroked the beaten animal while giving him a good looking over. He liked Cohasset's balance and fluid action through the shoulder; his intelligent head and big determined eye. From what Moses could tell, aside from a little underweight and a dull coat, Cohasset didn't appear to have any obvious afflictions that would account for his lackluster race efforts.

"'Don't knows fo' sho, but I don't tink dat hoss be hurtin'; he could be awright, Massah Mike.'

"The beating incident long faded into memory as deep autumn meant Suffolk's race meet was coming to a close. Many stables had already vanned to southern destinations. Trainers were culling sore and mediocre horses not up to grade for stronger winter meets, or had to free up stall space for incoming two-year-olds prepping for spring campaigns. Like now, a common practice for dumping stock was to enter horses at lower claiming ranks than normal, hoping to tempt smaller stables into claiming away a bargain.

"I remember it was a bright Saturday morning. Papa was in the tack room with his nose buried in the racing form as I helped Moses pin leg-wrappings and water the horses.

"One of Papa's five trainees had been claimed two weeks prior, another given away after pulling up lame with a torn suspensory. We were in dire need of replacements if we had any hope of earning a living in Louisiana.

"Papa was focused on a five-year-old gelding dropping in for thirty-five hundred, down from a tag as high as ten grand during the summer. He had two thousand from his claimed horse, plus a G-note he barely scraped together. But Papa kept staring at the form trying to resolve yet another problem— he was still five hundred short.

"'Wass yo readin' so hawd, boss?' Moses poked his head through the doorway as I came up beside him and looped my arm around his waist. We listened as Papa described his prospect— *and* his dilemma.

"Papa said, 'I know you got some rathole money stashed away. Any chance you got five hundred to lend?'

"Moses kept cash in a small tin box hidden in a shallow hole in the corner of a stall. He covered it with a shingle and masked it with straw, but shared his secret hideaway with us should anything ever happen to him. However meager his salary, he'd manage to squirrel away a deuce or a fiver here and there. Many times, he'd increase his stash if afforded tempting odds on horses catching his savvy eye during morning workouts. Moses said he thought he had enough money, but asked more details of Papa's targeted claim.

"'Oh lawdy, not Diggery Doc. He be dat big chessnut wit da white blaze dat Massah Lowe trains?' Moses stood in the doorway scratching his head as I sidled past to peek at Papa's notes. 'I dunnos 'bout dat one, Massah D. I tink dat be a *baaad* move.'

"Moses agreed the flashy chestnut had talent, and may have been turning heads at the track, but he seemed to favor a left fore ever so slight when setting it down in a slow walk. Moses suspected Diggery was about to bow a tendon, and urged Papa to reconsider.

"'You should listen to Grandpa,' I said. 'Grandpa showed me Diggery's problem a couple times already.' I reminded Papa a bad claim would destroy our finances. I again glanced at Papa's form, and got excited when I spotted an entry in the following race.

"'Hey Grandpa. Cohasset's in the sixth for five grand today.'

"Papa popped from his chair and knocked it over, thinking the two of us were deliberately conspiring to subvert his plans. 'What's so damned special about Cohasset?'

"Papa was fuming. He realized the colt was dropping in for twenty-five hundred less than previous starts, but the claim was also another *two* thousand more than he had for Diggery.

"'Besides, he's nothin' but a plodder!' Papa yelled; 'ain't even been closer than five lengths in his last dozen outs, for Christ's sake. Look!' Papa shoved the form at me, stabbing his finger at the stats; his face red with anger, and his mind made up; glowering at Moses.

"'Are you gonna give me any money or not?'

"I defied my father, and begged him to heed Moses' advice. All that time, Moses stood silent, torn between his loyalties versus wariness of Papa's decision. But Papa's glare was too much; he gave in and agreed to retrieve his savings.

"I grabbed Grandpa by the arm, and to the astonishment of my father, chastised Moses for turning tail. 'Don't do it,' I yelled, and urged Moses to ignore Papa. 'Go with your instincts like your Daddy always told you.' But instead, Moses ignored me. Getting no support, I whirled to plead further with Papa.

"'Grandpa knows, Papa. He can talk to horses, I tell ya; he *knows*.' I searched Papa's eyes, thinking a different tact might sway his decision.

"'If we have to, Papa, we can claim Cohasset out the next race. Grandpa likes him, too; I *seen* it.' I thought he might go for the compromise, but I was wrong.

"'Use your head, boy; you ain't thinking! I just said we ain't got enough for Diggery, so how in hell do we pay for the bastard when he's *two* grand more than I got?' Papa slammed the form on his desk so hard, it sent clouds of dust spiraling into the air.

"Moses got excited and hurried toward the first stall. 'Dunnos fo sho, Boss. But I mights have enough.'

"I chanced a last ditch effort using one of Papa's own precepts against him. 'You always told me a Grandpa can never lie, so *trust* him, Papa.' But my words had no effect. Papa brushed me aside as

Moses returned with the tin box. We stood in the doorway; our eyes locked on Papa sifting through wads of crumpled bills.

"'My word, Moses. You have thirty-eight hundred and change in here?' Papa handed him the box, but Moses refused.

"'No Massah D. You knows I cain't read or do figger'n. You be da boss o' diss fam'ly, so you minds it for ol' Moses, now hear?'

"Our motley faces were too much for Papa to contend with any longer. He pocketed a roll of bills and pushed me aside to snatch a halter and lead shank. Papa was still angry and stormed from the tack room, but stopped short of the barn's portal. He thrust a dangling shank at me and yelled once more.

"'Damn it to hell, boy! Are you comin' with me or not, 'cause if you don't have the stomach for it, then stay here and help Moses prepare a vacant stall 'til I get back.'

"I stood defiant. Papa turned his back on me, and stomped off to the track. I tried goading Moses into stopping Papa before it was too late, but Moses dismissed the notion with a wave of his hand.

"'Nossuh, Massah Mike. Nossuh. And doncha be frettin' none, boy. He be da boss man and dat's dat. We best do what he says.'

"More than two hours had passed while we waited in the tack room— brooding. Our reticent eyes met when hearing Papa yell for help. We heard snorting, regretting it was time to wash and cool out Papa's claim. I gathered soap, a sponge, and a bucket. Moses tossed me a squeegee and told me to scoot while he folded a horse blanket before shuffling out to the wash rack.

"Moses stopped only feet outside the shed row; his eyes widened in sync with an exuberant smile.

"'Why, lawd sakes alive. It be da '*Hasset*. Moses stood gazing at the prancing horse tugging at the lead shank, and then danced a little shuffle while I lathered Cohasset up. Papa greeted us with contempt, fumbling for words as he scrutinized the compact colt.

"'I hope you two nitwits are satisfied. Diggery *won* his race— by five! But this— this worthless son-of-a-bitch plodded home sixth, *just* like I said he would; beaten twelve lengths!'

"Moses ignored Papa. 'Aw, now Massah D, doncha be sayin' dat about da 'Hasset. Why he tain't no sumbitch. Nossuh. Why, he be da boss hoss now— yassah.'

"Moses whispered into the horse's nostrils, fixing his scent while stroking the colt's neck. 'Pay no 'tention to Massah D; he mean no hawm. Why, he knows you be a good'n.' Moses palmed the colt's muzzle, soothing him to a quieter stand as I rinsed him off.

"'You be talkin' to ol' Moses from now on. Why, you jess bin awaitin' on me to fix you up— aincha lil' fella? Yassah. Jess you wait 'n see, cuz ol' Moses be workin' his magic now, fo' sho.'

"Papa slowly slid experienced hands over the colt's knees and fetlocks, all the while mumbling. 'Christ, I'm gonna be the laughing stock of the whole damned meet.' Satisfied Cohasset's joints felt sound with no heat or filling, Papa warned us to be mindful of the colt's temperament; that he was a handful walking back to the barn.

"'He can be a bit ornery, but if you need me, I'll be at the track kitchen— gettin' stinkin' drunk!'

* * *

"Give us each a Hennessy and me both tabs," Robby ordered, and produced two cigars as Mike described how Moses worked on Cohasset for nearly two months before his next start.

"Papa went nuts," Mike said, laughing in retrospect. "He was furious over mounting feed and vet bills before he could even smell a chance at recovering purse money. But Papa gradually warmed up to Cohasset as his rich mahogany coat dappled to a healthy sheen.

"Days after the claim, Moses detected a hint of unusual odor in Cohasset's stools. He suspected the colt had heat ulcers— an ailment seldom diagnosed, let alone properly treated even by the best of modern trainers.

"Moses gained such knowledge from match-racing days in Louisiana. He taught us a secret remedy I *still* use; made with wild Cajun herbs mixed with corn meal, de-hulled oats, molasses, water, and then warmed the concoction to a soft mash.

"The horse looked better and took to training well after six weeks ingesting that '*mojo mush*.' The time came when Papa was about to enter Cohasset for the same claiming tag; hoping to get rid of the overhead. He prayed the colt's improved appearance and decent action during morning gallops would attract attention. But Moses pitched a fearsome fit.

"'Doncha be doin' dat, Massah D. Nossuh. Da 'Hasset done tol' me; he be *ready* dis time— fo' sho!'

"Moses stamped his foot predicting success, insisting Cohasset be entered for at *least* ten thousand, or risk losing him to a cheaper claim. 'And den ol' Moses be gone, too; fo' *sho!*' he threatened; never to set foot in Papa's barn again.

"Papa grumbled, but found a race for non-winners of two races lifetime, though the claiming price was much higher than he wanted; at twelve-five.

"Cohasset's form was pathetic at lower levels, let alone stepping up in class to nearly triple the value. The betting public confirmed it, sending Cohasset to the gate at 50-to-1 odds.

"Papa was irritated by onlookers taunting him in the saddling paddock, but held his tongue getting Cohasset ready for post parade. After boosting the jockey a leg up, Moses avoided Papa's sour mood and disappeared into the crowd shuffling toward the grandstands.

"You remember the tin box, Robby? Well, Papa took most of the money, but returned the box with over thirteen hundred still in it. I was proud of my father for not taking advantage of Moses' bankroll, but rather, he committed his own money for a half interest as the honorable thing to do. 'In for a penny— in for a pound,' Papa said; and a damned good thing, too," Mike chuckled.

"Cohasset made a mockery of the race; his stride smooth and steady, and after stalking the early pace, scored an easy four-length victory under a hand ride.

"That day was the first of only two times I ever saw my father cry. Not for the win," Mike paused, "but after Cohasset was bedded down for the night, you should have seen Papa's face when Moses handed him a thousand dollars in face-value win tickets."

"Holy, Jesus!" Robby computed. "At 50-to-1? That's fifty big ones; a *ton* o' dough back then."

"Yep. Fifty-two-thou to be exact." Mike drew slowly on his cigar. "Moses insisted on Papa cashing them."

"'Naw— ol' Moses needs no mawny, boss. I gots all I need right here,' and slid his good arm over my shoulder. 'You keeps it; for m'grandboy here.'

Mike gazed at the rain-soaked window. "That's when Papa's chin quivered and he lost it. The second time was finding a lifeless Moses curled up on his cot at first light. Grandpa died during the night about six months later.

"Moses' winnings improved everything— our living conditions *and* the stable," Mike recounted. "But that was only the beginning. Cohasset was okay; he improved and went on to win or place in a few more races until claimed away for a profit. But it was Papa's popularity that took off.

"Papa used Moses' money to expand the stable, and given his improving Cohasset and a few other shrewd claims, owners came around asking to be clients. The stable grew and even today, I train for some of Papa's bigger stables; like the prominent Kentucky farm who sent me Tiawah, and about dozen other top-bred prospects every year.

"So there you have it Robby; here I am fourth leading trainer in the nation, plenty of money, big stable of fine horses, and good owners— *all* because of a downtrodden old wretch, maligned as a worthless outcast who came into my life.

"I loved that old man. Besides Papa, he's all I ever knew or had to care for me; even adopted him as my true Grandpa, Robby. Yeah, ol' Moses sure worked his magic on me, or *I'd* be living in a tack room somewhere myself."

"Oh?" Robby challenged. "I'm not so sure about that entirely, Mike. I think you should give your father a great deal of credit, too." Robby was pleased he managed to induce a clueless expression on Mike's face.

"What do you mean?"

"Well, if you ask me, I think your father knew all along he had found his '*Biscuit*— only it *wasn't* a horse." Robby fanned emotional flames Mike had never before fathomed, but was curious why his father hadn't claimed Diggery in the first place.

"Ya know, I asked him that myself at the time. And all he said were three words: 'Grandpa's never lie,' and winked."

"Mm-hmm," Robby nodded. "I propose a toast. Here's to your Belmont second— *and* to your wise old Grandpa."

"I'll drink to that." Mike clinked glasses.

Robby smiled and maneuvered Mike's attention back to the window. "So your Grandpa says that's our window pane of life, huh? An amazing story, Mike. Makes me wonder which ones are us." Robby was intrigued as to who all the droplets might be.

"Don't know, but you can bet we're on there— fo' sho," Mike teased.

An alluring mystique pervaded Robby's mind as he browsed the rain-spattered glass; fantasizing how it could relate to his present life.

I wonder who I'm gonna bump into next, he mused.

Sinewy strands of bluish cigar smoke oozed from pursed lips as the two pals cradled snifters of cognac, and leaning back in their chairs, faced the window in silence as if waiting for a curtain rise.

Poet's Pantry
by D.R.Smith

The Morning Sun

The morning Sun left dreams undone
As eyes ope' to the dawn.
For rest there's none 'til chores are done
And darkness begs a yawn.

The day complete, I must retreat
To bedroom loft I go.
From window seat, a scene replete
So soft in Luna's glow.

O wondrous sight with fullness bright,
Arise majestic moon.
Infuse the night with silvern light
And flood thy chamber soon.

Once stationed high in midnight sky
Do bless me with your smile.
In bed I lie and softly sigh
To gaze at thee awhile.

As limbs embrace fresh linen lace,
In pillow's cleft I fade.
Thou tranquil grace shall bathe thy face
At peace 'neath window shade.

Yon moonlight seeps, 'round room it sweeps,
Sweet dreams once more begun.
Whilst slumber creeps, her vigil keeps
'Til early morning Sun.

The Broken Man

From town to town in fruitful land
Begged hungry hobo, hat in hand.
But people jeered his worn-out clothes
And snubbed his pleas with upturned nose.

Depression years saw banks foreclosed,
His savings lost and home disposed.
Tho' down and out, no grievance bears,
The only crime t'was no one cares.

Tired and hungry the pavements pound
But doors slammed shut, no jobs around
No dimes for soup much less a bed,
Trudged to the park, a week unfed.

No food or warmth for days that passed,
His feeble bones had walked their last.
Downtrodden man begged God forgive,
His spirit drained; no will to live.

In fetal curl on bed of leaves
With chin at rest on tattered sleeves,
Where once was life, now saddened sight,
His body found, first morning light.

Amidst the haves he walked disgraced,
Yet as God's child, his soul's embraced.
No more this broken man needs roam,
For Heaven's hearth is now his home.

Luna's Silent Scream

Mine eyes peruse the heavens to glean
Through crystalline air of autumn night.
Yon silvern glow, such luminous sheen,
Behold dear Luna, her fullness bright.

She peers remorseful t'ward kindred Earth,
Thou sadness shows, o' sorrowful moon.
Wed to sun and orbs that rule Man's birth,
Horrors seen, forewarns of Karmic doom.

'Tis a woeful message Munch unveils;
His genius oiled such haunting scene:
Of hands cradlin' face, the specter wails
When painting his masterpiece, "The Scream".

Fraught with dread, its pallid wafer face
Of hollowed mouth and desolate eyes,
Hails silent warnings thru void of space,
Yet Man hears naught, tho' harder he tries.

Woe, fate be damned if she's forsaken;
For Luna's cries to be heard— *not* seen,
Man must numb the senses, and waken
His callous heart to harken her scream.

Snows of Betrayal

Entwined in wedded bliss, passionate seeds were sown;
In Heaven's hearth God forged twin Cherubs in thy mold.
Nourished in summer's sun, by fall from nest have flown,
Thus rue the autumn frost that wilts thy fam'ly fold.

Lo, the knave cloud concealed 'hind gray horizon veil,
Her chill wind may smile, but betrayal snows approach.
A savored trust once sweet, now sours in love gone stale
As mute ears and blind eyes let wanton storms encroach.

Drawn by Siren's song to greener pastures taken,
Sacred vows uprooted, yield empty golden rings.
Thy jaded heart withers, its vibrant beat forsaken,
Fertile ground now barren, shall fallow in the spring.

Harrowed fields lie dormant to weather wintry days.
Bitter heartaches linger, thy hearth still lacking fire;
Yea, hopeful seedlings pine for coming solstice rays,
So idle pods may bloom once betrayal snows expire.

Must draw from inner strength and battle woeful throes,
For thy soul breeds contempt for tunnel void of light.
As bellows breaths whisper, a dying ember glows,
And ashen coals brought to life, flicker thru the night.

Alas, heat of rising sun lifts the mourning haze.
Aye, wakened eyes behold, two Cherubs sprouted fast.
As glint from gilded faces enrich thy harvest trays,
Proof that fruit conceived in love, shall survive the past.

Ne'er Do Us Part

Grieving for his soul mate, he set her urn adrift
Upon Atlantic Ocean surging 'neath the cliff.
From whence a mystic image sang from briny deep;
A lovely flaxen visage, begged his faith to keep.

Her soothing song spiraled o'er Fundy's tidal surf,
Consoling heavy heart in waves of rhythmic verse.
"O' husband, dear husband," whooshed the ocean roil,
Tamed by time-worn boulders bracing Scotia's soil.

A breeze bore her gentle kiss blown thru golden locks,
Twisting tawny sea foam, her curls amidst the rocks.
Supernal words continued chanting to his heart,
"Fear not my love, we mate etern', ne'er do us part."

Closing eyes when bidding true love's divine farewells,
His soul mate's apparitions faded from the swells.
"I shall e'er be with you," he answered tenderly,
And watched the phantom vision slip beneath the sea.

Eyes filled with lonely tears in sorrowful retreat,
Yet a parting whisper, her last rose from the deep.
For he heard her promise in final words sublime:
"We shall meet again my love, somewhere else in time."

Path of Evil
by Richard Sarles

A Walk Along Route 18

Raymond Dempsey scrambled up the steep ditch along Route 18, grabbing fistfuls of wildgrass and unearthing divots of mud with his work boots. Early morning sunlight stretched his lanky shadow far ahead of him, up and onto the road. Neither he nor his shadow would be anywhere near that old blacktop if he could help it, but Pinky lived up Route 18 and on the other side of it. At least that's where Pinky *used* to live, until about ten minutes ago, when Raymond shot him in the back of the head.

Raymond never killed anyone before and didn't plan on killing Pinky, but the guy knew things he shouldn't have. Things he had no business knowing. And now it was done, as sure as anything, as sure as those dark red spots on Raymond's jeans and T-shirt were Pinky's congealing blood. Yes, the old man was dead.

"Just get to your house, Ray; get to the house without anybody seeing you," he told himself between hoarse gasps for air. "Clean up. Get rid of these clothes. You're okay, you're okay." He crouched beside the road with his hand on a rickety fence post and listened. "You're okay," he repeated, "almost there, nobody's seen you. Cross over, climb back into the woods, and you're home free."

Hearing nothing other than his heart slamming against his chest, Ray lunged forward. And as Murphy's Law might predict, he took two steps, jammed his boot in a pothole, and crashed to the pavement.

"Shit!" he screamed, clutching his ankle with both hands and rocking back and forth atop the faded double-yellow line on the road. Between grunts he heard a car approaching.

According to the 2000 Census, Stillwater Township had a population of sixty-eight residents. Folks in that part of the country knew better: in 2000 it was actually seventy-three, at least until the Andersons packed up and moved to Grundy County, when it dropped to seventy. Since then, with a handful of births and a couple of deaths, it was back up to seventy-seven. Of course, if asked, Raymond could have told you that number was now officially seventy-*six*. Likewise, if asked, he could have told you damn near everything about the approaching car and its owner simply from the sound of its tired, four-cylinder engine.

He got to one knee and squinted into the sun, knowing he had no chance to crawl across the road before his neighbor, Ed Polanski, and his Toyota came into view.

Be calm, damnit! Don't do anything suspicious! Just taking a walk, that's all.

The rusted car slowed, brakes squealing. With the sun behind it Raymond couldn't see the driver, but he smiled anyway and stepped to the side of the road, trying not to wince at his throbbing ankle. He waved. "Hiya, Ed. Good morning!"

The car pulled to a stop. A brittle-looking man with a head of white hair that had gone yellow around the edges leaned out the window. "Mornin back at yah, Ray. Whatcha up to?" Ed asked.

Is he looking at me funny? Looking at the blood?

Ray brushed absently at his trousers. "Nothing much. Just grabbing an early walk before work," he replied, looking up and down the road, trying to appear as uninterested and innocent as possible.

"It's a peach of a day fer one." He motioned up the road in the direction of Pinky's place and said something Ray didn't catch.

Somebody found him already. The police are there right now, and that's where Ed's going. He'll tell them he saw me wandering here in the road, blood all over myself. Oh, Jesus!

"Well, did yah?" Ed asked, holding up a questioning hand.

Ray cleared his throat, scratched his cheek, and managed a forced yawn. "Did I what, Ed? I didn't hear yah." A tingle crept down his spine and into his gut.

Ed repeated himself, and over the pounding in Ray's ears, Ray only caught the words: *shoot a man.*

Although it felt like a bomb detonated in Ray's stomach, he laughed, casually at first, as he was certain any guiltless man would in the situation. "Shoot a man? What're you talking about?" He laughed a little harder, became aware of it sounding forced, maybe maniacal, and stopped abruptly. He scratched his cheek again and raised his eyebrows.

Ed's face wrinkled. "Shoot a man? Hell, you need to clean the earwax outta yer head, son. I said *fruit stand*. You have a chance to check out Mrs. Spradling's *fruit stand*?"

The laugh returned, this time with giddiness. "Oh, I musta misunderstood you." Ray paused and caught his breath. A wave of spent adrenaline weakened his bony knees and brought a tremble to his lip. He tried to swallow, but found his mouth dust dry. "I wouldn't miss it for the world. Haven't been down there yet, but I will, you can bet on that. Agnes always tends a wonderful garden, dear old woman. Ha, couldn't weigh more than ninety-five pounds that gal, but she sure is a workhorse, always running. She has lots of good stuff over there I bet. Best sweet corn in the county, you know. Terrific green tomatoes, too." His rambling trailed off, and he took a half-step sideways, felt his ankle buckle, and nearly dropped to the ground.

Ed frowned and dropped the Toyota into drive without taking his eyes from Ray. "You oughta get yourself home, neighbor. Get some rest before you gotta be at the shop this mornin. You look frazzled as anything," he said and drove away without waiting for a response.

Ray watched the car drive off, licked salty sweat and dust from the corners of his mouth, and began to entertain the idea that his goose was officially cooked.

Monday night's buck-a-card bingo at the Moose Lodge, at which Pinky was as much a staple as the brass cage of Ping-Pong balls and schooners of Old Style, was set to kick off just after sundown. It wouldn't take long for folks to notice him gone. One or two of them might even stagger over to check on him after the keg ran dry. And maybe Ed Polanski would be one of them. They'd show up on Pinky's porch, knock once or twice, then peek in to find the old guy there slumped forward in his recliner just the way Ray left him: dead. Not just dead, but murdered.

Sheriff Pearsall would show up, badge hanging out the pocket of the nightshirt he'd been sleeping in, and start asking questions. "Anybody see or hear anything out of the ordinary?" he might ask, rubbing his earlobe the way he does. And Ed, who maybe had forgotten how goofy Ray acted earlier, would perk up, cock his withered white head to the side, and reply: "Yeah, Sheriff. Yah know, on my way to town this mornin I came across Ray Dempsey stumblin over Route 18 all short of breath actin *real* out of the ordinary, talkin about shootin a man. And he had some stains on his jeans and shirt that looked like..."

"I'm screwed," Ray said, limping up the ivy-lined path that led to his house. But even though he said it, he didn't fully believe it. He wasn't ready to throw in the towel just yet. That wasn't his style.

Raymond Earns Fifty Cents

Before the walk, before the murder, Raymond's day had begun no differently than any other Monday in recent memory—with his butt planted on a rusted iron chair and a finger looped through the handle of a coffee mug. Out here, in what he called his *terrace*, is where he did his thinking, made his plans. The terrace wasn't much more than a clearing in an overgrown patch of tall weeds in Ray's backyard, but the guy had a way of dressing up things in his mind so they seemed something better than they were. He had a way of dressing up things in other people's minds too, which is why most everyone in Stillwater adored him.

As he sat on his terrace sipping black coffee and listening to acorns tumble off branches on their way to the ground, Ray recalled the conversation he'd overheard the previous night at Dusty's Tap.

Three or four old-timers who always played backgammon under the shelter in Thornton Park were seated around the cold, empty fireplace, trading stories about the Great Depression. One of the old-timers was Pinky.

Ray had his back to them, but he could hear them well enough from his barstool as he hovered over the Sunday crossword puzzle. He always did the Sunday crossword in public, at Dusty's or sometimes the Beehive Cafe, where people could see him. Thought it made him look smart.

Pinky's deep voice and slow, southern drawl were hard to miss. "Shoot, I'll never forget watchin my daddy cry into his hands on our porch swing, tellin Ma how the bank was gonna take our house away and there wasn't a thing he could do about it," Pinky said.

"Lost his job, huh?" another man asked, already knowing the answer.

Pinky grunted. "Lost his job and what money he had put away, all thanks to them bankers. Sons-a-bitches closed down the supply store he was workin' at, and when he went to pull the few bucks he had outta the bank, they said it was gone."

"Gone, huh?" the same voice asked. Again, with little interest. At the bar, Raymond tapped his pencil, struggling for a five-letter word for "cast out".

"Yep. Those bankers had put it into somethin that wasn't worth a damn, and when the stock market went... *poof!* went my pa's money. All of it. That's why to this day I don't like banks. Don't believe in 'em."

There was a mumbling of consensus from the old-timers, then Pinky: "Keep my money in an old tobacco tin underneath my bed. Always have, always will. Somebody like one of them bankers wants it, they gotta go through me and my Winchester to get it."

Pinky let out a phlegmy laugh and Raymond's pencil stopped tapping. He eyed Pinky through the mirror on the other side of the bar. With neon signs providing much of the bar's lighting, the old man's freckled, cherub face and carroty hair looked bright red. Brighter and redder than usual anyway. Raymond returned his gaze to the crossword, but his pencil only doodled in the margins.

Stillwater's a place where folks keep their doors and windows unlocked day and night whether anyone's home or not. Doors and windows are closed to keep out wind and rain and mosquitoes—not people. It's also a place where the word *trust* is rarely uttered, because it's pretty much a given amongst the townsfolk. You look out for your neighbors, your neighbors look out for you. Plain and simple.

On his terrace that next morning Ray tossed back the last gulp of coffee, rose from his lawn chair, stretched, and smiled wide, because he knew a thing or two about the way Stillwater worked. And one thing he knew as much as anybody in town was that every Monday morning, if Mother Nature allowed, you could find old Pinky on the banks of Culver Creek, fishing pole in his hands, briar pipe between his lips. With this thought in mind, Ray walked into the kitchen, rinsed out the coffee mug, and placed it upside down on a dishtowel. His thinking was complete, his plan in place. Time for a walk.

Then he heard someone coming.

Ray stood at his screen door and watched the Studebaker crawl up a driveway that consisted of two tracks parted by a hump of green grass. Fat tires rumbled over pebbles that cracked and popped under them, sending up plumes of gray dust. The screen door swung open and Ray stepped out, leading with a smile.

"Morning, Mrs. Hoffmeister!" he shouted toward the powder blue car that had rolled off the lines back when Eisenhower was still in his first term. The car's engine turned off, and Ray strode across his yard. With her gnarled spine and arthritic knees, it was always quicker to go to Mrs. Hoffmeister than wait for her to get to you.

She was working the window crank when Ray stopped beside her. As the window squeaked to a halt three-quarters of the way down she peered up at him over the top of her glasses. "Good morning to you, Ray-Ray." She paused, possibly to recollect the purpose of her visit. "You enjoy those cookies I brought you?"

Long-retired elementary school teacher and legendary ballbuster, Mrs. Hoffmeister baked two-dozen cookies each Christmas season and hand delivered them to Bailey's Auto Body where Ray-Ray was head mechanic. Of course, Christmas was eight months ago.

Ray didn't miss a beat. Bending at the waist and resting his hands on his blue jeans, he replied, "I sure did, Mrs. H. You bet I did." The only one of the old woman's ex-students to receive freshly baked goods, Ray-Ray was also the only person who could get away with calling her Mrs. H.

"Oh, wonderful, wonderful," Mrs. H returned, nodding before, during, and after she spoke. She paused, blinked. An acorn bounced off the hood of the car. "I had something I wanted to ask you, Ray-Ray, but I'll be darned if I can think of it."

Ray smiled wider, if that were possible. "Did it have something to do with this year's fundraiser?" he asked and winked.

Her face lit up. "Oh yes, of course!" She tapped her temple. "Sometimes it doesn't record the way it used to, you know. New things are the hardest for me, but the old stuff hasn't gone anywhere I promise you that. Why, I remember right where you used to sit in the classroom, Ray-Ray. You always were good at arithmetic, too. I remember that. And your parents. Wonderful people. How are your folks these days?"

"They're doing great, Mrs. H." They'd been dead for twelve years.

Ray glanced at the sun creeping up the sky and figured he had about an hour before he was supposed to punch in. He coughed into his fist. "You mentioned the fundraiser?"

"Yes, yes I did. Listen, Ray-Ray. I spoke at the PTA meeting last week, reminded them what a fine job you've done with it these last few years meeting our goals and all. We talked it over and agreed there's nobody we'd like more to have in the driver's seat than you again this year. If you can find the time, that is."

"Find the time? For you and the kids? Of course, Mrs. H. Count me in."

The old woman continued as though she hadn't heard Ray's response. "The ice cream social and flea market didn't pull in the money we'd hoped this summer, so we, well the kids really, need your help. If we fall short, I hear they're going to drop the spring music program, maybe even art."

Ray drummed his fingers on his pants leg. "Mrs. H.," he said, leaning closer to the window, smile frozen on his face, "I said I'd do it. I'm your man. No sales pitch necessary. There'll be plenty of music and art classes next spring. You can count on me."

Mrs. Hoffmeister clasped her hands together and shook them. "Oh, thank you! I knew you'd do it. Everyone will be thrilled. You are a dear man. A dear man! Oh!" She was giddy.

"No problem whatsoever. I'll stop by the school tonight and pick up the usual paperwork. Then tomorrow I'll start making calls, and the donations will be rolling in by the end of the week." He straightened and took a step back, trying to bring a hasty close to their meeting. "I have to get ready for work now."

"Of course, of course," the old woman said, composing herself and casually looking around her lap. She pulled something from a small handbag. "Before you go, Ray-Ray, I have something for you. Just a little something."

In her left hand, Mrs. Hoffmeister cupped a coin purse. With her right, she unclasped the tiny latch, and the thing popped open like a set of hungry jaws. She poked around inside and retrieved a silver half-dollar, which she dangled out the window. "Here you go, now. Buy yourself a chocolate bar. And when you do, think of me." Her face beamed, just as it did every time she made this humble offering to Ray-Ray.

Ray accepted the coin and rubbed it between his thumb and finger. Apparently no one told Mrs. Hoffmeister the price of a chocolate bar had increased considerably since she retired in 1977. Or maybe she'd forgotten. Nevertheless, Ray thanked her and she proudly drove off. He stood there grinning until the car turned onto Route 18.

The smile dissolved. Ray dropped the half-dollar in his shirt pocket and marched up the driveway, on his way to rob Pinky of his life savings.

A Confession of Sorts

Still catching his breath and occasionally rubbing his ankle, Ray stood alone in his kitchen and eyed the old rotary-dial phone.

After a few moments of thought he reached for it, noticed dry flakes of blood on his hand, and gagged. Ray had always had a weak stomach. He limped to the sink and scrubbed his hands and forearms with a Brillo Pad, mulling over his options again. After running into Ed while fleeing the murder scene, it seemed he only had one. He dried his hands on a dishtowel and returned to the phone.

To call the police.

Emergency 9-1-1 service hadn't made it to Stillwater yet, so Ray dialed the numbers on the sticker affixed to the phone's receiver. It rang through to the three-person police station in town.

A gruff voice rumbled in Ray's ear, "Stillwater PD, Pearsall speaking."

"Sheriff?" Ray squeaked.

"That's what it says on my badge. What can I do for you?"

"Sheriff, there's been an accident. A horrible accident." Ray's voice was uneven, shaking. He hoped he wasn't overdoing it.

It sounded like the sheriff moved the phone closer to his face. "Who is this? And what kind of accident?"

"It's Ray, Sheriff. There's been an awful accident. With a gun. I... I don't know what to do."

"Ray? Ray Dempsey? You say a gun?" He didn't wait for a reply. "Jesus, son, what the hell happened?"

Ray unconsciously wound the coiled phone cord around his finger, then his hand, then his wrist. "I was over there talking with him this morning about guns and he wanted me to see his. A shotgun. He handed it to me, said it was unloaded. I was looking at it, and it went off." As he spoke, Ray's mind teetered between the lie he was weaving and the gruesome reality he'd already created. Without warning, the latter took over. "Oh my God, oh my God. It was so loud. It shot him, man, right in the head. Holy Christ, he's in pieces, Sheriff. He's dead! Oh... God!" Though he hadn't planned on it, Ray found himself sobbing.

Unlike most folks in Stillwater, Sheriff Robert Pearsall was born and raised elsewhere, in a decent-sized city. Did his schooling and police training in an even bigger city. And he'd been on calls where people were hurt, dying, dead. A few too many calls—the flecks of gray sprinkled throughout his hair could testify to that—which is why he migrated south halfway across the state and settled in such a sleepy town. But in all his years, big city experience or not, Sheriff Pearsall had never gotten a call like this one, from somebody he *knew* talking about someone he *almost certainly knew*, who was now dead.

His voice was eerily calm. "Take it easy, breathe, breathe." He followed his own advice and exhaled loudly. "Now, where are you, Ray? Who got shot?"

Ambushed by emotion, Ray was helpless to the panic that clawed into his throat. "Pinky! Pinky's shot. Pinky's dead. It was an accident! I swear to God, Sheriff! I didn't mean to!"

A weak puff of air escaped the sheriff's lungs. "Aw, shit, Ray," he whispered, and for a while there was only a faint buzz on the line. Eventually, he spoke again. Sheriff Pearsall asked Ray where he was, then where Pinky was, then told him to stay put.

An ambulance was on its way to Pinky's. The sheriff was on his way to Ray's.

Something's Amiss at Pinky's

Ray's nerves were in shambles.

Waiting for the sheriff to arrive, he sat hunched over in his lawn chair, arms crossed firmly over his chest. He rocked slowly, whimpering, with snot pooling on his upper lip. Efforts to corral his frenzied, conflicting emotions had thus far failed miserably.

Not that he could stop if he wanted to, but Ray wondered if all this sniveling was a normal reaction for someone who *accidentally* killed a man. Hopefully the sheriff would see it that way. Or maybe he'd see the telltale sign of a murderer wrought with guilt. Or maybe simply a common response from a man who feared he might spend the rest of his life in jail.

The police cruiser turned into the driveway and rolled toward the house. To Ray's relief, the sheriff seemed in no rush to get there, and the car's red and blue lights were off.

That's a good sign, right?

Ray stood, dug both hands into his pockets, and took a few steps in the direction of the approaching car. Reflections of pine and oak slid up and over the windshield, obscuring Ray's view of the sheriff. He wiped his nose with his forearm and stared at the ground. His heart hammered away.

The cruiser came to a halt, and the door swung open. Out climbed Sheriff Pearsall, an enormous man in both height and girth, whose size and mannerisms somehow conveyed not intimidation, but rather gentle guardianship. In his uniform he looked something like an oversized teddy bear with a clean-shaven face.

The two walked slowly toward each other, and as Ray got close enough he saw tears hanging in the large man's eyes. Ray's stomach churned and his mouth filled with saliva. For a moment he thought he was going to puke right there on his work boots.

The sheriff's jaw flexed. "Ray."

Ray nodded, then shook his head and pursed his lips tight, trying not to start bawling.

Pearsall stopped a foot from him and put a hand on the younger man's shoulder. "You all right, son?"

The nausea passed, and a trickle of relief ran over Ray's conscience in seeing what looked to be concern from the sheriff. He cleared his throat and wiped the corners of his mouth. "I'm... okay. It's just... awful, Sheriff. I mean, it's horrible, a horrible accident. I... I keep seeing it..."

The sheriff patted Ray's shoulder twice. "It'll be okay, son. Everything'll be fine. I need to talk to you some, get a statement from you about what happened. But not here. Let's take a ride to the station," he said, stepping beside Ray and giving a gentle push in the direction of the car.

"The station?" Ray said, shuffling beside the sheriff.

"Sure, sure. Nothing to worry about, though. I'll ask a few questions, talk things over with you, get it all on tape. Standard procedure, you know. Then we'll go from there."

Go from there? Not, "let you go home"?

Ray felt the sheriff's eyes crawling all over him. Ray had decided against changing out of the blood-stained jeans and T-shirt, not wanting to look like he was hiding something. Now it seemed to him the *first* thing an innocent man would have done was rid himself of such grisly, soiled clothing. Nothing he could do about it now.

The two reached the side of the car, and Ray stopped at the passenger door. The sheriff continued a few feet farther.

"Uh, Ray, I need you to sit in back."

"The back?"

"The back."

"But it was an accident, Sheriff. You don't think I... that I could... that I meant to..."

Pearsall pulled the door open. "Ray, you confessed to killing a man. *On accident.* But killing someone, even on accident, is a crime. I'm not going to put cuffs on you and I'm not going to arrest you just yet, but please, climb on in the backseat so I can at least follow some bit of protocol here. Can you do that for me?" He motioned with his arm as though welcoming Ray to a party.

Ray's sniveling gained some momentum again, and he scuffed his feet across the gravel, squeezed between the door and Pearsall's sizeable gut, and flopped into the back of the cruiser.

A voice crackled over the walkie-talkie on the sheriff's belt: "Sheriff Pearsall, you there?"

The sheriff unsheathed his walkie-talkie and responded, "Go ahead."

He closed the back door and Ray heard the now-muffled walkie-talkie voice speak again: "Eh, we just got to Pinky's place, Sheriff, and eh, we need to talk."

The blood drained from Ray's face, gathered in the bottom of his stomach, and seemed to boil. Ray assumed the voice belonged to one of the ambulance guys who'd found something at Pinky's. But what? Maybe there were crime scene techs there, too. Maybe they did some preliminary work, discovered some kind of evidence, like fingerprints where they shouldn't be. Ray had watched enough CSI episodes on TV to know how good those guys were. Had Ray missed something? Forgotten something behind? He strained to hear the conversation, but the sheriff walked to the front of the car, back turned.

Pearsall nodded, tugged on his earlobe repeatedly, and then in one horrifying instant, spun and met Ray's eyes, which were open so wide they felt to him as if they might pop out and roll into his lap.

Ray turned away in a pathetic attempt to seem uninterested. Stomach acid bubbled in his throat.

After a minute, the sheriff returned the walkie-talkie to his belt and rubbed his earlobe again. He stared at Ray's house, off into the woods, then turned back to the car, the look on his face an utter mystery. Finally, he returned to the cruiser and climbed behind the wheel. He started the engine and turned around. His eyes narrowed, studying Ray.

"Anything you'd like to tell me before I start driving, son?"

Ray spoke with a voice that seemed to belong to someone else. "No, sir."

The big man turned back around, dropped the transmission into drive. "Okey dokey, then let's get moving," he said, his voice soft and sad. "We're going to take a little detour, though."

Ray's fingernails dug into the cloth seat.

The sheriff adjusted the rearview mirror and stared at Ray. "I want to stop by Pinky's."

It was a short drive—not much more than a mile. But before the sheriff could even complete a three-point turnaround to head up the driveway, Ray's mind whirled forward and back, back and forward, replaying his visit to Pinky's that morning. Something was obviously amiss at Pinky's place, and whatever it was, Ray knew he'd have to answer for it. In the next five minutes. He closed his eyes and tried to concentrate.

Hell Toupee

On the eastern outskirts of Stillwater, Route 18 slices its way through a patch of woodland a little too small to be considered a forest. Mostly oaks and Douglas firs, the towering trees border the road like canyon walls.

Ray trudged along parallel to the blacktop in the cover of the evergreens, morning dew beading atop motor oil on his boots. He whistled a cheerful tune while his mind drifted: the school fundraiser, the upcoming busy-season at the shop, and a few other projects. He stopped whistling as a sliver of Pinky's weather-beaten house came into view.

It wasn't set back as far from the road as Ray's place, so it was visible to anyone who might pass by going west into town or east to Grundy County. Ray stopped at the woods' edge which defined Pinky's backyard and watched the house for a moment.

Tattered shades covered the windows and Pinky didn't own a car, so from where Ray stood he had no way of telling if the old guy was home. But with routine and monotony as the cornerstones of Stillwater life, Ray was willing to bet that Pinky had tossed his fishing rod in the back of Jim Bartolucci's pickup and climbed into its cab that morning long before anyone else in town had even poured their first cup of coffee.

Just to be on the safe side Ray approached the backdoor with a spring in his step and a smile on his face. No need to look suspicious, even though he made damn sure he heard no cars approaching before he stepped out of the woods. He rapped the door with a neighborly, upbeat tempo.

He waited. Knocked again, and listened expectantly. No answer. He turned the doorknob, smiled, and stepped inside.

Ray had been in the house plenty of times over the years. Not so much recently, but when Ray was a kid, Pinky had been the go-to guy for knowledge on all topics of interest. He'd been in two wars, sailed on a ship, rebuilt carburetors for a living, pitched three innings in a minor league ball game, and once spent a brief stint in jail for a nasty barroom fight. Also a whiz at oiling bike chains, adjusting handlebars, and mounting baseball cards beside wheel spokes, Pinky always made it easier for Ray and his fourth-grade friends to pretend they cruised Thornton Park on motorcycles.

That was a long time ago.

Of the things that changed since then, neither the house nor its owner was one of them. Pinky was one of those people who'd been old for as long as anyone in town could remember. Dusty, sun-faded pictures hanging in the same place for a quarter-century showed Pinky looking just about like he did today. Thick, sagging jowls. Orangey hair undaunted by age. Freckled skin the color of calamine lotion. Eyes that narrowed to slits when he smiled. Crooked, brown-stained teeth that looked like toenails.

And nearly all the photographs showed Pinky with his briar pipe clutched in his hand, or dangling from his lips, or tucked in the ripped seam of a fishing hat he was fond of wearing. The house reeked of stale, cherry-oak tobacco, just like when Ray was a kid, and the odor still wrinkled his nose.

"Stinky old bastard," he said to the bedroom as he entered it. Even more cluttered than the other small rooms of the house, it looked like a garage sale from the 70s. Or maybe two garage sales from the 70s, piled atop one another. The drawn shades cast a stale yellow hue on everything. Ray shook his head in disgust and began shoving aside boxes, bags, piles of mildew-smelling clothes, books, records, magazines, and newspapers, trying to excavate a path to reach beneath Pinky's bed. To find the old man's stash.

In the small clearing he made, Ray dropped to his knees, then sprawled out on his belly.

Ray heard Pinky's voice in his head. *Keep my money in an old tobacco tin underneath my bed.* He didn't know exactly what a tobacco tin looked like, but how many of the things could there be under the guy's bed, anyway?

Turned out there were a couple hundred of them. Different shapes, sizes, colors, and brands which Ray guessed Pinky must have been collecting for the last forty, fifty, sixty years, or however long he'd been around smoking that pipe of his.

Ray dropped his forehead to his arm. "This'll take me forever," he mumbled and began grabbing random tins, shaking them, tossing them aside. After five minutes of burrowing through empty tins, he'd wormed his way under the bed so only his legs protruded.

And that's how Pinky found him.

"Help yah find somethin down there, young man?" Pinky said, nearly causing Ray's bladder to give way.

Ray was a guy who'd always been good at thinking on his feet. More specifically, he was a terrific bullshitter. If stuck in a pinch, he could create, retract, and revise a story to cover his butt quicker than most folks could say their name. And if you did manage to catch him in a lie, before you knew it he'd have you turned around, feeling guilty for not trusting him. Trying to corner Raymond Dempsey was like trying to mud wrestle a pig.

But here, wedged under Pinky's bed with dust bunnies in his hair, Ray was having a hell of a time coming up with anything. Through a wall of tobacco tins he could see the old man's boots shifting on the carpet.

"Pinky? That you?" he said, hoping to buy another second of time to think.

Pinky let out a half-cough, half-laugh. "The owner of that bed yer under? Yep, that'd be me, boy."

Ray eyed the tobacco tins. A dim light flickered in his mind. "Damn, Pinky, you weren't supposed to be home until later this morning," he said and wriggled backward on his stomach.

"I wasn't? Didn't know I had to make an appointment to come and go in my own home."

Ray worked his way from beneath the bed, up to his hands and knees. He swatted lint and cobwebs from his jeans, shirt, and hair, then nonchalantly looked over his shoulder. Pinky stood there in a plaid shirt, ubiquitous pipe set between his teeth. Ray sighed. "Well, I guess there's no way of getting out of it now." He stood up and smirked. "It was supposed to be a surprise... well, me and some of the guys in town wanted to do something for you. Something special." He paused for effect. "So we talked about it..."

"Somethin special for me?" the old man interrupted and worked the pipe with his teeth, setting it in motion from side to side.

Ray nodded.

Pinky smiled a little, and his nose twitched. He rubbed the rust-colored stubble on his chin and said, "By chance, was it somethin for my birthday?"

Ray's nodding became more exaggerated and he let out a quick, uneven laugh with edginess to it he didn't like at all. *This is too easy!* His heart thudded, seemingly for the first time since hearing Pinky enter the room. He sucked in a deep breath, almost choked on the pipe smoke, and said with as much confidence he could muster, "Yep, for your birthday. I should've figured you'd catch on. A bunch of us were sitting around the other day, and one of the fellas mentioned your birthday was coming up. We got to talking about it, and somebody else, maybe it was Ed, I'm not sure, mentioned your collection of tobacco tins. Thought maybe we could figure out which ones you didn't have and try to get you a few. To complete your collection. For your birthday." He gave a humble shrug. *Damn, you're good, Ray.*

Pinky's bushy eyebrows rose, the pipe tobacco glowed redder than his hair for an instant, and a cloud of smoke jetted from between his lips. He turned his back to Ray and sauntered toward the living room. "Well, this sure is a surprise, I tell yah. For my birthday, huh?" He seemed to be talking to himself. "That's odd. I didn't think anybody in town knew when my birthday was, 'cause it's been twenty years since I got so much as a card." He stopped in front of a recliner, turned around, and pointed lazily toward Ray, who now stood in the bedroom doorway.

"Plus, that *collection* as you called it, which nobody knew was under there besides me, ain't nothin but a heap of trash I haven't had the energy to take down to Dick's Scrap Metal. Oh, and my birthday came and went five months ago, by the way. So yeah, guess you could say I'm surprised," Pinky concluded, matter-of-factly.

For once, Ray was at a loss for words. He only stood there with a hand on the doorjamb, feeling his face flush and stomach swirl—conditions induced by a speck of embarrassment and guilt, and a mound of irritation and indignation. Part of what usually made Ray so believable, so convincing, was the passion with which he endorsed his lies. The instant someone dared question him or showed a hint of doubt in his motives, adrenaline surged through his veins as though his body truly believed the story his mind conjured out of thin air.

But he swallowed hard and did his best to remain calm. He held his hands up, palms outward. "Now, Pinky, I don't know what you think's going on here..."

Without words, Pinky derailed Ray's train of thought. The old man pulled the pipe from his mouth, cocked his head, and produced a heartfelt smile that shone from his eyes and cheeks and mouth which seemed to announce, "Come now, friend. Stop pulling my leg, because we both know *exactly* what's going on here."

Ray received Pinky's silence and smile as a show of arrogance, an attempt at gaining an advantage over him. He squeezed the doorjamb, the tendons in his wrist taut like piano wires. "What." He stepped into the living room. "What's with the ear-to-ear grin?"

The old man couldn't help but laugh. Again, it was a sincere laugh, not mocking. He turned on an old Philco radio beside the recliner, and Frankie Laine's ghostly voice filled the room as though it'd been trapped in that box for fifty years. Pinky laid down his pipe, then leaned on the olive green La-Z-Boy. The two remained silent for a moment, eyeing each other. Frankie sang about Tiger Wilson the Champ and Kid McCoy.

"Listen, Ray," Pinky began, "Known yah yer whole life, and I like yah. I'm willin to look the other way here, partly 'cause I'm old and tired, but mostly 'cause I like yah. But you aren't makin it easy on me. And I'll tell yah the truth: I'm standin here laughin 'cause I don't know how much more of yer BS I can stomach." Another quick laugh rattled in Pinky's throat. "I mean really, Raymond! I know damn well what yah were diggin for under my bed. Yah came straight over here after yah overheard me yappin at Dusty's last night. Shit, boy, I known yah yer whole life!"

Seemingly unfazed, Ray pursed his lips and hooked both thumbs in his pants pockets. "You're off your rocker, old man. You don't know what you're talking about. You don't know me. You might think you do, but you don't." A gust of laughter hissed out his nose.

Pinky stabbed the air with a gnarled finger. His eyes widened. "Oh, now see, that's where yer wrong, Mr. Dempsey. I know damn well what I'm talkin about. More than yah ever hope to know. Yah got just about everyone in this town hoodwinked, got 'em under your thumb, and I know that's your game. So be it. I ain't gonna meddle in that. But don't think yer gonna come over here, blow smoke up my ass, and expect to work me over the way yah do folks like Chip Bailey and that old teacher of yours."

As though slapped by an invisible hand, Ray's head jerked backward. His face darkened. He stepped forward. "What the hell's that s'posed to mean, old man?" he shouted.

Frankie belted out lyrics. *Come on, Kid, come on, Kid, let's hit him with a left and a right.*

Probably old enough to be his great-grandfather, Pinky looked close to tearing into Ray. But he didn't. He clenched both fists and relaxed them. The old man spoke, and his voice was calm, just above a whisper. "I know every secret yah hold in yer heart, boy. It's a dark place these days, but I know what's in there, yah can be sure of it. Yah got some power over folks in this town, some kinda spell, some kinda charm, but it ain't worth a damn to me. I see right through yah, right through that mask yah like to wear." He straightened and raised his chin an inch. "Quit while yer ahead, boy, that's all I have to say. Walk away while yah still got two legs to carry yah and while them secrets are still yers to keep."

Ray tried to shout again, but his voice caught in his throat and his words came out shaky and scratchy. "You're talking out your ass," he managed, his mind reeling.

The old man seemed to know a lot more than he should. Than anyone should. And here he was, threatening Raymond Dempsey, threatening to run off at the mouth and bring Ray's world crashing down. An ice pick of dread slid up Ray's spine to the base of his skull, pushing, piercing. That's when he saw the shotgun resting against the coat rack.

Pinky appeared to notice Ray spot the gun, but he simply made his way to the front of the recliner. "Go on now, boy. Run along. I've had enough of yah." He turned his back to Ray and eased into the chair awkwardly, his age showing. After a few seconds, he glanced back. Ray hadn't budged. "Don't push me no more boy, unless yer ready to hang all yer dirty laundry out on the line, let it air out a bit. Eh?" His eyes met Ray's icy gaze. Pinky smirked. "Whaddaya say, boy? Maybe we start with the Andersons? Lots of people still askin why a nice family like that packed up and moved away overnight. Any thoughts, Raymond?"

A switch flipped in Ray's head, igniting him. He pounced on the shotgun, swiped it from the floor, pumped it and pointed it at Pinky. "Close your mouth before I blow it off your face." Spittle clung to his lips, his chest heaved.

Frankie sang, *Go on, Kid, go on, Kid, but how were they to know it was the Kid's last fight?*

The old man continued to smirk, blinked once, then turned, resuming his original position in the chair. "Known yah yer whole life, Raymond. You ain't gonna do nothin of the sort. Now beat it, boy."

And for the first time that day, Pinky was wrong.

For Ray the next few seconds melded into a surreal collage of nightmarish patchwork. Blazing yellow flash, thundering explosion. Concussion from the gun jolting him backwards. Pinky's head snapping forward. The red cloud spraying in all directions. The stink of cordite from the spent shell. Ray on the ground, ears ringing, shotgun beside him with a tendril of smoke leaking from the barrel. Frankie Laine, fading away, *And the Champ is climbin through the golden ropes of the big ring up in the sky.*

Just like that, his rage defused. Ray sat spread-legged, staring up at the back of Pinky's chair. His jaw quivered. "Holy shit, holy shit," he said over and over. He climbed to one knee, and from there he could see everything he needed to see.

Pinky in his plaid shirt slumped forward in the La-Z-Boy, his neck wet and red, the back of his head missing. Droplets ran down a window shade like thick black rain.

Ray turned away, horror-struck. Panic swallowed him whole. He scrambled to his feet, grabbed the shotgun, and wiped it from top to bottom with a flannel jacket draped over the coat rack. He placed the murder weapon on the floor and did a quick search of the area, trying hard not to look at the body. Remembering the tobacco tins, he scurried to the bedroom, kicked them under the bed in no more a haphazard pile than he found them, replaced the bags and boxes and piles, and headed for the backdoor.

For as much as Ray didn't want to, some masochistic imp within him took control of his eyes as he hurried by the recliner. And there he found the back of Pinky's head. Still connected by a hinge of meat, red-headed scalp and shards of milk-white bone overhung the dead man's face, like someone about to surrender his toupee to a gust of wind.

Ray's gallop turned into a flailing sprint. It took everything in his power to keep from throwing up as he reached that backdoor, grabbed it using his T-shirt, and wiped the doorknob free of prints.

Out the door and off he went, squinting in the morning sun, tearing through the woods, the ringing in his ears eclipsing the birdsongs overhead.

Inspection of the Body

In the back of the police car, slick sweat covered Ray's face and neck. After replaying the incident in his mind and after the shudder passed, he opened his eyes and took a deep breath, feeling a little reassured about what the sheriff might find at Pinky's.

Ray already told him he was in the house and holding Pinky's gun when it unintentionally went off. As to why Ray's fingerprints weren't anywhere to be found, well, he could say he panicked, freaked out, wiped them away, and later confessed to the accident when he calmed down and got his wits about him.

Although a friend of nearly everyone in town, Pinky said visitors in his home were very infrequent. And the state of his housekeeping gave no cause for doubt. But if Ray were to tell the sheriff he strolled by the old guy's place and ran into Pinky outside, who's to say Pinky, Ray's long-time neighbor, didn't invite him inside to chat?

Oh, but there was Ed. Spotting Ray in the road like he did. That was a tough one. Ray had two options. He could massage the timeline, say he was on his way *to* Pinky's when Ed found him. *Did he see which direction you were coming from?* With Ed's awful eyesight probably not. *Think he saw the dark spots on your clothes? You were right in front of him.* Maybe he did, maybe he didn't. *Think he'll remember how strange you were acting?* Probably. *Or how you were limping? Who goes on long walks when they have a bum ankle?* Too many gaps in option one.

Option two, a simpler, neater option, relied again on the panic theme. Ray was in shock, that's all. Temporary insanity, if you will. Lost touch with reality for a few minutes, and that's why he didn't seek Ed's help or tell him what happened. Then it didn't matter if Ed saw the blood or not. Option two would also accommodate Ray's mumblings about shooting a man. Ed had even said, "You look frazzled as anything."

While Ray mulled over these two options, a third option peeked into his mind. An option whose time had already come and gone. *I should have killed Ed, right there in the middle of Route 18. Squeezed his saggy neck with both hands, and I wouldn't have to worry about any of this shit.* His consideration of option three, no matter how brief or inconceivable, scared the hell out of Ray, and he did his best to bury it away somewhere out of reach.

Another minute passed, and Ray's heart quieted down. *I don't know what Bob's up to stopping by Pinky's, but everything's covered. There's nothing to worry about, it's going to be okay. Just stick to your story, nobody can prove you wrong.*

Ray felt better until the cruiser rounded the last curve before Pinky's and he saw all the vehicles, all the people. Cars and trucks parked in the ditch and on the roadside with hazard lights blinking on, off, on, off. And with their cars and trucks stood men and women and children who knew *him*, Raymond Dempsey. The guy in the back of the police car pulling up to a crime scene.

News traveled fast in Stillwater. Nine out of ten households owned a Radio Shack scanner and left the thing on 24-7. Of course, nine out of ten emergency calls in Stillwater involved a kitchen grease fire, a shouting match at Dusty's Tap, or a cat marooned atop something tall. Nevertheless, just about every call on the police or fire frequency was answered in-person by a dozen interested, bored citizens. And as irony would have it, the first one on the scene for these calls, almost without fail, was Pinky. He was certainly the first at the scene on this day.

"Looks like we got an audience," Sheriff Pearsall announced as he rumbled onto Pinky's property, over the driveway, across the lawn, and stopped just short of the house. Beside them sat an ambulance parked backwards with its doors hanging open, engine and emergency lights off. Of course they were off. *Take your time, boys.*

The sheriff looked in the mirror. "Sit tight, son," he said, then exited the car. Without acknowledging the barrage of questions thrown at him from the onlookers, he walked up three stairs and disappeared into the sallow darkness of the house.

Ray laced his fingers and tried to control his breathing. He squinted at the open doorway but saw nothing beyond it. Peeking over his shoulder he found a row of familiar faces twenty yards back—at least they knew to keep their distance when gawking.

Like mannequins posed to exhibit an array of emotions they lingered at the roadside, some worried, some eager, some curious, some impatient. There was demure Agnes of local fruit stand fame, peering between shoulders, chewing at her knuckles. There was Ray's boss, Chip, with a child who'd probably just missed the first-hour school bell tucked under each arm. There was Mrs. H., wringing her hands. And of course, there was Ed Polanski, using a cupped hand to funnel gossip into hungry ears. *Ed, you prick! Mind your own—*

Movement in Ray's periphery drew his attention back to the doorway. Two ambulance guys, volunteers, both of whom Ray recognized as out-of-towners from the softball league he played in every Thursday night, stood on the porch. One lit a cigarette. Both stared at Ray with no look of recognition on their faces.

After a few minutes of talking under their breath and glancing into the house, they parted slightly. Sheriff Pearsall stepped between them. Looked at Ray.

The expression on his face was something Ray had never seen. A sickening blend of shock, woe, and pity. But there was something else to it. Something that didn't fit, didn't belong with those other bleak emotions. The look made Ray want to run far and fast and never turn back.

The large man walked to Ray's door an opened it. "Come on out here, son," he said, his husky voice unsteady.

Oh, shit, he's going to handcuff me.

Ray slid across the seat and stood before the sheriff, looking up into his eyes. "Yeah?"

A blanket of silence fell over the roadside bystanders.

The sheriff rubbed his face, plowing ripples of skin up and down his cheeks. "Ray," he said, "I need you to step inside the house for a minute."

Ray's knees liquefied. "Oh, Sheriff, no. Please, *Bob*, please don't make me. I already saw, I don't want to see again," Ray was saying, but the sheriff already had hold of his arm.

"I didn't think you'd want to Ray, but you have to. You don't have a choice."

"But why?"

Relying on the old parental adage, Sheriff Pearsall replied: "Because I said so."

Steered by the sheriff's firm grasp Ray ascended the porch steps and reached the doorway. He looked back and saw the audience in the ditch freshly animated and attentive. Beside him, the eyes of the ambulance guys were wide, expectant.

"Sheriff, I don't know if I can."

With a firm push, he could, and did.

It took a few seconds for Ray's eyes to adjust to the darker room. As they did, his other senses checked in. The Philco played on, although Frankie had been replaced by Elvis. The scent of Pinky's pipe lingered in the air.

Eyes focusing now—there's the recliner. A creak of a floor board. *Is somebody in here?* Becoming clearer—there's the body in the chair. Another creak. It's not slumped over as badly as it was. *They must have leaned him back.* The smell of the pipe is strong, too strong. The chair is moving, slowly rocking, creaking. The body's sitting straight up in one piece, and there's no blood, and the head's all together, and the pipe's in its mouth, and the mouth is smiling.

"G' mornin, Ray."

Folks in Stillwater talked about the scream for a long time. At the Moose Lodge, at church, at the Beehive Cafe, the one thing everyone on hand recalled from that day was the sound that came out of Raymond Dempsey when he walked into Pinky's house and found the old man enjoying the morning from his La-Z-Boy like he hadn't a care in the world. Like his skull hadn't just been torn apart with fiery buckshot.

Ray staggered back like a punch-drunk boxer and came close enough to fainting to see sparklers in the corners of his eyes. He ran square into the sheriff's chest and let out a grunt.

"Easy, Ray, easy," the sheriff said, grasping the younger man by the elbows. "Relax, catch your breath, it's going to be okay." He sounded like a father tending to a child awoken from a nightmare.

"No, no, no," Ray whimpered, shaking his head, eyes locked on Pinky. "He was dead, he was dead, I swear he was." His arm raised, a finger pointed. "You. You were dead. I shot you. I saw your head and your blood and you were dead. You're not alive." The words tumbled over Ray's tongue and dropped from his mouth like stones.

Pinky rocked lazily for a moment, then held out his arm. "You like to check my pulse, boy?"

Hearing Pinky's slow, deep drawl as he spoke, hearing breaths produced by lungs that had ceased to function an hour ago sent a wave of gooseflesh over Ray's skin. It was cold confirmation of one of two things: either Pinky had returned from the dead seemingly unscathed, or Ray had completely lost his mind. He pawed at Sheriff Pearsall's shirtsleeve.

The sheriff turned to the old man, "Pinky, please, don't be a smartass. Not now. Kid's obviously upset and... well, confused."

Ray, the thirty-one-year-old *kid*, studied Pinky, the chair, the surrounding area. Pinky wore different clothes than he had earlier. And he now donned his fishing hat, pulled down low. *Is his hair wet, darker in back? Is that blood back there?* The green vinyl chair was spotless. *He could have wiped it off, right?* The window shade bore no dark rivulets. *Isn't the whole thing cleaner? Not as dingy yellow as it was before?*

Sheriff Pearsall and Pinky remained silent, watching Ray mentally check off sections of the room.

Ray looked up at the sheriff, then down at his own clothes. He saw the tiny spots there. *But is it really blood? Pinky's blood? Are you sure?*

"But, I got his... blood on me here, Sheriff," he said, scratching a spot with his thumbnail, "and here, and here, and here."

The sheriff took a deep breath. "Well," he began and exhaled, "you have *something* on you there, son. Don't know if it's blood or not. But if it is I don't know where you got it, whose it is, because it sure doesn't seem to be Pinky's." His voice softened. "Pinky says he saw you last night at Dusty's, but it's been more'n a week since you two exchanged a word."

Ray's head shook again. "His shotgun, his shotgun. It went off. Get it and you'll be able to tell it was just fired," he said, voice louder, quaking.

Pinky pulled the pipe from his lips and continued to rock. "That old Winchester ain't been outta the attic in two years, Ray," he said. The hand that didn't hold the pipe lay atop his lap, closed in a loose fist.

"That's not true. I shot it. I was just here. He's lying, Sheriff! I was even in his bedroom, under the bed," Ray said, eyes pleading with the sheriff's. An instant later Ray felt a pang in his stomach, realizing he said more than he should about his visit. *Under his bed? For Christ's sake, Ray, shut the hell up!* But before that thought concluded, another feeling rushed over him: relief. *Pinky's fine! I'm off the hook, not guilty of anything!* Relief didn't last long either, as his mind began to grapple with the possibility he'd imagined the whole damn thing. *But I saw it, I heard it, I smelled it.*

"Man's got no reason to lie," the sheriff said, "You claim you shot and killed him. And here he is alive and well. Not much else to be said now is there?" His voice was flat and gentle. On the radio, The King stepped aside to make way for The Penguins.

Ray's mind raced, full of questions without answers. His gaze volleyed from Pinky to the sheriff, back to Pinky, then around the room searching for evidence or something or anything to prove he wasn't a raving lunatic. *The guy's alive, Ray, right here in front of you. People don't just put their head back together and go about their day like nothing happened.* Ray wanted the hell out of there.

Sheriff Pearsall draped a heavy arm over Ray's shoulders. "Let's go somewhere and chat a bit, son. Leave Pinky here alone to relax. EMTs shook him up pretty bad when they barged in the door."

Pinky chuckled around his pipe. "Hell's bells! They damn near *did* have a corpse on their hands. Just 'bout had a heart attack!" He patted his chest with the closed hand.

Laughter poured from Sheriff Pearsall like steam from a pressure valve. "I'll be in touch if I need anything else from you, Pinky," he said, still smiling while turning toward the door with Ray under his arm.

Ray looked back as he neared the doorway.

Pinky scratched at his hat and smiled. "You take care of yerself, Raymond." He opened his hand and shook it a little. Something shiny, metallic glistened there. Then he formed an "okay" symbol with the hand, and encircled by his thumb and forefinger was a half-dollar.

Mrs. Hoffmeister's half-dollar.

Ray slapped his shirt pocket. Gone.

Flew out when I fell. After I pulled the trigger. And killed him.

Pinky's fingers collapsed around the coin and he winked. "I'll be seein yah soon, friend."

Good thing the ambulance hadn't gone anywhere. Ray was in the doorway when consciousness departed, cutting his legs from beneath him on its way. Ray melted into the sheriff's arms, which prompted a collective gasp from the spectators.

The initial call over the scanners that morning reported a possible fatal shooting at Pinky's address. After Sheriff Pearsall escorted Ray into the house the crowd of bystanders thickened and grew frenetic, offering theories, demanding information, praying, gossiping. Now, as Pinky stood carelessly in his doorway watching the ambulance speed off with a sweaty, pale Raymond Dempsey and the sheriff inside, the onlookers stood in befuddled silence.

Pinky waited a minute then descended the steps and crossed his yard to meet with them and begin answering their questions about poor Ray.

A Bow for Raymond

"He had the half-dollar, Sheriff. Mrs. Hoffmeister's half-dollar. She gave it to me this morning, and I must've lost it when the shotgun blast knocked me down."

The ambulance engine roared, and Sheriff Pearsall steadied himself with a palm on the ceiling.

"Ray, I don't know what's happening in that head of yours, but you're making less sense as the day goes on. You didn't shoot the man, son. You didn't. To be honest I never seen Pinky looking better, and healthier, than he did this morning." He bent down and patted Ray's hand. His enormous, burly physique made the act especially touching. "Just rest your brain a few minutes."

The EMT softball player pressed two fingers against Ray's neck, measuring his heart rate. The guy smelled like cigarette smoke.

"Please listen to me, Sheriff. I know how nuts this all sounds, but Pinky's lying, I'm telling yah. Something's going on here, something I can't explain." Ray closed his eyes and swallowed through a thick knot.

Over time it's possible that Ray might have talked himself into believing he didn't shoot Pinky, that he dreamed the whole thing or experienced a vivid hallucination. Earlier he worried that he'd lost his mind, sure, but until Pinky flashed that half-dollar, a little *worry* was the only thing he had to deal with. Now Ray wasn't just worried, he was terrified.

"Nothing's going on, Ray. It's old Pinky for God's sake. I can't even imagine what a man would gain from denying he'd been shot." The sheriff pursed his lips and exhaled through his nose.

"Now, I'm not a psychiatrist, so I'm not sure what I'm supposed to be saying and not saying, but it seems to me something happened up here—" he tapped his own forehead "—and threw you off-kilter. Like you blew a fuse or something. Don't know what could do that to a fella. Maybe you got one of those blockages that happen sometimes. Ah, I don't know what the hell they're called—"

"Embolism," the EMT said.

"—yeah, well, anyway, I don't mean to scare you or nothing, Ray. I'm just saying I think you'll be okay once we get you looked at by folks who know what they're doing. They'll get you straightened out."

The sirens whined for a moment, and the ambulance motored up and over a railroad crossing. Town square was now behind them. The driver called into a walkie-talkie: "ETA eight minutes." The region's only medical facility was located along Culver Creek in the center of the county on the outskirts of Flat Rock Township.

"Dr. Hinkley's a nice fella, Ray. Smart guy. He'll take care of you. I'm giving orders for you to stay at least twenty-four hours so they can check you over good from top to bottom." The sheriff cleared his throat. "Plus, I don't think you should be alone right now."

"I'm not crazy, Sheriff. I'm not. I just want you to look into what I'm saying. Talk to Pinky some, look around his place. Please."

Sheriff Pearsall squatted beside Ray, his knees popping on the way down. "Listen, son. Since your folks passed on back in '92... Jesus, has it been that long... I've done my best to look out for you. Small community like ours we gotta be like family to each other, you know. We gotta lean on each other sometimes. So, I want to help you through this... this situation best I can. But I also have a job to do. I have a responsibility to the town. Given the speed of gossip around here and the way things unfolded down at Pinky's, the last thing I need to do is get dropped off at my car and stir up the hornets' nest with a bunch of questions and, in my honest opinion, *unnecessary* investigation."

Ray turned his head from side to side, shaking loose two tears that slid down his cheeks and puddled in his ears. "No, no, you don't understand. I don't know how any of this is happening, it makes no sense to me, but he's going to come after me, Sheriff. I know he is. I didn't just shoot him on accident, I killed him. I got pissed and scared and I *murdered* him. Now somehow he's okay and he knows what I did. You gotta help me because he's gonna come after me," he whimpered.

The EMT looked away before a smile overtook his face.

Albeit the oddest murder confession Sheriff Pearsall could have probably ever imagined, Ray's words seemed to do little more than evoke deeper sympathy in the man's heart. He only held Ray's hand until the ambulance pulled into the hospital parking lot, then he leaned down and said in a soft voice, "Hang in there, son. It'll be okay. I'll go by the shop and tell Chip you're taking a sick day today. I'm sure he'll… understand. For now, let the doctors do their thing. Play along, get some rest, and I'll come by first thing tomorrow. And if you still feel the same, I'll take some formal notes from you and look into it. On the down-low. How's that sound?"

Ray nodded almost imperceptibly. "Fine."

The doors swung open, and the EMT and a man in green scrubs slid Ray out the ambulance. Ray covered his face with his hands, hiding from the sun, or reality. He remained like that as the men rolled him away.

The doors swung shut and the sheriff cried out, "I'll see you tomorrow, Ray!"

Ray didn't hear him.

The sheriff was right: Dr. Hinkley *was* a nice fella. Ray met him in the emergency room a few minutes after being wheeled in and left alone behind a blue plastic curtain.

But smart or not, the doctor had a heck of a time finding the seam in the curtain, swatting at it like a nervous performer trying to find his way on stage. He finally emerged laughing at himself and strode forward to shake Ray's hand. It was a friendly, firm handshake—not the kind he'd give to the certifiably insane, Ray thought. Or that's the impression the man tried to give, anyway.

Dr. Hinkley, about three decades younger and a thousand times more pleasant to look at than the family doctor Ray had visited since he was an infant, told Ray his first and foremost concern was the possibility of a brain abnormality or injury. He ran through an exhaustive list of questions and symptoms, to which Ray repeated, "No, no, no," occasionally throwing in a "nope" or an "uh-uh" to mix things up. The doctor flashed his penlight in Ray's eyes, plugged a similar light into each ear, and for good measure, even put a tongue depressor to use.

After instructing Ray to walk toe-to-heel around the bed and having him perform a myriad of balancing acts, the doctor slapped Ray on the back and announced, "All systems are a go." Ray gave a weak smile and shrugged his shoulders.

The more Ray thought about the day's events the more certain he became that whatever took place had nothing to do with the condition of his brain or the question of his sanity. He acquiesced to the doctor's requests but thought only of Pinky. The things of which he spoke. The sight of him slumped over, skull mangled, dead. The gleam in his eye as he taunted Ray with the half-dollar: *I'll be seein yah soon, friend.*

"...so get comfy and we'll roll you upstairs for an MRI," Dr. Hinkley was saying, smiling wide as he scribbled something on a notepad. "Nothing to worry about. Twenty minutes of noise in a barrel so we can take pictures of your brain and see what it looks like," he explained as though Ray were a nine-year-old. Ray didn't notice.

I didn't need to give Pinky an MRI to see what his brain looked like.

"Everything checks out there, which I think it will, and I'll have Mrs. Fleming meet with you later this afternoon. She's a counselor. She's great. You'll like her," Doc said and capped his pen.

"Bob wants you to hang around for the day, so I'll have the nurse set you up in a room. Nice thing about our humble facility on the edge of nowhere-ville is there're always plenty of vacancies." He began to chuckle, but continued to talk. "You've had a doozie of a day, Mr. Dempsey, so I'll see you get a quiet bed where you can get some rest. You look like you could use it."

The doctor's smile never faltered, and when he speared his arm through the gap in the curtain and exited through it he let out another laugh and said, "Got 'er on the first try," as he walked away.

The MRI was uneventful as promised. The young lab tech in charge of the thing said he wasn't allowed to discuss the findings of the scan with Ray—that was the radiologist's job. But before the nurse wheeled Ray to his room, the tech winked, nodded, tapped the film, and gave the thumbs-up to Ray enough times to suggest perhaps the patient just might live to see another day.

It turned out that Mrs. Fleming couldn't keep her afternoon appointment with Ray so she rescheduled for Tuesday morning. Not that Ray cared. His mind was too occupied to care. Hours passed like minutes with him staring out the window of his room, eyes fixed, hardly blinking.

Across a sizable field of grass Culver Creek slithered around the hospital, at places coming within a hundred yards. And there at the closest point seated atop a pile of rocks with fishing rod in hand, sat Pinky.

The man I killed is fishing, Ray thought, started to laugh, but broke down instead. Frustration, confusion, and dread swarmed his mind. He wiped tears from his eyes and squinted. With the distance between them Ray couldn't be sure, but the man looked like he was smiling.

Eventually the afternoon grew old, and Jim Bartolucci and his pickup rumbled up a dirt lane beside the creek. Seeing his friend arrive, Pinky lumbered up the embankment, tackle box in one hand, rod in the other. After dropping them in the truck bed he paused, then turned in Ray's direction, tipped his fishing hat, and gave Ray a deep, gentlemanly bow before climbing in the cab and pulling away.

Alone, Ray watched the Monday sun melt down the sky and slip behind the trees. Golden shafts sliced between leaves and branches, doing their best to keep Ray's world warm and bright for a minute or two longer. But soon enough the orange-stained sky bled away. Shadows once chased into corners and beneath furniture by Day crept out in her absence, slowly at first but with greater courage as Night arrived, when they reclaimed all that was theirs.

In the bed, atop the sheets, Ray lay motionless. He no longer tried to make sense of the day's events. Further debate in his mind would reveal nothing to him. For many questions he was without answers, but of one thing he was certain: sooner or later, Pinky would come for him.

I'll be seein yah soon, friend.

Sooner

Although exhausted, Ray didn't want to sleep. Was afraid to sleep. He stared at the window, the ceiling, the walls, his senses tuned to the world on the other side of them. Every squeak of a shoe in some distant corridor was Pinky. Every muffled cough, every hushed voice, every whisper of a breeze—was Pinky.

But gradually Ray's eyelids grew weak and slipped shut. If asked, Ray would've said he didn't fall asleep, but he must've, because the stench of cherry-oak tobacco invaded his thoughts and imaginings, and when he opened his eyes he saw Pinky.

Bathed in chrome moonlight at the end of the hospital bed the old man sat in a chair with both hands folded comfortably over his knees. Ironically, he said to Ray, "Yah surprised me."

Ray sprung from his pillow like a Jack-in-the-box. "How'd you get in here," he asked in a blur. It sounded nothing like a question.

"Walked in the door. This is a hospital, not a prison. Besides, gal at the desk is sound asleep wearin a pair of headphones with a magazine layin across her chest. Nobody else on this end of the floor, yah know." A puff of smoke completed his response.

Ray sat rigidly upright like someone had replaced his spine with a two-by-four. The absurd notion flashed in his mind that Pinky could get into trouble for smoking in a hospital. He blinked hard and eyed the closed door, calculated its distance. "What do you want from me," he asked. Again, without inflection.

Pinky grinned around his pipe. "Don't be so darn skittish. Yah figured I was comin, didn't yah?" Pale moonlight bleached the color out of him, made him look like a mischievous ghost. "I dropped by to say yah surprised me today."

His relaxed manner and tone comforted some remote part of Ray's mind and gave it some scrap of hope on which to cling. He felt his heart beat a couple times. "Surprised you?"

The old man smoked in silence for a moment. "Yep. Yer farther along than I thought."

Ray thought about screaming for help, or lunging to the door, or going for Pinky's throat. But for the moment he only managed to follow suit. "Farther along what?"

"The path."

"What path?"

Pinky got to his feet, causing Ray's legs to sprawl and his hands to brace the mattress like he was about to launch through the ceiling. Pinky removed his pipe, chuckled, and turned sideways to face the window. "Simmer down, boy. I ain't gonna do nothin to yah."

Ray didn't move from his alert stance, but he breathed a quiet sigh.

"Path of evil, Ray. That's what path. Killin a man, 'specially one lookin the other way, is pretty far down that path. I know yah been makin yer way down it for a while, but yah surprised me pullin the trigger like yah did. I bet yah surprised yerself, too."

With the absurdity of the situation muddling Ray's thoughts, he could only come up with: "I didn't mean to."

Pinky cupped his pipe in one hand and scratched the back of his head with the other. "It itches back there, yah know?"

Remembering Pinky's torn-open scalp made Ray's arm hairs stand on end. Fresh tears stung his eyes, and he tried to speak through a sob. "How. How could you... your head... I saw it."

Still looking out the window, Pinky worked two fingers beneath his fishing cap and traced the site of the wound. "Almost healed. Wanna see?" he asked, lifting the hat an inch.

From the bed Ray couldn't see a thing but that didn't matter. The thought alone was more than enough, and before he could even turn his head he threw up into his lap. The puddle, like everything else in the room, was gray. He swatted threads of mucus from his face and tried to say something, but his jaw trembled too much to form the words.

Pinky seemed not to notice. "Yah know, I been fishin that creek fer years," he said, rapping the window with a knuckle. "There'll be days when I catch a bucketful. Practically jumpin in my lap." He paused to smoke, but his pipe had gone out. He stuck it in his hat and continued. "Then there'll be days, weeks, shoot, maybe even months, where I don't catch a thing. I try all sortsa superstitious stuff and I try to will those doggone fish to bite. But they don't, no matter what I do. Times like those I'm just an average Joe on the wrong side of luck.

"Then! When I ain't thinkin about nothin, I ain't even tryin—"
he felt the back of his head again "—I pull off some crazy, magic
stunt that just flat-out blows my mind." He smiled and glanced at
Ray. "No pun intended."

Pinky turned from the window and crossed the room, each step
tracked by Ray's eyes. He grabbed a towel from a shelf and tossed it
on the bed. "Looks like yah made a messa yerself."

Ray dabbed his mouth and chin and lap while Pinky returned to
his chair.

"Guess I lied to yah a couple minutes ago, Ray. Yah asked what
I wanted, what I came here for, and I lied. Didn't mean to, though.
Don't think I really knew until just now."

Ray's stomach lurched again.

"Came here to talk. Get a few things off my chest, I suppose. I
chat with folks all the time, and I know about their lives, about their
secrets, but none of 'em know mine." He stopped for a moment,
closed his eyes, and leaned back in his chair, falling behind the shaft
of moonlight.

Pinky went on, "Path of evil. You ain't the only one on it, yah
know. You'd be surprised how many folks find themselves there at
some point in their lives. Course, most only take a couple steps,
jump right off. But some stay on it, takin baby steps, gettin used to
it. A charmin personality don't hurt either—makes it easier to get
away with stuff. Before yah know it yer in over yer head." He leaned
forward into the light. "I bet if yah think hard yah can remember the
first time yah stepped down the path, can't yah?"

Although Ray watched the old man closely, a few seconds
passed before he realized Pinky was waiting for him to speak.

"What're you talking about?"

Pinky huffed and resumed staring out the window. "Right after
yer parents died in that car accident, if memory serves me. Don't
know what pushed yah there. Maybe yah were mad at the world,
mad at God—oh cruel world, oh woe is me, somethin like that.
Church basement on a Sunday night. Sound familiar?"

Ray said no, but he remembered. He remembered being down
there alone. Alone.

"Sure yah do. Wad of bills yah pulled from the collection box. Father Mackinaw had yah straighten it out, count it, put it in a lockbox, but some slipped into yer pocket. Wasn't much, maybe forty bucks, but a couple days later yah put it towards a car radio. And yah felt guilty as anything. Folks always feel guilty at first, but that goes away with time. Don't it?"

In typical fashion, Ray's initial thought was to refute the accusation, but the detail and Pinky's casual delivery made denial seem ridiculous. He scooted against his pillows. "How'd you know about that?"

"Ah, now we're gettin somewhere." A broad smile seized the old man, and the lines in his face cast deep shadows, forging a grotesque mask in the moonlight. "How'd I know, Ray? Just like I know everything about yah. The voices told me," he said, and let out a powerful laugh that quickly became a cough. He slapped his chest, trying to catch his breath.

Ray didn't laugh.

Pinky cleared his throat and continued with a phlegmy voice. "Ah, I don't know why that struck me so funny, but it did. Guess I never said it out loud before. But it's the truth, I swear it." He raised a hand beside him. "Scout's honor."

Amidst the storm of emotions and thoughts dominating Ray's mind, the oddest impression overtook Ray. He sensed Pinky reaching for some kind of camaraderie with him, sharing secrets in the dark the way he was. Ray didn't mind at all—the prospect came as a relief from his earlier fears of Pinky seeking revenge. And with questions piling in his mind, Ray couldn't help but try to make sense of the last twenty-four hours. To bring some feeling of control and sanity back to his existence.

"I know what I saw at your house, Pinky. What the hell is going on? How'd you do it?"

With his pipe in his hat the old man's hands and mouth took turns occupying themselves. Kneading his whiskers, Pinky said, "Yah know how I was sayin lots of folks step on the path of evil at some point in their lives? Well, truth is, I didn't step on it. Old Pinky was born on it."

It sounded like something that might scare a kid sitting in the dark aisles of a theater, but something an adult with a decent grasp of reason and logic would scoff at. But after all Ray had seen Pinky's words scared the shit out of him.

And Pinky knew it. "There yah go again, gettin jumpy. I ain't some kinda werewolf or vampire, boy. I ain't gonna eat yah. Not yet, anyway," he said and snickered quietly, then crossed his arms and composed himself.

"There's more to it than I could hope to tell yah. More than I could hope to understand myself. And I'll be damned if I'm gonna go into some hocus-pocus explanation of the world, talkin about auras and karma and the like, but plain and simple there's more to this place than you'll ever know. Count yerself lucky for it.

"Me, I ain't so lucky. Got people talkin to me all the time. People I can't see tellin me stuff I never wanted to hear. Don't really know if they're people, but they got voices, that's fer sure. Ever since I was a kid they talk to me all times of day and night. When I was real young I thought they lived in the chimbley of my house. Now I ain't so sure they don't live up here," he said, tapping his head.

Ray wanted to say something, but didn't know what exactly, so he said nothing. The room felt colder, and he pulled the bed sheet over his legs.

"Most of the time I hear people's secrets, the dark ones. That's the kind secrets usually are, anyway. Dark. Seems my job round town is chiefly to listen and see and know... and here yah probably thought I was just a busybody like Ed Polanski, stickin my nose everywhere it don't belong. Not my choice, though. Every now and again they give me an errand, make me get involved, but mostly I'm just the ears and eyes for the thing with the voices."

The thing with the voices? You gotta be kidding me.

Pinky took his pipe in his hands and stroked it with a thumb. "There's a balance in the world, Ray. And some folks were put here for the purpose of helpin to keep it balanced. I imagine for every one like me out there stuck dealin with the bad, there's somebody else gettin bombarded by good. To tell yah the truth I don't know which'd be worse," he said and couldn't help but smile. "It's all about checks and balances, evil and good. One gets the upper hand,

and the powers that be tip the scale a little to right it. Don't usually need any help, but like I said, every now and again I gotta get my hands dirty."

The more Pinky talked, the less threatened Ray felt. Ray began to see him not as some ominous fiend from the far side of the Twilight Zone but instead for what he obviously was: a tired, used up old man with a head full of stories and a touch of dementia to boot. Increasingly reassured, Ray's mind again sought to anchor itself with rational explanations.

Pinky continued to talk. "Don't get me wrong—life I got ain't so bad, and it's the only one I know. Plus, it has its perks." He formed a pistol with his index finger and thumb, pointed it at his head, and pulled an imaginary trigger. "Never healed up like that before. That's a new one for me. Took a bullet once, but nothin like that. Livin the life I have, I ain't all that surprised, though. Had a lot of near misses in my day. Seems I'm meant to hang around for a while." His eyebrows lifted and his finger pointed upward. "Yah see, when it's my time to go, it'll be *them* who decide, nobody else." He paused for a moment.

"If yah knew how old I was you'd fall over right where yer sittin, boy." He smiled his crooked-tooth smile. "Hell, I'm not even sure any more. Oldest memory I have nowadays is ridin a train with my folks to the World's Fair in New Orleans, and I'm pretty sure I was in my teens by then."

Ray's eyes widened. "New Orleans? I went to the World's Fair there when I was in fourth grade. But I remember them saying the last one held there was like..." He did the math in his head, and the result exceeded even Ray's high tolerance for bullshit. "Oh come on! It was like a hundred years ago!"

"1884, actually," he said, setting his cold pipe beside him on the nightstand.

The idea Ray had fallen into such a state of disarray over the day's events suddenly angered him. There had to be a simple and logical account for what happened at Pinky's. Had to be. The more Pinky spun this ridiculous yarn the more Ray became convinced that Pinky had masterminded the entire ordeal as some kind of setup, beginning with his tobacco tin story at Dusty's.

Ray wet his lips. "What about the Great Depression? That was in the 30s. Last night you were talking about seeing your dad cry after losing his job and house back then. I guess everybody in your family lives forever, huh?"

"Nope, and I didn't say I was gonna live forever, smartass. But when yah been around as long as I have yah gotta tweak yer stories fer yer audience to stay one step ahead. Yer pretty good at that yerself, ain't yah?" He let the comment hang in the air for a moment. "Anyway, the fella cryin in that story was my grandson. May he rest in peace."

Oh, gimme a break! "So all these years you been walking around, nobody ever thought twice about it, never once questioned how you could be so damn old?" Ray asked, voice laced with ridicule.

"Think about it, boy. Nobody knows how old I am, but who's gonna question the age of some old-timer? I never have to show identification for nothin, and I don't think there's a soul alive who knows my real name or even cares about it. Besides, I think that about the time somebody starts wonderin why I'm still alive and kickin, they pass on themselves." He pulled a handkerchief from his back pocket, blew his nose, and while still dabbing continued in a nasally tone. "I usually try to keep outta pictures so I don't have to answer questions later on, but the few really old black-n-whites of me out there I explain away as bein my pa or grandpa or whatever." He stuffed the kerchief back into his pocket. "Who the hell is gonna question such a thing?"

Ray only shook his head. *He lured me to his house talking about his hidden money, put some kind of blanks in the shotgun, figuring he could get me riled enough to use it. But the blood, the wound, you saw it. Did I? The mind's a powerful machine, capable of filling details a person expects to see. No, no. The blood on my clothes. His skull was shredded. Some kind of prop he rigged up? Remember, you panicked, weren't thinking straight, so maybe it was fake. Like something from the movies. Just listen to his fairytale for Christ's sake!*

"Damn it feels good to air out some of this stuff. My place in the world doesn't allow for much in the way of free will when it comes to certain things. Can't do nothin to upset the balance, yah see, and that usually includes openin my mouth. In fact I scared myself some earlier when yah were at my place. Let my temper get the best of me, said a few things I shouldn't have. Coulda cost me dearly."

Pinky slapped his hands together. "But then yah came along and made an ass of yerself, didn't yah! Callin up Bob, draggin him and the ambulance over to my place. And fer what? To go screamin and passin out like yah did, front and center, fer all the world to see." Pinky's throaty, wet laugh gurgled through the room. "Whole town thinks yer nuts now and ain't gonna listen to a thing yah say... 'specially bout me." His laugh dwindled. "Boy I'm glad I thought to clean up after yah left. Made things so much more fun, didn't it?"

Ray had heard enough, and he spun to plant both feet on the floor. "Okay, game's up. I want answers and I want 'em now. What the hell are you up to? What's this is all about? And no more of your bullshit. You got some hunches about my comings and goings around Stillwater. So what. You knew about me pocketing a couple bucks a dozen years ago. So what. For all I know I got drunk at Dusty's one night and blabbed the whole thing. I don't know how you pulled the shit you did at your house today, but it ain't witchcraft, that's for damn sure. And you ain't some senior citizen demon, hearing voices from the great beyond. I know that much. You got me unnerved pretty bad earlier, I'll give you that," he said, tugging at his soiled pants. "But I'm tired of it. So let's hear it. What do you want? You playing guardian angel for all the morons around here who can't take care of themselves? Trying to run me out of town?"

The old man laced his fingers, rolled his thumbs. "Guardian angel?" His voice was calm and soft. "I'm anything but an angel, Ray. Just 'cause you always see me smilin and gettin along with folks don't mean nothin—even serial killers kiss their mom g'night, yah know? Yah only seen one side of me, but I got others. Others you'd like much less than the one sittin in front of yah.

"Remember, boy, I've spent a long life strollin down this path. Stuff I seen and done would make yah do more than just puke on yerself, I guarantee that. I've passed by lots of folks, heard their sins, but it's my job to just turn my head and look the other way, unless I'm called upon. So you connivin and schemin the townfolk ain't no business of mine, never was." He cracked his knuckles. "But you messin with *me*? Now *that's* a whole nother story."

Ray licked his lips, but his tongue had gone dry. *Look at him! Frail, sloppy old man is trying to back you down!* "Yeah? So what're you planning on doing about it?" The words came with much less conviction than he intended.

Silence lingered for a moment, then parted for Pinky's response, which he delivered in a composed, straightforward manner: "Why, I'm gonna kill yah, Raymond."

Beat the hell out of him! Do it, now! As much as Ray wanted to leap from the bed it felt as though a thousand needles pinned him to it. "Just a crazy old man, that's all you are. Outta your damn mind. You don't scare me."

"No? Hmf." Pinky took his pipe from the nightstand, stood halfway, and dug in his jeans pocket. He removed a lighter and worked at relighting the tobacco. Between puffs, he mumbled around the mouthpiece. "Ever wonder what happened to Melissa, Ray?"

"Who?"

Smoke rose from Pinky's mouth and nose, and he reclined in the chair, flipping the lighter's lid open, closed. "Who. Yah know damned well who. Fourth of July, Thornton Park. Ring a bell?" Open, closed.

The memory, which Ray had successfully kept at bay the last four years, resurfaced, and Ray could only reply, "That wasn't me."

"Oh, it sure as shit was, Mr. Dempsey!" The tobacco blazed red for a few seconds. "Melissa Anderson. Sweet young girl, makin eyes at yah all the time," he said, smoke mingling with his words. "Never good to throw temptation in front of a man who's been tradin away morals and self-control for instant reward, now is it?"

Ray sank into the bed, closed his eyes, and wished he could close his ears.

"Year the Jaycees called off the fireworks. Rained like a son of a bitch. Came down in sheets so bad it dug holes. You two under the shelter, water bouncin off the metal slide so hard yah could barely hear her sayin to stop. But yah heard it, Ray. God knows yah did, I know yah did. Nothin but a roll in the hay for you, though, wasn't it. Sent her home, jeans all muddy, arms all bruised, cryin to her ma that she fell down, she fell down hard. Too scared to say what happened. What yah did to her."

Ray made no response, only sat there watching crystal tears drop from his eyes to the floor.

"Of course, none of that's news to you. Got most of it right from the shadows of yer heart. But that young gal's got her own secrets too, Ray. A few yah don't know."

Ray's breath halted.

Pinky continued, "She's a tough gal, Melissa is. I know you didn't see much of her after that night, but she held it together, carried on, didn't make a peep to nobody. Then three months later, a friend drives her to Grundy County—they got a big Wal-Mart over there yah know—and she buys one of them pregnancy tests."

Ray looked up.

"Yep, yah heard me. Turns out she's with child and has to tell her folks about the night yah raped her."

Before Ray could object or even make a sound, Pinky held up a hand. "No, she didn't mention you. Said she didn't know who it was. Guy wore a mask, she said. For some goddamn reason she had feelins for yah, looked up to yah, hoped yah'd come round when yah found out." Pinky let out a scoff. "Well, her folks solved yer end of equation. They knew she'd get her reputation dragged through the mud and wouldn't stand a chance in Stillwater. Fifteen-year-old gettin knocked up, regardless of her part in it, would have the whole county buzzin. So just like that, her folks pack up, move an hour away, start home schooling their only daughter." Pinky stood from his chair. "Yer son turned three last spring, Mr. Dempsey."

Ray's heart, mind, and body were defeated. He still sat at the edge of the bed, but his face now lay in his hands. If Pinky were there to harm him, kill him, he hadn't the energy or will to defend himself.

The old man paced from window to door and back again, hands folded behind him, pipe hanging from his lips. He stopped by the door and leaned against it with his hand resting on the knob. "Like I told yah this mornin. I know all the secrets in yer heart. I really ain't here to preach about what yah got in there, cause yah know well enough. Just wanted to remind yah that yah been ruinin more lives than just yer own these past dozen years. It's easy to forget sometimes, to only look forward on the path, never back." He turned the doorknob.

Ray looked up, his face blotchy and wet. *He's not going to hurt me, he's not going to kill me.*

As if Pinky heard Ray's thoughts, which he might have, Pinky pointed at him and said, "I told yah I'm gonna end yer life, boy, and by God, I meant it. Got a lot of creative ways to do it, too. But the *when* ain't up to me. Gotta wait til I get the call—they'll whisper in my ear when it's time. You messin with me, one of their own, I'm bettin they'll let me tend to you myself—there's a little dose of that karma stuff I said I wasn't gonna talk about. Could be years, could be months. But hell, could be tomorrow. Guess we'll have to wait and see." Pinky smiled and pulled the door open. Hall light poured into the room, making Ray squint.

"Go on about yer days as best yah can. Yah never know when you'll be on yer last. Next time I come knockin, you'll know I got the call, and you'll know why I'm there. What I come for." Pinky backed out the door and held it open with his foot while he pulled something from his shirt pocket. "In the meantime," he said, flinging it across the room, "buy yerself a chocolate bar. And when yah do, think of *me*, Ray-Ray."

The half-dollar bounced off Ray's shoulder, and Pinky laughed hard as the door swung shut, returning the room to darkness. Ray plugged his ears but heard the old man's laughter until long after the sun came up.

Christmas with an Old Friend

A string of large, colored bulbs, the kind discontinued years ago because they often burned down folks' Christmas trees and houses, framed the view of a gloomy Stillwater morning. Sheriff Pearsall slid into the booth and scooted close to the window. Sitting in the middle of that seat you not only sank nearly to the floor, you also stood a good chance of getting goosed by a busted spring. Across the table sat Ed Polanski, already on his second cup of coffee. A heavyset waitress approached.

"Mornin, Bob. The usual?" she said, pen and pad at the ready.

"No, I don't think so," the sheriff replied, craning his neck around the woman. "You have any of those cinnamon sticky-buns today?"

Ed glanced up from his mug, and the waitress snorted. "Yeah, but I thought Doc Hinkley told you those were off limits."

"Give me two of them. And a coffee. Black."

"Sure thing, hon," she said, her eyes lingering on him as she turned away.

The waitress left. Ed asked, "Somethin botherin yah, Sheriff?"

The sheriff studied the downtown street, rubbed his earlobe. "Just got the oil changed on the cruiser. Over at Chip's place."

"Uh huh?"

"While I was there old Mrs. Hoffmeister stopped in, wanting to drop off a basket of sugar cookies for Ray Dempsey."

Ed set his mug down. "Ray Dempsey? Yer kiddin."

Sheriff Pearsall shook his head, his gaze still cast out the window. "I feel sorry for the old woman. But part of me's jealous."

The waitress approached the table, and the sheriff leaned back to make way for his breakfast. "Need anything else, hon?" she asked while filling Ed's cup.

"No ma'am," both men replied, and she walked away.

The sheriff tucked a paper napkin into his shirt collar and adjusted the plate in front of him. Ed watched him and asked, "You were sayin about Mrs. Hoffmeister?"

Instead of answering, the sheriff took two huge bites of a glistening, swirled roll and chewed with his eyes closed. Ten seconds later he opened them, took a sip of coffee, and said, "I feel bad because the poor old gal's mind is all but gone. It's been almost four months since Ray disappeared, and she took it pretty hard when she first heard. Now she brings cookies for him like she does every other Christmas, and cried when I broke the news to her. Again." He slid the sugar dispenser across the table, poured a generous helping into his coffee.

"Yah said somethin about bein jealous?" Ed asked.

The sheriff's face saddened. "Yep. I'm jealous she can forget so easily, Ed. I wish like hell I could." He stirred the coffee, clanking the spoon around the rim.

"You mean about Ray?"

The sheriff nodded and took another bite. Still chewing, he said, "I can't tell you how much sleep I've lost over the whole thing."

"I think a lot of folks can sympathize with yah."

"Sure, sure. But that's what really hurts, yah know. I feel like I let a lot of people down. Like I should've known," he said, tapping the star on his uniform.

"Aw, Bob, don't be so hard on yerself. You're a damn fine sheriff."

Bob looked his friend in the eyes. "I wasn't pointing to my badge, Ed. I was pointing at what's beneath it." He picked up his mug. "I feel like I should've known better. In my heart."

Ed scratched his white hair. "Well, he pulled the wool over damn near everybody's eyes, so yah can't take it personally."

The sheriff turned to the window again and seemed to talk to his reflection. "Worse part is that looking back on it now, I realize there were signs here and there, but I paid them no mind. I gave him the benefit of the doubt. Blind trust, you might say."

"That's what this town of ours is built on, Sheriff. Trust. And the kid used it against us. Damn shame."

"He's not a kid, Ed. Not anymore." The sheriff paused. "He sure grew up fast after his parents passed on. That wasn't long after I moved down here. I hardly knew you back then. Christ, Ed, you remember that night? The accident?"

Ed frowned and nodded. "Down the road a spell from the Geiger's place. I was second one out there, right after Pinky."

The sheriff wrung his hands. "One of the first bad calls I got in this county. Maybe the worst I've seen."

Ed said, "Yep. Brakes went out and they rolled down into the dry creek bed. Pinky said it was already burnin when he came up on it. Old guy was out walkin alone, didn't have any way of callin you or the paramedics. Guess it was too late anyway with the fire and everything, but he said another five minutes passed before a car came along that he could send into town for help. I heard it on the scanner and beat the ambulance over there. Pinky was pretty shaken up."

Outside, beneath the faded Beehive Cafe sign, Mrs. Spradling hurried along, bundled up against the uncommonly chilly air. She saw Ed and the sheriff in the window, smiled, and pulled her hand from her coat pocket long enough to give a quick wave.

Both men returned the smile and wave, and though it seemed forced, the act pushed their conversation forward.

"So anything else surface lately? Any other skeletons in Mr. Dempsey's closet?" Ed asked, his tone laced not with concern but a thirst for juicy info.

The sheriff shrugged. "Not really. I dipped into the petty cash to hire an accountant to do an official audit of the school's books. But I think we all know what that'll turn up."

Ed nodded. Old gossip.

"After I took over the fund raising and more than doubled the annual donations from each of the last four years-without making a single phone call, mind you—it didn't take a sleuth to figure Ray was somehow monkeying with the ledgers," he said, tossing the last bite of breakfast into his mouth. "And pocketing a couple thousand bucks of school money in the process."

Ed grumbled. "And with those measly yearly goals, the kid looked like whiz, meetin 'em without a problem. Who set those goals, anyway?"

"I'll give you three guesses, and the first two don't count."

The waitress stopped by, poured steaming coffee into their mugs, and took the sheriff's plate.

"Yah done with that, hon?" she asked, pointing at the paper napkin hanging like a starched sail from the man's neck.

The sheriff pulled the napkin free and touched it to the corners of his mouth before relinquishing it. He then reached for the sugar, but found Ed already sliding it toward him.

"Thanks." He poured and stirred at the same time. "Yah know, after Mrs. Hoffmeister left the shop this morning, I got talking to Chip about Ray."

Ed perked up. "Oh yeah?"

"Yeah, he said he was going to look into it, but he was pretty sure his deposits were up quite a bit from this time last year, even though business has been about the same. He said he'd kept it mostly to himself because he didn't want to give folks around town anything else to get bent out of shape about. I have a feeling it had more to do with him not wanting to look foolish, getting bamboozled by Ray like he did."

From behind his coffee cup and a rising curtain of steam, Ed said, "That kid had his fingers in a lot of pies, didn't he?" He lowered the cup. "I'll tell yah though, Sheriff. I ain't sayin I had him figured out, but I always knew in my gut that somethin wasn't quite right about him."

The sheriff raised his eyebrows and tilted his head forward. "Is that so?"

Ed nodded. "Yep. I keep my ear to the ground, yah know. My sight ain't worth a damn, but my hearing's tip-top. So I'm always listenin, tryin to stay on top of things. Plus," he said, "I'm a first-rate judge of character."

"Really," Sheriff Pearsall said, his gaze wandering to the street.

"That day I come up on him in the road, I knew right off somethin was wrong with him. Real wrong. You ever find anything out about all that?"

"Nope. Nothing new. Our quick search didn't turn up anything in those woods, and wherever Ray ran off to he took his blood-splattered clothes with him, so I doubt we'll ever know what that whole ordeal was about. Or if it was even blood for that matter. But something or someone rattled his cage, that's for sure, because after we left Pinky's in the ambulance he was talking all kinds of nonsense and paranoia. And that's the last I saw of him. Nurse that night said he was there when she peeked in at midnight, but gone by two."

Ed propped his elbows on the table and shook his head. "So after practically milkin the town dry he runs off to who-knows-where, probably livin like a king from the money he swindled. Ain't there any justice in this world?" He paused, and a corner of his mouth grinned. "Boy, for whatever reason he sure did break down at Pinky's though, didn't he? Screamin like a banshee, then fallin on yah when he conked out." He huffed. "Pinky, that poor old guy. He's seen a lot of crazy shit in his day."

The sheriff's eyes lit up and a warm smile brightened his face. He pointed into the street. "Well, speak of the devil!"

Wearing a flannel coat that looked like a giant checkerboard, Pinky shuffled across Main Street, carrying a black box of some sort under his arm. Smoke chugged from his pipe. The wind suddenly picked up, fluttering his hair and snapping his pants against his legs.

Just looking at the man drew Ed's hands around his warm coffee mug.

"What the hell's he doing out on a day like this?" Sheriff Pearsall said and pounded on the glass.

As Pinky neared the Beehive he looked at the window and smiled, but it was obvious he couldn't see who was on the other side pounding on it. Both men motioned for him to come in, and when Pinky got close enough to see them he nodded and headed for the entrance.

The bell over the door tinkled and a gust of December blew through the tiny restaurant, turning heads and ruffling newspapers. After dishing out smiles and waves to everyone seated at the counter, Pinky turned to his friends in the booth.

"Mornin, gents," Pinky said, plodding in their direction.

"Mornin yerself," the sheriff returned. He and Ed eyed what the old man carried in his right hand.

Pinky lifted it up and pointed at it. "Yah like it? Ain't seen the light of day in thirty years, I reckon."

Pinky held an old-fashioned travel bag that resembled a very deep, sturdy briefcase clasped on the side with an oversized brass buckle. Comically adorned with faded bumper stickers and bygone campaign slogans, it looked like a suitcase one of the Three Stooges might have owned.

"Whatcha got in there, Pinky?" Ed asked.

"Change of clothes," he said and leaned on the back of Ed's side of the booth.

"Oh," replied Ed.

Sheriff Pearsall patted the booth. "Grab a seat, old-timer."

"Can't stay. And even if I could, I wouldn't sit in that deathtrap. Hurts my rump just thinkin about it," he said and grinned, his rotten teeth a perfect match for the dismal morning.

"You goin somewheres?" Ed asked, his tone falling somewhere between surprise and worry.

Pinky lugged the suitcase up on the backrest and crossed his arms atop it. "Sure am. Got a call last night, and I'm goin to see an old friend."

Neither Ed nor the sheriff seemed to think twice about the fact Pinky didn't own a phone. Both only sat there smiling the same goofy smile. The idea the old guy knew somebody outside the Stillwater town limits was enough to bewilder almost anyone into looking like that.

"Old friend yah say?" Ed asked.

"Yep, I been waitin a while for this day. He probably don't think I'm gonna follow through with it, and it's a long ride, but I know the look on his face'll more than make it worth my effort. Besides, I promised him I'd come knockin when I got the call, and I'm a man who sticks by his word."

"That you are," the sheriff said, glancing at Ed, who fidgeted with his empty coffee mug, looking like he was about to burst with curiosity.

But before Ed could open fire with questions, Pinky slapped the suitcase and announced, "I gotta scoot, fellas. Bus'll be here any minute." He took a step back.

Ed twisted a hundred-and-eighty degrees. "Where yah headed?"

Turning toward the door Pinky replied, "Little town up north. Looks a lot like this one in fact. Just over the state line."

"How long yah goin for?" Ed asked, volume a little louder.

Pinky grabbed the doorknob. "Just a day. Two, tops."

"So you'll be back in time for bingo? Last one before Christmas, yah know."

Pinky yanked open the door, rang the bell. "There ain't nothin in this world could keep me from my bingo, Ed," he said and winked. "I'll be there. Promise." The door closed behind him with a final jingle and a handful of well-wishes from the Beehive patrons and staff.

Sheriff Pearsall and Ed watched in silence as the old man made his way to the town's lone bus stop, which was served only by a regional Greyhound that came through once a day. Pinky set his suitcase on the bench and stood beside it.

With his finger, Ed poked at the air in Pinky's direction. "Now *that*," he said, "is a real class act. A straight shooter—who yah see is who yah get. And with Pinky, yah get a good man, inside and out." Ed was practically gushing.

The sheriff nodded. "Mm-hm."

"And like I said a couple minutes ago," Ed began, then paused to wait for the sheriff's eyes to meet his. "I'm a first-rate judge of character."

Snowflakes danced in the air like cottonseed. Stillwater was far enough south for snow to be met with jubilation and wonderment, and the doorways of the five other Main Street businesses filled with wide eyes and eager smiles. Pinky turned and faced the restaurant with an open hand held before him, palm up. From their warm booth, Ed and the sheriff smiled and gave him an enthusiastic thumbs-up. A plump snowflake dissolved in Pinky's hand, and the old man smirked and shrugged.

A minute later the Greyhound pulled to a stop, scuffing its tires on the curb. The Plexiglas doors folded open, and the single Stillwater passenger boarded. Pinky took a seat up front and waved to anyone in the Beehive who may have been looking. The bus pulled away and turned onto Route 18, its wipers swatting melted flakes from the windshield.

Truth is, Pinky had always disliked cold weather, and he downright hated snow. But as he settled into the seat and stared out the window, on his way to pay Raymond Dempsey one last surprise visit, the red-haired man smiled wider than he had in a long, long time.

➦➧

The *New* Yorkshire Times
by D.R.Smith

Old English nursery rhymes are still popular and often quipped today. Ages ago, they were commonly used for mocking noted people and events, for easy commitment to memory given the high rate of illiteracy, aid town criers, help parents teach children, or designed to parody sensitive political issues and Royal families when an outspoken dissent could mean death.

The brutal "Bloody Mary"

Though attributed to having multiple origins at times, most rhymes had well defined, and sometimes austere roots. For example: Mary, the contrarian gardener, as well as her victims (such as the *three blind mice...* a trio of Protestant Nobleman) were satirical verses of the staunch Catholic, the sinister Queen Mary Tudor.

Her infamous "garden" was actually a graveyard; home to those who dared adhere to the Protestant movement. Many were burned at the stake while others were subjected to *"silver bells and cockle shells"*;

horrible instruments of torture. Others were beheaded by guillotine, a device first used in England and not France as commonly thought. The English colloquial name for it was "Maiden", only shortened as in: *"pretty Maids all in a row."*

"Jack and Jill" of French Aristocracy

Historical figures and events in France were also popularized in verse as well. During France's Reign of Terror in the late 1700's, "Jack and Jill" memorialized the beheading of King Louis XVI who *"lost his crown"* to the guillotine; followed by his Queen, Marie Antoinette, who *"came tumbling after."*

The not-so-rosy plague, a big-ass cannon, & others

Other rhymes had little to do with people, but were of *things—* like "Ring a Ring o' Rosies" describing the tell-tale circular markings of the Bubonic plague on the skin.

Another lyric still popular today is that of "Humpty Dumpty", a colloquial expression for obesity during England's Civil War period of the mid 17th century.

"Humpty" was the nickname of a massive cannon in defense of the walled town of Colchester, a Royalist stronghold. Adjacent to the castle stood St. Mary's Church where the cannon was affixed to its wall. While under siege, a chance shot by the Parliamentarian "Roundhead's" hit the foundation beneath it, the wall crumbled, and 'Humpty had a great fall'. The Royalists, *"with all the King's horses, and all the King's men;"* failed to raise the heavy beast, and thus: *"couldn't put Humpty together again;"* forcing the Royalists to lay down their arms in surrender.

More rhymes were dedicated to reflect common occurrences, such as craftsman like "Simple Simon," hawking his pies at County fairs. Other parables spoofed sensitive political issues, such as "Baa Baa Black Sheep". Its origins date to the 13th century when England's wool trade was a major economic resource for King Edward I to impose an unpopular export tax. He demanded duty on wool leaving from any port, hence: of *"three bags full, one for the Master"* was set aside to fatten Royal coffers.

Modern day *crooked little men*

In keeping with the spirit of olden verse, The *New* Yorkshire Times is a lampoon of current headlines. Since history has shown how early rhymes have survived long after parodied people or events have passed... who knows: perhaps five hundred years hence, Ol' Bard Joel's recitals below may become just as familiar; a spoof of society's *crooked little men?*

* * *

The *New* Yorkshire Times

In days of old, town criers told the news of English times,
Of Lords and Kings and other things, by citing clever rhymes.
Reality shows, where anything goes has set new precedents.
Thus olden verse needs new rehearse for modern day events.

Old bard Joel, was a worldly-wise soul, and a witty old bard was he.
Said to little wife of Mabel, while he sat at breakfast table
Eating porridge with his early morning tea:

"Since my aim is to amuse, I shall read the daily news
Using ancient rhymes deranged."
So he spoofed amoral capers, paraphrasing from the papers,
Of how wacky times have changed.

TV preacher, bible teacher,
Fleeced his flocks, cleaned their clocks.
Chased another looker, turned out was a hooker.
Sinful shrew. Shame on you.

Simple Simon was a pieman making lots of dough.
"But not with pies," said Simple Si,
"My shop's a front for blow."
All day long came user, loser, triggerman, thief.
Came boozer, bruiser, underworld chief.

Little Jack Horner, went to the corner
To watch for black and whites.
Hookers baring wares, drew his lustful stares,
Now his gang is being read their rights.

"Basement Barry, apothecary, why do your sun lamps glow?"
"So sprouting weeds and coca leaves,
Midst poppy pods all can grow.
My metered flasks and filtered masks,
For making meth and blow."

The Prez ran 'round the Oval Room,
'Til getting caught with Moni.
"Impeachment looms," First Lady fumed,
"The press revealed your honey."
But now that she's in big-boy shoes,
The press report with snickers;
"His game's the same," amused the news;
"Still chasin' White House knickers."

Mary's in a little jamb, her drug test proved up snow.
Now everywhere that Mary went, the Feds were sure to show.
They followed her to school of course, where likely she got high.
And there the sheriff nabbed her source, now Mary's out supply.

Peter Peter, repeat beater,
Had a wife he'd last mistreat her.
Fell asleep upon the couch,
Woke up less his testes pouch.

Sing a song of plenty, a pocket full of dough.
Five new fancy T-Birds stripped in a row.
As the parts are processed, the fence he gladly pays.
Off to shopping malls again, need four-door Chevrolets.

Petty crime thief had lost his teeth
In fisticuffs with a cell mate.
Now minus his bite, refuses to fight
With anyone twice his weight.

There was an old woman too old to turn tricks;
Too old to work in brothels, much less compete with chicks.
So she sent her oldest daughter, and brother Moe as pimp,
Out to work the corner stoop so she won't have to scrimp.

Oh piddle piddle! nay dealer in the middle,
But a g-man undercover.
Found guilty by his peers, judge gave him twenty years,
Now he's in the slammer as Big Bubba's lover.

Tom Taum, the biker's son.
Stole a Hog and tried to run.
But fled the scene in rainy weather,
Found him crushed in sun-dried leather.

"Says here my little Mabel, that in Motown by the lake,
Half the cops are under paid, the rest are on the take."

"Hey hey black man, have you any smack?"
"Yes sir, yes sir, triple dime sac.
Dime for my dealer, another for my pay,
One for the cruiser cops to look the other way.

There was a crooked Mayor, who milked the crooked trades
By rigging crooked contracts, and bribing crooked aides.
He paid off crooked judges, and twice as crooked clerks,
And forced his crooked bagmen, to split their crooked perks.

Slippery, slithery Don,
The only witness gone.
The judge agreed, "mistrial indeed,"
Snickering, sniggering Don.

Two doper dodos, went to the ghettos
To buy a few baggies of crack.
Got robbed of their dough, including their blow,
And all but the clothes on their back.

Mobster's lawyer paid the judge off.
Mobster's lawyer got the case tossed.
All the Don's power, all his button men,
Kept the wily gangster out of State pen.

Three trained vice; three stained vice.
No more legit, see how they split.
They're seizing the coke from collared guys,
Then pocket the spoils not tagged as buys.
Have you ever wondered how narcs survive,
As three blind vice.

Handed teller open tote, demanding all her cash.
Five and twenty bank notes, she gave him half her stash.
Bragging he's in clover, but die pack snuck in place.
Now he's red all over, it blew up in his face.

"Now the papers say out west, where the sunsets are the best
And the ocean meets the sand,
'Tis a place called tinsel town where the *strangest* ones are found,
Running loose 'round La La land."

All across the border they fled,
The Juan's that stole the diesel.
They found the rat who tipped the Feds,
POP! they whacked the weasel.

Father Joe is not around, gone downtown, wears a frown
Charged with a felony.
Another priest is goin' down, offed his gown, kissed kid's crown,
While in his rectory.

Wee Willie Winkie, liked to show his pinkie.
A pervert out again on bond, teased the boys of which he's fond.
He'd flash his digit as a lure; t'was not his finger, *that's* for sure.

Tooty Fruity, twinkled toed dude.
Kissed the boys but girls refused.
In the bars where lots o' men stag,
Tooty Fruity's dressed in drag.

Madge and Meg went off to bed, holding hands together.
Madge lay down as Meg came round
With whips and gothic leather.
With braided thongs and rubber dongs,
They both climaxed each other.

Little Miss Wanda, revving up a Honda
Daring any dragster that she saw.
Along came a Spyder and peeled out beside her,
And both got caught speeding by the law.

Psycho man, freed from jail,
Delayed killer case out on bail
With a black jack, slash 'n hack;
Victim number four.
Why's this nut out stalking more?

"Now I'm sorry to disclose, but there's no more newsy prose.
But if wait 'til evenin' tea, sixty channels on TV
Will flood the air with freaks and crime-filled shows."

Authors Forum

Beaches of Belmont is a collection of fiction designed to be a reader's ticket to enjoyable literary journeys through time, emotion, imaginary interaction with characters and themes.

Works include novellas and short stories, sprinkled with a taste of poetic genres free from hardcore vulgarities and bare-all reality-type rehashing— a leisurely stroll for pure entertainment.

One goal we all hope to achieve, is that our efforts have enabled you a memorable escape from mundane demands of daily life; for spiking your imagination, thought, evoking a smile, tear, laughter, and so on. If so, mission accomplished.

D.R. Smith: a pseudonym in honor of my grandfather who helped raise me. I grew up on the coast of New England, made Chicago home for most of my business life, and now reside in Kentucky to build ambrex.org. Have two novels in progress: "Tree of the Great Long Leaves", an epic on the powers of human bonding, and, "Dante's Threshold", an arcane twist to mankind's prophetic apocalypse. Feel free to say hello: authordrsmith@aol.com

 Jerry Powell: The father of eight, grandfather of four, and a retired member of the Dallas Police Force. He currently owns a staffing agency, and when time and the muse permit, he enjoys writing novellas and short stories from his office. Though no novels in progress at the moment, Jerry prefers genres in shorter fiction revolving around family, police action, and tales of rural life set along the Arkansas River south of Little Rock.

 Harold 'Butch' Kempka: I was born in Des Moines, Iowa, and grew up in St. Paul, Minnesota. I joined the Marines after high school, and spent six years on active duty, and awarded three Purple Hearts in Vietnam. After my discharge, I settled in southern California where I now reside with my lovely wife, Celeste, son Derek, and four grandchildren. Aside from this anthology, I've had poetry and short stories published in the Leatherneck and Circle magazines, and currently have a Vietnam-based novel in progress.

 Xin Wang: Born in China and moved to the United States at the age of eight, and lived in Florida, North Carolina, and currently in South Carolina in pursuit of a pharmaceutical degree. I began writing as a hobby, and partly because I realized that it would be a great excuse for putting off things I should be doing (i.e. studying for exams, et al). My other interests include reading, surfing the web, and generally goofing off.

Richard Sarles: Born and raised in a small Illinois town, now living in southern California with my fiancee, Samantha. As an only child, I wrote and illustrated my first short story at age ten. Adolescence brought with it colorful experiences and characters from rural America which would eventually populate my writings. In college, I excelled academically, graduating near the top my class earning a master's degree in psychology. I've authored several short stories and novellas, and am presently working on my first full-length novel. Say hello; richardsarles@hotmail.com

Deborah L. Kloeppel: I'm a mother of three from St. Charles, Missouri, and a published professional editor, freelance writer, and author. During the past fifteen years, my writing focus has been on children's items, education, and curriculum development, with a side of short stories and historical fiction. More recent works include home how-to's, and my latest: *The Photogenic Kitchen*, a niche cookbook in progress. When not writing, I'm an in-depth editor helping guide and improve style, technique, and grammar for aspiring authors. Feel free to reach me at: debwritesitall@yahoo.com

Cover & Layout Design

Lincoln Adams: A resident of Akron, Ohio with my wife, Dorothy, and daughters, Cicely and Naomi. I graduated with a BFA from the Cleveland Institute of Art in 1998, and in my early days, embellished stories and illuminated magazine articles as an illustrator. I also did graphic design work assisting in marketing and promotion of small and large businesses. In recent years, my portfolio has grown to include painting portraits: www.lincolnadamsillustration.com.